S0-ASO-903

SOLITUDE
A Philosophical Encounter

SOLITUDE
A Philosophical Encounter

Philip Koch

Open 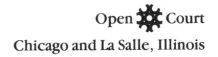 Court

Chicago and La Salle, Illinois

OPEN COURT and the above logo are registered in the U.S.
Patent and Trademark Office.

© 1994 by Open Court Publishing Company

First printing 1994
Second printing 1994

All rights reserved. No part of this publication may be
reproduced, stored in a retrieval system, or transmitted, in any
form or by any means, electronic, mechanical, photocopying,
recording, or otherwise, without the prior written permission of
the publisher, Open Court Publishing Company, 315 Fifth Street,
P.O. Box 599, Peru, Illinois 61354-0599.

Printed and bound in the United States of America.

Library of Congress Cataloging-in-Publication Data

Koch, Philip, 1942–
    Solitude :   a philosophical encounter/Philip Koch.
      p.   cm.
    Includes bibliographical references and index.
    ISBN 0-8126-9242-X   (cloth).   — ISBN 0-8126-9243-8   (paper)
    1. Solitude.   I. Title.
  BJ1499.S6K59   1994
  128'.4—dc20   94-8836
                                                      CIP

To my father and mother,
Philip L. Koch and Gertrude E. Koch,
who, each in their own way,
equipped me well for fruitful solitude.

CONTENTS

ACKNOWLEDGMENTS

With Gratitude,

How ironic, that a solitary man, writing a solitary book, owes so much to so many people. "Acknowledgement" is too astringently grudging to properly thank the grace, the kindness, the wisdom that has been given, asking nothing, glad to help the work prosper; and the extent of my indebtedness can certainly not be captured by a few brief words. Nevertheless, I can at least record my grateful realization of the gifts given by:

Norman Malcolm and Robert Richman, philosophers in the oldest and truest sense, who taught me through their personal lives how to be a whole thinking person, cost what it may;

Don and Anne Mazer, who gave me (along with everything else) my first journal many years ago, a journal which was briefly an enemy, then a companion, then a source for much that is written here;

Professors Kenneth Butler, Ken Clatterbaugh, Charles Holmes, Graeme Hunter, Elizabeth Percival, Terry Pratt, John Smith and Peter Trnka, whose kind observations on earlier versions of the manuscript encouraged me to aim higher, yet speak always in my own voice;

Christine Couturier and Huang Hua-liang, who arranged meetings with Chinese scholars in Beijing which deepened my understanding of ancient Taoism and modern human nature;

Virginia Kopachevsky, whose mastery of the machinery of inter-library loan made our small library seem limitless;

Ann and Howard Schonberger, Mike and Lynn Foster, Steve and Pat Patten, Wayne Attoe, Buzz and Marge Holmgren, Tim and Marian Nelson, Brenda Young, Lucina Baryluk, Jean-Louis Herivault and Barry Bartmann, who contained my solitude in their friendly concern, enabling me to think and write rather than to shrink into myself;

Kerri Mommer, my editor, whose confidence in the work and its author, together with a most gentle yet acute critical faculty, made the final stages of the project a time of completion rather than compromise;

Peter Koch, my son, always wise beyond his years, who taught me lessons about the transparency and yet opacity of unconditional love, whose presence has given me much of the joy of human encounter these last 22 years, and whose absence has never been far from the heart in my solitude;

Nadine Smith, who for five years has nurtured the writer of this manuscript and his ideas, giving better than she got in searching discussions, editing the manuscript with the greatest care while graciously minimizing her own contributions, teaching me the compatibility of solitude and relationship through countless daily acts of care and letting alone, helping me to remember, always, what love and solitude can give to each other.

I most humbly thank you all.

What is solitude? What is its meaning, its value, its place in a human life?

The reflections that fill the following pages have been accumulating since my thoughts began to turn upon themselves in childhood. At first the wondering was more inchoate than philosophical: a boy always on the run between family and friends began to notice empty places along the well-worn pathways. Strange, puzzling, a little scary; yet soon enough familiar, accepted, and not much later, sought (here I try to recall the difference between being eight and being eleven). Secure, alone, in the sheltered corner of the screened porch during thunderstorms, I knew nothing yet of the Sturm-und-Drangers who went before me, struggling to craggy heights and lashing themselves to towering trees in order to merge with the awesome thundering power of the storm. But, in a boy's way, I felt that power and that ecstatic awe; and I watched expectantly for revelations in the lightning flashes.

Time elapsed and there were lonely student years, times when solitude's quiet wonders seemed but weak solace for the friendships and romantic transports I painfully lacked. True, there was the silence late at night when the dormitory slept; then ordinary things assumed a strange presence before the young chemical engineer who was discovering his disinterest in chemistry: the pen thrown upon the matted papers became, suddenly, WRITING, and the calculus book NUMBER, and the slide rule LAW. Later, when I read Derrida and Pythagoras and Plato, the partial understanding I gained would spring from the traces of those late night solitudes. But then, at the time, still innocent of the realities of adult relationship, I shook my head sadly at what seemed sad substitute gifts, so much second best to what I craved. And I felt a thousand years old.

Loves did come, finally, and then marriage, a child and years of family life. They were wonderful, when they were not unbearable, but now solitude began to urgently reassert itself. How could that tender student have imagined that his business with solitude would now become a struggle to *find* it, and then to build stockades around the few small clearings? I stole solitude then as everyone so placed steals it: escaping into chores, driving alone to work, standing alone at the hockey rink appearing to watch my son's team, listening to the house creak and the wind moan through the darkness of the hours of the wolf. Still the uncanny nature of the silence, still the power. And new thoughts began to grow in their own dark soil: maybe these silent spaces where ordinary things become numinous, where feelings become spruce boughs and scattered stars—maybe this, not relationship, is where I should find my place. Where any one should, if they had enough longing for the deepest reality and enough courage to pursue it.

Those reflections produced results, though I would not now cite courage as the dominant motive as I did in those desperate days. There followed years as a single parent, Peter and I forming a paired solitude in the hilltop house that looked southwest across descending grainfields towards the sea. So much together there, I was yet struck by the varieties of absence we could practice in each other's presence: were not the games during which one mind was elsewhere really solitudes of a peculiar sort? Perhaps protected solitudes: for later, though I was alone by the fire with a book, did not the dim awareness that all the while he slept in the back bedroom create a kind of containment for my solitude, rendering it less absolute?

When he grew up and left for a school far away I was really alone with the house and the fire, the spruces and the wind. It was a different solitude than those that went before, open now in all directions. Sometimes it was lonely, sometimes it was so lonely that I gasped with fright, sucked and spinning into a terrible vortex of emptiness. But not very often. Mostly the need I had for others was satisfied by warm musings about Peter and my parents, about friends and lovers not far distant in time or place, remembered, elaborated and woven densely into a future. And there was something else, which every solitary knows well: the world we "half create and half perceive" (Wordsworth), where every natural thing rises up to assume a human form. Loading in wood in the late afternoon, I saw a pair of maple logs ignore each other; dumped together by brusque hands, however, they became solid neighbors. What a delight it was to pursue these imaginings as I wished! How amusing, these logs, each a character, each demanding a perfect personal fit in the stack.

But suddenly I would think that I was becoming a crank. A severe inner voice would observe coldly:

"This poor creature fills his bleak impoverished world with phantasms as a desperate substitute for the real relationships every human needs. A sick life, a tragic life! What he has here are illusory engagements with shadow-people, and yet he has somehow managed to deceive himself into thinking that this is the deepest reality in which a human might live! Solitude has gotten the best of him."

I did not like that voice at all; but, upon reflection, was not all it said true? Was there not something twisted, something distorted, something pathetic in preferring imagined company to real company? After all the living with people, after all the years of living alone and reflecting upon it, could I have failed finally to understand solitude? Yes, it could be. Think again, think harder, think to refute the cold voice.

Think of Pop, perhaps, as you think of refutations. He cared for Mom twenty-two years while the Multiple Sclerosis slowly wore her away, stealing a few sinews of strength each day until It had them all. That closest being-with, being-for, surely could not endure the final parting. Yet it did. For seven more years he lived as heartily as his seventy-year-old organs allowed, alone. Of course we visited him, but he never pressed for more visits; invited, he came, but never stayed very long. What did he do, those long retired days and nights? And what if, my guilt and fear rose loudly crying, he should die alone? It was my question, not his. The solitude was simply there, factual. If death came, well then he supposed he would have to die it; thinking the whole matter out, that he'd leave to me. It arrived, as usually happens, unexpectedly. I flew in to be there. But how exactly was I there in his fading autumn world? True, I held the taut hand which shuddered in the puzzled dreams; yes, the fluttering eyes sometimes fixed upon me in the easy recognition come of forty-eight years of loving sight. Yet then he would smile, nod weakly and close his eyes again, and I had the strong sense that he had important business elsewhere, solitary business, as though he only needed to be reassured that I was all right before ambling off on his own. Then he left me, as he raised me, thinking.

The thinking continues. These last few years have brought a complex mixture of solitudes and encounters, new loves and old friendships performing their elaborations before the great silent background of changing light and seasonal wind. And always the questions with so many threads: what is solitude? what is its meaning, its value, its place in my life?

These pages record the substance of those reflections, organized now as a philosophical structure, hounded by a logician, connected by a historian to the centuries of solitaries who have gone before, brushed tenderly with the poetry I wish that I had written. I commit them to paper with a hope: that you and I might meet and pause here for a moment, joining in the celebrations yet critically alert before the arguments; meet long enough to feel a shy recognition before we wander off again into our own particular regions of the silence.

INTRODUCTION

What is solitude? What compound of space and self and silence and time is this that forms experiences so profound yet so humble, so reflectively rich yet so obliviously immersed in nature, so exhilarating yet so peaceful? Is it possible to say what solitude is?

My thoughts run at once to famous solitaries. Take St. Antony, for example, "the father of monastics." Around AD 269 this son of Egyptian peasant farmers wandered into a church where the Gospel was being read, "Go, sell all that you have, give it to the poor and come." At that moment, the words heard so often before struck him as perfectly new and inexorably binding. Setting to work making himself poorer and more ascetic, at last he escaped alone into the desert. There, in a cave hastily vacated by the resident snakes, he secluded himself for twenty years, locked in solitary mortal combat with the legions of The Enemy.[1]

Consider also the three young English nuns who, around 1250, undertook to have themselves walled into small cells attached to the outside of the local church. There, after a ceremony approximating a requiem mass, each of the Sisters was sealed in with brick and mortar, left with only one small window opening into the church and another out upon the village; there, dead to the world around her, each would pray and do penance in a solitude that would last for the rest of her natural life.

Five hundred years later, Daniel Defoe produced his immortal tale of a hapless seaman named Crusoe, washed up on a deserted island off the coast of South America. Few can resist admiring this "shrewd middle class solidly matter-of-fact intelligence," as Virginia Woolf called him, who contrived to survive and prosper utterly alone for ten long years.

Then there was rambling, bumptious, paradoxical, profound Thoreau. His older friend and mentor, Emerson, owned forty acres of woodland around Walden Pond just outside Concord, Massachusetts, and there young Henry went in 1845 to build his own shelter and "live deliberately." The experiment lasted two years, two years of observation and reflection, of hoeing beans and cultivating the journal whose first entry was entitled "Solitude."

Writing brings to mind Franz Kafka, waiting impatiently for his parents and sisters to go to bed so that he could have the dining room table for writing, writing that ran away into the night, every night for most of his adult life. Only in that solitary silence could he relax and breathe, only there could he write through and write beyond the ever-present anxiety. And for that writing, "one can never be alone enough . . . there can never be enough silence around one . . . even night is not night enough."[2]

Another explorer of another night, Admiral Richard Byrd, volunteered to operate Bolling Advance Weather Base alone during the Antarctic winter of 1934. Four hundred miles inland towards the pole from Little America, the risks were substantial:

> Whoever should elect to inhabit such a spot must reconcile themselves to enduring the bitterest temperatures in nature, a long night as black as that on the dark side of the moon, and an isolation which no power on earth could lift for at least six months.[3]

There, in a small hut buried under feet of snow, month after month, with a failing radio in the deepening Antarctic night, he charted the weather and measured the sort of man he was.

Now I am envisioning the massive cedar trees and lone totem poles of British Columbia painted by Emily Carr. They exude the solitude of the coastal forests where she worked alone for many of her later years, living with a menagerie of pets in an old caravan. At night she recorded the struggles of the days' work:

> October 5th: Oh that mountain! I'm dead beat tonight with struggling. I repainted almost the whole show. It's still a bad, horrid, awful, mean little tussock. No strength, nobility, solidarity.

> Sept. 8th: Did good work this morning. Did poor work this afternoon. I am looking for something indescribable, so light it can be crushed by a heavy thought, so tender even our enthusiasm can wilt it, as mysterious as a tear.[4]

Where is such a thing to be found, let alone painted? In solitude, she thought.

But for all of these examples, it is still not clear what solitude itself is. True, an essential element has appeared: all of these heroes of solitude were, in their solitude, alone. But that is not enough: for loneliness, isolation, alienation, and schizophrenia are also modalities of aloneness, yet none are equivalent to solitude. Is it possible to articulate exactly what it is that makes solitude different?

One should not be overconfident. There is, at the beginning, Thoreau's stern warning: "The silence cannot be done into English." True, he did set out "to crow like a chanticleer" in a book about his solitary life, and crowed for more than two hundred pages. However crowing is not philosophical analysis, and even the *Walden* chapter on solitude is lacking in any attempt at definition. Nevertheless the crowing helps: when we have read "Solitude," and the rest of *Walden,* and "Walking," and "Wild Apples," it is clearer what solitude is and what there can be in it. Crowing about solitude is one expressive path towards enlightenment, and the following pages collect many such poetic songs. Yet the songs do not yield a finished comprehension, for they raise their own questions. Thoreau exclaimed, "I never found the companion that was so companionable as solitude." Companionable? But then is it a solitude, if the loons and the raindrops are companions? Nor is this merely an eccentric remark by a man who loved paradox; for you can find in Byron's *Childe Harold* a very similar exclamation

> Then stirs the feeling infinite, so felt
> In solitude, where we are least alone;[5]

and you can read the same sentiment in Petrarch, who objects that St. Ambrose stole it from Scipio.[6] What did they all mean, exactly?

Then too, these crowings about solitude sometimes conflict with each other. Wordsworth wrote often of solitude in words like these:

> . . . we are laid asleep
> in body, and become a living soul:
> while with an eye made quiet by the power
> of harmony, and the deep power of joy,
> we see into the life of things.

> (from "Lines Composed A
> Few Miles Above Tintern Abbey")

Yet he also wrote the "Elegiac Stanza" of 1805:

Farewell, farewell the heart that lives alone,
Housed in a dream, at distance from the Kind!
Such happiness, wherever it be known,
Is to be pitied; for 'tis surely blind.

Sight or blindness, which is solitude? Indeed, the conflicts grow worse. Compare, for example, Proust's famous drearity,

Notwithstanding the illusion by which we would
fain be cheated and with which, out of
friendship, politeness, deference and duty, we
cheat other people, we exist alone.[7]

with D. H. Lawrence's insistence that

Everything, even individuality itself, depends
on relationship . . . The light shines only when
the circuit is completed.
My individualism is really an illusion. I am
part of the great whole, and I can never
escape.[8]

Once the possibility of general illusion is raised, even solid ground begins to feel shaky. Perhaps those famous solitudes just recalled were not really solitudes after all? True, St. Antony lived alone in a cave for twenty years; but they were twenty years of prayer, and if prayer is communion with God, and if God is conceived as a personage . . . where is the solitude? Or take the immured Sisters: if they could see into the church and follow the service at the altar, if they could look out upon daily village life outside the cell, if they were surrounded on all sides by people with whom they felt some connection . . . what then? Is it so absurd to call their solitude illusory, as Lawrence appears to wish to do? Or consider Kafka. Is writing, at some level, always writing-for-others, and so a kind of quasi-engagement? Is living in the characters as one creates them a kind of surrogate encounter? If so, would it follow that Kafka was not really alone in that silence all those nights?

Proust might seem easier to dismiss, but his descriptions of the isolated detachment of what ought to be intimate personal encounters certainly make one cringe:

> I might, if I chose, take Albertine upon my knee, take her head in my hands; I might caress her, passing my hands slowly over her, but, just as if I had been handling a stone which encloses the salt of immemorial oceans or the light of a star, I felt that I was touching no more than the sealed envelope of a person who inwardly reached to infinity.[9]

If this is how intimate encounters really are, stripped of illusions, is it not possible to call them solitudes? And if this is true of the most engaged of our engagements, what else is there than solitude?

I feel certain that neither Proust nor Lawrence are right. But where do they go wrong? It will be necessary to burrow much more deeply into the natures of solitude and encounter if we are ever to understand the truth and the falsity in these disturbing claims. And understanding such things seems to be crucial for understanding the nature of a human life. A great deal of energy has been expended of late years in trying to say what *relationship*—especially intimate relationship—really is. Men and women want to know whether their own garbled versions are the real thing, to know how they measure up. Whether or not anything ought to be done, independent of all projects for action and change, they simply want to know. It is the philosopher in them. One of the reasons for burrowing into the nature of solitude is exactly parallel and equally compelling.

But as we are knowers, so are we actors. The concern for understanding the nature of solitude is also motivated by our ongoing stumbling project to discover the best way to live. If Lawrence and Proust are wrong and there is the possibility of choice for or against solitude, which to choose? We need to assess the value of these quiet moments, to consider what gifts they offer that encounter cannot give so well. That was the question Byrd set out to answer: his self-isolation was propelled by

> one man's desire to know that kind of experience to the full, to be by himself for a while and to taste peace and quiet and solitude long enough to find out how good they really are.[10]

One good that solitude provides is indisputable: it gives respite and restoration, a time and a place to lick the wounds of social strife; "he leadeth me beside the still waters; he restoreth my soul." That is a great good, but is it all there is to the value of solitude, which functions merely as a restful retreat between the interpersonal encounters which contain the real meaning of human existence? I cannot believe it. I think of Lao Tzu:

> At the age of 160 Lao Tzu grew disgusted with the decay of the Chou dynasty and resolved to pursue virtue in a more congenial atmosphere. Riding in a chariot drawn by a black ox, he left the Middle Kingdom through the Han-ku Pass which leads westward from Loyang. The Keeper of the Pass, Yin Hsi, who, from the state of the weather had expected a sage, addressed him as follows: "You are about to withdraw yourself from sight. I pray you to compose a book for me." Lao Tzu thereupon wrote the 5000 characters which we call the Tao Teh Ching. After completing the book, he departed for the west.[11]

From the solitary westering he never returned. Why, if solitude is but a restorative? I know this is only a legend: but why does the legend say it?[12]

How indeed can solitude function as a restorative if it does not provide its own intrinsic values? What exactly are they? As I have read over twenty-five centuries of celebrations of solitude, through Lao Tzu, Hesiod, Plato, Jesus, Seneca, Marcus Aurelius, Petrarch, St. Teresa of Avila, Montaigne, Rousseau, Goethe, Wordsworth, Byron, Shelley, Hazlitt, Hugo, Emerson, Thoreau, Dickinson, Whitman, Muir, Proust, Rilke, Byrd, Stevens, Eiseley, Carr, Tillich, Sarton, Camus, Storr, Kohák, and Koller, certain praises are repeated again and again. In part 2 of this volume I collect and organize them around five central ideas: Freedom, Attunement to Self, Attunement to Nature, Reflective Perspective, Creativity. Then I worry about them. Take Freedom, for example. Petrarch wrote in *De Vita Solitaria* (The Life of Solitude),

> For it is not the mere name of solitude but the good things which are proper to it that I praise. And it is not so much the solitary recesses and the silence that delight me as the leisure and freedom that dwell within them.[13]

So true, a wonderful freedom does characterize solitude; but what is the distinctive nature of that freedom? How does it compare, for example, with political freedom, which seems to be devoid of value in solitude? Is one freedom broader or deeper, in any coherent sense, than the other? Such questions will take us to the very core of the values of solitude.

But where there are virtues there are surely vices, and the Western tradition has not been lax in raising objections to solitude. Pericles remarked in the "Funeral Oration" that Athenians regard the man who takes no part in public affairs, not as one who minds his own business, but as good for nothing.[14]

Dr. Johnson took a stern view of the likes of Lao Tzu:

> There is a higher order of men . . . (who) ought to consider themselves as appointed the guardians of mankind: they are placed in an evil world to exhibit public examples of good life; and may be said, when they withdraw to solitude, to desert the station which Providence assigned them.[15]

Indeed, especially when one turns from the evaluation of episodes of solitude to the assessment of the place of solitude in a whole life, one raises issues that Western culture has viewed with marked ambivalence. Opposing voices are already to be heard in our ancient sources, the Bible and Greek literature. Tillich noticed that Adam's aloneness was the first thing that God found not good (Gen. 2:18), and Eccles. 4:10 moans "Woe to him that is alone! For if he falleth, there is none to raise him up." On the other hand, Moses, John the Baptist, and Jesus found in solitude the great moral visions that became their lives. Furthermore, the New Testament identifies true prayer with inner prayer, the prayer of the heart said in solitude, and not the prayer of the Pharisees cried aloud in the market place. The Sermon on the Mount admonishes the faithful,

> when thou prayest, enter into thy closet, and when thou hast shut thy door, pray to thy Father which is in secret; and thy Father which seeth in secret shall reward thee openly. (Matt. 6:6)

On the other hand, as the medieval clerics argued against the monastics, Saint John demanded, "he that loveth not his brother whom he hath seen, how can he love God whom he hath not seen?" (I John 4:20). Ah, said the monastics, but did not Christ say, "My kingdom is not of this world" (John 18:36), and furthermore that "The kingdom of God is within" (Luke 17:21)? And so it went.

A similar ambivalence manifests itself when we turn to the Greeks. The myths and legends, it is true, do not appear to accord much value to solitude: the gods live together on Mt. Olympus, and their escapades are amorous or political, not solitary. As for mortals, both Achilles and Odysseus chafe at their solitudes, Narcissus is punished for his solitary disdain for maidens, and Atalanta's plan to remain unmarried is thwarted by the gods. Indeed solitude seems to be part of the punishment in many of the tales: Io is compelled to wander forlornly over the earth by Hera, and the three great offenders whose punishments so powerfully impressed themselves on Western thought—Prometheus chained to the side of the mountain, Tantalus forever thirsty in the pool of cool clear water, and Sisyphus condemned to roll the great stone uphill forever—each of these punishments seems increased by the solitude of the victim.

However, the ancient Greek view is not so clear-cut as might be deduced from these examples. Antigone, I recall, buried her brother alone. Joseph Campbell has remarked upon a hero-theme running through the myths which involves a solitary quest: a young hero must prove himself alone, and then receives some gift or power which enables him to aid his people (Theseus and Bellerophon come to mind). Along different lines, the stories of Hercules and Oedipus develop a theme of redemptive atonement in solitude, suggesting that only in isolation can guilt, remorse, and redemption run their full course.

The same ambivalence regarding the value of solitude is present in the philosophers. In the *Phaedrus,* Plato gives us a Socrates that would rather discuss philosophy with men than ramble alone through nature:

> You must forgive me, dear friend; I'm a lover of learning, and trees and open country won't teach me anything, whereas men in town do.[16]

Yet even he withdraws occasionally into a kind of trance-like meditation which, though unexplained in the dialogues, is mentioned too often to be devoid of importance. As for Plato himself, taking the middle and late dialogues as representing his own position, individual solitude is little mentioned and might not seem of any importance; yet the highest good of the highest life is consistently said to lie in the contemplation of the Forms, a clearly solitary activity.

Aristotle reveals the same ambivalence. Some of his most famous remarks in the *Nicomachean Ethics* mitigate against solitude: "to live alone, a man must be either a beast or a god" (obviously real men are neither). Discussing the role friendship plays in happiness, he writes:

> Surely it is strange, too, to make the supremely happy man a solitary; for no one would choose the whole world on condition of being alone, since man is a political creature and one whose nature is to live with others.[17]

Yet Aristotle could never align himself with Pericles and the man of the polis at the cost of turning his back on the older philosophers, and as the *Nicomachean Ethics* winds to a close he argues that the highest good for this *zoon politicon* is contemplation:

> If happiness is activity in accordance with virtue, it is reasonable that it should be in accordance with the highest virtue; and this will be that of the best thing in us. . . . That this activity is contemplation we have already said.[18]

But the contemplation intended was a solitary activity. Aristotle was of two minds about solitude.

That was 2300 years ago, but the ambivalences have persevered. As the twentieth century draws to a close, we are still not sure what place solitude ought to have in our lives. We are becoming more communal, more political, more communicative, but we are also flying apart, fascinated with the varieties of the "return to nature" possible in activities such as gardening, wilderness camping, sunlight meditation. The divorce rate is rising but marriages are keeping pace. The true and balanced place of solitude in a human life is a philosophical question which has, for us, now, urgency.

The reflections that fill the following pages focus upon these problems of essence and value. For those who like ponderosities, there will emerge a phenomenology and an axiology of solitude. I prefer to speak plainly, to ask: how much of the experience of solitude can be articulated? Which claims for its value can survive rational scrutiny?

I ask these questions of solitude for personal reasons. All the while, through the arguments and the poetic evocations, I stalk the creatures of my own ambivalence: should I, as the days pile into years around me, move ever closer to other people, giving now out of the rich stores of past solitudes? Or should I quietly, unobtrusively, head out westward through the Han-ku pass?

PART 1

THE NATURE OF SOLITUDE

What sort of space is that which separates a man from his fellows and makes him solitary?

—HENRY DAVID THOREAU

CHAPTER 1

Dimensions

I f I aim to say what solitude is, it seems best to begin by scrutinizing an example. I need an experience of solitude to interrogate, and which better than the one Thoreau describes in the opening lines of "Solitude" in *Walden?*

> This is a delicious evening, when the whole body is one sense, and imbibes delight through every pore. I go and come with a strange liberty in Nature, a part of herself. As I walk along the stony shore of the pond in my shirt sleeves, though it is cool as well as cloudy and windy, and I see nothing special to attract me, all the elements are unusually congenial to me. The bullfrogs trump to usher in the night, and the note of the whippoorwill is borne on the rippling wind from over the water. Sympathy with the fluttering alder and poplar leaves almost takes away my breath; yet, like the lake, my serenity is rippled but not ruffled. These small waves raised by the evening wind are as remote from storm as the smooth reflecting surface. Though it is now dark, the wind still blows and roars in the wood, the waves still dash, and some creatures lull the rest with their notes. The repose is never complete. The wildest animals do not repose, but seek their prey now; the fox, and skunk, and rabbit, now roam the fields and woods without fear. They are Nature's watchmen—links which connect the days of animated life.[1]

Three features which I intuitively associate with solitude are apparent in this description:

1. Physical Isolation. Thoreau is alone by the pond in the simple physical sense: there are no human beings within possible sensing distance of his body.
2. Social Disengagement. Experientially, he is not engaged with other humans: he is not aware of anyone nearby, not searching for anyone or hiding from anyone, not longing for anyone or remembering anyone. His mind is filled with his surroundings, surroundings devoid of people.
3. Reflectiveness. Although most of the passage describes a state of absorption in the sights and sounds of the evening, the last line signals a reflective distancing from the directly perceptually given: reflection now provides a symbolic meaning for Thoreau—"Nature's Watchmen" and "links in a chain."

When all three of these features characterize an extended experience, a "time," it is certainly a solitude. But are all three necessary conditions for solitude, the sort of attributes which could yield at once a definition of the concept? Unfortunately, matters are not so simple, for there are varieties of solitude in which each of the features seems to be absent (or rather incidental).

1. Physical Isolation? Can there be solitude in the presence of other people? Thoreau thought so: "The really diligent student in one of the crowded hives of Cambridge College is as solitary as a dervish in the desert." Or consider the meditative state attained by this ancient Taoist sage:

> Tzu-Ch'i of South Wall sat leaning on his armrest, staring up at the sky and breathing—vacant and far away, as though he'd lost his companion. Yen Ch'eng Tzu-yu, who was standing by his side in attendance, said, What is this? Can you really make the body like a withered tree and the mind like dead ashes? The man leaning on the armrest now is not the one who leaned on it before![2]

No doubt the majority of solitudes involve physical isolation from others, no doubt it is very difficult to achieve solitude with a chattering disciple at your side; but the minority and the difficult should not be excluded by definition.

2. Social Disengagement? One is struck throughout Thoreau's essays by his tendency to anthropomorphize natural things—indeed nature itself—and thus experience himself as engaged:

> Sympathy with the fluttering alder and poplar leaves almost takes away my breath;

> . . . the most sweet and tender, the most innocent and encouraging society may be found in any natural object . . .[3]

And there were other presences at the pond: he delighted in the "old settler" who told stories on winter evenings and the "elderly dame" who told mythic fables while he strolled in her garden—both presumably creations of his imagination, but powerful sources of delight nonetheless. Commonly, those who prefer solitude to society are able to people their silent worlds with a wealth of imagined encounters and silent conversations which satisfy completely the need for companionship. Is this not a kind of engagement with others, however?

3. Reflectiveness? Had Thoreau remained immersed in the perceptual experience, simply flowing empathically with the eve-

ning sights and sounds, would it not have been a solitude? An architecture student sits sketching for hours, unaware of the passing time as the facade of the building emerges on her sketchpad; a carpenter bends over the table leg he is carving, fully absorbed in the pressure and resistance of the chisel: surely these are solitudes, but where is the reflection? It is important not to overintellectualize solitude, as though only writers and philosophers belong there. No, our quarry is right there in the ordinary lives of ordinary people. Here is Richard Triumpho exulting in a farmer's solitude; and although some of his solitudes are reflective, this one is not:

> All day I have been riding the droning tractor, planting sudan grass on the sloping 19 acres we call Rivenburg Hill, named after some long forgotten landowner. The sun is hot; the ground is dusty. My face, arms and clothes are covered with a thick layer of grime—a combination of sweat, good field dust and fertilizer powder. . . . But I am happy. Since sunup I have driven round and round this field with a one-track mind, like one possessed . . . round and round I go with one thought uppermost in my mind—putting in the seed.[4]

Reflection upon these very different solitary experiences has convinced me, finally, that the most promising place to look for the core of solitude is in the realm of social disengagement, our second factor. To be sure, solitude is most usually and most easily achieved in physical isolation, but that appears to be because most of us are too little able to disengage consciousness from the powerful stimuli of present others. Again, although solitude does provoke and nourish kinds of reflection that are most intimately connected with the intrinsic values of the state, as we shall see later on, this need not necessarily occur. Solitude is, most ultimately, simply an experiential world in which other people are absent: that is enough for solitude, that is constant through all solitudes. Other people may be physically present, provided that our minds are disengaged from them; and the full range of disengaged activities, from reflective withdrawal to complete immersion in the tumbling rush of sensations, find their places along the spectrum of solitudes. As for the exact nature of this state of disengagement, as for the problems which imaginative modes of engagement seem to raise about solitude, much more will have to be said.

The three features we have just been examining may be the first and clearest ideas called to mind by the mention of solitude, but they are not all that term suggests. Freedom seems implicated too: must not true solitude be freely chosen? and is it not also a state distinguished by a distinctive freedom of activity? "I come and go with a strange liberty in Nature," wrote Thoreau, and Francis Bacon remarked that "the most ordinary cause of a single life is liberty." Then there is the suggestion of quiet, of stillness, of silence: a recent author remarks that "genuine solitude is a 'coming to terms with' silence and aloneness in life."[5] Again, the expression 'the world of solitude' comes so easily to the lips, suggesting that solitude is a peculiar sort of "place," with its own distinctive experiences of time and space. These suggestions must be pursued.

The idea that a time of disengagement from others should only be called a solitude if it is freely chosen has an initial attraction when we think of solitaries like Thoreau and Muir and Rilke, but must be modified when we recall some famous prisoners.

Anicius Manlius Severinus Boethius (AD 475–525) was born to a wealthy patrician family during the last years of the Roman Empire. Remarkable for scholarship as a youth, he entered public life around thirty years of age and soon became a consul, holding that position successfully for ten years until he returned to scholarly interests. The retirement was interrupted, however: Theodoric the Ostrogoth had just succeeded in conquering Italy, and sought to conciliate the Roman Senate by returning to office this honored public servant. For several years Boethius enjoyed Theodoric's confidence, but in 523 things changed abruptly: Theodoric became convinced that Boethius was the force behind some treasonable actions of the Senate, and without warning threw the old man into prison. There Boethius languished for two long years while Theodoric skirmished with the Senate. Finally in 525, Theodoric had Boethius taken from prison, tortured, and bludgeoned to death. It was during those final two years of darkness and despair, however, that Boethius wrote *The Consolation of Philosophy,* an enduring testament to his solitude.

Dr. Viktor Frankl, deported to Auschwitz by the Nazis, survived for three terrible years in the degrading brutality of the camp. In *Man's Search for Meaning* he describes how he managed, incredibly, to steal some brief moments of solitude:

> There were times, of course, when it was possible, and even necessary, to keep away from the crowd. . . . The prisoner craved to be alone with himself and his

thoughts. He yearned for privacy and for solitude. After my transportation to a so-called "rest-camp" I had the rare fortune to find solitude for about five minutes at a time. Behind the earthen hut where I worked and in which were crowded about fifty delirious patients, there was a quiet spot in a corner of the double fence of barbed wire surrounding the camp. A tent had been improvised there with a few poles and branches of trees in order to shelter a half-dozen corpses (the daily death rate in the camp). There was also a shaft leading to the water pipes. I squatted on the wooden lid of this shaft whenever my services were not needed. I just sat and looked out at the green flowering slopes and the distant blue hills of the Bavarian landscape, framed by the meshes of barbed wire. I dreamed longingly, and my thoughts wandered north and northeast, in the direction of my home, but I could only see clouds.

The corpses near me, crawling with lice, did not bother me. Only the steps of passing guards could rouse me from my dreams.[6]

Robert Stroud, The Birdman of Alcatraz, was only nineteen when he shot the man who raped his girl friend. Convicted and sentenced to twelve years in prison, he was incarcerated in the maximum security federal prison in Leavenworth, Kansas. The first view of that prison, which would contain so much of his adult life, was calculated to fill hardened hearts with despair:

Rising sheer from a slight elevation of the friendly prairie, enclosing sixteen acres, the wall sat like a flat square snake of brick and mortar, its face a front of granite centered with a nose-like dome and portico. Ranging from thirty to forty-two feet high, the wall had been erected by the prisoners themselves, working in the thousands in steady shifts since 1899. The wall's history immediately became known to the inmates and it was an ever-present and awesome reality to convicts and guards alike. The wall contained the encysted sweat of prisoners forced to immure themselves under the rifles of guards. Periodically some guard would quit, saying, "The Wall got me" . . .[7]

It got to Stroud too: four years later a brutal guard tried to club him into submission, and Stroud stabbed the guard to death. For this he was immediately removed to solitary confinement, and then sentenced to death. Moved by the tireless pleading of Stroud's mother, however, President Woodrow Wilson finally commuted the sentence to life imprisonment—in solitary confinement. Thus began fifty years of confinement alone, first at Leavenworth and then on "The Rock" in San Francisco Bay.

His cells in both places were similar in their isolation and their bleakness:

Behind the enormous stone facade of Leavenworth, past the great cell blocks, the Isolation Building huddled alone. On the first floor, the rear half of the structure held eighteen segregation cells, nine on each side. It was a prison within a prison.

Stroud's cell was twelve feet long and six feet wide, and the thick plaster walls were painted gray. At the rear was a small barred window. The door was of heavy steel bars covered by wire netting. There was a second door of solid wood which could be swung upon the steel door, shutting out light and air. In the cell stood a lavatory, washbasin and a narrow bed. From the high ceiling dangled a twenty-five watt bulb.[8]

One June day in 1920, out for his one hour of exercise alone in the prison yard, Stroud came upon a fallen bird's nest containing four weak baby sparrows. Carrying them gently back to his cell, he fashioned a nest out of rags, and, with permission from a sympathetic warden, nursed them to maturity. Thus began the series of acute observations of the habits, breeding, and diseases of small birds that was to totally absorb him for the next twenty years. During that time he raised and studied thousands of canaries, publishing a number of articles in the *Roller Canary Journal* and producing two full-length books on canary diseases. When this world of fruitful solitary study was shattered by a sudden and vindictive transfer to Alcatraz in 1940, Stroud began to research and write a massive historical analysis of the United States penal system. This remarkable work, which captured the sympathy of many people outside the prison walls for dozens of years, was accomplished in solitude, in six-foot by twelve-foot cells.

It would be absurd to deny the solitude of these three men on grounds that their isolation was not freely chosen. Yet in the second suggested meaning of freedom in solitude, a time of free activity, there seems some merit. Notice how each of the three prisoners deliberately constructed their solitudes: they took charge—to write, to sequester themselves, to study birds. Spheres of freedom remained available to them in their imprisonment, and they found the strength to exercise those freedoms. Take away all choice, all control, and the word 'solitude' sounds wrong. If one thinks of victims of torture, lying overwhelmed, aching, terrified, and exhausted in the darkness alone, it seems as semantically wrong as it does morally indecent to call their states "solitudes"; and the reason appears to be the suggestion the word has of freedom and control.[9]

Quiet, stillness, silence—these do come invariably to mind when one thinks of solitude. "The most beautiful thing about my burrow is the stillness," exults the solitary animal in Kafka's eerie tale *The Burrow*. Indeed, profound stillness and silence can almost seem to make of themselves a solitude. Is this bedside vigil of Walt Whitman's a solitude or not?

> I have been sitting late to-night by the bedside of a wounded captain, a special friend of mine, lying with a painful fracture of left leg in one of the hospitals, in a large ward partially vacant. The lights were put out, all but a little candle, far from where I sat. The full moon shone in through the windows, making long, slanting silvery patches on the floor. All was still, my friend too was silent, but could not sleep; so I sat there by him, slowly wafting the fan, and occupied with the musings that arose out of the scene, the long shadowy ward, the beautiful ghostly moonlight on the floor, the white beds, here and there an occupant with huddled form, the bed-clothes thrown off.[10]

Yet surely solitude need not of necessity be quiet and silent; for who would not recognize a familiar solitude in Robert Louis Stevenson's remembrance of falling asleep in a forest encampment?

> The wind among the trees was my lullaby. Sometimes it sounded for minutes together with a steady even rush, not rising nor abating; and again it would swell and burst like a great crashing breaker, and the trees would patter me all over with big drops from the rain of the afternoon. Night after night, in my own bedroom in the country, I have given ear to this perturbing concert of the wind among the woods; but whether it was a difference in the trees, or the lie of the ground, or because I was myself outside and in the midst of it, the fact remains that the wind sang to a different tune among these woods of Gevaudan. I hearkened and hearkened; and meanwhile sleep took gradual possession of my body and subdued my thoughts and senses; but still my last waking effort was to listen and distinguish, and my last conscious state was one of wonder at the foreign clamour in my ears.[11]

Confusion enters our thinking about the necessity for stillness, quiet, and silence in solitude because of several ambiguities in the terms. In the first place, 'quiet' and 'still' can refer either to a state of noiselessness or to a state of passive calmness. These two states are distinguishable—Stevenson was himself quiet although the wind in the trees was not—but they have a striking facility for producing and interfusing each other. Oliver Morgan felt this quiet agency:

> I am sitting at my desk and looking out the bay window at some swaying trees and those bright autumn leaves that have not yet fallen to the ground. It is quiet, and I am alone. At this moment I choose to allow the quiet to surround and penetrate me. I can feel the concerns, and plans, and details of an ordinary, busy day recede for a time. I can feel myself quieting down . . .[12]

Here, quiet in the sense of passive calmness is produced by relaxing into resonance with the quiet of the noiseless room.

Still, neither the quiet of noiselessness nor the quiet of passive calmness are essential for solitude. The solitary world is also a place of activity, sometimes the best place for an activity, and the action may be noisy. Think of John Muir alone, high in the California Sierras, running whooping down a great morrain of glacier-strewn boulders, feeling the music of their placement in his feet.

But there is another ambiguity here as well. We use the term 'quiet' sometimes to refer to the absence of any noise, sometimes to the absence of *human* noises, especially speech; in this latter sense, the grassy bank of a gurgling stream which flows under rustling boughs can be said to be a quiet place so long as there are no voices to be heard there. And now one can see that quiet in the sense of absence of human noise *is* connected to solitude through the core feature noted earlier, disengagement from other people: the less one hears of human noise, the more disengaged from people one is, and so the deeper the solitude.

What about silence, that which Thoreau despaired of doing into English? Here the writings on solitude reveal a considerable elasticity of usage. 'Silent' conveys to me the absence of all sound, human or otherwise: it seems natural to say that the silence was *broken* by the sudden rustling of the wind in the leaves or by the cry of a bird. Alice Koller, however, admits nature's sounds to the silence:

> I surround myself with silence. The silence is within me, permeates my house, reaches beyond the surfaces of the outer walls and into the bordering woods. It is one silence, continuous from within me outward in all directions: above, beneath, forward, rearward, sideward. In the silence I listen, I watch, I sense, I attend. I observe. I require this silence. I search it out. The finely drawn treble song of a white-throated sparrow is part of it. Invasions of it by the noise of engines are torments to me.
> This is my solitude.[13]

Charles Alexander Eastman, a Sioux who wrote during the last decades of the nineteenth century about the traditional culture he remembered from his youth, stretched the term silence to refer to a way of life:

> Silence is the absolute poise or balance of body, mind, and spirit. The man who preserves his selfhood ever calm and unshaken by the storms of existence—not a leaf, as it were, astir on the tree; not a ripple upon the surface of shining pool—his, in the mind of the unlettered sage, is the ideal attitude and conduct of life.[14]

Absence of noise, absence of the sounds of humans and their artifacts, inner calmness, balance and poise, a place where all of these meet and interfuse—no wonder Thoreau despaired of doing the thing into English![15] In the end, however, the conceptual connections between solitude and silence (in a reasonably restrained sense of the latter term) seem to parallel those between solitude and quiet. Consider, for example, this plausible intuition: as silence deepens, solitude deepens. If silence refers to the absence of human sounds—voices, footsteps, automobiles—the intuition proves out because solitude *is* this sort of absence of others in one's experiential world. On the other hand, the claim that the silencing of nonhuman sounds marks a deepening solitude does not prove out; far from being conceptually opposed to such sounds, solitude is in fact the best place to truly enjoy them.

The last suggested meaning of solitude I will consider emerges in the frequent references to solitude as a "realm" or "world," a place where time and space are experienced very differently than in society. Wordsworth remembered his heedless youthful solitary explorations as

> . . . a time when meadow, grove and stream,
> The earth, and every common sight,
> To me did seem
> Apparelled in celestial light,
> The glory and the freshness of a dream.[16]

To speak first of time, it is striking how many celebrations of solitude emphasize the difference in its perceived temporality: Thoreau wrote that

> Sometimes, in a summer morning, having taken my accustomed bath, I sat in my sunny doorway from sunrise till noon, rapt in a revery, amidst the pines and hickories and sumacs, in undisturbed solitude and stillness, while the birds sang around or flitted noiseless through the house, until by the sun falling in at my west window, or the noise of some traveller's wagon on the distant highway, I was reminded of the lapse of time. I grew in those seasons like corn in the night. . . . For the most part, I minded not how the hours went. The day advanced as if to light some work of mine; it was morning, and lo, now it is evening. . . . My days were not days of the week, bearing the stamp of any heathen deity, nor were they minced into hours and fretted by the ticking of a clock.[17]

May Sarton wrote one evening in her *Journal of a Solitude,*

> I began the day with Vaughan Williams' *Mass* sung by the King's College choir. There are days when only religious music will do. Under the light of eternity

things, the daily trivia, the daily frustrations, fall away. It's all a matter of getting to the center of the beam.[18]

But what is time wrapped in revery, unfolding under the light of eternity? It is time which flows more from within than from without, time that is conditioned by the subject's unique constellation of interests, hopes, and anxieties—subjective time, in one sense of that vague philosopher's term.[19] Objective time, the time of most interpersonal activities but especially of science, technics, and commerce, is clock time: it has a uniform and interpersonally repeatable metric, an invariant order and an irreversible direction. Each of its attributes are established through social agreements which recognize certain natural processes as privileged—the oscillation of a pendulum of a certain length, the atomic decay of a well-known substance. Although objective time has a direction, its repeatable sequence of discrete units has no intrinsic beginning or ending. And it has no essential reference to any particular human subject.

Subjective time, time as experienced by the subject, is quite a different matter. For one thing, it *endures,* as Bergson emphasized long ago:

> There is no doubt but that for us time is at first identical with the continuity of our inner life. What is this continuity? That of a flow or passage, but a self-sufficient flow or passage, the flow not implying a thing that flows, and the passing not presupposing states through which we pass; the *thing* and the *state* are only artificially taken snapshots of the transition; and this transition, all that is naturally experienced, is duration itself. . . . A melody to which we listen with our eyes closed, heeding it alone, comes close to coinciding with this time which is the very fluidity of our inner life . . .[20]

This flowing personal time is not metrically regular: sometimes swift and sometimes slow, it rushes through emotional narrows, settles down into widening pools, sinks slowly into unconsciousness. Moreover its "times" are neither uniform nor repeatable, and often can not be assigned precise beginning or end points. It carries a weighting from memory, and is, if Heidegger is correct, ever shadowed by anxiety over its ending in death. Our memory and our death: we are the demiurges of our own subjective time.

Social situations, however, are fraught with the need to correlate our subjectivity with other people's. The more people involved and the more correlation required—think of air traffic controllers—the greater the pull towards objective time as described above. Of course some encounters with others are easy and empathic, each party giving themselves freely to the temporality springing from their own subjectivity: lovers feel this as a spontaneous attunement. Yet even lovers feel some blocks and hindrances to the flow of subjective time, whereas solitude, the complete disengagement from others and their desiring pursuits, gives subjective time free rein. Not only is there a lightening sense of escape from the clock-time framework of social engagements and from the interested time of other subjects, there is an opening upon a different set of temporal dimensions. As Schutz and Luckerman expressed it in *The Structure of the Life-World,*

> the subjective time of the stream of consciousness (of inner duration) intersects with the rhythm of the body as 'biological time' in general, and with the seasons as world time in general. . . . We live in all these dimensions simultaneously.[21]

How far-removed is the temporality of this solitary realm from the ticking mechanical clock! Erazim Kohák beautifully captures its sensations in this description of the gathering twilight on his New Hampshire homestead:

> The night comes softly, beyond the powerline and the blacktop, where the long-abandoned wagon road fades amid the new growth. It does not crowd the lingering day. There is a time of passage as the bright light of the summer day, cool green and intensely blue, slowly yields to the deep, virgin darkness. Quietly, the darkness grows in the forest, seeping into the clearing and penetrating the soul, all-healing, all-reconciling, renewing the world for a new day. Were there no darkness to restore the soul, humans would quickly burn out their finite store of dreams.[22]

Kohák is reluctant to use the term "subjective time" to describe such experiences, partly because they are not automatically available to modern subjects, dazed as they are by too much "objectivity," and partly because the rhythms of the evening are real natural rhythms, not merely the private inner constructions of a subject.[23] True enough, but the sense of time in these experiences is also strongly determined by the subject's particular inner bent; Marlow, in Joseph Conrad's *Heart of Darkness,* felt a very different sense of time before a dark forest as he steamed up the Congo, the dark aeonic time of an evil dream:

Going up that river was like travelling back to the earliest beginnings of the world, when vegetation rioted on the earth and the big trees were kings. An empty stream, a great silence, an impenetrable forest. The air was warm, thick, heavy, sluggish. . . . And this stillness of life did not in the least resemble a peace. It was the stillness of an implacable force brooding over an inscrutable intention. It looked at you with a vengeful aspect.[24]

It seems most useful, therefore, to think of subjective time as a complex product of individual passion and interest operating selectively upon independent givens.[25] I prefer the term 'attentive time,' which emphasizes the way in which the sense of time is determined by both the inner subject which attends and the independent object of that attention. The contributions of each element of attentive time to the experiential whole are well conveyed by this description of a fisherman's river:

No two successive hours are alike to the angler, for the brook or river is changing its form and hue in every instant, and his mind and mood and artistry are affected by every yard of the gliding Protean stream. He is watching it, not with the sentimentalist's preoccupation with pure beauty, but rather with the fisherman's trained perception of the effect of wind and light, of deeper or darker-colored water, of eddy or shallow, upon the next cast of his fly.[26]

With this understanding of the idea of attentive time, the implications for solitude emerge easily: with its dependence upon individual passion and interest, attentive time intensifies and spreads as disengagement from others becomes more complete. Thus an important experiential truth lies behind the intuitive phrase, 'a time of solitude.'

What about space: is it experienced differently in solitude than among people? Thoreau's wry boast, "I have travelled a great deal in Concord," reminds us of one striking phenomenon, the way in which a space expands when there is freedom and time to explore it at leisure. Anyone who has spent long periods of time in a house—even a room, perhaps a sick-room, perhaps a study—knows this well. Later we will see how Emily Dickinson's solitude was formed by the space of the house in Amherst, how other women confined to the house have managed to expand their horizons.

Obviously too, the points just made regarding attentive time are easily transfered to space. Solitude can shrink distances, as when warmly imagined friends, thousands of miles away, seem just over the hill; conversely, the town in which one has no interest recedes into the distance. In solitude, the attentive imagination constructs a sense of place out of stories: there is an overgrown orchard near my house which Johnny Appleseed must have planted, so it must be within walking distance of Illinois; the marsh down by the shore is both easterly and hospitable to hydras, so Hercules must have come this way long ago. In such solitudes, Greece feels near.

Less obvious, perhaps, are those distinctive features of the space of solitude which spring from the complex ways in which experienced space is coordinated. George Lakoff and Mark Johnson have recently explored the genesis of our most basic spatial concepts—and then the derivative spatial metaphors based upon them—from bodily experience.

> We have bodies and we stand erect. Almost every movement we make involves a motor program that either changes our up-down orientation, maintains it, presupposes it, or takes it into account in some way. . . . The centrality of up-down orientation in our motor programs and everyday functioning might make one think that there could be no alternative to this orientational concept. Objectively speaking, however, there are many possible frameworks for spatial orientation, including Cartesian coordinates, that don't in themselves have up-down orientation. Human spatial concepts, however, include UP-DOWN, FRONT-BACK, IN-OUT, NEAR-FAR, etc. It is these that are relevant to our continual everyday bodily functioning, and this gives them priority over other possible structurings of space—for us.[27]

To illustrate, if I am gazing at a daffodil two meters from my eyes, its experienced spatial location is *in front, ahead and a little to the left, down there.* The new leaves on the sugar maple above it are *to the left side and higher,* and so on as all the objects of the perceptual field arrange themselves around me.

Things change, however, with the arrival of The Intruder. People are, of course, objects in our perceptual field, like the flowers and trees, but they are also experienced by us as themselves coordinate-centers, new loci of front/back, right/left, up/down. This dramatically alters our experience of space: not simply cluttered with one more object, it is now more complexly referenced. William James remarked once about the uncanny feeling that comes over a lone hiker if he suddenly notices another hiker in the distance, what a change it makes in the feel of the wilderness. Closer to home lie many illustrations. What was a direct relationship between me and the daffodil has become a three-way affair: my rapport with the flower is lost as I feel it giving me only half its attention. Further, my sense of the flower's nearness becomes unsettled: roughly calculating its nearness to the intruder and my nearness to him, triangularizing myself as I feel him triangularizing me and the flower, nearness falls into limbo.[28]

This complex referencing of space which other people automatically produce has a marked effect upon our experience of space even when, as I have been imagining, the other bears no particular burden of emotional weight. Of course people almost always figure in our world as friendly or threatening, helpful or hindering, significant or unimportant, and these weightings stretch or compress lived space in their own ways. Sartre taught us to see this in his discussion of the way space would alter if the shaming gaze of a stranger caught one peering through a keyhole. More ingeniously, there was his insistence that the bare *look* of the other freezes one in object-hood, miring the self in materiality, chaining the spirit in space. Certainly the chapter on The Look in *Being and Nothingness*[29] is Sartre at his most fascinating, and my few reflections here concerning spatiality and intersubjectivity find their inspiration in his words. They find a dark confirmation too in the repeated experience of women that the appearance of a man in a lonely environment coordinates the space along axes of fear and flight; when they find it impossible to shake this sense of potential threat while alone, their solitude is crippled. What I have wished to emphasize here, however, is the important role the other plays in our experience of space simply as an independent perceiving subject.[30]

When this referencing to others is eliminated in solitude, how altered is the feel of space! One becomes an unconfused center, flowing easily out to the horizon, an alert clarity around which all objects dance. This feeling of rapport between the myriad forms of the universe and the lone self at its center was remembered vividly by Walt Whitman:

> As the night advanced it changed its spirit and garments to ampler stateliness. I was almost conscious of a definite presence, Nature silently near. The great constellation of the Water-Serpent stretched its coils over more than half the heavens. The Swan with outspread wings was flying down the Milky Way. The northern Crown, the Eagle, Lyra, all three in their places. From the whole dome shot down points of light, rapport with me, through the clear blue-black.[31]

It is this rapport, I think, which is most distinctive of the space of solitude, a rapport which explains the special power of solitude to connect us with nature.[32] Disengagement from other subjects is its essence, and that is also the essence of solitude.

What, then, is solitude? It is a time in which experience is disengaged from other people. All of the other features of solitude that come intuitively to mind, the physical isolation, the reflective cast of mind, the freedom, the silence, the distinctive feel of space and time—all of these flow from that core feature, the absence of others in one's experiential world. Of course much remains to be said about this disengaged experience, this curious region spreading out behind time's back in which you gaze from the absolute center of the world and your thinking is the only human voice. Perhaps, though, the possibilities—and limitations!—of doing solitude into English have emerged?

CHAPTER 2

Near Relations: Loneliness, Isolation, Privacy, Alienation

Solitude, I understand you better now. Or do I? After all, loneliness, isolation, privacy, and alienation are also states of social disengagement, although none of them seem to be the same thing as solitude. What are the distinctions here? Why must they be respected?

As I have read over the wide range of philosophical, psychological, sociological, and theological writings on human aloneness, three obstacles to clear thought have plagued me. First, there is the striking diversity of usages. In his useful survey, *Isolation: Clinical and Experimental Approaches,* the psychologist Charles Brownfield detected twenty-five different expressions used to describe sensory deprivation or perceptual isolation, among them 'solitude.'[1] More disturbingly, while Paul Halmos defines solitude as "the lack of desired social contact,"[2] Rubin Gotesky's definition appears to actually *exclude* such states:

> Solitude is that state or condition of living alone, in any of its many forms, without the pain of loneliness or isolation being an intrinsic component of that state or condition.[3]

A second stumbling block for philosophers is a frequent careless gliding from one distinct concept to another. Thomas Parkinson glides from solitude to loneliness in the following remark: "The writing of poetry is a solitary operation. But that very loneliness is among the primary rewards of the poet".[4] A similar glide appears in the opening lines of Ralph Harper's chapter "Self-Isolation" in *The Seventh Solitude:* "Solitude is not new. There have always been men and women born to be lonely."[5] Sixty years ago, when philosophers still wrote in a magisterial style, John Cowper Powys glided cavalierly in *A Philosophy of Solitude* between such apparently different terms as 'alone' and 'lonely':

Every human being is alone in the core of the mind. When we are born we cry; and that cry is the cry of loneliness.

. . . the conscious "I am I" within us is absolutely alone. It is alone from the first moment of its awareness of life to its last moment on the threshold of what may be its final extinction.
   The drifting, brainless, gregariousness of so many human beings, imitating one another, conciliating one another, admiring, desiring, envying, competing, tormenting one another, is an attempt to escape from this inherent loneliness of the self.[6]

And, at about the same time, in *Solitude and Society*[7] the Russian existentialist Nicolas Berdyaev treated 'solitude,' 'loneliness,' and 'alienation' as synonyms—a usage which would have surprised Thoreau, who remarked in *Walden,* "I am never lonely here."

A third problem bedevils the search for the precise meaning of 'solitude': something about human aloneness seems to provoke writers to hyperbole. Paul Tillich exclaims, "Man is alone because he is man,"[8] and Clark Moustakas laments, "Man is ultimately and forever lonely."[9] This hyperbole even becomes a philosophy in several authors: Parkinson argues that "the subject of all poetry is loneliness" and Ben Mijuscovik defends "an image of man as intrinsically alone and irredeemably lost, man as continually struggling to escape the solipsistic prison of his frightening solitude."[10] Arguments are advanced, which we will have to consider, but all the while I am thinking, "surely this writer exaggerates?"

Given these three maddening proclivities, a search for the "real" meanings of the terms designating various forms of aloneness might seem futile. I think, however, that it is not futile; aloneness does have joints, and I think my knife can find them. In any event, an author must explain his own usage, and that is the task to which I now turn. The approach, dictated by my interest in the experiential nature of solitude, will be to distinguish it from lonely or isolated or alienated modes of experience. The guiding assumption is that, whatever the similarities, it would be very odd indeed if five different terms had exactly the same meaning.

Loneliness

Loneliness, in the first and clearest sense, is an emotion. Emotions are things you feel,[11] though they are not simply bodily feelings. Additionally, they are structures of belief and evaluation: anger, for example, does not *cause* the judgment that one has been wronged, it *is* (in part) the judgment that one has been wronged—just as shame essentially involves the assessment that one has done something humiliating, and Weltschmertz ("world-sadness") involves the global assessment that things are, all in all, sad. Generally, emotions also involve desires—e.g. to confront the object of one's wrath, to cover one's shame—and they also manifest distinctive modes of attention: "Great feelings take with them their own universe . . . They light up with their passion an exclusive world in which they recognize their climate."[12] Camus's words remind us that the attentional focus of anger is different from that of shame or Weltschmertz: when one is angry, the manifold world simplifies and condenses into the object of anger, whereas with shame the center of attention is the self (though other people may seem painfully near); Weltschmertz, quite differently, beholds a broad undifferentiated world, the self and every other object dulled equally in its weak light.

Emotions, then, are constellations of bodily feelings, evaluative judgments, desires, and modes of attention. Returning now to loneliness, let me offer a definition, then an illustration, then an analysis. *Loneliness is the unpleasant feeling of longing for some kind of human interaction.*[13] Here is a typical episode:

> *Out for a breath of warm wind after a long afternoon at the typewriter, his thoughts wandered. Fresh air—certainly fresher than the last chapter! Unfamiliar faces going their own ways. My unknown public?—the thought amused him, then was forgotten as a stone lion, caught forever in the darkened limestone facade, drew his attention.*
>
> *Approaching the park, he noticed a young couple sitting on a low wall, talking quietly, legs touching lightly, hands resting easily together. And some emanation from them, like the shadow of a March cloud racing over the ground, overtook him, something rose up inside to meet it, and they whirled emptily where they met. As he*

walked more briskly on, he felt a tension all through his body—the inner sides of his arms, the chest, the facial muscles. He grew taller. Insistently but inarticulately, the wind seemed to address him: he leaned into it to make out the voice. If one had looked closely, one would have noticed that the ironic light had gone from his eyes; now, compressed in a squint, they darted up questioningly at each passing face. As he walked on across the park, one could see him shaking his head slightly, lips pursed: "How desolate it is here!" he thought, noticing how few returned his gaze. That gaze, previously lighter, was now darker, and seemed to focus far away: Karen? . . . the boy? No, impossible now.

Across the park at last and waiting to cross the street, he sagged. How stupid it all is, he thought, not bothering to kick the coffee cup that rolled crazily in the cold March wind.

Here was an attack of a common sort of loneliness, though perhaps uncommonly brief. Lengthy enough, though, for us to identify the four characteristic components of an emotion.

First, the writer's experience was one of unsatisfied desire for someone: the longing welled up in him, and carried him on through the park; it fueled his searching looks, the listening to the wind, the painful remembrances, and it was not satisfied. When it finally died on the sidewalk, the loneliness had decayed into dejection. What exactly did he want with another? We cannot say, and perhaps neither could he: . . . "I don't know . . . you know, somebody."

Second, he was feeling the world in different ways before, during, and after the episode. To take one item, the wind felt warm and cleansing before the park, simply cold afterwards; but while the loneliness lasted it manifested itself differently, calling and quickening him like Shelley's wild West Wind. Along a somewhat different dimension of bodily feeling, he felt relaxed, then felt something "well up," felt tense, alert, poised, and then finally enervated, empty, drained. Tense hollowness, that is a familiar "feel" of loneliness.

Third, the loneliness altered the way in which he was attending to the world. Eyes which had previously wandered haphazardly over the scene now scrutinized faces: he was set for people, not for stone lions. True, as the loneliness wore on, his gaze focused farther away; but the buildings seen in the distance were only half-seen, serving merely as backdrops for the human images to which he was attending. Afterwards at the streetlight, hope of any encounter having been abandoned, the shuffling hurrying bodies sank to the dull level of passing cars and rolling coffee cups.

Fourth, as he moved through the states of amused observation, loneliness and dejection, his evaluative construal of the world changed. Perhaps as he ambled along towards the park he perceived himself as simply one individual among others; they were different, to be sure, and unfamiliar—but not so different or unfamiliar after all. This assessment changed in the park: there the sense of himself as separated from others sharpened, the gap became dismayingly large. Finally, as he slouched at the streetlight, the gap had become unbridgeable: one couldn't hope for anything from these people.

Something very much like these desires, bodily feelings, attentions, and evaluations—unified and interactive—make up the emotion of loneliness. Solitude, however, is not an emotion. Even if a solitude and a loneliness lasted for the same amount of time, they are not logically the same sort of thing. For solitude does not entail any specific desires, feelings, or attentional sets: it is an open state receptive to every variety of feeling and reflection (with the possible exception, as will appear, of overpowering desires for other people). Most importantly, whereas loneliness is intrinsically painful, solitude is equally open to both pleasant and painful feelings. Tillich errs, consequently, in treating it as an emotional state parallel, though opposite, to loneliness: "loneliness . . . the pain of being alone . . . solitude . . . the glory of being alone."[14] Feeling glorious is not definitionally tied to solitude in the way that feeling pained (whether mildly or severely) is tied to loneliness, and neither is any other feeling. The same applies to moods. Rubin Gotesky's otherwise excellent analysis errs in identifying solitude with one particular mood: "His mood in all of these instances of aloneness is one of serenity, inward serenity."[15] But solitude is not, in its essence, either serene or not serene: it may be especially propitious for attaining serenity, but is not itself a kind of serenity. Sometimes it is turbulent, sometimes threatening, sometimes exhilarating.

As a final reflection, the walker was alone during the whole period, but lonely only during the middle segment. Indeed, it was during that lonely segment that he was most engaged with other people—the gazing, the darting glances, the small gestures of availability—and so least socially disengaged and so least solitary. Solitude and loneliness, it is beginning to appear, are not merely different but in a way opposed.

Isolation

Since isolating something means to separate it from other things, the feeling of isolation would be the experiential sense that one was separated from other people; it also seems to involve the sense that the separation cannot at once or easily be overcome. As a case in point, there comes to mind almost automatically

> *The Life and Strange Surprising Adventures of Robinson Crusoe, of York, Mariner:* Who lived Eight and Twenty Years, all alone in an uninhabited Island on the Coast of America, near the Mouth of the Great River of Oroonoque; having been cast on Shore by Shipwreck, wherein all the Men perished but himself. [from a facsimile of the title page of the first edition of 1719][16]

Crusoe realized from the first the extent of his isolation:

> I had a dismal prospect for my condition, for as I was not cast away upon that island without being driven, as is said, by a violent storm quite out of the course of our intended voyage, and a great way, vis. some hundreds of leagues, out of the ordinary course of the trade of mankind, I had great reason to consider it as a determination of Heaven, that in this desolate place and in this desolate manner I should end my life.[17]

This realization produced at first great anguish:

> the tears would run plentifully down my face when I made these reflections, and sometimes I would expostulate with my self, why Providence should thus completely ruin its creatures, and render them so absolutely miserable, so without help abandoned, so entirely depressed, that it could hardly be rational to be thankful for such a life.[18]

However such agonies were surprisingly brief:

> but something always returned swift upon me to check these thoughts, and to reprove me. . . . Well, you are in a desolate condition, 'tis true, but pray

remember, where are the rest of you? . . . Then it occurred to me again, how well I was furnished for my subsistence, and what would have been my case if it had not happened.[19]

Very quickly he would conclude that "all evils are to be considered with the good that is in them," and proceed with the practical matters at hand, tending his goats, repairing the fortifications or making new pots.

In short, the sense of isolation and the feeling of loneliness are not the same thing: the painful longing of the latter need not characterize the former. As many authors have remarked, Crusoe is quintessentially a practical economic man. Virginia Woolf remarked (a little unkindly),

The waves, the seamen, the sky, the ship—all are seen through those shrewd, middle-class, unimaginative eyes. . . . Everything appears as it would appear to that naturally cautious, apprehensive, conventional and solidly matter-of-fact intelligence.[20]

The qualities of his experiences in isolation were largely determined by the successes and failures in the saga of economic independence and self-reliance. Crusoe was not one to brood much, and when he did become meditative about his isolation the issues were usually resolved along the lines quoted above. On the whole, he seemed to be resigned to the isolation. Almost content.

Of course a period of isolation can be lonely, and Crusoe had some powerful attacks. The worst was brought on during his twenty-third year on the island by the sound of a gun at sea. Racing to the top of a hill, he lit a great signal fire, stoking it all through the night, only to find in the morning a wrecked ship lying off in the water, caught up on the concealed rocks. When it became clear that there were no survivors,

I cannot explain by any possible energy of words what a strange longing or hankering of desires I felt in my soul upon this sight; breaking out sometimes thus: 'O that there had been but one or two; nay only but one soul saved out of this ship, to have escaped to me, that I might but have had one companion, one fellow-creature to have spoken to me, and to have conversed with!' In all the time of my solitary life, I never felt so earnest, so strong a desire after the society of my fellow-creatures, or so deep a regret at the want of it. . . . I believe I repeated the words, 'O that it had been but one!' a thousand times: and the desires were so moved by it, that when I spoke the words, my hands would clinch together, and my fingers press the palms of my hands, that if I had any soft thing in my hand, it would have crushed it involuntarily; and my teeth in my head would strike together, and set against one another so strong, that for some time I could not part them again.[21]

A terrible disappointment, which set off two years of plotting how to escape. Yet just prior to the sighting he had apparently come to a comfortable acceptance of the isolation:

> . . . now in my twenty-third year of residence in this island, [I] was so naturalized to the place, and to the manner of living, that could I have but enjoyed the certainty that no savages would come to the place to disturb me, I could have been content to have capitulated for spending the rest of my time there. . . . I had also arrived to some little diversions and amusements, which made the time pass more pleasantly with me a great deal than it did before.[22]

Robinson Crusoe never was, of course; the character was a fiction Defoe created around the mishaps of a real Scottish sailor, Alexander Selkirk.[23] But I have quoted from his "life" so extensively because the mixed emotions of his isolation ring so true: sometimes despairing of the isolation, sometimes revelling in it, much of the time he was simply busy with other things. The same variations could be traced through the diary of Admiral Byrd's ten months of isolation in the Antarctic, or Christianne Ritter's periods of isolation in a cabin in northern Norway.[24] The lesson for our purposes is that the experience of isolation, the sense/feeling/awareness of being separated from other people without any immediate recourse, is not in itself an emotional state: it does not entail any particular desires or evaluations or pleasures or pains. All this makes isolation sound a great deal like solitude, and indeed the difference I will detect below in the senses of the two terms may seem slight. For now, it will be enough to observe that the awareness of his separation from society seemed to have been omnipresent with Crusoe, whether lightly or darkly colored with emotion: England, shipwrecked sailors and cannibals were always on his mind. But solitude has its mind on other things.

Privacy

Isolation, at least the isolation from prying invading eyes, calls to mind the idea of privacy: is not privacy, after all, just being let alone separate from others, a state in which they cannot engage with us or our secret thoughts? And isn't that just the disengagement of solitude? Paul Halmos's definition of privacy, "freedom from social contact and observation when these are not desired" seems to fit solitude as well; and Sue Halpern writes in *Migrations to Solitude* that she is going to study "the experience of being left alone":

> It is here that privacy, which in broad terms is the state of being free from the observations, disclosures, and intrusions of others, and solitude, which is the condition of being apart, merge.[25]

This sounds plausible, and yet some thoughts give me pause. William James is hiking in the wild uplands: a lone hiker appears in the distance, sees James, waves, and moves off. James notes the way his feeling of solitude is broken. But he would not say that his privacy was violated: for it is not just observation, or even unwanted observation, that violates privacy, but unwanted observation of something a person wishes to keep unobserved and *feels entitled to keep unobserved.* This is brutally evident in Halpern's chapter on the violations of privacy which the homeless endure, here described by a man who lost his job after his wife died and was struggling to cope with a family shelter:

> I'm all alone there, in this place with about two hundred cots packed side by side. Men, women, and children, all together. No dividers. There's no curtains and no screens. I have to dress my kids with people watching. When my girls go to the toilet, I can't take them, and they're scared to go alone.[26]

This is the degrading feeling of the lack of privacy. The feeling of privacy, by implication, would be the feeling that there are no unwanted observers of one's *rightfully*[27] reserved thoughts, words, activities: privacy has built into it a sense of entitlement that solitude lacks.

Moreover the sense or feeling of privacy is, as the feeling of solitude is not, commonly experienced as involving other people. Think of private conversations in bars, private business discussions, therapeutic sessions, friendly walks along the beach. Indeed it is tempting to think of privacy alone as a kind of limiting case of privacy in society. Was Crusoe, utterly cut off from other people, enjoying privacy? It sounds odd to my ears to say so. Even when we exclaim "that's my own private business," it is almost invariably a "business" we share with some confidant—doctor, lawyer, best friend, etc. The upshot is that privacy seems to have a social context that solitude escapes.[28]

Finally, the sense or feeling of privacy does not characterize all experiences of solitude; the latter may be so disengaged from other people as to not even consider the issue of concealment from prying eyes.[29] Indeed, it is characteristically so.

Alienation

By now I hope that you are wondering why I pause to discuss alienation. After all, is not alienation a painful, unhappy condition imposed upon a victim, a condition felt within society (though perhaps on its fringes), whereas solitude is sought, away from society, for its calm joys? The answer must be that since a number of contemporary studies run the two terms together, concocting thereby what look like critiques of solitude, we have to pause a minute and note the important distinctions. I am referring, for example, to Paul Halmos's *Solitude and Privacy*, whose chapters study "the aeteology of social isolation," "desocialization," "Isolation and Anxiety"—all of which sound like alienation and none of which sound like solitude. I am also disturbed by Robert Sayre's erudite neo-Marxist study of the conceptual history of solitude, *Solitude in Society;* for his introduction defines the subject in a way that seems to run together solitude and alienation:

> Solitude in society—that is, a generalized and radical social fragmentation that causes the isolation of each individual within the social framework, his inability to communicate adequately with others—is one aspect of the fundamental crisis of capitalism: 'alienation.'[30]

I believe that most people would understand something quite different by the phrase "solitude in society," and would balk at calling that different thing any sort of alienation. But are their intuitions defensible against these professors? Only an investigation of alienation can decide the matter.

Considering that a recent author described modern literature since Kierkegaard and Dostoevsky as "effectively an exploration of aliena-tion," and considering that since Marx the concept has been widely used in social/political/economic analysis, it is going to be hard to isolate one clear meaning for the term. Nor does intuition speak as immediately or clearly about alienation as it does about loneliness. As Richard Schacht remarks at the beginning of his comprehensive study, *Alienation:*

> The average person depends almost entirely for his understanding of the term upon his direct or indirect acquaintance with the writings of certain philosophers, psychologists, and social scientists. It is the latter, therefore, whose uses of the term are most significant. . . . To analyze what it means to say of someone that he is 'alienated' is primarily to observe how those who have introduced the term into contemporary discussion have used it.[31]

We had better have a look at the analyses of the most famous "introducers," then—both to appreciate the diversity of meanings the concept has enjoyed and to remind ourselves of its frequent systemic connections with specific social theories.

But before theory, etymology. Drawing again on Schacht's study,

> The Latin origin of 'alienation' is *alienatio.* This noun derives its meaning from the verb *alienare* (to make something another's, to take away, remove). *Alienare,* in turn, derives from *alienus* (belonging or pertaining to another). And *alienus* derives ultimately from *alius* (meaning 'other' as an adjective, or 'another' as a noun.[32]

Schacht discovered three traditional uses of the Latin term. First,

> one of the principal Latin uses of *alienare* is in connection with property: 'to transfer the ownership of something to another person' . . . Thus in the fifteenth century a man could be ordered to 'make no alienation of no parcel of land' . . .

Second, there is a standard usage which refers to interpersonal estrangement:

> *alienare* can mean, 'to cause a warm relationship with another to cool; to cause a separation to occur; to make oneself disliked.' And *alienation* can refer either to this process or to the resulting condition. These Latin terms are applicable in ordinary interpersonal contexts. In Middle English, however, the derivative use of 'alien' and 'alienation' was confined primarily to theological contexts.

Finally, there was a less common usage in which "one could speak of *alienation mentis,* or simply *alienation,* in connection with the state of unconsciousness, and the paralysis or loss of one's mental powers or senses."

According to Schacht, before Hegel the concept of alienation had theoretical importance primarily in the first of the above senses. Grotius, Hobbes, and Rousseau each held it a necessary condition for the establishment of political society that the individual divest himself of autonomy in the exercise of personal will and power. The concept in its second sense, interpersonal estrangement, was not of particular importance or widespread use.

All of this changed with Hegel, who Walter Kaufmann calls "the father of the contemporary discussion." Alienation is a central concept in the *Phenomenology of Spirit*—or two central concepts, as Schacht notes:

> At times he uses it to refer to a separation or discordant relation, such as might obtain between the individual and the social substance, or (as in 'self-alienation') between one's actual condition and essential nature.' . . . (but) He also uses it to refer to a surrender or sacrifice of particularity and willfulness, in connection with the overcoming of alienation (in the first sense) and the reattainment of unity.[33]

Initially, in Hegel's view, an individual is in an ego-less pre-reflective harmony with the institutions and modes of the culture—the social substance, as he calls it. This realm is the product of spiritual activity, and thus is essentially spiritual. However in order for the individual's essential nature as self-conscious spirit to be realized, a dynamic progression involving the two modes of alienation must occur. First, s/he must separate from the social substance and emerge as a distinct and independent individual; this involves an alienation (in the first sense) both from the objective spirit of culture and from the initial self, since s/he is partly the maker of spiritual culture and partly universal spirit. This necessary development produces an unhappy state, since it separates the individual from his/her own cultural forms and from the universal Love and Reason flowing through those forms. However, a transcendent reunification is achieved in the final stage of self-development through the second form of alienation, the relinquishing of the separate willful self in the act of merging the now-self-conscious self with the universal will. This is every individual's highest destiny because each partakes of the universal, the infinite, the rational, and only in these can the self fully unfold its essence.

Hegel's analysis goes deeper and broader, as he kneads phenomenology into logic into psychology into metaphysics; but enough has been said to give some sense of the complexities of his use of the notion of alienation and its connection with all the other elements of the system. Perhaps it is also clear how tenuous the connections are between his senses of alienation and the ordinary garden-variety solitude that so interests us; for solitude need not involve either discordant separation from culture and the self, or the relinquishing of self-hood to Universal anything.[34]

The other *locus classicus* of reflections upon alienation is of course the man who "stood Hegel on his head," Karl Marx. It is in the early writings, most notably the *Economic and Philosophical Manuscripts* of 1844, that alienation appears as a crucial analytic concept; later it is replaced by "reification" and is even referred to derogatorily in the Communist Manifesto. However, there are those who find the earlier and later theories materially the same, and if they are right he abandoned only the word, not the concept.

It is important to remember from the outset that Marx's theory of alienation was developed with an economist's eye on labor and production. Although social life and sensuous life are also parts of man's species-character or essence, Marx places the greatest emphasis upon productive work: "labor, productive life . . . is man's species life." Self-realization is inseparably linked with production, and production is inescapably social:

> Man is in the most literal sense a zoon politicon, not merely a political animal, but an animal which can develop into an individual only in society. Production by isolated individuals outside of society—something which might happen as an exception to a civilized man who by accident got into the wilderness and already dynamically possessed within himself the forces of society—is as great an absurdity as the idea of the development of language without individuals living together and talking to one another.[35]

Accordingly, evils which attack productive life are the fundamental evils for human beings, and alienation, in Marx's conception, is just such an evil.

Marxian alienation, in all of its forms, essentially consists of the severing or practical breakdown of the interconnectedness which makes a whole, natural person. In Bertell Ollman's succinct summary,

> The distortion [alienation] in what Marx takes to be human nature is generally referred to in language which suggests that an essential tie has been cut in the middle. Man is spoken of as being separated from his work (he plays no part in deciding what to do or how to do it)—a break between the individual and his life activity. Man is said to be separated from his own products (he has no control over what he makes or what becomes of it afterwards)—a break between the individual and the material world. He is also said to be separated from his fellow men (competition and class hostility have rendered most forms of cooperation impossible)—a break between man and man. In each instance, a relation that

distinguishes the human species has disappeared and its constituent elements have been reorganized to appear as something else . . . (alienated man) has been reduced to performing undifferentiated work on humanly indistinguishable objects among people deprived of their human variety and compassion.[36]

Separation-with-distorted-connection, loss of power and control, fragmentation, these are the key elements in Marx's conception of alienation. But they are not necessarily, indeed not even usually, elements of solitude. Fair enough, for Marx was not interested in solitude, and one looks in vain through his writings for serious discussions of our subject. Like most of the sociologists that followed him, Marx apparently considered solitude an utterly marginal phenomenon.

Let us turn to more recent developments. Kaufmann notes that, with a few exceptions (most notably Martin Buber and Bertold Brecht), during the first half of the twentieth century

the time was not yet ripe for 'alienation'. Less than a year after the publication of Marx's early manuscripts (1932) the Nazis came to power in Germany and put an end to scholarly discussions of Marx's thought. And the Soviet hierarchy accepted the (derogatory) view of alienation put forth in *The Communist Manifesto*.[37]

It was in the postwar period, especially the fifties, that use of the concept mushroomed, thanks to the writings of existentialists like Camus and Sartre, Marxists like Lukacs, and Humanists like Fromm and Arendt. By 1959, the sociologist Melvin Seeman could identify five different senses of the term in current use: "(a) powerlessness, (b) meaninglessness, (c) normlessness, (d) isolation, and (e) self-estrangement."[38] Seeman wanted to distinguish between what he took to be incompatible meanings, and though they do not appear to be incompatible they certainly are logically distinct (with the possible exception, depending on precise definitions, of b and c). But then which is the real meaning of alienation? What are we to make out of 180 years of conflicting theories?

The situation is not as hopeless as it may seem. A core concept with some determinate content can be extracted from the many formulations. It is approached closely by another sociologist, Robert Weiss: according to him, alienation is "the social or psychological estrangement of an individual from an activity or social form with which he is nevertheless at least nominally associated."[39] An alien is a stranger, and the feeling of alienation is a feeling of estrangement, estrangement from some person or group (or their "activities or social forms," as Weiss has it). Further, it seems to be part of the concept that the victim feels himself in some way linked with the persons/activities/forms from which he is estranged, though perhaps only distantly or "nominally": the alienated failure of contact—whether in action or feeling or understanding—is an estrangement from one's friend, family, generation, God, etc. Being a stranger to a group is merely being separate from it if you do not belong, and not alienation.

The only complaint one might lodge against Weiss's excellent definition is that it does not make sufficiently explicit the painful negative quality of alienation.[40] Even separation from a group to which one nominally belongs is not alienation if it is not painful: think of being awarded your group's annual prize for excellence. But, with the addition of this element (perhaps Weiss understood it as contained in the sense of 'estrangement'), the definition seems both general enough to do justice to the historical sources and specific enough to make the important distinctions. It would not be hard, given a little time, to connect the five characteristics Seeman mentions to this core definition. For example, given the powerful way in which social connections create networks of meanings, feeling cut off from a group and their network would certainly be an experience of loss of meaning, of meaninglessness. However, our concern here is with solitude.

What differences have emerged between solitude and alienation? Two points seem especially salient. First, like loneliness alienation is intrinsically an unpleasant condition, whereas solitude is not. Second, alienation involves a fracture of relationship with another *who is yet felt as part of the experience:* feeling alienated from your co-worker, for example, is a way of being aware of that person, a modality of *consciousness-of-other,* if we wanted to talk that way. This is not so of solitude, which is not any kind of consciousness-of-other, but rather a consciousness-without-other.

Solitude

Solitude has begun to emerge from the family portrait. It is open with regard to pleasure or pain—not intrinsically either pleasant or unpleasant—and equally open to the widest variety of emotions and moods. But there is something more. Notice that in each of the other types of experience alone, consciousness was conditioned by others: it yearned lonesomely for them or was sickened and repelled by them; it gazed about warily for intruders to its privacy or felt the distance of all humans in its isolation. In each case, experience was defined and structured by other people—"bipolar," to use Robert Solomon's felicitous phrase, a consciousness of self-in-relation-to-other. Here lies a crucial difference with solitude: for there one pole has vanished from experience, the other is absent. The mind has disengaged itself from other people and is absorbed elsewhere, in the earth being shovelled, in the ripples on the river, in the implications of a line of thought. Let this stand, then, as a brief definition: *solitude is the state in which experience is disengaged from other people.*

Of course, like all brief definitions, this one will require elaboration and clarification, a process that will occupy the next few chapters. Here I will add just two qualifications. My notion of solitude is of an extended experiential state, a "time"; a moment of distraction from a conversation does not make a solitude. Yet because of this very durational feature, a solitude can tolerate minor interpersonal interruptions without losing its title. Moreover, solitary disengagement seems to be a matter of degree: it can permit some vague awareness of others, some noting of them through its peripheral vision and still be disengaged enough to count as a solitude. It seems to me that the word 'disengagement' nicely captures the experience we are examining: it suggests a gear wheel that is disconnected from other wheels, even if near them, even if built onto the same machine. Thus insofar as a person is able to disengage from other people while among them, as did Tzu Ch'i of South Wall, the state can fairly be called a solitude.

No author can construct a definition without carping at its rivals. With some, I have very little quarrel: Gotesky's, cited above, is acceptable, except for the narrowing caused by referring to *living* alone, which might be taken to exclude the solitary rambles of housemates. Tristam Englehardt errs a little more seriously, I think, in building in the requirement of self-reflection:

> Solitude as such is a dimension of mental life found in inwardly directed consciousness—the self, while considering itself in isolation, in contrast to consciousness explicitly directed outward to others.[41]

It is a mistake to conceive of solitude as necessarily directed inwardly, since a common joy of solitude is immersion in the (outer) natural world[42]: Thoreau's experience as he walked by the pond in the evening seems not to have been either "inward" or self-considering. It is also unwise to think of solitude as necessarily focused on the self, because one of the celebrated virtues of solitude has been its propitiousness for transcendence of the self. Nor is solitude as empty as Peter Munz would have it in *Relationship and Solitude:* there he claims that "Solitude means the withdrawal from others to the point at which such withdrawal becomes absolute," this absolute state being attained when "one's consciousness has been emptied of all contents and attachments."[43] But this is too extreme: all attachments, yes; all contents, no. Things become really confused by Paul Halmos's definitions in *Solitude and Privacy:* "Privacy is freedom from social contact and observation when these are not desired, and Solitude is the lack of desired social contact."[44] What he calls Solitude is in fact loneliness!

Why does it matter what he calls what? It matters, for one thing, because these misdefinitions make his whole book confusing: the reader interested in solitude—which is, after all, the book's designated subject—is called upon, page after page, to convert Halmos's claims about Solitude and Privacy into statements about good old-fashioned solitude. Irritating. But far worse, misdefining solitude frustrates our deeper need to understand the *value* of solitude. We wish to know, finally, whether solitude is a good or an evil, how good or evil and how so. Now if you begin by misdefining solitude as loneliness, the inherent negativity of loneliness is going to lead you to stigmatize solitude; but then it will be unclear as to whether you have attained some bold new insight into the subject—or simply changed it.

But words wreak their own vengeance: for solitude does have its ordinary meaning, and the author who redefines it cannot help slipping back into ordinary usage from time to time. Halmos appears to do just that in his stingy assessment of the proper place of solitude in human life: "Sleep has only one writ: to regenerate life for its continued living; willed solitude has only one function: to regenerate social life for its more harmonious living."[45] Here, I think, he must be using solitude in the ordinary sense and not according to his own definition: for how would willed loneliness be regenerative?[46]

These same problems of definition and evaluation mar Robert

Sayre's otherwise enlightening study. Already, on the dustcover, some disturbing slippage appears:

> In contrast to the existentialist interpretation of *alienation* (in which *isolation* is the external dilemma of Man), [his] Marxist analysis interprets *solitude* in society as precisely a modern phenomenon . . . [my emphasis].

Page one provides what certainly looks like a definition:

> Solitude in society—that is, a generalized and radical social fragmentation that causes the isolation of each individual within the social framework, his inability to communicate adequately with others—is one aspect of the fundamental crisis of capitalism: 'alienation'.

Later in the introduction he writes in reference to the varieties of alienation in Marx, "It is with this latter aspect, the alienation of human relations, that I am primarily concerned here"; and later still, "it at the same time alienates them. Thus the contradiction of Solitude in society." In short, the book appears to be about alienation, and not about solitude.

This appearance is not entirely born out; for part 1 consists of a historical study of both solitude in the ordinary sense and alienation, and sheds considerable light on both. Part 2 is also useful in revealing —through analyses of the novels of Proust, Malraux, Bernanos, Camus, and Sarraute—the variety of ways in which modern monopoly capitalism has effected the replacement of fruitful solitude by alienation. Unfortunately, the confusion of subject never goes away. So when he finally comes to claim, in the Afterword, that

> It can no longer be convincingly claimed that solitude contributes to the richness of human existence, precisely because in the twentieth century that richness has been undermined.[47]

one doesn't know whether to argue with him or not, and, if so, how to argue, in favor of solitude or in favor of alienation?

I have singled out Halmos and Sayre because their books have been widely read (at least by scholars); but their terminological transgressions are far from uncommon. I could as well have complained of Ralph Harper's *The Seventh Solitude,* whose subtitle reveals that the book is in fact about "Metaphysical Homelessness in Kierkegaard, Dostoevsky and Nietzsche."[48] There is a mystery and a power to the term 'Solitude' that leads authors to choose it for their titles regardless of appropriateness: by my rough count, less than half the books listed in the National Library data-bank under 'Solitude' are actually about solitude in the ordinary sense. This phenomenon causes distress to those readers who really want to pursue solitude, and not some other subject.

To those readers, a reassurance: this book will continue to search for an understanding of solitude.

CHAPTER 3

Disengagement

Solitude is consciousness disengaged from other people, the mind wandering along its pathways alone. The experiences that come to it now are not structured by the imperious presence of other people. But neither need they be structured by any explicit sense or feeling of the absence of others: disengagement from people does not entail awareness of being disengaged, for one can be totally absorbed in the small waves raised by the evening wind over the pond, the stony shore, the scampering in the woods.

But suppose, in your solitude, you did begin to think of someone: would that spoil the solitude—spoil its title, that is, to being called a solitude? What if memory seats an old friend on the boulder next to you, felt now as a living presence, diffusing the familiar careless warmth over shore and water and sky? Or what if you knew at the back of your mind that there was someone to return to when it grew dark at the pond? And suppose you did return to the cabin late, lay down beside her quietly and listened drowsily to her even breathing, letting your last tired thoughts drift. . . . Engaged or disengaged?

We cannot really be satisfied with matters as they stand. The notion that experience is either engaged or disengaged is far too simplistic to do justice to the richness of human consciousness. For the mind can move on different planes simultaneously, and may accordingly be partially engaged and partially disengaged. Moreover memory and imagination construct experience as much as does bare perception. Some years ago the woman I loved left to work on the other coast for a year; I lived alone, worked mostly at home, saw scarcely anyone, walked for long hours through the wooded hills alone. A solitude, surely? Yet I lived all through those months in *our* world: the plants in the house, the pictures, the chairs, the refinished cabinets, the views across the hills, the walking trails—they were all ours, saturated with common memories and plans. And late at night when I wrote to her alone in the silence, the thing I kept repeating had its truth: "I'm never alone here; you're always with me."[1]

Or consider Henry Bugbee's remark:

> I think solitude is essentially a bringing to consciousness of the manner of our being in the world with other beings and of engagement in the working out of the import continually and cumulatively borne upon us of this participation.[2]

If I am right, it is not *essentially* this; but perhaps it is often this, perhaps profoundly this, and it will not do at all to simply deny that such experiences are solitudes because there is a kind of engagement with others at work in them. No, we must burrow deeper into the nature of disengaged experience.

Imagine two friends leaning forward intently over their coffee mugs, talking of personal follies. Talking, listening, suddenly a feeling of ironic triumph seizes one of the pair: bending forward, he jabs a finger at his poor victim with mock outrage and scolds, "I *told* you she would do that two years ago! You wouldn't listen! You're always so smart!"

Scolder and victim, Branch and Bough, as I shall name them, provide a clear example of an ordinary sort of engagement. But ordinary does not mean simple: notice four different aspects of this engagement, referring only to Branch for clarity's sake.

1. Perceptual awareness: he is peering intently at Bough, listening keenly, breathing in his coffee'd breath.

2. Cognitive focus: his mind is fully absorbed by their conversation; concentrating on Bough's words, he imagines the scenes they conjure and examines them with gentle irony.

3. Emotional contact: the feelings and emotions flowing through him have Bough, or Bough's remarks, as their object. Just now he is filled with mock outrage at his friend.

4. Active involvement: he is leaning towards Bough, listening and talking to him, jabbing a finger at his chest.

Perceiving, thinking, feeling, and acting are hardly independent categories at deeper levels of analysis—we were just remembering the cognitive elements in loneliness—but for the present purpose they will serve well enough. That purpose is to explore the complexities of consciousness in engagement and disengagement, to remember how, for example, you can be looking at someone but not thinking about him, feeling a longing but not doing anything about it, doing something when your heart isn't in it and your mind is elsewhere. Analytically, we could speak of modes of intentionality with differing intentional objects, which would please some philosophers but not others and certainly not anyone else. More profitably, we might speak of four modes of *attention* and use the metaphor of focus: in the fullest kind of engagement, perception, cognition, emotion, and action are all focused on some other person.

But back to our story. Imagine, now, the unravelling of this all-absorbing engagement, a progressive disengagement:

Fresh coffee arrives, and it needs to be stirred. Branch's mind wanders slightly: he has to ask Bough to repeat a point. Shortly after, he permits himself a brief glance at a new arrival in the doorway, a faint flurry of curious interest. Now, leaning back in his chair, he regards his friend with the slight distance of a kindly observer: dear Bough, how do you and I, so different, remain so close? Dear Bough—but to tell the truth the conversation has gone on for a long time and he is beginning to feel restless. The waterfall: suddenly remembered, a plan begins to crystallize around it. And soon, with a few mumbled apologies and the familiar farewell clap on the shoulder, he is on his feet towards the door. The engagement is broken.

But not entirely broken: for the first quarter-hour of the drive along the shore finds him rehashing the conversation, often scarcely noticing the road. Finally, however, the inner dialog wears itself out, and his thoughts rove aimlessly over sea and sky and gathering woodland.

Stepping out of the car at the end of the lane, the clearness of the forest air seems to open his senses. An exciting feeling of gathering energy propels him along the trail, winding now through richer colors and more vibrant forms, until at last he hears ahead the unmistakable sounds of the falls. Emerging abruptly in the dripping clearing where the rocky base pool foams, he is stopped short, seized and drawn up through the noise and mist into the awesome relentlessness of the torrential falling. He stands and stands and stands. Now he is mist rising and thunder falling, glorious.

This progressive disengagement from the other, this journey from Encounter into Solitude, tempts us to think of solitude and encounter as the two end-places of a continuum, each experience shading off towards the other along a single line of change. There is some truth in this image: it is possible to represent solitude and encounter as polar opposites on a continuum—I have just done so. But the fourfold character of disengagement makes apparent the oversimplification this image also conveys. For with multiple criteria of anything, conflicts can occur; and the story illustrates some of the ways in which they do occur. Listening in a distant way to Bough while thinking of the waterfall, Branch was partially engaged and partially disengaged, and the same may be said of his first quarter-hour driving along the shore road. Understanding the fourfold nature of engagement/ disengagement, we can understand our difficulty in classifying these cases: are they really solitudes or not? Yes, but in a way, no. And there are so many mixed cases. Indeed, it is not too much to say that the *ordinary* state of human consciousness is a mixed case: oneself, other people, and diverse objects in the world are constantly vying for attention, and they all usually receive some during any experience lasting for more than a minute.

My conclusion is that only when all four criteria of disengagement —perceptual, cognitive, emotional, actional—are satisfied do we have a chemically pure case of solitude. And such chemically pure cases are rare: the vast majority of solitudes are at least slightly adulterated with attentions to other people in one of the four modalities cited. But this adulteration seems to be allowed within the concept of solitude—and of encounter, insofar as the two are understood as opposites: partially engaged solitudes still are solitudes, just as encounters remain encounters in spite of the parallel impurities that commonly diminish their total engagement. Of course there are limits, points at which the adulterating attentions become strong enough to challenge the others for dominance. How strongly must they vie, and for how long, before the opposite term becomes appropriate, before encounter (solitude) becomes solitude (encounter)? These questions do not seem to be neatly decided in our concepts of solitude and encounter. The semantic situation appears to be that when one of the criteria of disengagement is satisfied, there is a toehold for ascriptions of solitude: the solitude of the emotionally absent, the solitude of the passively disengaged, the solitude of the vacant look, and so on. The more criteria satisfied, and the more powerfully each conditions the experience, the more appropriate it is to speak of solitude; but it is not decided in the concepts themselves precisely when the toehold becomes solid footing, when encounter becomes solitude.

This seems to be the logic of the situation, but it does not entirely satisfy me. My mind keeps returning to certain cases, struggling to decide whether or not they are really solitudes. Here are three that have especially puzzled me: Kafka, Wordsworth, and Raskolnikov.

Writing far into the night at the dining room table, with his parents and sisters sleeping just down the hallway, Franz Kafka was able to disengage to a degree that only he can fully convey:

> What I need for my writing is seclusion, not 'like a hermit,' that would not be sufficient, but like the dead. Writing in this sense is a sleep deeper than death; and just as one could not and would not drag a corpse out of his grave, I cannot be made to leave my desk at night either.[3]

What a solitude, what an obliviousness surrounds this writing! Let us quietly draw near, peer over the bent shoulder and follow the thin hurrying hand.

> "Am I well covered up now?" asked his father, as if he were not able to see whether his feet were properly tucked in or not.
>
> "So you find it snug in bed already," said Georg, and tucked the blankets more closely round him.
>
> "Am I well covered up?" asked the father once more, seeming to be strangely intent upon the answer.
>
> "Don't worry, you're well covered up."
>
> "No!" cried his father, cutting short the answer, threw the blankets off with a strength that sent them all flying in a moment and sprang erect in bed. Only one hand lightly touched the ceiling to steady him.
>
> "You wanted to cover me up, I know, my young sprig, but I'm far from being covered up yet. And even if this is the last strength I have, its enough for you, too much for you."[4]

The writer has been absorbed into the stuffy room of "The Judgment," creating father and son out of himself but at the same time listening to each and feeling the force of their words. The engagement is so intense that to break it would be like dragging a corpse back from death. Can this really be a solitude? And another thought troubles me: is not this writing really directed at his sleeping father just as surely as the famous "Letter to My Father"? Is it not a projectile hurled from the solitude at the real judge of "The Judgment"?[5] And if this is so, is Kafka not more engaged with his father than he would be if he walked down the hallway and gazed at the tired old warhorse snoring in bed?

A second kind of solitary experience to which my reflections keep returning is the powerful experience of *presence*. What do we make of cases like my own discussed above, when aloneness is suffused with the presence of the beloved? To say that the lover thinks constantly of the beloved would be to woefully understate the case. No, she is there everywhere in the sense and texture of things, a presence most eloquently expressed by Wordsworth, though he was not writing about a human lover:

> And I have felt
> A presence that disturbs me with the joy
> Of elevated thoughts; a sense sublime
> Of something far more deeply interfused,
> Whose dwelling is the light of setting suns,
> And the round ocean and the living air,
> And the blue sky and in the mind of man:
> A motion and a spirit, that impels
> All thinking things, all objects of all thought,
> And rolls through all things.
>
> (from "Lines Composed A Few Miles
> Above Tintern Abbey")

Wordsworth was here giving voice to what he elsewhere called "natural piety," the sense of an immanent spiritual presence diffused throughout the works of nature; but his words also convey wonderfully the sense of sublime presence that parted lovers often feel, a presence absolutely unbounded that rolls through all things.

These lines from Wordsworth were written above the ruins of an abbey, and that causes me to reflect upon the religious solitudes of more traditional Christian monks: might it be that they experience the divine personage in just such an interfused way? Thomas Merton, the contemporary Dominican monk who wrote so much about the nature of monastic existence, explained the monastic hermit's vocation in this way:

> The hermit's whole life is a life of silent adoration. His very solitude keeps him ever in the presence of God. . . . His whole day, in the silence of his cell, or his garden looking out upon the forest, is a prolonged Communion.[6]

This adoring communion with a transcendent being whose presence irradiates the cell and garden and forest is no doubt different from the felt presence of an absent human. But in so far as that presence is felt as personal, as a divine personage, can we still speak of the experiences as solitudes?

A final case to ponder, one with a darker cast—for solitude is not always bright and sweet, but sometimes dark and bitter—Dostoevsky's Raskolnikov. The impoverished student had tossed for hours on the filthy couch in his "tiny cupboard of a room about six paces in length." Haunted by daydreams, a clock striking somewhere in the city aroused him with a start—how late it was already! At once the preparations must be made and the wild plan dreamed in months of starving fantasy put into action—though even as he began he did not believe in its reality, did not believe that this fantasy could actually run its course to the very end.

> But the preparations to be made were few. He concentrated all his energies on thinking of everything and forgetting nothing; and his heart kept beating and thumping so that he could hardly breathe. First he had to make a noose and sew it into his overcoat—a work of a moment. He rummaged under his pillow and picked out amongst the linen stuffed away under it, a worn out, old unwashed shirt. From its rags he tore a long strip, a couple of inches wide and about sixteen inches long. He folded this strip in two, took off his wide strong summer overcoat of some stout cotton material (his only outer garment) and began sewing the two ends of the rag on the inside, under the left armhole. His hands shook as he sewed, but he did it successfully so that nothing showed outside when he put the coat on again. The needle and thread he had got ready long before and they lay on his table in a piece of paper. As for the noose, it was a very ingenious device of his own; the noose was intended for the axe. It was impossible for him to carry the axe through the street in his hands.[7]

Raskolnikov is totally absorbed in preparing the noose—all action, now, with no time for the angry obsessive thoughts that have poisoned him week after week. All alone in the miserable room with its dusty yellow paper peeling off the walls, there is no one near him to see or hear, no presence to feel. Even thought dare not look ahead to the old woman to whom he is going with the axe in the noose under the overcoat. Surely this is a solitude, though feverish and obsessed? Does he not work alone? Yet the action that totally absorbs him is aimed at a person, and in some way he always knows it. And is this sewing not an integral part of the whole terrible crime, connived in the solitude of the cupboard room, the murder of the old pawnbroker? Is it not the first motion of an action he has been aiming at the old woman for months, now an arrow loosed on its way? Is this solitude too actively engaged with the old woman to remain a solitude?

Kafka, Wordsworth, Raskolnikov—why do these cases haunt me? Is it the intensity of the absorption in each case? Or is it the eerie indescribable way in which each person is engaged with a personage that is experientially present, powerfully present, yet absent in body? If only there were a theory of the imagination that were equal to these phenomena, that could explain the full depth of these experiences! Walking alone with the beloved in one's heart is a deep way of being together, deeper certainly than many actual walkings together: the one is not merely a "faint impression" of the other, as is proved by the fact that lovers sometimes choose the solitary way of being with their beloved over a flesh and blood engagement. No doubt to understand the imagination better would be to understand this presence-in-absence better, and consequently the relations between solitude and encounter.

Now I am letting myself dream of a more final understanding than can probably be had, however. Philosophical analysis does provide illumination, certainly, but it always seems to raise new questions, revealing new sources for wonder in the phenomena, and so returning us to those phenomena with a growing sense of awe. As I labor over definitions, distinctions, and dimensional analyses, Kafka and Wordsworth and Raskolinkov return me in this way, return me to solitude itself,

> The measureless untouchable source
> Of its images,
> The measureless untouchable source
> Of its substances,
> The source which, while it appears dark emptiness,
> Brims with a quick force[8]

CHAPTER 4

Engaged Disengagement

A solitude is a stretch of experience disengaged from other people in perception, thought, emotion, and action. True, but not yet clear or subtle enough; for there are modes of diminished engagement, thus far unexplored, which have the greatest importance for understanding the experience of solitude. I am thinking of a number of ways in which solitary experiences can involve an *indirect* or *substitutive* engagement with persons.

Objects as Reservoirs

The phenomenon I have in mind here is a deflection of consciousness from objects to persons more implicit than those surveyed in the last chapter. How exactly did it happen that a solitary man experienced his absent lover as a presence? Part of the explanation is that the objects in the house, the rocks and the trees outside, were not termini of attention but acted like mirrors, deflecting his thoughts towards her. And just as it is the object seen in the mirror which is the focus of attention and concern, even though one is aware at some level that it is a reflection, so it was the emotionally charged image of her that dominated his attention as he slowly turned the stone in his hand. Dominated: one cannot understand solitude without appreciating the way in which perceptions can deflect into reflections and imaginings which, *while co-present with those perceptions,* are so vivid and potent that they dominate the experiential whole. The solitude of the aged seems especially characterized by this process, as Margaret Lawrence shows us in *The Stone Angel:* her ninety-year-old protagonist, Hagar Shipley, exclaims alone, "Now I am rampant with memory," and the memories comprise 95 percent of the book.

But consciousness is not always explicit. Objects connected with persons may radiate a warm personal substance without propelling the mind to the source. The difference between deflection towards others and merely feeling their radiance becomes clearer if you imagine a mirror and a rock lying together on the ground in the sunshine: the mirror reflects the sun, itself almost vanishing in the piercing glare, and the ray can burn you. The rock is opaque and dense, and your gaze stops there; but you can feel its warmth, moreover feel the warmth without ever thinking of the sun which produced it.

So too does it happen in solitude that we live in the personal warmth stored in objects, seldom turning our minds to the sources.

Here in the study, sitting at the desk, things feel companionable, familiar, in-place, right. If I stop to remember the history of any of these objects, it is easy to bring back the time in which the thing became a part of this special place because of some other person. The curtains which swell and fall gently—I remember where she and I found the material, the argument about the inch or two longer or shorter, her sewing, my misinstalling them upside down, standing back with final approval of the job. The desk itself, a slab door hastily braced up twelve years ago when friends were arriving on short notice—have those crude braces held for twelve years? Why the angle-braces and not legs? Oh yes, so there would be room for two chairs, so He could sit beside me and scribble with his own pad and pencil. When he wasn't banging on the typewriter. That typewriter, which spoke to so many friends over all those long years, has been retired by the word processor, but it still sits there in the corner, just in its right place, making the room comfortable and right.

Even though it may be possible to call to mind the engagements which lie stored in these silent reservoirs (sometimes it is not possible), one need not do so to feel their residual warmth. It is an engagement at another step removed from the mirroring phenomenon we discussed in the last chapter, but an engagement all the same. And its effects can be powerful, as Marcel felt near the beginning of *Swann's Way:*

And soon, mechanically weary after a dull day with the prospect of a depressing morrow, I raised to my lips a spoonful of the tea in which I had soaked a morsel of the cake. No sooner had the warm liquid, and the crumbs with it, touched my palate than a shudder ran through my whole body, and I stopped, intent upon the extraordinary changes that were taking place. An exquisite pleasure had invaded my senses, but individual, detached, with no suggestion of its origin.[1]

Marcel does succeed in tracing the origin of this emotion, however, by focusing his memory upon the sensations of that first moment's mouthful of tea:

> And suddenly the memory returns. The taste was that of the little crumb of madeleine which on Sunday mornings at Combray (because on those mornings I did not go out before church-time), when I went to say good day to her in her bedroom, my aunt Leonie used to give me, dipping it first in her own cup of real or of lime-flower tea.[2]

Locked in the taste of the tea, for this weary man, was the image of the kindly aunt; and savoring it was, indirectly and at first unknowingly, savoring her again.

Places too can become reservoirs of personhood, exuding a kind of inaudible invisible presence. One favorite place for solitary reflections has always been the empty church and adjoining graveyard: Gray's "Elegy" and Wordsworth's "Tintern Abbey" were, Eleanor Sickels tells us in *The Gloomy Egoist*,[3] only the most famous of a large body of melancholy poetry reporting such solitary ruminations. Why would these places seem particularily attractive? Without it ever becoming explicit, there is even for non-believers a sense of human spirit, the air filled with a silence made weighty by the repose of generations. Philip Larkin brings to words this implicit sense of presence in "Churchgoing." It pleases him to visit empty churches,

> . . . tending to this cross of ground
> Through suburb scrub because it held unspilt
> So long and equably what since is found
> Only in separation—marriage, and birth,
> And death, and thoughts of these . . .

> A serious house on serious earth it is,
> In whose blent air all our compulsions meet,
> Are recognized, and robed as destinies.
> And that much never can be obsolete,
> Since someone will forever be surprising

A hunger in himself to be more serious,
And gravitating with it to this ground,
Which, he once heard, was proper to grow wise in,
If only that so many dead lie round.[4]

Personification

There is something primitive within us, little changed perhaps from
the Ice Age, that wants to see nonhuman things as persons. Personifying metaphors merely give voice to this anthropomorphizing genius:
when Blake insists that "The owl that calls upon the Night/Speaks the
Unbeliever's fright," when Wordsworth calls the river Wye "Tho
wanderer thru the woods," when Shelley exclaims "Oh wild West
Wind, thou breath of Autumn's being," the metaphors work because
we actually do experience the natural objects as personlike in these
ways. Metaphors are no mere literary devices: there is metaphor
because there is metaphorical experience. And this way of experiencing is so pervasive in solitude that it is worth exploring in detail.

George Lakoff and Mark Johnson have done more than any other
recent philosophers to reveal the ways in which our conceptual
scheme and the experiences it forms are thoroughly and profoundly
metaphorical. Since personification is a type of experiential metaphor,
it is worth our while to examine their theory as to how these metaphors
arise and work.

In *Metaphors We Live By,* they argue that "Our ordinary conceptual
system, in terms of which we both think and act, is fundamentally
metaphorical in nature."[5] Not only thinking and acting, but also feeling
and perceptual experience are structured by metaphors:

> The concepts that govern our thought are not just matters of the intellect. They
> also govern our everyday functioning, down to the minutest details. Our concepts
> structure what we perceive, how we get around in the world, and how we relate to
> people.[6]

Arguing that our conceptual scheme is revealed in the language we
use, they marshal linguistic evidence to show that, in general, both
individual concepts and the connections between them are structured

by metaphors. What exactly does this mean? Their favorite illustration is the conceptual metaphor ARGUMENT IS WAR.

This metaphor is reflected in our everyday language by a wide variety of expressions:

ARGUMENT IS WAR
Your claims are *indefensible.*
He *attacked every weak point* in my argument.
His criticisms were *right on target.*
I *demolished* his argument.
I've never *won* an argument with him.
You disagree? Okay, *shoot.*
If you use that *strategy,* he'll *wipe you out.*
He *shot down* all my arguments.

It is important to see that we don't just *talk* about arguments in terms of war. We can actually win or lose arguments. We see the person we are arguing with as an opponent. We attack his positions and we defend our own. . . . It is in this sense that the ARGUMENT IS WAR metaphor is one that we live by in this culture; it structures the actions we perform in arguing.[7]

Metaphor is not, then, merely a linguistic phenomenon: "The essence of metaphor is understanding and experiencing one kind of thing in terms of another." But why do we do this? How can this process yield understanding? Lakoff and Johnson answer that metaphors help us get a handle on complex phenomena by lending a structure, or gestalt, which is more directly familiar in our experience:

Such gestalts are *experientially basic* because they characterize structured wholes within recurrent human experiences. They represent coherent organizations of our experiences in terms of natural dimensions (parts, stages, causes, etc.) . . .

Concepts like LOVE, TIME, ARGUMENT, HAPPINESS

require metaphorical definition, since they are not clearly enough delineated in their own terms to satisfy the purposes of our day-to-day functioning. [On the other hand, concepts like UP-DOWN, OBJECT, CONTAINER, FOOD, BUILDING, WAR, JOURNEY] provide the right kind of structure to allow us to get a handle on those natural kinds of experience that are less concrete or less clearly delineated in their own terms.[8]

Argument, to take their favorite illustration, is a rather complex rational/intellectual activity, but "fighting is found everywhere, in the animal kingdom and nowhere so much as among human animals"

(p. 61). Moreover, the strategies and practices of fighting are widely and easily apparent across the whole spectrum of animal behavior: between brutes, between children, between adults of all cultures we find similar and familiar practices of "issuing challenges for the sake of intimidation, of establishing and defending territory, attacking, defending, counterattacking, retreating, and surrendering" (p. 62). These facts enable fighting to make sense of argument: the metaphor ARGUMENT IS WAR connects the simpler and more pervasive to the more complex and unique.

Returning to personification, Lakoff's and Johnson's theory is able to explain both the pervasiveness of the experience in solitude and its efficacy in making personal sense of that world. For one of the most powerful of our experiential gestalts, omnipresent to us since the early years in which conceptualizing begins, is that of PERSON. In personification, when we experience nonhuman things metaphorically as persons or personlike, we bring to bear the vast solid familiarity of our countless experiences of mother, father, siblings, and friends, not to mention our intimate knowledge of our own motivations, desires, emotions, and habits. The vastness of this category of experience gives to PERSON the same sort of explanatory/organizing power that UP/DOWN and BUILDING and CONTAINER have.[9] It is, however, a far richer metaphor, owing to the large variety of emotions, desires, motivations, goals, character traits, etc., which persons exhibit, and so is particularly useful for organizing our experiences of nonhuman things. Personification, in the light of Lakoff's and Johnson's work, emerges as a central feature of human experience and conceptualization; one would expect it, accordingly, to play an important role in solitude. And so it does.

Almost everyone personifies pets, especially in solitude, even that sturdy middle class Englishman on his island:

> I had taught my Poll, as I noted before, to speak; and he did it so familiarly and talked so articulately and plain, that it was very pleasant to me. . . . My dog was a very pleasant and loving companion to me for no less than sixteen years of my time . . . as for my cats, they multiply'd as I have observed . . . and these were part of my family.[10]

Loving members of a family: that is certainly how Alice Koller would describe the German Shepherds that have been her companions during her years of solitude (although insofar as personification involves the attribution of personal characteristics to things that are *not* persons, I suspect that she would object to the term). Certainly some of the most moving passages in her recent book, *The Stations of Solitude,* are expressions of love for her dogs, an attentive and perceptive love that makes charges of projectionism seem simplistic. Listen to her describe the intricacies she finds in her first dog's behavior:

> Logos refuses ever to admit that something he has done is wrong. The most he will acknowledge is that I'm big enough to be able to enforce a command, if I happen to be close enough to do so. When his ears go back, it is only a formality; deep down he does not recognize anyone as having rightful power over him. Unlike Ousia in similar circumstances, his heart is not breaking, nor does he construe my displeasure as the withdrawal of my love. Perhaps the reason is that long ago he learned that he can always change the subject: he can find some way to make me laugh. Faced with the actuality of a loud lecture, Logos wags the last four inches of the tip of his tail. He does it tentatively: out and back, then stop. If I have not noticed, he tries again. Of course I have seen it the first time: I have simply been trying to sustain my authority. No use. The experiment in apology always works, and he knows it . . .[11]

Even if a faithful dog is not capable of the full range of intellectual and passional responses that a human person—even a fairly young human person—can manage, in some cases they are clearly able to supply what human beings need by way of love and friendship. When these needs are met by a being that is not capable of the full range of personal activities and sensibilities, I suggest that the mechanisms of personification "fill in the blanks": we permit ourselves to imagine that the baby or the dog is *skeptical* of our promise, ignoring for the moment (what we otherwise know) that neither baby nor dog have the conceptual wherewithal to manage the mental complexities of skepticism. There is personification, but of a more subtle nature: now it is the attribution of *a more complex level* of a personal attribute to a being that is partly, yet not fully, a person.[12]

It is fascinating to trace personification back through the history of solitude. For a boundless sense of the world as personal, probably no one has ever matched St. Francis of Assisi. The little saint moved so freely between the personal and the nonpersonal realms that he could refer repeatedly to his own body, so overworked and underfed, as "poor donkey," yet treat all other created things as brothers and sisters. Thomas of Celano, commissioned shortly after St. Francis's death by Pope Gregory IX to write a biography of the saint, tells us that

When he would come on a vast field of flowers, he would preach to them and exhort them to praise God as if they could understand his words. He would likewise exhort cornfields, vineyards, stones, fields, springs of water, green plants in gardens, earth, fire, and water to a praise and love for the Creator. In short, he called all creatures by the name of *brother* . . .[13]

We have the record, in the *Little Flowers* of one of these lovely sermons, the one he preached spontaneously to "a great company of birds" met while travelling along the road:

> My little sisters, the birds, much bounden are ye unto God, your Creator, and always in every place ought ye to praise Him, for that He hath given you liberty to fly about everywhere, and hath also given you double and triple raiment. Still more are ye beholden to Him for the element of the air which He hath appointed for you; beyond all this, ye sow not, neither do you reap; and God feedeth you, and giveth you the streams and fountains for your drink, the mountains and the valleys for your refuge, and the high trees whereon to make your nests; and because ye know not how to spin or sew, God clotheth you, you and your children; wherefore your creator loveth you much, seeing that he hath bestowed on you so many benefits; and therefore, my little sisters, beware of the sin of ingratitude, and study always to give praises unto God[14] . . .

St. Francis was there alone with the birds, yet a kind of interpersonal experience was unfolding. I smile at him—always such an extremist! —but the personifications of his exhuberant love do not really seem so very strange when considered in solitude. The impulse to speak to a bird, an animal, a tree is so natural a feature of solitude that it could pass unnoticed. It is worth noticing, however, as a substitutive mode of engagement with other people.

Personification is not always delightful, though, as the life of St. Antony reveals. In his case, it was the forces of Evil that were personified, demons enraged by the iron-willed asceticism of the saint. Since he is one of the most famous solitaries of all time (his story, as told by Bishop Athanasius, was a bestseller of its day), and since he came to be regarded as the father of monasticism—Western culture's strongest defender of solitude—it is worth investigating the role which personification played in his solitudes.

Antony was still a youth, living alone near his own village, when the devil launched his first campaign:

> First he attempted to lead him away from the discipline by suggesting memories of his possessions, the guardianship of his sister, the bonds of kinship, love of money

and of glory, the manifold pleasure of food, the relaxations of life, and, finally, the rigor of virtue, and how great the labor is that earns it, suggesting also the bodily weakness and the length of time involved. So he raised in his mind a great dust cloud of considerations.[15]

When this strategy did not prevail against Anthony's pious resolves, the devil tried lechery:

> he advanced against the youth, noisily disturbing him by night and so troubling him in the daytime that even those who watched were aware of the bout that occupied them both. The one hurled foul thoughts and the other overturned them through his prayers . . . the beleaguered devil undertook one night to assume the form of a woman and to imitate her every gesture, solely in order that he might beguile Antony. But in thinking about the Christ and considering the excellence won through him, and the intellectual part of the soul, Antony extinguished the fire of his opponent's deception.[16]

Finally, the devil capitulated. Manifesting himself as a black boy[17] and using a human voice, he complained to Antony, "I tricked many and I vanquished many, but just now, waging my attack on you and your labors, as I have upon many others, I was too weak." Antony demanded to know who exactly was addressing him, and upon hearing gave thanks to the Lord, telling the devil boldly how he despised him.

> Hearing these words, the black one immediately fled, cowering at the words and afraid even to approach the man. This was Antony's first contest against the devil.[18]

But it was not the last. Shortly thereafter, seeking greater opportunities for ascetic discipline, Antony had a friend lock him into some tombs outside the village, with only a bit of bread for sustenance. This brazen contempt for the devil's power maddened the Enemy—and worried him too: this Antony "might before long fill the desert with the discipline" (Athanasius). He set fiercely upon the young ascetic one night and "whipped him with such force that he lay on the earth, speechless from the tortures." Luckily the next day friends arrived bringing more loaves, and Antony was hauled back to town half-dead. Reviving speedily, however, he departed again for battle in the tombs. And battle it was: beat to his knees by the devil's blows, he still cried out "Here I am—Antony! I do not run from your blows." The devil amplified his efforts:

> When it was night-time they made such a crashing noise that the whole place seemed to be shaken by a quake. The demons, as if breaking through the

building's four walls, and seeming to enter through them, were changed into the forms of beast and reptiles. The place immediately was filled with the appearances of lions, bears, leopards, bulls and serpents, asps, scorpions and wolves, and each of these moved in accordance with its form . . . and altogether the sounds of all the creatures that appeared were terrible, and their ragings were fierce.

Struck and wounded by this horde, Antony groaned with pain, but still mocked them:

If there were some power among you, it would have been enough for only one of you to come. But since the Lord has broken your strength, you attempt to terrify me by any means with the mob; it is a mark of your weakness that you mimic the shapes of irrational beasts.[19]

Of course there was no answering this defiant logic, and the beast-devils evaporated in impotent rage.

Shortly thereafter Antony set out for the mountains to pursue his solitary battles. There in a deserted fortress (hastily abandoned by the resident snakes at the mere sight of the saint) he stayed for twenty years, neither going out nor allowing visitors to come in. Many were the battles waged and won: "Antony remained and suffered no injury from the demons, and neither did he grow tired of the contest," wrote Athanasius. In later years, when crowds in a city pressed close to touch the old hermit, he was quite undisturbed, remarking "These are no more numerous than those demons with whom we wrestle on the mountain."

An agnostic mind will construe Antony's attackers as personifications of the eerie shadows in the tombs, gusts of wind whistling in the cracks, lizards scampering over the walls—all transformed into demons by the severity of the asceticism and the fierce imagination of a hermit determined to wage war without quarter.[20] Modern psychology will be fascinated by the way in which inner temptations are split off from the self and projected outside as Tempters, as when Antony's own lust is reified in "the form of a woman." But then perhaps real demons are called forth by great holiness. I am not concerned here to argue the matter, but only to point out that in either case the solitude of the Father of Hermits was filled with almost-human presences.

As monasticism and eremitism developed over the next thousand years, there was a growing awareness of the sophistication of the devil's strategies for conquering the spirits of solitaries. Consider, as an illustration, the *Ancrene Wisse:* it was written around 1220 by an

English cleric as a guide for three young anchoresses who had immured themselves in cells built onto the walls of the local church. This work is of interest to us for what it reveals about personification in the medieval religious mind, still manifested largely in struggles with the devil. Linda Georgianna's masterful study of the guide highlights how skilled the Enemy had become:

> The devil, in the *Ancrene Wisse* as in most other medieval writings, is a being with a real existence who tempts the anchoress, though the *Wisse* author is careful to point out repeatedly that he has no power over her except by her own consent. If the anchoress can only recognize the devil in all his disguises, she can defeat him. But therein lies the difficulty . . . (for) the devil becomes an expert in the anchoritic life, making himself the 'trusty counselor' of the anchoress.[21]

Thus the *Wisse* author writes:

> There is most need to fear when the deceiver of hell incites one to something which seems very good but which is destruction to the soul leading to mortal sin. . . . 'No,' he says, 'I cannot make this one sin through gluttony, but I will push her further to the side towards which she is already leaning, and throw her on that side and suddenly fall upon her when she least expects it.' He urges her on to such great abstinence that she becomes the less strong in God's service, and to lead so hard a life and to make her body suffer so much that her soul itself dies.[22]

Or again,

> When you have been keeping vigil for a long time, and ought to go to sleep, he will say, 'It would be virtuous to keep awake now that it is difficult. Say another nocturn.' Why does he do this? So that you will fall asleep later, when it is time to get up.[23]

An unceasing inner interrogation was thus demanded of these *inclusi*. When one's inmost thoughts and desires, even desires for holiness, may in fact be the whispering voice of the devil, great vigilance must be exercised: listen to the tone of the thought, the bent of the yearning, see if you can detect the false concern of the Deceiver. Moreover, this interrogation was no mere aspect of the inclusion, but one of its central purposes: solitude was sought in order to discover more completely the devil's incursions into the soul, to disengage from them, and to thereby move closer towards God. The recluse's very purpose, thus, was to construct a disengagement propitious for a kind of engagement.

Perhaps someone will remark, "but the personification which loomed so large in the experience of these religious recluses was simply a sign of derangement: the endless solitude, the obsession with rooting sin out of the soul finally tore their minds to pieces." This diagnosis is mild when compared to Gibbon's view of St. Antony:

> A hideous, distorted and emaciated maniac, without knowledge, without patriotism, without natural affection, spending his life in a long routine of useless and atrocious self-torture, and quailing before the ghastly phantoms of his delirious brain, had become the ideal of nations which had known the writings of Plato and Cicero and the lives of Socrates and Cato.[24]

Considering how Gibbon prized solitude for his own work[25] this seems unsympathetic; and after many hours spent reading about the spiritual journeys of these holy men and women, even an agnostic mind may find these sorts of accusations simplistic and unconvincing. Surely we are all fellow explorers in the vast realms of solitude? Surely we can feel as much warm fellow feeling in the face of difference as modern hikers do when meeting strangers along the trail?

However, by way of an argumentative reply to the contempt sometimes levelled against the religious hermits, let us consider Thoreau. Certainly he was richly endowed with the personifying propensity under discussion. Again and again he insisted that there at the pond he was among companions:

> I never met the companion that was as companionable as solitude . . .

> . . . the most sweet and tender, the most innocent and encouraging society may be found in any natural object . . .

> I was suddenly sensible of such sweet and beneficent society in Nature, in the very pattering of the drops, and in every sight and sound around my house, an infinite and unaccountable friendliness all at once like an atmosphere sustaining me . . .

> I was so distinctly made aware of the presence of something kindred to me, even in scenes which we are accustomed to call wild and dreary, and also that the nearest of blood to me and humanest was not a person nor a villager.

> I am not more lonely than the loon in the pond that laughs so loud, or than Walden Pond itself. What company has that lonely lake, I pray? . . . I am no more lonely than a single mullein or dandelion in a pasture or a bean leaf, or sorrel, or a horsefly, or a humblebee.[26]

There seems to me a great similarity here to the world of St. Francis: does not Thoreau sing just as gladly about Brother Loon and Sister Humblebee? And as for the splitting and externalization of the inner self we observed in connection with the religious recluses, consider this passage which has so exercised Thoreau scholars:

(I) am sensible of a certain doubleness by which I can stand as remote from myself as from another. However intense my experience, I am conscious of the presence and criticism of a part of me, which, as it were, is not a part of me, but spectator, sharing no experience, but taking note of it; and that is no more I than it is you.[27]

It would not be a great step to identify this spectator as "conscience" or "devil," though Thoreau was not interested in taking such steps. His spirituality was of a different cast than Antony's or the medieval Sisters', yet not entirely dissimilar.

For an even more recent illustration of the ways personification can articulate the spirituality of solitude, consider Martin Buber. Famous for distinguishing the experience of an "It" from the experience of a "Thou," one would expect him to give personification no quarter. Yet early in *Ich und Du* there is a beautiful description of a mystical transformation in which an It (a tree) *becomes* a Thou:

> But it can also happen, if will and grace are joined, that as I contemplate the tree I am drawn into a relation, and the tree ceases to be an It. This does not require me to forego any of the modes of contemplation. There is nothing that I must forget. Rather is everything, picture and movement, species and instance, law and number included and inseparably fused. Whatever belongs to the tree is included: its form and its mechanics, its colors and its chemistry, its conversation with the elements and its conversation with the stars—all this in its entirety. The tree is no impression, no play of my imagination, no aspect of a mood; it confronts me bodily and has to deal with me as I must deal with it—only differently.[28]

Conversing, confronting, dealing: Buber's tree has become a personage. I think that this existential mystic is not dazed or deranged. I think we can recognize the presence he describes from our own solitudes: Brother Tree.[29]

Containment

Even when solitary consciousness is not feeling the stored warmth of other people, not personifying the objects of its attention, it is usually structured by an implicit sense of containment in some human community. May Sarton sees this clearly as she settles down to write at home in her study:

> Mildred is here cleaning. . . . The solitude is animated but not broken. I sit at my desk and work better because I know her sensitive hands are busy dusting and making order again.[30]

Here the sense of containment has risen to awareness; but as she begins to write it will recede into the background, sensed somewhat as background music is sensed. When other people are not the focus of consciousness, their backgrounding presence can go unnoticed: a poet who is totally absorbed in an *important* metrical problem, may never explicitly recognize that the feeling of *importance* derives from the expectation of an audience. Similarly, changes in the containing personal background can reverberate throughout the experience without ever coming explicitly to one's attention: if Mildred were either noisier or quieter than usual, Sarton might have felt somehow disturbed, felt that something was . . . not right . . . though never stopping to consider exactly what.

Containment is a general phenomenon of consciousness which gestalt psychology has taught us to see: the importance within experience of border and background. Think of the difference matting and frame can make to the mood of a painting. Or think of the way a certain grove of trees can seem ominous: you don't stop to ponder why, to identify what exactly is causing the feeling, but you move on feeling a vague uneasiness. Some time later it occurs to you that it was the peculiar reaching quality of the branches that unnerved you, the way they suddenly looked like giant, grasping arms. But, at the time, you were intent on other matters and only felt a vague inchoate sense of uneasiness. Or, to take another illustration, think of the way just-heard musical notes are present in one's experience of a melody (one of Husserl's favorite examples of the way in which the past is present to us): although the notes have vanished, they are still a presence which gives form to the stream of presently perceived notes, constituting them as this particular melody.

Social relations, real or imagined, can also serve this backgrounding or containing function. Because of the implicit level of consciousness at which these phenomena of containment operate, the forming and bounding of solitary experience by social relations is most forcefully brought to attention when the containing web is broken. The solitude is so sweet that you immerse yourself in it more and more, finally severing connections with the friends who "intrude"—only to discover that without their background presence the solitude has soured into loneliness.

If this is the phenomenon of containment, what sort of importance does it have in solitary experience? Let us return to our famous solitaries, looking this time, you might say, behind their backs.

For all his solitude, St. Antony lived within a web of human relations. As a novice ascetic he visited the various hermits who lived just outside his town, collecting "a word" and a virtue from each to explore in solitude. Then there were the admiring supporters, lowering bread regularly and resuscitating him when necessary. Surely, too, in those twenty years of struggle he must have felt a comradeship with the Old Testament heroes of solitude—Elias, Osee, Habacuk, Isaias, Jeremias, Ezechiel, etc.—as well as with John the Baptist who wandered forty years in the desert, and Christ who was tempted there for forty days.

When St. Antony finally emerged from the twenty years' seclusion, the wilderness around his cell had become crowded with other holy men and women determined to emulate his struggles. Antony undertook to organize and instruct them, creating thereby the beginnings of monasticism—no easy task, considering the numbers involved. One student of the period describes Antony as "overwhelmed with disciples," and Palladius, writing about the time of Antony, says that at Nitria, one of the early gathering places of hermits in northern Egypt, "lived some 5000 men with different modes of life, each living in accordance with his own powers and wishes, . . . alone or with another, or with a number of others."[31] We do not know exactly how many disciples, admirers, and curiosity seekers Antony had to deal with, but we know that the numbers were large and we know that Antony accepted the task of fathering them. In words remarkable for the hermit of hermits, he once insisted, "Our life and our death is with our neighbour. If we gain our brother, we have gained God, but if we scandalize our brother, we have sinned against Christ."[32] Several times he left the desert, once to minister to the victims of a plague and once to help Bishop Athanasius in his war against the Arian heresy. Throughout his life, then, Antony was enmeshed in a variety of social relationships, some very direct, some indirect. The long solitudes unfolded in these containing frameworks, whose subtle influences on the quality of his experiences it seems impossible to doubt.

The sense of containment felt in these early communities of hermits is worth pursuing a little further, not only for the light it sheds upon religious solitude but also for the sense of normal humanity it gives to these often ridiculed holy men and women. A passage from the *Historia Monachorum,* a contemporary description by Rufus Tyrrannius, gives us a fine sense of the "community in isolation" of these desert ascetics. When the Nitrean mountains became too crowded with monks and visitors, Tyrrannius tells us, some of the hermits moved nine miles further into the desert:

> this place, by reason of the multitude of cells dispersed throughout the desert, they call *Cellia* (the cells) . . . the cells are separated from one another by so wide a space, that none is in sight of his neighbour, nor can any voice be heard. One by one they abide in their cells, a mighty silence and a great quiet among them; only on the Saturday and the Sunday do they come together in the church, and there they see each other face to face as folk restored in heaven. If by any chance anyone is missing in that gathering, straightaway they understand that he has been detained by some unevenness of body and they all go to visit him, . . . But for no other cause dare they disturb the silence of his neighbour, unless perhaps to encourage by a kind word, or to anoint him with the comfort of counsel the athletes set for their struggle. . . . Many of them walk three or four miles to church, and the distance dividing the cells from one another is no less great; but so much love is in them and by such intense affection are they bound towards one another and towards all the brethren that they set an example and cause wonder to all.[33]

Even the inevitable curiosity seekers were treated well:

> The old men of the desert received guests as Christ would receive them. They might live austerely themselves, but when visitors came they hid their austerity and welcomed them. A brother said, "Forgive me, father, for I have made you break your rule," but the old man said, "My rule is to receive you with hospitality and send you on your way in peace."[34]

These quotations emphasize one element of the containing relationships in which the hermits lived, brotherly love, but there was a strong element of rivalry too. In *The Evolution of the Monastic Ideal* Herbert Workman emphasizes the difference between these first collections of self-directed spirits and the tightly organized communities of obedience and self-effacement which soon became characteristic of monasticism in the West. Citing with approval another scholar's assertion that "The dominating principle that pervaded Egyptian monachism in all its manifestations . . . was a spirit of strongly-marked individualism," Workman continues:

> The very extravagances and eccentricities which later writers have held up to scorn, were but the manifestations of this pronounced individualism in a rivalry of asceticism. Against the essential solidarity of the Catholic Church, as against the all-pervading tyranny of the organization of the Empire, the monk placed that individualism.[35]

The character of both the asceticism and the rivalry prevailing amongst the desert hermits, suggesting the containing influence of the latter on the former, can be seen in two extreme and famous examples, Macarius of Alexandria and St. Simeon Stylites.

> Of Macarius of Alexandria we read that "if ever he heard of any one having performed a work of asceticism he was all on fire to do the same"—an attempt to "break the record" in subduing the flesh. One day Macarius of Alexandria was stung by a gnat. In his impatience he killed it. Conscious of a lost opportunity of bearing mortification with resignation, he deliberately lived for six months in the marshes of the Nile near Scete, maddened by gnats "whose sting can pierce the hides of boars."[36]

I note that Macarius was attentive to news of other ascetics, on fire to match or surpass their works, and careless enough to have done so in a sufficiently public way for the word to be spread. When he visited the monks of Tabennisi near Thebes, ostensibly to learn "their great method of life," I do not doubt that he would allow his own austerities to be known. And earlier, there in the marshes of the Nile, was there not an ineffable sense of an audience?

The containment of ascetic solitude in a human world is even more clearly manifest in that most famous ascetic of them all, St. Simeon Stylites, who lived in Syria about a generation after Macarius and two generations after Antony. Some of his early exploits reveal the background presence of admirers, and manifest an extremism which does suggest motives of rivalry:

> He began his monastic life as an enclosed anchorite (AD 413–423) by dwelling for forty days in a cave with his right leg fastened by an iron chain to a stone. . . . When the bit of leather which protected his skin from the iron was removed, admirers counted in it twenty fat bugs which Simeon had refused to disturb. At another time he dug a trench in a garden and daily buried himself in it up to his head through a whole summer. His fame as a saint was unequalled throughout the East.[37]

The feat for which he was most celebrated, however—by both the the devoted and the curious—was his retirement to the top of a pillar for the last thirty-seven years of his life. The pillar, Workman tells us,

> which the devotion of his admirers or his own desire to escape their attentions, gradually raised from [six feet to sixty feet] in height, and which seemed to an eye-witness but [4 feet] in breadth

probably had a cage on top to prevent falls, even though he was chained in place. There he sat, alone, for thirty-seven years.

Why choose to do such a thing?[38] Apparently Simeon was moved by the biblical injunction to be the light of the world:

> a lamp is not lighted to be put away under a bushel measure; it is put on the lampstand, to give light to all the people of the house; and your light must shine so brightly before men that they can see your good works, and glorify your father who is in heaven. (Matt. 5. 14–16)

In this he was greatly successful: the curious came from as far away as Britain and Spain to gaze upon him and listen for a holy word. Some were even so bold as to put ladders up against the pillar and climb up to seek advice, advice which he apparently was quite willing to give; indeed the Emperor Theodosius II consulted thus with the holy man. Simeon also dictated letters to his disciples, and was kept informed of developments in the councils of the day. Certainly there was a great deal of solitude left, hours of wind and hours of darkness high on the pillared platform; but one imagines those solitudes firmly contained in a complex web of human relationships.

With the turning to cenobitic (the term comes from 'koinos bios,' "common life") monasticism effected by St. Basil (AD 330–379) and St. Benedict (AD 480–543), eremitic isolation became a thing more rare, though still prized as the final achievement of the Christian spiritual life. Attempting to follow the complicated history of monastic solitude through the centuries is beyond the scope of this study, but perhaps no one will doubt the role of containment in the experience of solitude in a community of hermits. What of the solitude of the inclusi, though, those anchorites and anchoresses who had themselves sealed permanently into cells? Emerging as a common phenomenon during the twelfth century, the inclusi hoped to become more alive to Christ by becoming dead to the world. The cell was conceived, Peter Anson tells us, as a grave in which the recluse was prematurely buried, and the ceremony surrounding the immurement repeatedly expressed this meaning. Beginning often with a requiem mass, the ceremony proceeded with a reaffirmation of the recluse's vows of poverty, chastity, obedience, and "stability" in the church.

> There followed a procession to the cell, with even more stress on burial, because the choir sometimes chanted 'In paradisum deducant te angeli,' concluding with the 'Libera me Domine.' . . . Very often ashes were sprinkled over the living tomb.
> At last came the dramatic climax of the function. The solitary entered the 'tomb,' and the door was locked, after which the bishop, abbot or priest sealed the

key-hole. There were occasions when the opening of the door was built up with bricks, so that there was no means of entrance or exit.[39]

Contained within the walls of their grave-cells, dead to the world outside, the solitude which was theirs now for life must interest us by its very extremity: can there have been any significant social forming left in this radically anti-social consciousness? Can their solitudes have been in any meaningful sense contained?

Georgianna casts considerable light upon the psychology of these dwellers in darkness, and the resulting picture is of a very complex structuring of solitude by social connectedness. To begin with the cell itself, following the practice all over Europe during the twelfth and thirteenth centuries, it would have been built onto the outside wall of the church.[40] This fact had a social significance which neither anchoress nor passing villager could forget: as the *Wisse* author expressed it, abandoning etymology for simile,

> It is for this reason that an anchoress is called an anchoress, and anchored under a church like an anchor under the side of a ship, to hold it, so that the waves and storms do not pitch it over. So all Holy Church, which is called a ship, shall be anchored to the anchoress, and she shall hold it secure so that the puffing and blowing of the devil, that is, temptations, do not pitch it over.[41]

Georgianna remarks that, "Though [the anchoress] herself lives the most private of lives, her name and the position of her anchorhold proclaim a sort of public contract to support the Church." Through both her intercessive prayers and her struggles with the devil, the anchoress rendered constant service to the community, a service received with reverence and gratitude by the townspeople. Nor are we speaking of a few unusual localities: Anson concluded that, "Almost every large town in Europe appears to have had its anchorite or anchoress throughout the Middle Ages."

But to return to our three English anchoresses and their cells: as important as the walls which sealed them in were the windows which connected them to the world. One window faced inward towards the altar of the church, where the anchoress could watch the daily services. Another faced into the parlor of the church, where informal conversations among visitors could be heard, sometimes even joined. The third small window opened out upon the town; through it the anchoress could watch the daily life of the town, and even enter into it in ways which the *Wisse* author finds it necessary to discuss. His most famous directive shows the surprising involvements that recluses sometimes undertook:

> Ye shall not possess any beast, my dear sisters, except only a cat. An anchoress that hath cattle appeareth as Martha was, a better housewife than anchoress; nor can she be any wise as Mary, without peacefulness of heart. For she must think of her cow's fodder, and of the herdsman's hire, flatter the hayward, defend herself when her cattle is shut up in the penfold, and moreover pay for the damage. Christ knoweth, it is an odious thing when people in the town complain of an anchoress's cattle. If however, anyone must needs have a cow, let her take care that she neither annoys or harms any one, and that her thoughts be not fixed thereon.[42]

The interesting point here, Georgianna argues, is not simply that anchoresses enjoyed more sociality than was previously thought; rather it is that the spiritual guide who wrote the *Wisse* believed firmly that the world is ultimately inescapable for the anchoress. With a fine psychological sensitivity he realized that she entered the anchorhold steeped in all of the memories and habits of a social woman, maintained awareness of the village life surrounding her, and could not realistically expect to escape these human connections. Nor need she despair over this: for worldly connections could actually serve important spiritual purposes. For one thing,

> the minute details of creation [can] teach or mirror spiritual things. Thus no incident or desire is too worldly to illustrate God's love and the ways the anchoress can return that love. Barnyard animals, the habits of thieves, the calls of soap merchants, wrestlers' favorite holds, mothers' games with their children, and husbands' relations with their wives—all can be seen as illustrations of God's ways. In a negative sense, the anchoress *cannot* ignore these worldly activities because they exist not only outside her window but within her memory. But in a positive sense she *should* not ignore them because they are her only mode of reference, the only objective correlative for her relationship with God.[43]

But secondly, the anchoress can make psychological use of worldly concerns in advancing her own spiritual growth. She can, when struggling against particularly recalcitrant temptations, call up thoughts which inspire fear, wonder, joy, and sorrow for the purpose of extinguishing the temptations:

> For example, think what you would do if . . . people were shouting "Fire! Fire!" because the church was burning . . . or if you were to see Jesus Christ and hear Him asking you what you would like best, next to your own salvation and that of your dearest friends . . . or if anyone were to come and tell you that a man most dear to you had by some miracle, say a voice from heaven, been elected pope . . . [44]

Georgianna remarks,

> Such mundane concerns, which might at other times draw her into sin, here give her comfort when she feels most alone. In this instance, it is not so much that the author shows his sensitivity to the solitary's loneliness by, as one critic puts it, "imaginatively breaking down the walls of the cell" to people the anchoress's lonely world with desert heroes and saints; rather, and more to the point, the author effectively reminds the anchoress that she has within her memory and imagination the resources to do the job herself. . . . Here, paradoxically, the anchoress's attachment to the world—thoughts about family, friends, and security —is precisely what keeps her unstained by sin.[45]

Finally, both acknowledging and sanctioning the psychological realities, the *Wisse* author encourages the anchoress to develop her relationship with Christ "in terms of the human relationships she has willingly foregone, though the desire for them remains and accumulates" (Georgianna):

> Stretch out your love to Jesus Christ. You have won Him! Touch Him with as much love as you sometimes feel for a man. He is yours to do with all that you will.[46]

Throughout the pages of the work, Georgianna notes,

> the love relationship between Christ and the anchoress is explicitly defined in terms of various human love relationships. The most famous, of course, is the extended image of Christ as the knightly wooer. But Christ is also described here as the most forgiving husband, the sacrificing mother, and generous friend.[47]

The picture that emerges from the *Ancrene Wisse,* thanks to Georgianna's careful reading, is of a solitude threaded through and hemmed about with social connection. The point is *not* that the anchoress does not really live in solitude, that would be absurd; rather it is that containment as I have defined it is characteristic of even the most extreme religious solitudes.

But these were religious solitudes, and they all happened long ago. How generalizable is the containment of the solitudes of St. Antony and St. Simeon and the three nuns to secular minds and more modern sensibilities? How about, for example, Thoreau: was his solitude at the pond, to any significant extent, contained in the sense I have been investigating?

It comes as something of a shock to learn how much Thoreau had to with people during his two years at the pond. First there was the setting: the pond was only a mile and a half from Concord, and from one of his hills he could see—if he stood on tiptoe—"some portion of the village." A railroad ran "half a mile distant," and the Walden Road was close by. In addition to the occasional farmer or fisherman who wandered into his encampment, visitors would come to the pond (sometimes twenty at a time!) and Thoreau seems to have received them all as hospitably as the old desert fathers. He also went visiting, rambling around the countryside and into town to dine with his mother once a week, on other days with friends. Those friends kept an eye on his "backyard experiment," and their presence must have been felt back at the pond. And of course a central project at the pond was the journal, writing for himself but also with the roughly formed intention of publishing some version of his life there. All in all, the solitude at Walden Pond appears to have been solidly contained.

Finally, listen to Alice Koller describe the way her dog, Logos, contained her solitude:

> When he had to stay at the vet's for a few hours or overnight, his absence became the leading edge on whatever else I was doing until he was back with me again. When I left him at home while I spent the day in a library or kept a city appointment in the heat of the summer, I was as aware of his not being with me as of his presence when he was; and on the drive away from the house without him I kept having the feeling that I had forgotten something I should have brought with me. That sense of his absence was itself a presence, as though a draft were blowing into a window that someone had left open but that I could not shut.[48]

To sum up the results of this chapter: disengaged solitude, in both its secular and religious forms, is regularly threaded through and hemmed around by diminished modes of engagement. These partial, indirect, substitutive engagements, our involvements with reservoir-objects, personifications, and implicit background structures of personal involvement, must not become too powerful, too direct or too explicit if we are to continue to speak of a solitude; perhaps the more acute forms of St. Antony's combats with the demons strain our willingness to think of them as solitudes. Yet in their subtle and diminished forms, they certainly do not disqualify an experience as a solitude—it would be absurd to deny the solitude of St. Antony, the immured anchoresses or Thoreau. Indeed these indirect/substitutive engagements can now be seen to pervade most solitudes. Typically: I do not wish to claim that these elements of engagement are necessary or inescapable: some kinds of meditation appear to achieve completely pure disengagement. But it is important to remember how rare and difficult of achievement such pure states are, and how briefly they endure. If the phenomena which have occupied us in this chapter are called impurities, virtually every solitude has its impurities, even the great solitudes of the greatest solitary spirits. And for that very reason, I dislike calling these threads of engagement impurities: do they not, afterall, like the additives which make alloys of gold, render the substance stronger and more lustrous?

CHAPTER 5

The Symmetry of Engagement and Disengagement

A terrible thing may be happening: my reflections upon the ways in which diminished or substitutive engagements pervade most solitudes may be leading the reader to conclude that solitude is a derivative mode of human experience, secondary to and parasitic upon social relations. Derivative, secondary, parasitic—three metaphors which diminish solitude and banish it to the outer hide of reality. Just such a view of solitude has been taken by some famous thinkers. I recall D. H. Lawrence's exclamation,

> Everything, even individuality itself, depends on relationship. . . . The light shines only when the circuit is complete. . . . In absolute isolation, I doubt if any individual amounts to much; or if any soul is worth saving, or even having.
> My individualism is really an illusion. I am part of the great whole, and I can never escape. But I can *deny* my connections, break them, and become a fragment. Then I am wretched.[1]

Of course it is hard to know exactly what Lawrence meant by these words; perhaps he had no quarrel with the claims of solitude to ontic equality with encounter; perhaps he only wished to speak about the individualism which unfolds in solitude as an illusion and not the solitude itself. Perhaps. But if, as many people think, solitude is the state in which one most fully explores one's individuality, and if the "individuality" so explored is really an illusion, it would be hard not to attribute something illusory or unreal to the solitude itself. Not sharply logical, of course, but very tempting. I think many writers have done this.

More formidable philosophically, though deeply ambiguous, are Heidegger's thoughts on the ontic status of disengaged consciousness. On the one hand, he writes:

> Being-with is an existential characteristic of Dasein even when factically no Other is present-at-hand or perceived. Even Dasein's Being-alone is being-with in the world. The Other can *be missing* only *in* and *for* a Being-with. Being-alone is a deficient mode of Being-with.[2]

On the other hand, he argues elsewhere that authentic existence continually grapples with death, an inherently solitary crisis: "No one can take the other's dying away from him," and "In dying, it is shown that mineness and existence are ontologically constitutive for death."[3]

Ashley Montagu provides an anthropologist's version of the diminishment of solitude:

> What human beings desire most of all is to have their needs satisfied, to be made secure. They also want to feel dependent, either upon some mother-ideal, deity, or other persons, or, pathologically, narcissistically upon themselves, but dependent they must feel. Man does not want to be independent, free, in the sense of functioning independently of the interests of his fellows.[4]

Depending on onself as "pathologically narcissistic"?—the words make me cringe.

Can my own reflections of the last two chapters possibly be taken to support these views of Lawrence and Heidegger and Montagu? Do they go any distance towards showing that solitary disengagement is an illusion, or a deficient mode of being-with, or a pathological condition? I feel certain that they do not, but how is this to be shown? Well, one way would be to point out the illegitimate category-crossing at work in many such writings. Lawrence, for example, glides between metaphysical truths regarding individuality and relationship and psychological claims about the false consciousness of certain kinds of feelings about individuality. Such gliding is all too common among writers on human aloneness, and revealing its illegitimacy will be a major task of the remaining pages of this book. For it *is* illegitimate: the fact that metaphysically I am a distinct individual has no necessary connection with how completely I feel bound up with other people, how I experience myself in relation to them, or any other phenomenological point of the sort we have just been making about engagement and disengagement—except for the minute truth that being a separate entity is a precondition for feeling *oneself* to be anything. I hesitate to accuse Heidegger of conflating metaphysics and phenomenology, partly because of the brilliance of his thought and partly because of its obscurity, but must confess to suspicions.[5]

One could also rise to do battle with Lawrence et al. on the metaphysical plane, pointing out that individuality and relationship are mutually implicative ideas. If individuality entails some difference between the individual and the other, then there must be relations of difference, true enough. But then exactly the same argument shows that there can be relationships only if there are individuals. Tu quoque!

Or one could go about it a different way. Figuring that it is not so much metaphysical arguments that lead people to denigrate solitude as it is their awareness of the impurities we have just been considering, one could undertake to show that engagement characteristically has its own impurities, that it is split apart and hollowed out by modes of disengagement. That at least would dispense with all diminishments of solitude based on its impurities; and perhaps that is the only way, finally, to argue with Heidegger.[6]

Branch and Bough have already revealed how disengaged thoughts, feelings, actions, and perceptions can spoil the clinical purity of an encounter: thinking of the waterfall while Bough talked on, a crack of disengagement opened in Branch's engagement. Needless to produce more examples; in an age which never wearies of complaining of the distance, the distraction, the part-quality of all human encounters, it is hardly necessary to argue that these sorts of impurities are as characteristic of engagement as their counterparts are of disengagement. So far, then, there does seem to be a symmetry of impurity between the great body of experiences of engagement and disengagement, of encounter and solitude. Can we go further?

In the last chapter solitary experience emerged as pervasively threaded and bounded by diminished modes of engagement; it moves among objects which have become reservoirs of personal meaning, it personifies external things and elements of itself through the workings of experiential metaphor, and it lives in a containing world of human connections. Now, upon reflection, it occurs to one that the opposites or negatives of these processes are equally pervasive in our engagements with others—not necessarily, not inescapably, yet regularly.

Mirrors and Reservoirs

How commonly do our daily involvements reveal a mirroring deflection away from people towards things. You hold the sack open and I shovel in the sand: not unaware of the cooperative nature of our activity, we are mainly focused on the shovel and the sack and the sand. Or to speak of more intimate engagements, so many of them involve the intimates quietly contemplating together other things, the music, the firelight, the dinner being savored. Or think of listening: if the speaker is eloquent, a kind of erasure occurs in which we are transported through the person into the world of her referents. In all of these familiar kinds of engagements we are aware of the mirroring person, yet deflected beyond towards objects which draw our attention away from the mirror; there is still engagement, but now in a slightly diminished way. (Diminished only in the sense at issue; I do not wish to claim that these experiences are less real or less rich—indeed quite the contrary, as will appear.)

Is there a parallel in encounter to the phenomenon of the object-reservoir in solitary experience? The analogous phenomenon would seem to be this: one experiences a person as a reservoir of something impersonal, of thingness, and that sense of the thing colors the experience to some degree, making it a little less purely an engagement with a person, without ever becoming very explicit in consciousness. Does this happen?

Yes, often. To see how it happens, and how often, it will be useful to think first of impersonal relations with other people, those non-intimate utilitarian dealings which loom so large in everyday life. Then we can take up the question of the presence of The Object in more intimate relations.

Impersonal relations are those in which our primary concern[7] is with making use of, or being of use to, another. Here the dominant motive is the accomplishment of some task: getting a tooth filled, paying a parking ticket, finding a piece of matching yellow cloth, improving the comfort of a sick patient. I say "making use of" and not "using": the latter term should be reserved for the morally impermissible ways of making use of others. Specifying the conditions which convert (mere) making-use-of into *using* proves a difficult task, as Lawrence Blum's fertile study, "Deceiving, Hurting and Using,"[8] revealed some years ago. However, it is clear that there is a valid distinction here, that we do very often make use of people without *using* them. As Walter Kaufmann expressed it,

> Innumerable are the ways in which I treat you as a means. I ask for information, I may buy from you or buy what you have made, and you sometimes dispel my

loneliness. . . . Even when you treat me only as a means I do not always mind. A genuine encounter can be quite exhausting, even when it is exhilarating, and I do not always want to give myself.[9]

Personal relations, what Kaufmann perhaps means by "genuine encounters," are those in which our primary interest is in the person, not in what s/he can do for us. The extent to which we are personally involved with another is the extent to which the full range of their self is our concern. Here we are not so much interested in getting from A to B with M as we are in being as fully with M as we (and M) are able—regardless of whether it gets us anywhere.

With this distinction between personal and impersonal relations roughly drawn, I return to phenomenon of the "reservoir" in encounter. It is not difficult to detect it in our impersonal experiences of people: their "sense" and "feel" are often conditioned by associated objects which, though contributing to the experience, do not draw attention to themselves. I think now of the way the constellation of assembled probes implicitly condition my sense of my dentist, the sense of soil and steel tools emanating from the gnarled hands of the landscaper I consult, the way the crisp uniform of a Mountie bespeaks lines drawn in the social dirt, lines of impersonal Law. I remember that salespeople are taught to incorporate a romanticized image of the product in their own manners of speaking, gesturing, dressing: the solidly stylish demeanor and the Mercedes must merge.

Here it would not be to the point to object that this is an alienated or dehumanizing way of perceiving dentists or landscapers or salespeople. This is not an ethics of engagement, but a phenomenology: finding traces of engagement in St. Antony's solitude was not to denigrate it but simply to see it more clearly for what it was. All the same, it seems to me that much anguished writing on contemporary alienation does not take sufficiently into account the pervasiveness of these phenomena of partial disengagement in ordinary everyday intercourse between people. People are often useful to us because of their involvement with objects; those objects can become internal to our experience of the person so that our encounter with the other is partially an involvement with objects, and that is that. Of course, matters can go too far in this direction, so that the personhood of the other vanishes, but they must go some considerable distance before that happens. Kant's great moral imperative, I remember, incorporated this insight: it did not forbid us to treat people as means, but insisted that we treat them "always also as ends."

What about personal relations, those more intimate engagements which might be expected to reveal most clearly the essence of interpersonal encounter: do we find there the same dim sense of objecthood? FRIENDSHIP, LOVE, the words conjure up almost mystical states of pure relation with the beloved: but what are the realities?

It is no sin against a true romanticism to insist that friends and lovers are creatures of their world, that they bring that world to us in both the mundane and the ethereal moments of relationship. Friends are always bound up with places, the school where we met, the apartment that we shared, the city which we explored together on long Sundays. If I should sit down to write such a friend, if I should dream of him at night, all those places would be opaquely incorporated in his presence: I could call them to mind if anyone asked me to, but ordinarily they lie in the background, quietly generating the sense of the richness of the relationship. A dear person, however, has become partly places and things.

Of the mystical experience of the other on the high plains of erotic encounter I am reticent to speak. I know one remarkable thing, though: the gentle gathering of the elements into the beloved, the way a smiling face in the twilight can become light breeze and lilac and darkening soil. At such moments, as Joyce Carol Oates says,

> The visible world collapses
> and repeats itself in our bodies;
> All visible things repeat themselves
> into permanence.[10]

Personification and Objectification

Underlying the personification explored in the last chapter is our ability to experience metaphorically, to experience one thing as another. Everyone understands the phenomenon in the realm of vision, having since childhood been fascinated by the way clouds can be seen as dragons, as mountain peaks, as hobnobbing giants, etc. But metaphorical experiencing occurs in all the other senses too: wind sounds are sometimes heard as moans, and Leonardo da Vinci spoke of "those bells in which you can hear every named word." In metaphors of touch, rain is felt as a flailing attack, nausea as oceanic waves.

But this ability of consciousness operates symmetrically in solitude and encounter: just as objects can be personified, so persons can be experienced as objects (or object-like)—"objectified" in this, and only this, sense of the term. Take the case of vision, the metaphorical experience of seeing-as: just as seaweed can be seen as slimy hair, wet hair can be seen as seaweed; just as trees can be seen as sturdy sentinels (sentinel pines), so sentinels can be seen as trees; just as hills at twilight can be seen as breasts, breasts can be seen, from certain privileged perspectives, as soft hills. However, seeing things as other things is only the metaphor of one sense: there are also hearing-as, smelling-as, and touching-as. Just as voices can be heard in the wind, a tiresome speaker becomes a bee droning at the front of the hall. Just as the outer membrane of a plum becomes its skin, so a rough hand becomes sandpaper. And just as the ancient Greeks felt the awesome powers of nature as Zeus Thunderer and Poseidon Earth-Shaker, so in our own time particularly fortunate sexual encounters are sometimes experienced as thunderstorms and earthquakes.

Nor are these eccentric, isolated experiences. Since the earliest years of life, people and their parts have been objects in our world, to be seized, sucked, pushed aside, clambered over, curled against. Even the own-body presents itself to the infant as a set of foreign objects, the manipulation of which has to be learned in frustration. Apparently, then, there is the same sort of experiential primacy in the concepts of OBJECT and CONTAINER as Lakoff and Johnson found in UP/DOWN and we found in PERSON. OBJECT and CONTAINER are primary ways of organizing experiences for us because we are ourselves—and experience ourselves as—objects and containers; this is our embodiment. But of course we are embodied *persons:* objectification of the personal is not *more* primary than personification of objects. I have only meant to suggest an equal primacy for both ways of grasping reality, a symmetrical forming of solitude and encounter.

The extent of personification and objectification in experience really is surprising. Undeniable, though, when you look at the extensive collections of metaphors Lakoff and Johnson have assembled from the ordinary everyday ways we talk about human activities. Take human thoughts and ideas, for example: one of the pervasive ways we talk about, conceive, and experience them is as food;

> What he said *left a bad taste in my mouth*. All this paper has in it are *raw facts, half baked ideas, and warmed-over theories*. There are too many facts here for me to *digest* them all. I just can't *swallow* that claim. That argument *smells fishy*. Let me *stew* over that for a while. Now there's a theory you can really *sink your teeth into*. We need to let that idea *percolate* for a while. That's *food for thought*. He's a *voracious* reader. We don't need to *spoon-feed* our students. He *devoured* the book. Let's let that idea *simmer on the back burner* for a while. This is the *meaty* part of the paper. Let that idea *jell* for a while. That idea has been *fermenting* for years.[11]

These authors are also able to provide similarly extensive lists of common ways of speaking about ideas as plants ("Mathematics has many *branches*"), products ("He *produces* new ideas at an astounding rate"), commodities ("He won't *buy* that"), and cutting instruments ("That was a *cutting* remark. He's *sharp.*"). As they emphasize, these are the normal everyday ways of talking about thinkers and thinking; and they argue persuasively that as we speak so do we conceptualize and experience. The upshot is that our engagements with other people are pervasively (albeit subtly) characterized by modes of objectification.

An important caution: I have called this activity of consciousness "objectification" because the term seems to accurately describe the phenomenon; but I am aware that there are other uses of the term, especially in Marxist and feminist analyses, where it has a strong pejorative sense. As I understand that usage, "objectification" is the dehumanizing practice of seeing and treating other people *merely* or *exclusively* as objects, not also as persons. Employers objectify workers when they see them only as production units; men objectify women when they see them solely as collections of sexual parts, or when their sexual behavior remains fixated solely upon those parts and does not express or seek emotional connection. However, these attitudes and behaviors, although depressingly familiar, represent a pathology of the psychic processes I have been discussing, an exaggeration of the object-aspect together with a blindness to the personal inhabitation of the object. Whereas my concern throughout these last two chapters has been to capture the richness created in human experience by the mind's ability to *simultaneously* mingle object and person, a mingling which appears to work equally and symetrically in both solitude and encounter.[12]

Containment and Autonomy

In the last chapter I used the word "containment" to refer to the variety of ways in which solitary experience is formed by an implicit sense of connectedness with other people, a diminished or background sense of engagement with others. The symmetrically opposite phenomenon in the realm of engagement would appear to be this: the engagement is contextualized by an implicit sense of disengagement from the other, a backgrounding sense of the self as a separate thing only partially involved in this engagement. That such a sense of disengaged autonomy is indeed characteristic of our engagements is perhaps best shown in two ways: first, by considering the rare wonder of those few experiences in which it is gladly superseded, and secondly, by noticing the upsetting irritating character of encounters which place the dim sense of autonomy under threat.

Mystical ecstasy is a state in which all sense of disengagement from the object evaporates. Meister Eckhart provides us with a description of one such experience, of becoming absorbed into the Godhead so that his soul was

> more intimate with Him than a drop of water put into a vat of wine, for that would still be water and wine; but here, one is changed into the other so that no creature could ever again detect a difference between them.[13]

Something like this total absorption can happen with other human beings too, times in which "our eyes did thread upon a common beam." It is this mysticism of the other that Martin Buber struggles to articulate in the darkly beautiful descriptions of *I and Thou:*

> The basic word I-You can only be spoken with one's whole being.
> He is no longer He or She, limited by other Hes and Shes, a dot in the world grid of space and time, nor a condition that can be experienced and described, a loose bundle of named qualities. Neighborless and seamless, he is You and fills the firmament. Not as if there were nothing but he; but everything else lives in *his* light.
> As long as the firmament of the You is spread over me, the tempests of causality cower at my heels, and the whirl of doom congeals.[14]

I read these words with a thrill of recognition: yes, I have known that union, lived in that world lit only with her light . . . yes, it was like that! But if one speaks honestly of love, the moments are transient, as Buber himself laments:

> This, however, is the sublime melancholy of our lot that every You must become an It in our world. However exclusively present it may have been in the direct relationship—as soon as the relationship has run its course or is permeated by *means,* the You becomes an object among objects. . . . Genuine contemplation never lasts long; the natural being that only now revealed itself to me in the mystery of reciprocity has again become describable, analyzable, classifiable. . . . And even love cannot persist in direct relation; it endures, but only in the alternation of actuality and latency. . . . Every you in the world is doomed by its nature to become a thing or at least to enter into thinghood again and again.[15]

A melancholy fact, a part of our doom, so Buber perceives the disengaged distance which most commonly underlies our experiences of other people.

Total absorption is not always wonderful, however. Just as solitude often becomes unbearable when the background sense of containment vanishes, so encounter can become unnerving when all sense of autonomous distance vanishes. One feels a sort of hypnotic eeriness in this episode described by Lawrence in *The Rainbow:* Tom Brangwen, a farmer, has surprised Lydia Lensky, the vicar's housekeeper, with a stiff, brief proposal of marriage; and as she looks uncertainly at him,

> The expression of his eyes changed, became less impersonal, as if he were looking almost at her, for the truth of her. Steady and intent they were, as if they would never change. They seemed to fix and resolve her. She quivered, feeling herself created, will-less, lapsing into him, into a common will with him.[16]

The novelty of the experience reminds us that typically we do *not* lapse into the other during our engagements, which generally proceed with a firm background sense of differentness and separation. The negative reactions of threat and indignation when someone becomes overfamiliar are also revealing here: the intruder, with his presumption to know just what we feel or think, has overstepped the boundaries that protect our disengaged autonomy. The background refuge of private safety, necessary for a sense of control in encounter, is being invaded by strangers.

Nor is this sense of overfamiliarity, of intrusion upon the autonomous self, a problem only with strangers. Intimacy must also learn to defend against invasion, to establish bearable boundaries to disclosure. W. H. Auden grumbles about the problem in "You":

Really, must you,
Overfamiliar
Dense companion,
Be there always?
The bond between us
Is chimerical, surely:
Yet I cannot break it. . . .

Totally stupid?
Would you were!
But, no, you plague me
With tastes I was fool enough
Once to believe in:
Bah, blockhead,
I know where you learned them. . . .

It is time to summarize and appraise the findings of these last three chapters. Solitude and encounter have emerged as regularly threaded with their opposites, each experience unfolding in an experiential world implicitly structured by the other. First, there was the interweaving of engagement and disengagement produced by our ability to operate along four dimensions of attention simultaneously. Then a deeper probing revealed that even when solitude achieves a univocal focus, it typically experiences its objects as reservoirs of personal meaning, personifies them, and moves among them with a dim implicit sense of containment in a web of human relations. But the same inter-threading with the opposite appears to characterize encounter: from the most impersonal to the most personal, human engagements manifest an infusion of objects, the metaphorical objectification of persons and the backgrounding (barricading) sense of one's disengaged autonomy. The same criteria establish the presence of these backgrounding structures, the same sense of anxiety accompanies their erasure.

A philosopher must be careful here, however. It would be too strong to say that solitude and encounter, as modalities of experience, *necessarily contain* or *presuppose* each other; for the pure states of each do seem attainable, as several of our striking examples have indicated.[17] But how rare indeed such pure states are, how commonly and pervasively solitude and encounter are threaded with each other. Of course the way of encounter is not the way of solitude; but the distance between those paths does not appear as large as it once did. Nor, incidentally, does the distance between the secular and the religious paths of solitude. St. Antony in his fortress in the desert hills and Admiral Byrd in his cave under the Antarctic ice, St. Francis singing of Brother Wind and Sister Water and Thoreau observing the forms of thawing sand and clay until he exclaimed, "There is nothing inorganic," all of these solitudes have revealed their hidden engagements. I feel a kinship with them all.

How are we to understand these permeations of solitude and encounter with each other? A darker view and a brighter one suggest themselves. The former sees a pair of failures, a depressing distractedness of human consciousness: only a Thoreau can even approach pure solitude, and how denatured were his achievements; only a Buber can reach the fullness of total encounter, and even Buber admits forlornly that "every you in the world is doomed by its nature to become a thing."[18]

There is a brighter view, however. It discerns, in the interpenetrations of solitude and encounter, the workings of a playful demiurge in the psyche, ever at work marrying opposites together, kneading the Many into One and then rolling the One out again into Many. We have become accustomed to looking for this power only in the transcendent moments of mystical ecstasy, moments reserved for extraordinary spirits like Plotinus, Meister Eckhardt, and St. Theresa. But this is too farsighted: for now one sees The Mystical playing everywhere with the separateness of things, transmuting people into objects into people, lightly or forcefully, playing now in solitude and now in encounter, unpredictably but unceasingly.

CHAPTER 6

Images of Solitude

A bstract thought longs for images, as philosophers have always known but seldom acknowledged: think of Heracleitus's river, Plato's cave, the Stoic's stage, Locke's dark room, Leibniz's windowless monads, Hume's theater of perceptions, Wittgenstein's toolbox. These images summarize, simplify, and make vivid what is diffuse, complex, and abstract. Is there an image of solitude that could serve us in this fashion?

The first image I grasped for, the continuum line of engagement and disengagement with Encounter and Solitude as its extremities, did not prove very satisfactory. First, there was the fourfold complexity of engagement/disengagement which did not map well onto a single line. Then there were all those impurities in solitude and encounter, fine threads in what had appeared to be whole cloth, structures of one giving form to the other. There must be a better image.

Objects standing alone in nature can wonderfully capture one's *sense* of solitude, a sense that naturally differs from person to person, as some famous poetic images remind us. Compare Hermann Hesse's "Steppenwolf" with T. S. Eliot's vision: "I should have been a pair of ragged claws, Scuttling across the floors of silent seas."[1] What a different image Walt Whitman conveys!

> I saw in Louisiana a live-oak growing,
> All alone stood it, and the moss hung down from the
>   branches;
> Without any companion it grew there, uttering joyous
>   leaves of dark green,
> And its look, rude, unbending, lusty, made me think of
>   myself[2]

These visions are powerful, but too personal. Is there a more universal image?

An interest in Chinese philosophy has led me to appreciate the aptness of the ancient Tai Chi diagram for representing, in a simple yet powerful way, many truths about solitude and encounter:

SOLITUDE

ENCOUNTER

It is an image of symmetry and harmony between opposites, reminding us of an often unnoticed feature of opposition. The impurities of solitude and encounter are visible here in the streakings of light and darkness in each half, and the wrap of each segment around the other suggests the ways in which containment and autonomy condition solitude and encounter respectively. As for the dark spot at the center of encounter and the spot of light in the center of solitude, these remind me that engagement/disengagement can suddenly sound out of the very depths of solitude/encounter. Meister Eckhart went deeper and deeper into the isolation, shrunk away from the world into a drop of pure self—and then dropped into the vat of Godhead. And is there not a parallel phenomenon deep within engagement? I am thinking of those erotic mystics who report, at the extreme of erotic encounter, a sudden transcendence of any sense of self or other, an oceanic feeling of utter unboundedness.

Read in this way, the diagram is an icon of the logical-constitutive relationships between two kinds of experience, encounter and solitude. But the diagram could also be read in a different way, as a portrayal of the way in which those experiences relate temporally, how they grow out of each other through time. I think this is a fruitful and suggestive reading: I have felt a common dynamic within both solitude and encounter, a desire for more and more that, if it is unimpeded, achieves at last a satiation out of which is born a desire for the opposite. Here I think of Empedocles, who conceived the progress of all things as cyclical, driven by the waxing and waning of the forces of Amity and Strife:

> Double is the birth of mortal things and
> double their demise.
> For the coming together of all both causes
> their birth
> and destroys them; and separation nurtured in
> their being
> makes them fly apart. These things never stop
> changing
> throughout, at times coming together through
> Amity in one
> whole,
> at other times being violently separated by
> Strife.[3]

Even when Amity (engagement) reigns, there is a seed force of Strife (disengagement) remaining, which will grow according to dark inexorable laws until only the thinnest threads of Amity remain to connect the separated elements, threads which will then begin to thicken, drawing all beings back together into "one whole." Empedocles called this whole the "Sphairos" or sphere, an image suggesting uncannily the Tai Chi diagram. To develop this interpretation of the diagram, however, would lead us off into empirical psychology and archaic psycho-cosmology, away from more pressing concerns.

For a third reading of the diagram is fruitful: it can be seen as portraying the proper places of solitude and encounter in a human life, as revealing the relative importance of the two ways of experiencing the world, the meaning of each kind of experience for human existence. It is to these questions of meaning and value and place that I shall now turn.

PART 2

EVALUATING SOLITUDE

For it is not the mere name of solitude but the good things which are proper to it that I praise.

—PETRARCH

Yes, solitude is greater than I anticipated. My sense of values is changing, and many things which before were in solution in my mind now seem to be crystallizing.

—ADM. RICHARD BYRD

CHAPTER 7

The Virtues of Solitude

W hy do they go there, the seekers? What is it that they find in that silence, what does the solitude give them that encounter cannot give so well? And these treasured gifts, how do they compare with the undeniable joys of human relationship? How much are they really worth?

My own struggle to articulate the wonders of solitude—notes scrawled in various journals over many years, a few successes and more failures—sent me searching into the written records of solitary experiences past. As I read myself deeper into solitude after solitude, certain expressions of delight, certain reverent testaments repeated themselves again and again. Variations were played on common themes, themes I recognized at once in the fragmented record of my own journals. Here I give them names: Freedom, Attunement to Self, Attunement to Nature, Reflective Perspective, Creativity. In this chapter I listen to the variations and offer observations on the themes.

As I reflected upon these virtues of solitude, however, interrogating the experiences from a philosopher's perspective, a conviction grew stronger: these very virtues of solitude, so precious in themselves, yet find varieties of completion in encounter. Chapter 8, which explores these phenomena of completion, thus provides a more finished picture of the virtues of solitude.

The sense of balance and commerce between solitude and encounter which emerges from these two chapters, which emerged in part 1 as well, now faces a horde of philosophical objections: solitude, one camp passionately insists, has ontological, epistemological, existential pride of place over encounter; how we are then, alone, is at the deepest level "how it really is" for mortal humans. The arguments for this fascinating claim are many and confusing, and it will take chapters 9 and 10 to unravel them. Then, having chastened any overweening pretentions of solitude, I return to its defense, taking on the perennial objections that pursuing life alone is self-indulgent, selfish, irresponsible, neurotic, etc. I shall have much to say, as well, about the insinuations by various cultural relativists that even if solitude does provide some valuable experiences, it does so only for certain historically specific groups and is by no means of universal value. After replying to these charges, there will be time for a brief final word before I return to the silence.

The virtues of solitude—but what is a virtue? I use the term, as Aristotle did in the *Nicomachean Ethics,* to refer to that which a thing does exclusively or best: the virtue of a knife is its ability to cut well, and the virtue of a Phillips-head screwdriver is its ability to drive Phillips-head screws well. In the latter case, the virtue is almost exclusive: there is no other tool in the box which will do the job, as I have sadly learned from experience. In the former case, the virtue is not exclusive: a knife is the best thing for cutting, but you can get the job done in a pinch, crudely, with a small saw or a sharp chisel.

My question is going to be, accordingly: what good things, what valued states or activities is solitude *best* for realizing? Exclusivity is rare for any virtue, and it does not seem to characterize the virtues of solitude; all of the things which lovers of solitude have praised can be gained to some extent, sometimes even to a large extent, in encounter: you can appreciate the way sunlight refracts itself in flowing water with a friend at your side, though you can do it better in solitude.

Can one really appreciate the visual delight of flowing water better alone? How could such a claim be proved? Well, it's very difficult. For one thing, there seems to be an inherent roughness to general claims about virtue. Books are especially useful for learning ideas, but there are some people who simply cannot learn that way. Those few people do not destroy the generalization that books are the best way to learn ideas, but they dull its sharpness. Similarly with our subject: I believe that most people find—have always found—solitude particularly propitious for achieving the values I will be enumerating; but some people simply don't find those values best in solitude. One might try to defend the sharp generality of the virtues of solitude by arguing that unappreciative people are alienated, psychologically blocked, spiritually emaciated, etc., and, although I tend to believe this, I am doubtful that such arguments would be decisive for every case. Better, perhaps, to draw an analogy to the virtues/values of works of art: most people find Rembrandt's portraits quietly moving but some do not, and most people find Greek temples inspiring though some do not. The numbers of the unappreciative can be greatly reduced by patient education, but a few unregenerates will remain. The fact that there are a few such people, however, does not destroy the virtuosity of those artistic works, their lustrous richness and timeless nobility; just so, the fact that a few people do not observe nature best alone does not prove that attunement to nature is not a special virtue of solitude. That it *is* such a virtue, the following pages of celebration and reflection undertake to establish.

Solitude as Retreat, Respite, and Restorative

One of the most fervently celebrated virtues of solitude is its ability to provide a place of refuge from the beleaguering toils of social life. "It seems to me," wrote Petrarch at the beginning of *De Vita Solitaria,*

> that I can demonstrate the blessedness of solitude by exhibiting the troubles and afflictions of a populous environment, reviewing the actions of men whom one kind of life preserves in peace and tranquility and the other kind keeps agitated and careworn and breathless.[1]

He then proceeds to detail "the wretchedness of the busy man," who is immersed in the corruptions of social living:

> The busy man, a hapless dweller of the city, awakes in the middle of the night, his sleep interrupted by his cares or the cries of his clients, often even by fear of the light and by terror of nightly visions. No sooner is he up than he settles his body to the miserable bench and applies his mind to falsehood. On treachery his heart is wholly fixed—whether he meditates driving a corrupt bargain, betraying his friend or his ward, assailing with his seductions his neighbor's wife whose only refuge is her chastity, spreading the veil of justice over a litigious quarrel, or whatever other mischief of a public or private character he intends. Now eager with passion and aflame with desire, and now frozen with desperation, like a very bad workman, he begins before dawn the web of the daily toil in which he shall involve others with himself.[2]

From morning until night scheming and corruption engross this cosmopolitan until finally, when it is time for sleep, he is

> full of troubles, replete with dining and wining, gripped by fear and envy, dispirited by the checks he has encountered or vainly elated by his successes, afflicted with melancholy, busting with wrath, at war with himself, not master of his own mind. . . . His life is like that of the fiends; he is hateful to his neighbors, oppressive to his fellow-citizens, an object of terror or derision to his own people.[3]

When our world seems too full of people who fit Petrarch's description, when "every meeting with another human being has been a collision" (Sarton), we need the green pastures and still waters of solitude to restore our souls. There we can feel the *vis medicatrix naturae,* the healing power of nature. Erazim Kohák feels it while alone in a forest clearing, beyond the powerline and the paved road:

> The dominant colors of a forest clearing are green and light blue, both of which, as empirical psychology can attest, have a distinctly soothing effect on humans. The decibel levels here are geared to the tolerances of the human nervous system. The effort required by daily tasks, whether drawing water, building a fire, or making wood, provides regular physical exercise and has a beneficial psychological effect as well, building a sense of competence and confidence—the "mastery" of psychological lore. The diurnal cycle, undisturbed by electric power, assures a healthful alternation of activity and rest, while, together with the phases of the moon and the seasons of the year, it gives life a rhythm it lacks in the unchanging urban environment. The environing world of a forest clearing is calm and unjarring, living its own familiar life, so unlike the threatening, unpredictable environment of the artifact world.[4]

Escaping to such a solitary place—often called a retreat[5]—provides respite, relief, a time for the healing of wounds. Thoreau called solitude "medicine to the soul," and Montaigne even recommended it as a kind of stoic preventative medicine:

> In this retreat we should . . . talk and laugh, as if we had neither wife, nor children, nor worldly goods, retinue or servants: to the end that, should we happen to lose them, it may be no new thing to do without them.[6]

In more recent times, the Japanese physician Shoma Morita has developed a form of psychotherapy, based in the principles of Zen Buddhism, which eschews therapist intervention in favor of the healing power of solitary reflection:

> Upon his arrival at the hospital, the neurotic patient—overt psychotics are not accepted—must have complete bed rest for up to a week. During this time he is not permitted to associate with anyone else. He must not read or write, smoke, telephone, listen to the radio, or watch television. The patient is left alone with his illness until he and his illness become one—he has to accept his illness in complete solitude.[7]

Restoration is indeed one of the great gifts of solitude, but that is not the whole story. For important as this virtue is, it is a derivative value: it is because solitude provides us with certain intrinsically valuable things that it is able to function as a restorative. What are these intrinsic values? Until we articulate them, it will remain a mystery as to *how* solitude works its regeneration. Kohák's description of the forest clearing contains clues, but there is much more to tell.

Moreover there is a danger in emphasizing the restorative virtue of solitude: it can lead one to think of this profound experience as a mere instrumentality of relationship. Such a view is suggested in an image from Montaigne, "They have only stepped back to take a better jump and to hurl themselves with a stronger impetus further into the crowd"[8] and also in a mixed metaphor from Miguel de Unamuno:

> it is good to withdraw oneself, but [only] after having spilled oneself out, and in order to spill oneself out.[9]

The conviction that solitude is ultimately of value only for restoring us to society is put most uncompromisingly, however, by Halmos:

> Sleep has only one writ: to regenerate life for its continued living; willed solitude has only one function: to regenerate social life for its more harmonious living.[10]

What is it like to be asleep? Who knows, who cares?

Such a view is, of course, repugnant to lovers of solitude, and in any case fails to withstand scrutiny. It can make no sense of the indisputable fact that people often choose solitude over opportunities for warm and harmonious social relations: in such cases they are not fleeing from an evil but electing a greater good. The *Tao Teh Ching* asks knowingly, "Who will prefer the jingle of jade pendants if He once has heard stone growing in a cliff?"[11] Notice too that the restorative view, especially in Halmos's reductionist version, betrays an unargued prejudice in favor of sociality: for if it is true that solitude equips us for social living, it is equally true that society equips us for more fruitful solitude. This reciprocity struck Emerson: "The soul environs itself with friends, that it may enter into a grander self-acquaintance or solitude; and it goes alone for a season, that it may exalt its conversation or society."[12] And perhaps he understates the case: perhaps solitude, and not social engagement, is the most valuable state of human being; perhaps Halmos has the instrumentalities reversed?

Thus I am led, by the logic of the enquiry but as much by simple animal curiosity, to delve into the intrinsic virtues of solitude. What *is* it, really, to hear stone growing in a cliff? I am anxious to learn what words can capture of the richness of these silent hours, mindful, however, of Charles Olsen's warning:

the too strong grasping of it,
when it is pressed together and condensed,
loses it.

(from "The Kingfishers")

The First Virtue: Freedom

> For it is not the mere name of solitude but the good things which are proper to it that I praise. And it is not so much the solitary recesses and the silence that delight me as the leisure and freedom that dwell within them.[13]

Petrarch wrote these words in 1346, and his assessment has often been repeated. Three hundred years later, Francis Bacon remarked sardonically in "Of Marriage and the Single Life,"

> But the most ordinary cause of a single life is liberty, especially in certain self-pleasing and humorous minds, which are so sensible of every restraint as they will go near to think their girdles and garters to be bonds and shackles.[14]

William Hazlitt loved walking alone largely for its freedom:

> The soul of a [solitary] journey is liberty, perfect liberty, to think, feel, do, just as one pleases. . . . I want to see my vague notions float like the down of the thistle before the breeze, and not to have them entangled in the briars and thorns of controversy. For once, I like to have it all my own way; and this is impossible unless you are alone.[15]

Freedom of physical movement and freedom of thought seem to be the perfect expression of each other: one imagines Hazlitt now hurrying, now ambling, now pressing forward and now dawdling as his thoughts race and slow, connect and disconnect, all at their own pace. Certainly freedom of movement is a universal metaphor for the spiritual freedom of solitude, where our spirits *wander* or *ramble* or *leap* or *soar*.[16] These were the images chosen by Chuang Tzu around 300 BC to express the wonderful freedom the solitary spirit finds in the Tao (the Way). The first chapter of his book is entitled "Free and Easy Wandering," and one of its recurring themes is that those who do not understand Tao cannot achieve perfect freedom:

> Lieh Tzu [a fabled sage] could ride the wind and go soaring around with cool and breezy skill, but after fifteen days he came back to earth. As far as the search for good fortune went, he didn't fret and worry. He escaped the trouble of walking,

but he still had to depend on something to get around. If he had only mounted on the truth of Heaven and Earth, ridden the changes of the six breaths, and thus wandered through the boundless, then what would he have had to depend on?[17]

Wandering through the boundless and soaring with cool and breezy skill are true delights of solitude, available even in the most ordinary everyday circumstances. Virginia Woolf's Mrs. Ramsay could wander through the boundless when the family left her alone with her knitting:

> She could be by herself, by herself. . . . All the being and doing, expansive, glittering, vocal, evaporated; and one shrunk, with a sense of solemnity, to being oneself, a wedge-shaped core of darkness, something invisible to others. Although she continued to knit, and sat upright, it was thus that she felt herself; and this self having shed its attachments was free for the strangest adventures. When life sank down for a moment, the range of experience seemed limitless.[18]

Thoreau remarked, "I go and come with a strange liberty in nature." So true, but why? An obvious point is the escape from the social controls which govern all interpersonal life: in solitude you can cry "Fire!" anytime you like, and you can do it stark naked. More interesting, if harder to see, is the way in which other people, for all their friendliness and generosity, represent structures of demands: demands to be listened to with an interest commensurate with *their* expectations, cared for according to *their* requirements, followed or led along the trail at *their* own pace. Engagement accordingly requires self-governance by a variety of sensitive control systems, vigilance lest they malfunction, alertness to clues bearing on their need for adjustment, and skill at making them appear nonexistent. No one, to my mind, better captures the convoluted nature of even familiar relations than R. D. Laing:

> They are not having fun.
> I can't have fun if they don't.
> If I get them to have fun, then I can have fun with them.
> Getting them to have fun, is not fun. It is hard work.
> I might get fun out of finding out why they're not.
> I'm not supposed to get fun out of working out why they're not.[19]

Laing sees brilliantly the social constraints upon even having fun, the constricting impositions even friends and lovers make upon encounter. Rilke cried out in the Paris notebook, "To be loved means to be consumed in flames." What he meant, wrote William H. Gass, was this:

> Because you are loved . . . you are expected to serve your lover, whose feelings have been left like a kitten in your care. Because you are loved, you become the

victim of many benevolences which your lover wishes to bestow upon you, but which you are scarcely prepared to receive. Because you are loved, your work, which is a rival much admired but not more jealously betrayed for all that, will have to step aside so that the loving one can be comforted by your attention, assured of your devotion by the degree to which you are prepared to neglect yourself, abandon your principles, release your dreams. Because you are loved you will be offered a physical intimacy which will be perceived as conferring spiritual rights. Because you are loved, you are now fuel for another's fire . . .[20]

Rilke and Gass exaggerate, of course, but the constraints of love are familiar enough—present even when you can "just be yourself." Constraints and a considerable expenditure of energy just to keep abreast of the complexities of the human heart, as Laing's vignettes force us to recognize:

JILL: I am frightened
JACK: Don't be frightened
JILL: I am frightened to be frightened when you tell me I ought not to feel frightened.[21]

When all this is removed in solitude, a great weight is lifted. Free! It feels strange at first, no one bounding you on any side. Sue Halpern conveys the feeling with admirable honesty in *Migrations to Solitude*: on a solo camping trip, the solitude of her campsite is disturbed by a fisherman out in the lake; finally, though,

The man in the aluminum boat leaves the neighborhood pursued by a cloud of greasy blue smoke, and I am alone again, and not sure what to do.
    If the forest were a room with a door, I'd probably be inside, reading. But the open wood demands something else. A hike up the ridge, an hour with the chickadees—something like that. Solitude would appear to be defined by place as well as dependent upon it. What passes for being alone at home, say, wouldn't pass here. You don't pitch a tent to curl up with a novel.[22]

Then she remembers what she is about, "the confrontation of the self by the self, which is solitude's true vocation." If you softened "confrontation" into "exploration," you would capture one of Rilke's remembrances of childhood, a description which makes the free "feel" of solitude palpable:

No one will find it surprising that I pulled all these clothes out and took them into the light; that I held one of them up to my chest or wrapped another one around me; that I hastily tried on some costume that might fit me and, curious and excited, ran to the nearest guest room, in front of the tall, narrow mirror . . . how I trembled to be there, and how thrilling when I was; . . . I had imagination on my side, as long as I wanted.[23]

Hearing a door slam downstairs would have spoiled that free space as surely as another fisherman chugging into sight would have spoiled Halpern's.

Notice how deeply time is implicated in these freedoms of solitude: part of the freedom to sing and dance upon the beach is the conviction that no one is around to laugh, but equally important is the certainty that there is time to do either or both. Free time, in this sense, is time liberated from socially imposed constraints, the clocks, the deadlines, the need-schedules of other people. May Sarton revels in this sense of time alone at home on a winter morning:

> Today I feel centered and time is a friend instead of the old enemy. It was zero this morning. I have a fire burning in my study, yellow roses and mimosa on my desk. There is an atmosphere of festival, of release, in the house. We are one, the house and I, and I am happy to be alone—time to think, time to be. This kind of open-ended time is the only luxury that really counts and I feel stupendously rich to have it.[24]

However, it would be a mistake to think that the time of solitude is just the time of sociality in larger and more assured quantities; for as we remembered earlier there is a different sense of time that comes in solitude—attentive time, I called it—a time controlled solely by the object itself and one's interest in it. Consider the free imaginative pretending that accounts for so much of the fun of solitude. Imagine, for instance, pretending to be a duck (as I was once brazenly challenged to do by a marshland mallard in Wisconsin). How would you do it? How long would it take? The answers to these questions depend upon how determined you are to be a duck, but also upon what you know about ducks: there would be quacking to try, and waddling, and looking sideways with a green eye and (I found this the hardest of all) preening. How long each act takes, the duration of the whole experience, is between you and that strange constellation of memory traces which I suppose they call in California one's "inner duck." Attentive time is so different from objective social time: just think if I had invited you to imagine being a duck *for two minutes;* you would be half-watching the clock all the time, and half-lose your duck. And you would feel so much less free.

A frivolous experience? What a pinched objection! I prefer "play-ful." Certainly the delight is no trivial thing, at least not to St. Augustine, who was hardly a frivolous man:

> Behold in the plains and caves and caverns of my memory, innumerable and innumerably full of innumerable kinds of things . . . over all these do I run, I fly; I dive on this side and on that, as far as I can, and there is no end.[25]

Indeed solitude's ability to restructure time contributes so powerfully to the sense of freedom that it can even mitigate the anguish of solitary confinement. Christopher Burney, who spent eighteen months in isolation cells in Nazi-occupied France, wrote that he found himself rejecting the overtures of other prisoners because they threatened the free attentive time:

> Later that evening the man in the cell next to mine started to tap on the wall. When I understood that he was signalling to me I wanted him to stop . . . I was selfish and prized my silence, especially the silence of night. For the night, to those who have used it for privacy and sleep rather than as a trysting-place for ghosts and demons, is by instinct and experience a peaceful time, when your surroundings disappear and you may go where you will, and even the deadliest fear is tamed and may be touched and played with.[26]

Nor should we forget the solitary confinement of the hospital bed. David Grayson wonderfully captures the salvation that free imagination brings to the bedridden patient, as well as the distinctive "break" with the objective time of hospital operations, in this remembrance of his long confinement:

> My morning experiences were not only a source of comfort and delight to me in that sorrowy place, but they opened the way to new adventures. Adventures abroad in bed! The nurse did not see me, nor the doctors know of it, nor was it written down in the sober sheets of my daily record, but I was going out again! Though covered to the chin with a white counterpane, apparently quite helpless, I was in reality often abroad among my own hills, or in my garden, or walking the pleasant elm-shaded streets of the little town I love best of all. I don't mean by this any mere darting memories, full of sadness or regret, I mean that I was *there*. I was there to complete absorption, so that I was not conscious for the time being of the gabled room where I lay, nor of the hospital, nor of my own illness.[27]

The freedom of the imagination unfolding its own objects in its own time—what a precious gift of solitude! How unbearable human life would be without it.

A final word on the freedom of solitude will lead us toward the next virtue. I have been speaking of the freedom of unrestraint, the glorious feeling of the evaporation of social control, the open liberty of pursuing your own desires as they arise. But Alice Koller reminds us of another meaning of the idea of freedom, a meaning which philosophers know as the autonomy of Kant's ethical theory:

> Free: not only having no restraints, but also being self-governing according to laws of your own choosing. And even though acting in accordance with those laws can carry consequences you might not choose for their own sakes, you acquiesce in those consequences because they are the price of the laws you *have* chosen. You mistake freedom when you focus only on the first, the being unhindered. A spoiled child governs herself only by the whim of the moment, having no conception of her most intimate purposes, and thus having no conception of the consequences that will ensue from her actions. Heedless of them, she will be at their mercy, for they will occur, will she, nil she. Because the second holds the key, clarifies the interrelationship of both. Not being bound by anything except what you choose, where your choices spring from a genuine sense of what your life is and can become: that's the connection between there being no constraints and your being self-determined.[28]

But what purposes *are* your own, really? Which inner voices should be given authority if one is to be self-determined? An attuning to self is going to be necessary if these questions are to be answered, and that attunement to self occurs most readily in solitude: it is the second virtue to be explored.

The Second Virtue: Attunement to Self

> Adventure most unto itself
> The Soul condemned to be—
> Attended by a single Hound
> Its own identity.
>
> (Emily Dickinson, Sonnet #822)

Attunement to self is not an idea that is immediately clear: what, really, is the self, this secret watcher who becomes more elusive the more you try to capture him? And if it is just me, plain and simple, how could I *fail* to be attuned to it? Dickinson's terse sonnet raises all of these questions: hound? single? attended? condemned?

Philosophical psychology has produced a sea of conflicting answers to these questions since Plato divided the soul into three parts in the fourth century BC. Peering into those turbulent waters, however, it is important to remember that we do have, preanalytically, a pretty good idea of what is meant by attunement to self, and a pretty unequivocal sense of how good it is. What a relief when the station finally emerges from the static! How good it is to hear a clear unfearful voice instantly recognizable as *your own*. What I have in mind by "attunement to self" is best characterized by the image of free flow, the flowing into awarenessness of thoughts, desires, and emotions with no sense of censorship or management, together with a free-flowing access backwards towards their origins. Oliver Morgan nicely captures the sense of growing freedom of flow, flowing out and flowing backward towards the source, which is so distinctive of the attuning process: he is sitting alone at his desk after a busy day, looking out the window at some autumn leaves:

> At this moment I choose to allow the quiet to surround and penetrate me. . . . I can sense that my "person" is pulling back from its scattering into the details and plans of today, like a wave rolling from sand and shore back to its ocean source—collecting itself into the unity of "ocean."
>
> "I" am here, present to myself, and available for a possible revelation of what is inside me—feelings, images of self, my loves and aversions, my hopes and fears. I am present, too, for experiences of those guiding, inner images (personal metaphors, archetypes) that I sense shape my values, actions, judgements, and decisions during the rest of the time.[29]

May Sarton experienced the attuning process as a return: alone in the house for days after a difficult relationship had ended, she wrote in her journal, "I begin to have intimations, now, of a return to some deep self that has been too absorbed and too battered to function for a long time."[30] A constant theme of Sarton's *Journal of a Solitude* is the scattering of self produced by extended encounters with others, requiring a self-collection in solitude:

> for me, being with people or even with one beloved person for any length of time without solitude is even worse [than loneliness]. I feel dispersed, scattered, in pieces. I must have time alone in which to mull over any encounter and to extract its juice, its essence, to understand what has really happened to me as a consequence of it.[31]

Solitude is also the place for contacting the deeper springs of self that the writer so relies upon:

> There has been a long hiatus in this journal because I have had no days here alone, no days when time opened out before me. I find that when I have any appointment, even an afternoon one, it changes the whole quality of time. I feel overcharged. There is no space for what wells up from the subconscious: those

dreams and images live in deep still water and simply submerge when the day gets scattered.[32]

Why does encounter produce this scattering and submersion of the self? I suspect it is largely a matter of safety. For in the presence of others we are always, with more or less conscious effort, maintaining a variety of lines of defense: defense against potential assaults upon the self by adversaries, critics, manipulators; defense of certain crucial images of the self (e.g. maintaining an image of adult responsibility before one's child); defense against loss of self through absorption into loving others. Suppose, for instance, that while speaking to a colleague a man is suddenly struck by the inscrutable blue of her eyes: the urge to exclaim as much must pass two defensive censors, one who fears that she will ridicule him or indignantly repudiate an overfamiliarity, another who fears that she will make too much of the exclamation, turning it into "an approach." Caught between the clamoring censors, the feeling disintegrates in confusion. No wonder there is a feeling of blockage in such encounters! In solitude, safe from threats of battering and absorption, the defensive guardians can be dismissed and the whole array of inner feelings—savory and unsavory—let loose. Yearnings, rages, jealousies, dependencies, and estrangements can be safely lived through when the persons upon whom we might wrongly (or dangerously, or foolishly) unleash them are absent. Inner conflicts and ambivalences can be felt back-and-forth when there is no longer a need to present a unified, consistent, predictable self to the world. Walt Whitman dared to exclaim, "Do I contradict myself? Very well then, I contradict myself," but few of us would dare to do so to another.

Safety is not the only condition for self-attunement in solitude, however. Equally important is the freedom from interruption (parents especially know this). For then one can wait patiently and listen, "present to myself" in Morgan's words: then the true object of a feeling, its obscure symbolisms, its reverberations in other corridors of the soul, can emerge as they will. And now, having entered the uninterrupted temporality of listening presence, the rapport with self can grow into a gathered sense of completeness; Rousseau describes the experience in his *Musings of a Solitary Stroller:*

> But if there is a state where the soul finds a solid enough base to rest itself entirely and gather together there its entire being without having to recall the past or to step over into the future; where time is nothing for it, where the present lasts

always, without, however, marking its duration and without any trace of succession, without any other feeling—of privation or joy, of pleasure or pain, of desire or fear—than that alone of our existence, and this feeling alone can fill it completely; [then] as long as this state lasts, whoever finds himself in it can call himself happy, not with an imperfect happiness poor and relative such as what one finds in the pleasures of life, but with a sufficient happiness perfect and full which leaves in the soul no void which it feels the need of filling . . .

What does one enjoy in such a situation? Nothing exterior to the self, nothing except the self and one's own experience.[33]

I would not be misunderstood, however. This state of inner attunement is not always joyful or serene—you do not always like what you hear when the radio is tuned. Sometimes it involves feeling with devastating intensity the conflicts, the rages, the intimations of mortality we have been trying to deny. That was how it was for Alice Koller, who fled to Nantucket in her thirty-seventh winter, battered and dazed, desperate to find out who she was and how to continue:

For a good part of each day, particularly when Logos and I were walking, most particularly when I stopped to sit on a certain log that had been washed up on the sand, I compelled myself to become aware. . . . And one day I came upon the purpose I had been pursuing all the preceeding years. I had not known I had been doing that thing: I had believed I had been doing something quite different. So it was a huge thing to learn. Understandable, but ugly. Not palatable in any way.

When the thing I had been concealing from myself emerged, I raged, I screamed, I wept. After a time I said, "So that's how it is." Not too much later I said, "No longer."[34]

It would also be misleading to call this gift of solitude "inner harmony" or "integration," since the voices of desire do not always sing together. Nor is the much-used metaphor "centered" very satisfactory, since it ignores the multiplicity and conflict one finds deep within, powerful forces emanating from different epicenters, as it were. Self-attunement is not necessarily, or not yet, a state of *self-knowledge* or *self-understanding*—at least insofar as those ideas imply access to all of the elements of the self and the possession of some explanatory scheme which connects those elements into a coherent whole. No, I am thus far only talking about an attunement, a free and attentive receiving which has given up defensive guarding and is open to the revelations of the self—deep or shallow as they may be. Of course, this kind of attunement is a prerequisite for inner harmony, integration, centeredness, and self-knowledge, and indisputably valuable for those reasons. But it is also valuable simply in and for itself, without any promise of serenity or salvation. For in spite of the pain which may accompany self-attunement, a powerful sense of wholeness arises which human beings long to feel. We have heard it celebrated by Morgan and Sarton and Rousseau; listen now to Anne Morrow Lindberg, writing in *Gift of the Sea* about the few weeks a year she spent at a seaside cabin away from busy family life:

> Parting is inevitably painful even for a short time. It is like an amputation, I feel. A limb is being torn off, without which I shall be unable to function. And yet, once it is done, I find there is a quality to being alone that is incredibly precious. Life rushes back into the void, richer, more vivid, fuller than before. It is as if in parting one did actually lose an arm. And then, like the starfish, one grows it anew; one is whole again, complete and round—more whole, even, than before, when the other people had pieces of one.[35]

The self attuned to itself may be a disorganized whole or a conflicted whole but even so we wish to feel it all.

Why do we wish to feel it all? Thomas Merton answered from a spiritual perspective:[36]

> Not all men are called to be hermits, but all men need enough silence and solitude in their lives to enable the deep inner voice of their own true self to be heard at least occasionally. When that inner voice is not heard, when man cannot attain to the spiritual peace that comes from being perfectly at one with his true self, his life is always miserable and exhausting. For he cannot go on happily for long unless he is in contact with the springs of spiritual life which are hidden in the depths of his own soul. If man is constantly exiled from his own home, locked out of his own spiritual solitude, he ceases to be a true person. He no longer lives as a man.[37]

Holmes Rolston, a contemporary environmental philosopher, develops a similar theme in some meditations upon solitude in wilderness: without the attunement to self that disengagement in nature best brings, the self is at mortal risk:

> there is a relative solitude that is essential for personal integration—a separateness complementary to human community, its polar opposite. Nature does not define humans in order that they may be cultured, but neither can humans depend upon society to make us human. Each must finish himself. As an eminently political animal, man has the curious capacity to individualize personal worth. But distance is essential for this individualization. So, paradoxically, unless one can come by a lakeside such as this, and let physical distance loosen the hold of society upon him, he cannot find space and sanity within which to establish and maintain the boundaries of the self. Without such spaces there is no togetherness —merely fusion and homogeneity. Alone we cannot be human. Yet we cannot be human until we are alone . . . though tolerances differ, each has a threshold of

crowding beyond which he is crippled, for he has not the space for himself which is emblematic of his person.[38]

If, in this space emblematic of the person, "the spiritual peace that comes from being perfectly at one with the true self" is the goal we seek, it is a goal only fleetingly attained, as I think Merton and Rolston would agree. Nevertheless, even when the quest produces a tumult of self rather than serenity, it is a good and valuable thing: the ancient inscription did not read "Know thyself in order to be happy."

So much about the nature and value of attunement to self is, once remembered and contemplated, perhaps not likely to be disputed. But a more probing reflection reveals difficulties. The trouble begins with the metaphor of depth, an image used by Sarton and Merton and indeed just about everyone who has ever discussed the phenomena of self-awareness. There is a surface self and a deep self, and the relations between the two are problematic.[39] Richard Zaner nicely expresses one aspect of the problem—giving a very different view of the depths than Merton's:

> "Going into one's deeps," one finds figures, symbols, ideas, which, far from having the sense of being "mine," are simply found, perhaps (as with poets, artists, but also the rest of us) with an urgency to be said, but always with a sense of astonishment, delight, or anxiety, embarrassment, even terror. . . . [Though these feelings, etc., are in one sense "mine," yet] in another way there are within my reflectively disclosed self hosts of feelings, thinkings, urgings, etc., which I can only wonder at as being or as occurring "in me," only enigmatically "mine" if at all . . .[40]

But how could there be, deep within *me,* not-me? Isn't it all self down there? Look! Something just scuttled across the bottom! Under a rock now, can't make it out.

The depth metaphor is so apt, I think, because it facilitates the discussion of two central problems for self-attunement, accessibility and understanding. The closer something is to the boat on the surface, the easier it is to reach; things down deep have to be fished for, and if they are very deep you may need professionals with technical gear. The other problem is one of accurate appraisal: near the surface the water is clear, but down in the depths it is murky; objects there are hard to make out: some are distorted by the medium, and some simply can't be seen at all.

Reflecting upon these problems for self-attunement, I imagine the following objection to my assertions in this section:

You say that attunement to self is better accomplished in solitude than in encounter, but you ignore the necessary role of others in its processes. Since Freud, no one can possibly deny the operation of defenses within the self against the self, defenses which prevent inner material from coming to light: sometimes only an astute friend or a skilled therapist can break down those defenses and give you access to that buried material. Moreover, not to speak of pain and defense, there is normal human blindness: emotions are really terribly complex, and a friend can help you see their faces in the bramble bushes. Talking into the night with a friend, that is the way to tune in to yourself—not spinning in the darkness alone.

A strong objection! What might solitude answer in reply?

It ought to insist on the distinction between *attunement* and *understanding*. It is true that therapists and friends can greatly aid our understanding of ourselves, but this is a step beyond the attunement to self which I have been exploring. I go to my friend with some feelings in-hand, wanting to explore their sources, their connections to other feelings, the light they shed upon conceptions of myself that I find tempting, the consequences a fair mind might draw about the moral character of their owner.[41] This talking into the night gives me words to name the feelings, organizations to contain them, reassurance that I am accepted for all of them; it encourages me thereby to remain open to the attuning processes. But those processes, in my experience (though the same may not be true of pathological cases), proceed best alone; then I attend most fully to the emergent material, free of the not inconsiderable distraction produced by the desire to please/confirm my friend. By the way, I also believe that the final test of the understanding achieved in dialogue is its durability in solitude: disengaged from all others, fully attending to my own feelings, does the explanation still satisfy? I say this from personal experience, but note that even Freud held that the final criterion of therapeutic success was acceptance of the analysis by the patient. But what would be the criterion of such acceptance—certainly not simply agreeing with the analyst during a session, no matter how genuinely or vigorously?

The distinction I am urging between attunement and understanding can be brought out in a personal example.

It was only the afternoon of Good Friday on a long Easter weekend, but time was dragging. So I went out for a walk. Gusts of cold April wind, rain heavy and then light, fields covered with crushed weeds from the recently melted snow. Up I stumped, up the slope of the hill rising behind the house until finally I reached the high point where the ocean can be seen on three sides. Low spirits, tired of the winter, tired of the rain, tired of the aloneness, tired of myself. I stood there for awhile, poking at some loose bark on a birch tree. Then I noticed that something was changing. The wind was shifting to the northwest; the cloud cover was starting to break up, and thin streaks of sunlight were shining through. I checked my watch, 3:00 P.M. It occurred to me that this was the time at which the Good Friday service I used to attend as a teenager finished. And suddenly there came over me a very odd feeling of, I would say, triumph; filled beyond containment, I began to run down the grassy hill, galloping with arms stretched out above me, yelling wildly all the way down.

At the bottom, feeling sheepish and hoping nobody saw, I felt purged and triumphant and happy.

For days I wondered about the experience: what exactly did it mean? The feelings were no longer accessible to me: they had rushed through and vanished. Yet as I remembered them, in spite of their opacity one thing seemed important: the way they wanted to flow out in that strange galloping. But what was the significance of that? If ever there was spontaneous symbolism, this was it; but what schema of interpretation could I trust? In some way, no doubt, the triumph and the upstretched arms were a residue of early religious experiences; but what could they mean in a man who has not believed for thirty years? They might express a feeling of triumph over reliance on other-worldly means of personal salvation, the sense that hillside and sea and thin sunlight are finally enough; but, quite to the contrary, they might really reveal the self-deception involved in imagining that my identification with Christ has ceased. Surely not, not after thirty years? But it might be. I walked back there several times in the next few days, but nothing happened. How could something so fleeting and baffling feel so important?

Which psychology of the self, which hermeneutic of the passions makes the best sense of that brief but powerful experience? I do not know. My reflections on attunement to self have not, I think, been superficial (another depth metaphor!), but they only go half way: one would have to plunge deeper into psychological and philosophical analyses of the self to fully understand the complex nature of this process.[42] But if you decide to dive deeper into these dark waters, take the truths about attunement that we have been remembering as torchlights, holding them close to each theory of the self and asking: does this really make sense of solitary self-attunement?

And I will make a closing observation. My experience on the hillside on that raw April day did not lead me to self-understanding or integration or serenity or grace; but the free-flowing down that hill filled me with joyful release and triumph, and has remained a profound life-memory. And I would not have done it if you were there.

The Third Virtue: Attunement to Nature

Who publishes the sheet-music of winds or the written music of water written in river lines?

—John Muir

Extraordinary connections to the natural world are formed in solitude, sensations more acute, more engrossing, more infused with passion than are usually possible among other people. Wordsworth remembered his childhood solitude as

> . . . a time when meadow, grove and stream,
> The earth, and every common sight,
> To me did seem
> Apparelled in celestial light,
> The glory and the freshness of a dream.
>
> (from "Ode: Intimations of Immortality")

Forty years later, Victor Hugo paused in the twilight on a street in Nemours:

> For a long time, I remained motionless, letting myself be penetrated gently by this unspeakable ensemble, by the serenity of the sky and the melancholy of the

moment. I do not know what was going on in my mind, and I could not express it; it was one of those ineffable moments when one feels something in himself which is going to sleep and something which is awakening.[43]

Intense emotion seems characteristic of these sensate moments: Thoreau exclaimed "sympathy with the fluttering alder and poplar almost takes away my breath," and May Sarton recalled that, "when I saw light on half that granite boulder, I felt a stab of pure joy . . . seeing it was like getting a transfusion of autumn light right to the vein."[44] Sometimes, however, the attunement becomes a total immersion which seems almost beyond emotion: I think of Loren Eiseley's experience while on a solitary field trip along the Platte river:

> Standing quietly in the water, feeling the sand shifting away under my toes . . . I lay back in the floating position that left my face to the sky, and shoved off. The sky wheeled over me. For an instant, as I bobbed into the main channel, I had the sensation of sliding down the vast tilted face of the continent. It was then that I felt the cold needles of the alpine springs at my fingertips, and the warmth of the Gulf pulling me southward. Moving with me, leaving its taste upon my mouth and spouting under me in dancing springs of sand, was the immense body of the continent itself, flowing like the river was flowing, grain by grain, mountain by mountain, down to the sea. I was streaming over ancient sea beds thrust aloft where giant reptiles had once sported; I was wearing down the face of time and trundling cloud-wreathed ranges into oblivion. . . . I was streaming alive through the hot and working ferment of the sun, or oozing secretively through shady thickets. I was water . . . [45]

Shedding clock time as he shed his clothes, Eiseley floated into water time: his words remind us that immersion in the natural world is immersion in its own intrinsic rhythms.

Reflecting upon these quotations, and many similar celebrations of solitary attunement to nature, it has seemed to me that three distinguishable sorts of experience can be detected:

1. Clear, undistracted, sensitized perception;
2. Symbolic perception: perceiving nature as signifying or symbolizing other things;
3. Fusion/interfusion: the loss of the sense of barriers between oneself and nature, the sense of flowing out into it as it simultaneously flows through oneself.

Each of these is a special gift of solitude in its own right, with a distinctive attentional stance and emotional "feel"—some part of which I shall now attempt to convey. And yet there is a natural progression through the three states, with clear perception serving to transport the spirit into the higher realms of symbolic experience and mystical union.

1. CLEAR PERCEPTION

John Muir, the American naturalist who founded the Sierra Club, who once called himself a "poetico-trampo-geologist-bot. and ornith-natural, etc.!-!-!,"[46] was a loner in love with wilderness from his boyhood. Immigrating with his family in 1849 from Scotland to the Wisconsin frontier, long hours of farm work established early a pattern of continuous contact with fields and marshes and woodlands. Chafing eventually at his father's fundamentalist and utilitarian evaluation of nature, young Muir left the farm for the university town of Madison, studying the natural sciences while imbibing the Transcendentalism that flourished among the professors. Intending to leave "the Wisconsin University for the University of the Wilderness," a side-trip into the world of commerce was fateful. Muir was a mechanical genius, and a machine shop enticed him into employment. But there he nearly lost his eyesight when a sharp file slipped and pierced one of his eyeballs. During a long dark month of recuperation, thinking over the future behind bandaged eyes, a life-decision congealed: "God has to nearly kill us sometimes to teach us a lesson," Muir wrote later.[47] As soon as the eye healed, he set off southward on a thousand-mile walk through the southern states, learning biology from the wildflowers along the way and reading a tattered copy of Emerson's essays at night by the campfire. The wilderness he passed through whetted his appetite for more, drawing him a few years later to California: when his ship landed in San Francisco, Muir walked down the gangplank and asked a dockhand for the quickest road out of town. That road took him eastward into the California Sierras, a wilderness of forests and mountains and glaciers which he never really left. For forty-four years he haunted the territory, exploring, measuring, mapping, theorizing, eulogizing, and defending its wonders.[48] There he began the great battle for wilderness preservation, there he invited his hero Emerson, who finally accepted an invitation and came for a brief visit.

Muir was probably the most solitary naturalist who ever wrote books. He would set off with a knapsack containing only a notebook, matches, hard bread, and tea, and disappear into the mountains for weeks at a time. There he roamed freely but inquisitively, gauging the extent of species of trees, carefully noting the varieties of lichen, seeking the formative genesis of the great valleys and crafting a theory of glacial geology. His joy in observing nature—with a total disregard for what most people would call minimal comfort—and the fresh keenness of the experiences themselves come out beautifully in this passage from *Travels in Alaska:*

> It was raining hard when I awoke, but I made up my mind to disregard the weather, put on my dripping clothing, glad to know it was fresh and clean; ate biscuits and a piece of dried salmon without attempting to make a tea fire; filled a bag with hardtack, slung it over my shoulder, and with my indispensable ice-axe plunged once more into the dripping jungle. I found my bridge holding bravely in place against the swollen torrent, crossed it and beat my way around pools and logs and through two hours of tangle back to the moraine on the north side of the outlet,—a wet, weary battle but not without enjoyment. The smell of the washed ground and vegetation made every breath a pleasure, and I found *Calypso borealis,* the first I had seen on this side of the continent, one of my darlings, worth any amount of hardship; and I saw one of my Douglas squirrels on the margin of a grassy pool. The drip of the rain on the various leaves was pleasant to hear. More especially marked were the flat low-toned bumps and splashes of large drops from the trees on the broad horizontal leaves of *Echinopanax horridum,* like the drumming of thunder-shower drops on veratrum and palm leaves, while the mosses were indescribably beautiful, so fresh, so bright, so cheerily green, and all so low and calm and silent, however heavy and wild the wind and the rain blowing and pouring above them. Surely never a particle of dust has touched leaf or crown of all these blessed mosses; and how bright were the red rims of the cladonia cups beside them, and the fruit of the dwarf cornel![49]

It is impossible to imagine Muir or anybody else enjoying such a sustained and detailed observation of the rain forest with a companion.[50] The concentration of attention possible when alone is surely an important part of the explanation of the keenness of these perceptual experiences. Interestingly, Muir found the concentration of attention produced by danger particularly powerful and rewarding:

> In climbing where danger is real, all attention has to be given to the ground step by step, leaving nothing for beauty by the way. But this care, so keenly and narrowly concentrated, is not without advantages. One is thoroughly aroused. Compared with the alertness of the senses and corresponding precision and power of the muscles on such occasions, one may be said to sleep all the rest of the year. The mind and body remain awake for some time after the dangerous ground is passed, so that arriving on the summit with that grand outlook—all the world spread below—one is able to see it better, and brings to the feast a far

keener vision, and reaps richer harvests than would have been possible ere the presence of danger summoned him to life.[51]

Yet paradoxically it is sometimes precisely this concentrated control which must be abandoned if one is to experience nature fully: in this vein, Muir wrote the following directive to those who might doubt that earthquakes arrange boulders harmoniously:

> In this beauty work, every boulder is prepared and measured and put in its place more thoughtfully than are the stones of temples. If for a moment you are inclined to regard these taluses as mere draggled, chaotic dumps, climb to the top of one of them, tie your mountain shoes firmly over the instep, and with braced nerves run down without any haggling, puttering hesitation, boldly jumping from boulder to boulder with even speed. You will then find your feet playing a tune, and quickly discover the music and poetry of rock-piles.[52]

Keenly aware of the importance of solitude for these glorious moments, Muir felt considerable ambivalence about publishing his experiences: on the one hand, he had dedicated his life to publicizing the expansive joys of wilderness: "I care to live only to entice people to look at Nature's loveliness"; but on the other hand he was apprehensive that *his* wilderness would be overrun by greenhorns, "the moiling, squirming, fog-breathing public" with their "blank fleshly apathy," riding through his beloved Yosemite Valley "with about as much emotion as the horses they ride upon."[53] They were "seeing the valley," but hardly *seeing* it at all, and he feared they would destroy it.

2. SYMBOLIC PERCEPTION

Thoreau was certainly as careful an observer as Muir[54]: listen to this collection of observations of the colors of Walden pond:

> Walden is blue at one time and green at another, even from the same point of view. Lying between the earth and the heavens, it partakes of the color of both. Viewed from a hill-top it reflects the color of the sky; but near at hand it is of a yellowish tint next the shore where you can see the sand, then a light green, which gradually deepens to a uniform dark green in the body of the pond In some lights viewed even from a hill-top, it is of a vivid green next the shore. Some have referred this to the reflection of the verdure; but it is equally green there against the railroad sand-bank, and in the spring, before the leaves are expanded, and it may be simply the result of the prevailing blue mixed with the yellow of the sand. Such is the color of its iris . . . [55]

Yet he cannot help seeing things representationally: even in this scientific account the pond suddenly becomes the iris of an eye. A few pages later the image is made explicit:

> A lake is the landscape's most beautiful and expressive feature. It is earth's eye; looking into which the beholder measures the depth of his own nature. The fluviatile trees next the shore are the slender eyelashes which fringe it, and the wooded hills and cliffs around are its overhanging brow.[56]

This kind of perception, seeing through things to their symbolic source, was the kind that mattered most to Thoreau. When a farmer offered to bring him a two-headed calf as an item of interest, he declined: "I am not interested in mere phenomena."[57] To understand why, we need to remember why he went to the pond:

> I went to the woods because I wished to live deliberately, to front only the essential facts of life, and see if I could not learn what it had to teach, and not, when I came to die, discover that I had not lived.[58]

The teaching he was most interested in was that concerning his deeper self, the self which had become so encrusted with Emerson and the Transcendentalists,[59] Concord, New York, literary setbacks, making pencils, and so forth, that its true lineaments were no longer clear. There at the pond he felt free at last to see[60]; and what he especially saw, as Geoffrey O'Brien has observed, was an unbounded array of natural correspondences to the self:

> I watched a pair of hen-hawks . . . as if they were the embodiment of my own thoughts;

> sympathy with the fluttering alder and poplar leaves almost takes away my breath . . .

> Let me suggest a few comparisons, that some one may can convey an idea of my situation. I am no more lonely than the loon in the pond that laughs so loud, or than Walden Pond itself.[61]

The fact that the pond had no visible inlet or outlet delighted Thoreau because "by living thus reserved and austere, like a hermit in the woods" it mirrored his own seclusion. There seemed to be no end to the symbolic meaning of the pond: it was mirror, and eye, and "God's drop"; it was his own pristine eternal self, as its shore was his actual self. Peering into its depths, he saw his own thoughts in the pickerel gliding about, and the reputed bottomlessness of the pond served to confirm his hunches about the depths of the self he had set out to appropriate.

But the symbolism also took him (as it took the other Transcendentalists) beyond the self onto wider plains. Nature was a language, a text that could be read by those who had purified the gates of perception and developed "the discipline of looking always at what is to be seen." Thus prepared, we can read the symbolic utterances of nature because we are of a common substance with it[62]: "Shall I not have intelligence with the earth? Am I not partly leaves and vegetable mould myself?" In spring, Thoreau beholds thawing sand and clay flowing down the sides of a railway cut and is seized by a feeling of the identity of process and energy between oozing sand and organic growth:

> It is wonderful how rapidly yet perfectly the sand organizes itself as it flows, using the best material its mass affords to form the sharp edges of its channel. Such are the sources of rivers. In the silicious matter which the water deposits is perhaps the bony system, and in the still finer soil and organic matter the fleshy fibre or cellular tissue. What is man but a mass of thawing clay? The fingers and toes flow to their extent from the thawing mass of the body. . . . Each rounded lobe of the vegetable leaf, too, is a thick and now loitering drop, larger or smaller; the lobes are the fingers of the leaf; and as many lobes as it has, in so many directions it tends to flow. . . . There is nothing inorganic.
>
> Thus it seemed that this one hillside illustrated the principle of all the operations of nature. The Maker of this earth but patented a leaf. What Champollion will decipher this hieroglyphic for us, that we may turn over a new leaf at last?[63]

Why Henry David Thoreau, of course. He is the one who can decipher what is there to be read, for example, in the eyes of partridge chicks:

> The remarkably adult yet innocent expression of their open and serene eyes is very memorable. All intelligence seems reflected in them. They suggest not merely the purity of infancy, but a wisdom clarified by experience. Such an eye was not born when the bird was, but is coeval with the sky it reflects.[64]

And there is a representational meaning in the hooting of owls:

> I rejoice that there are owls. Let them do the idiotic and maniacal hooting for men. It is a sound admirably suited to swamps and twilight woods which no day illustrates, suggesting a vast and undeveloped nature which men have not recognized. They represent the stark twilight and unsatisfied thoughts which all have.[65]

Thoreau actually saw and felt the world this way, and did not merely adopt a stylized rhetorical conceit. Of course, he was not above an occasional classical allusion in the style of the times:

> Morning brings back the heroic ages. I was as much affected by the faint hum of a mosquito making its invisible and unimaginable tour through my apartment at earliest dawn, when I was sitting with door and windows open, as I could be by any trumpet that ever sang of fame. It was Homer's requiem; itself an Iliad and Odyssey in the air, singing its own wrath and wanderings.[66]

But generally, as Sherman Paul remarked, "he adopted symbolism because he had seen his universe symbolically." Bronson Alcott wrote of his friend Henry,

> He is less thinker than observer; a naturalist in tendency but of a mystic habit, and a genius for detecting the essence in form and giving forth the soul of things seen. . . . His mysticism is alike solid and organic, animal and ideal. He is the mythologist of these last days.[67]

Thoreau was a writer, to be sure, but always as a messenger reporting from the front, determined "to hear what was in the wind, to hear and carry it express! . . . watching from the observatory of some cliff or tree, to telegraph any new arrival."[68] The great pride and triumph of these messages springs from symbolic perception in solitude. The messages ring true because we are also mythologists in solitude, if less gifted in expression than Thoreau. Looking down at brook water rushing away over stones, suddenly you see Time rushing away and feel an empty sadness; or you see Life hurrying on, clear bright energy, eternal delight; or you see the two large boulders, immovable, impervious to all the rushing, and in that moment see your parents again as you had seen them with the eyes of a child. So many other things are there, separately and together, that you wonder if there is anything that is *not* right there in the brook. But you couldn't adequately convey these symbolic visions to another; they form in solitude, rich but fragile, and they vanish leaving only a warmth in the heart when you return to camp.

3. FUSION

In deep solitude it can happen that the boundaries between self and nature dissolve: uncontainable feelings flow out through the world, as natural forces rush into the soul. May Sarton felt a transfusion of sunlight flowing through her veins, and Loren Eiseley "was water." However, it was the poets of the European Romantic period who most fervently worshiped this mode of attunement. Shelley's immortal cry to the West Wind comes at once to mind:

> Be thou, Spirit fierce,
> My spirit! Be thou me, impetuous one!

A great poet's words, but is the experience not familiar? Have you not felt, on some hillside on some turbulent day, the wind blowing through you, taking you up into itself until you blow over the hillside and stream out towards the clouds? Or on another day, felt lost in the loud surf, swept along in a great breaking wave, felt yourself become water? I think too of the Sturm-und-Drangers ("storm-and-stress–ers") among the German Romantics: they would clamber to the rocky heights during wild storms and lash themselves to the trunks of the frantically tossing trees in order to feel merged with the storm. What extremists! Yet to hear it is to want to try it![69]

The young Goethe captured the full force of this passion for fusion with nature in *The Sorrows of Young Werther.* Late in the novel the troubled protagonist recounts how he felt before the unhappy passion for Charlotte destroyed his felicity:

> When I used to gaze from these rocks upon the mountains across the river and upon the green valley before me, and saw every thing around budding and bursting; the hills clothed from foot to peak with tall, thick trees; the valleys in all their variety, shaded with the loveliest woods; and the river gently gliding along among the whispering reeds, mirroring the clouds which the soft evening breeze wafted across the sky—when I heard the groves about me melodious with the music of birds, and saw the million swarms of insects dancing in the last golden beams of the sun, whose setting rays awoke the humming beetles from their grassy beds . . . —all this conveyed to me the holy fire which animates all Nature, and filled and glowed within my heart. I felt myself exalted by this overflowing fullness to the perception of the Godhead, and the glorious forms of an infinite universe stirred within my soul![70]

Goethe knew, though, that the yearning for immersion in nature also has a darker side, the longing for extinction. Near the end of the novel, hopes for possessing Charlotte at an end, Werther is morbidly oppressed at heart, tormented by "an inexpressible inner fury which seems to tear up my heart and choke me." Then reports reach him that run-off from a storm is flooding the valley:

> I rushed out after eleven o'clock. I beheld a terrible sight. The furious torrents rolled from the mountains in the moonlight—fields, trees, and hedges were torn up, and the entire valley was one deep lake, agitated by the roaring wind! And when the moon shone forth, and tinged the black clouds, and the wild torrent at my feet foamed and resounded with awful and grand impetuosity, I was overcome by feelings of fear and delight at once. With arms extended, I looked down into the yawning abyss, and cried, "Down! Down!" For a moment I was lost in the intense delight of ending my sorrows and my sufferings by a plunge into that gulf![71]

A terrible longing at a terrible time! Yet in spite of the terror, the longing to merge produced "intense delight."

Fusion with nature can launch the spirit upon the mystical flight towards union with the All. Tradition refers to this path of ascent as the Via Positiva, the Positive Way; in contrast to the Via Negativa, which involves emptying consciousness of all contents so that Being can flow in to fill it, the Via Positiva fills consciousness with sights and sounds and feelings until the transcendent unity of all things illuminates the whole. Here is an example Cohen and Phipps selected from the archives of the Religious Experience Research Unit at Oxford:

> I was sitting on a low wall on the outskirts of the town of Chittagong. Across the road was a wayside teashop stall, with the proprietor in full view serving two customers. The branches of two small trees next to the stall waved in the moderately strong breeze and the sun shone with some glare on the white dusty road, along which came some fishermen with baskets of fish on their heads. From the second storey of a nearby building I could hear a nautch tune. Then, as the fishermen came abreast of me, one fish, still alive, flapped up and seemed to stand on its tail and bow. I felt great compassion for the fish.
>
> Suddenly everything was transformed, transfigured, translated, transcended. All was fused into one. I was the fish. The sun sang and the road sang. The music shone. The hands of the stall-keeper danced. All in time with the same music. They were the music and I was the music and I was the fish, the fishermen, the hands of the stall-keeper, the trees, the branches, the road, the sun, the music; all one and nothing separate. Not parts of the one but the one itself.[72]

The writer began in a solitude of disengaged observation, but by the time the fusion had reached its heights he (felt that he) *was* the fishermen and shopkeeper and every other thing.

"Was it still a solitude, then?"

Ordinary words collapse before the mystical.

The Fourth Virtue: Reflective Perspective

I am finding that life here has become largely a life of the mind. Unhurried reflection is a sort of companion.

—Adm. Richard Byrd

There are other rewards of solitude that require withdrawal from the experiential immersion in freedom, self, and nature to the plains of Mind. From playful musing to the sober "recollection in tranquility" that Wordsworth called the fountain of poetry, from analytic reflection to the silent deeps of contemplation, perspectives on existence are acquired which provide powerful experiences of value. Independently of their final truth (an issue to be raised in the next chapter), each of these achievements of perspective is a true pleasure; and each is generally best achieved in solitude.

Autobiographical records of solitudes are full of musings—brief, light reflections upon this or that of no very great moment. There is, for example, a great deal of the following sort of reflection in Richard Katz's *Solitary Life:*

> It would be a desirable compromise between man and dog if human beings could get rid of their peculiarities which are a worry to the dog, and vice versa. Human beings should renounce their nerves, their sudden anger and their egoism. Dogs should abjure uncleanliness, snappiness and greed. Unfortunately the one is just as impossible as the other. Nevertheless, since true friendship between men and dogs is so often to be seen, this means that the adaptability of the dog is greater than that of the man.[73]

At some indefinable point, as musing become more serious, purposeful, and sustained, the word 'reflection' becomes more appropriate. Here the quiet open time of solitude is used to assemble before the mind all of the elements of some object of concern, gathering them into a well-related and meaningful whole. Here is Thoreau reflecting upon connections and meanings:

> The gentle rain which waters my beans and keeps me in the house today is not dreary and melancholy, but good for me too. Though it prevents my hoeing them, it is of far more worth than my hoeing. If it should continue so long as to cause the seed to rot in the ground and destroy the potatoes in the lowlands, it would still be good for the grass on the uplands, and, being good for the grass, it would be good for me.[74]

Since *Walden,* reflections penned in solitude have developed into a genre—I think of such gifted writers as John Muir, John Burroughs, Joseph Wood Krutch, and more recently, Loren Eiseley, Niko Tinbergen, and Annie Dillard. Richard Triumpho reminds us, however, that reflections like these are not restricted to "writers" and "philosophers," but are part of the everyday disengaged life of everyone:

> The attraction of berry picking is that it offers time for quiet contemplation. If the mosquitos and deer flies aren't biting, and if the heat isn't intolerably humid, a person can enjoy an hour or two of busy solitude . . .
>
> While the fingers are busy plucking berries, the mind is free to wander. Your thoughts go skipping, seemingly aimlessly, contemplating the briars, the plump berries, the song of a bird, the satisfactions and frustrations that happened to you last week. Such reflection puts perspective on one's life, makes you realize where

you have been, gives awareness of the forces that shape you into the kind of person you are, makes you better able to deal with where you are going.

In order to get to know yourself, a person needs to be alone with his thoughts now and then.[75]

The processes of recollection are crucial in such reflective life-assessments. With deliberate voluntary memory, past experiences are assembled before the mind's eye so as to provide a setting for the present—in Bugbee's lovely words, "the gathering of the remote into the presence of things near, and a receding of the near into the vastness of the far."[76] There are also the sudden unbidden intrusions of past time which bring a gathering of the time-strewn self, enabling us to contemplate our lives as wholes. In Max Scheler's words,

Nothing "in particular" is recalled in these moments, but everything is somehow "there" and "operative." We are, in these cases, not empty but, indeed, "full" and "rich." Here we are truly "at home with ourselves." Operative-effective experiences address us from all points of our life. Innumerable soft "appeals" from the past and future sound within us. We look over our *total I* in all of its manifoldness or we experience it as a whole in an act, a deed, or a work.[77]

The more given to reflection a person is, the more a philosopher: and when, in addition, the objective of reflection is a connected vision of the whole of reality, we have a philosopher in the strongest sense of the term. One thinks of Descartes, for example, who turned a day of confinement into a search for the most general principles for "rightly conducting the intellect":

I was then in Germany, to which country I had been attracted by the wars which are not yet at an end. And as I was returning from the coronation of the Emperor to join the army, the setting in of winter detained me in a quarter where, since I found no society to divert me, while fortunately I had also no cares or passions to trouble me, I remained the whole day shut up alone in a stove-heated room, where I had complete leisure to occupy myself with my own thoughts. One of the first of the considerations that occurred to me was that there is very often less perfection in works composed of several portions, and carried out by the hands of various masters, than in those on which one individual alone has worked . . . [78]

The scope, as well as the insistent logicality, of philosophical reflection[79] is nowhere more clearly exemplified than in his short *Meditations on First Philosophy,* which begins also in solitude:

Today, then, as I have suitably freed my mind from all cares, and have secured for myself an assured leisure in peaceful solitude, I shall at last apply myself earnestly and freely to the general overthrow of all my former opinions. In doing so, it will not be necessary for me to show that they are one and all false . . . The withdrawal of foundations involves the downfall of whatever rests on these foundations, and what I shall therefore begin by examining are the principles on which my former beliefs rested.[80]

His subsequent attempt to organize the entire realm of human knowledge according to its foundational principles situates him near the high limit of rational reflection.

But there is possible in solitary reflection, it is repeatedly reported, something higher still. Called variously "contemplation" or "enlightenment," it is described as a kind of beholding or gazing which arises beyond the limits of willful rational inquiry. Perhaps the most famous (and beautiful) description of the ascent of the soul to final enlightenment is given by Plato in the *Symposium*

> this is the way, the only way, he must approach, or be led toward, the sanctuary of Love. Starting from individual beauties, the quest for the universal beauty must find him ever mounting the heavenly ladder, stepping from rung to rung—that is, from one to two, and from two to every lovely body, from bodily beauty to the beauty of institutions, from institutions to learning, and from learning in general to the special lore that pertains to nothing but the beautiful itself—until at last he comes to know what beauty is.

> And now, Socrates, there bursts upon him that wondrous vision which is the very soul of the beauty he has toiled so long for. It is an everlasting loveliness which neither comes nor goes, which neither flowers nor fades, for such beauty is the same on every hand, the same then as now, here as there, this way as that way, the same to every worshipper as it is to every other.[81]

While for Plato, contemplation of the Form of Beauty comes as the culmination of philosophical reflection, Taoism and Buddhism insist that contemplative enlightenment demands the repudiation of logical discriminating thinking. In *The Book of Chuang Tzu* Yen Hui finally wins the approval of Confucius when he announces,

> "I can sit down and forget everything!"
> Confucius looked very startled and said, "What do you mean, sit down and forget everything?"
> Yen Hui said, "I smash up my limbs and body, drive out perception and intellect, cast off form, do away with understanding, and make myself identical with the Great Thoroughfare. This is what I mean by sitting down and forgetting everything."[82]

The Buddhist classic, *Lankavatara Sutra* expresses a similar conception of growing enlightenment:

> As Bodhisattvas advance along the stages, they more and more become sensitive to the arising of these false discriminations [of conceptual thought] and more and

more quickly react against them, and become more and more skilful in employing expedient means for checking them arising and ignoring them if they arise. Until at last they come to a state of awareness in which they are able to keep far away from even the most refined conceptions, knowing that Essential Mind is permanent and abiding in its purity. This is a state of perfect accommodation; it can truly be called enlightenment.[83]

Whereas these philosophies emphasize the need for mental discipline in attaining enlightenment, Gregory the Great emphasized moral discipline, the purging of sin from the seeker's soul. In what was to become the generally accepted definition of contemplation in the medieval church, he wrote:

And when the eyes of our heart are purged from sin, that joy of our heavenly home is disclosed to them that we may first wash away by sorrow what we have done, and afterwards gain in our transports a clearer view of what we are seeking after. For the intervening mist of sin is first wiped away from the eye of the mind by burning sorrow; and it is then enlightened by the bright coruscations of the boundless light swiftly flashing upon it. At which sight, seen after its measure, it is absorbed in a kind of rapturous security, and carried beyond itself, as though the present life had ceased to be, it is refreshed in a manner by a kind of new being.[84]

This sense of elevation to a new kind of being is found earlier in Plotinus, where the ascent towards mystical enlightenment which he called the "flight of the Alone to the Alone" culminates in a unitive absorption:

Then the soul neither sees, nor distinguishes by seeing, nor imagines that there are two things. . . . It belongs to God and is one with Him . . . in this conjunction with Deity there were not two things, but the perceiver was one with the thing perceived.[85]

By now it is apparent that the terms "contemplation" and "enlightenment" have been used to refer to a very diverse assortment of experiences. No one would venture now to speak with the categorical confidence that Richard of St. Victor could muster in the twelfth century:

Thinking, slow-footed, wanders hither and thither along bypaths, caring not where they will lead. Meditation, with great mental industry, plods along the steep and laborious road keeping the end in view. Contemplation, on a free wing, circles around with great nimbleness wherever the impulse takes it. . . . Thinking roams about; meditation investigates; contemplation wonders.[86]

And when we include the phenomena of musing, recollecting, and reflecting, it must seem questionable indeed to include them all under a single rubric. I have done so firstly because all of these phenomena involve a thoughtful approach to the elements of experience, secondly because in each case an organization or perspective on those elements is achieved, and thirdly because each achievement is felt to be valuable in itself. A fourth point is almost too obvious to mention: they all come best in solitude.

The Fifth Virtue: Creativity

I have at last got the little room I have wanted so long, and am very happy about it. It does me good to be alone, and Mother has made it very pretty and neat for me. My work-basket and desk are by the window, and my closet is full of dried herbs that smell very nice.

—Louisa May Alcott, age 13

One of the best ways to understand the role of solitude in creativity is to listen to gifted creators talk about the solitary places of their creating, and I love to listen to Annie Dillard:

> Every morning you climb several flights of stairs, enter your study, open the French doors, and slide your desk and chair out into the middle of the air. The desk and chair float thirty feet from the ground, between the crowns of maple trees. The furniture is in place; you go back for your thermos of coffee. Then, wincing, you step out again through the French doors and sit down on the chair and look over the desktop. You can see clear to the river from here in winter. You pour yourself a cup of coffee.
>
> Birds fly under your chair. In spring, when the leaves open in the maples' crowns, your view stops in the treetops just beyond the desk; yellow warblers hiss and whisper on the high twigs, and catch flies. Get to work. Your work is to keep cranking the flywheel that turns the gears that spin the belt in the engine of belief that keeps you and your desk in mid-air.[87]

Or listen to William Carlos Williams cavorting in a poet's solitude (can a poet choose the wrong word, "lonely"? yes he can!):

If I when my wife is sleeping
and the baby and Kathleen
are sleeping
and the sun is a flame-white disc
in silken mists
above shining trees,—
if I in my north room

dance naked, grotesquely
before my mirror
waving my shirt round my head
and singing softly to myself:
"I am lonely, lonely.
I was born to be lonely,
I am best so!"
If I admire my arms, my face
my shoulders, flanks, buttocks
against the yellow drawn shades,—

Who shall say I am not
the happy genius of my household?

("Danse Russe," 1951)[88]

Here is Georgia O'Keeffe at the desert retreat in New Mexico where she went alone every summer to paint the white bones and wild flowers:

> The wind is blowing hard . . . I have been painting all day—a painting that should be very good if I can really get it right—another cedar tree—a dead one, against red earth, but the red earth is more difficult—if this one doesn't go I'll try it again. At five I walked—I climbed way up on a pale green hill where I could look all around at the red, yellow, purple formations—miles all around—the color all intensified by the pale grey green I was standing on. It was wonderful.[89]

Creative people have often been explicit about their need for solitude. Kafka's rebuff to Felice returns to mind, as does Sarton's insistence that the dreams and images upon which the poet depends "live in deep still water." Here is Rilke's advice to a young poet

> What is needed is just this. Loneliness, vast inner loneliness. To walk in one's self and to meet no one for hours on end. That is what one must be able to attain. To be lonely the way one was lonely as a child, when the grown-ups moved about, involved in things that appeared important and big because the big ones looked so busy and because one understood nothing of what they were doing. If one day one comes to perceive that their occupations are miserable, their professions moribund and no longer related to life, why not go on regarding them like a child as something alien, looking out from the depths of one's own world from the expanse of one's own loneliness which is itself work and rank and profession.[90]

Georgia O'Keeffe made her own need for solitude powerfully clear. Her husband, the photographer Alfred Stieglitz, missed her intensely during her annual summer sojourns to the desert ranch in New Mexico, but he always recognized their necessity for her work. Old and sick in 1946, he wrote her the first letter of the summer before she had even left New York:

> It is very hard for me to realize that within a few hours you will have left. . . . But there is no choice. You need what "Your Place" will give you. Yes you need that sorely. And I'll be with you, cape and all.[91]

O'Keeffe knew D. H. Lawrence, who lived and wrote for a time in New Mexico. The following lines written by him sound rather different from those we heard earlier on about lights shining only when social circuits are completed:

> Be alone, and feel the trees silently growing.
> Be alone, and see the moonlight, white and busy and silent.
> Be quite alone, and feel the living cosmos softly rocking . . . [92]

Considering the relationships between solitude and creativity more systematically, Elizabeth Cobb studied the autobiographies of three hundred geniuses; she found that a powerful solitary revelation in childhood played an important role in their creative lives:

> . . . the natural world [was] experienced in some highly evocative way, producing in the child a sense of profound continuity with natural processes. . . . These writers say they return in memory [to such experiences] in order to renew the power and impulse to create at its very source, a source which they describe as the experience of emerging not only into the light of consciousness but into a living sense of dynamic relationship with the outer world. In these memories the child appears to experience both a sense of discontinuity, an awareness of his own unique separateness and identity, and also a continuity, a renewal of relationship with nature as process.[93]

Anthony Storr has also studied the importance of childhood solitude for adult creativity in his recent book *Solitude: A Return to the Self.* With erudition and insight this psychologist probes the extant biographical facts of the lives of such writers as Franz Kafka, Anthony Trollope, Beatrix Potter, Edward Lear, Rudyard Kipling, H. H. Munro (Saki), and P. G. Wodehouse. He concludes that

> It is legitimate to assume that, in these examples, the development of such highly complex imaginative worlds was the consequence of being cut off from the emotional fulfillment which children with more ordinary backgrounds experience in their relations with parents and other care-takers. . . .
> However, what began as compensation for deprivation became a rewarding way of life . . . as valid as any other and more interesting than most. Even if their

intimate attachments were not the hub around which their lives revolved, there is no reason to suppose that these lives were unfulfilled.[94]

Storr notes that when these writers lost contact with their childhood solitudes or became enmeshed in family relations, creativity tended to decline.

I will close reflection on this virtue by relating the creative potential of solitude to the four virtues that have already been examined. Creative activity goes beyond centering, attunement, and reflection upon the already-existent, and it imposes a programmatic ordering upon its freedom of action: thus creativity is a virtue beyond the first four. And yet these other virtues are indispensably bound up in the success of the creative attempt: the freedom to do and undo and do again as the medium and imagination demand, the sureness and directness of one's inner responses, the "becoming one with" the material which enables the artist to sense the finished form in the rough block, the reflective gathering of disparate elements into the conceptual statement of the new work—all of these must fuse in the attentive time of creative need. Creativity best achieves its goals when it maximizes these virtues, and they are the virtues of solitude.

Yet it would be a mistake to think of creativity in solitude as limited to Artists, Writers, and Inventors, or to tangible Works of Art.[95] I was reminded of this when speaking with an old friend, Ed Baillie, retired for many years, widowed for most of them. "In solitude," he said thoughtfully, "you develop your own resources; you learn how to use resources that are there." I think of him creating a day out of many hours with few of the friendly interruptions most of us rely upon, devising schemes to trick his failing eyesight into delivering a few more pages of the book in progress, musing, pondering, puzzling along strange paths of thought, arranging and then rearranging the pieces of ninety years of gentle life. This creativity will leave no product, its figures will not be performed again. And yet in his resourcefulness, in his courage in the face of failing health, in his imposition of a unique form upon the raw materials of life, I see a creator at work.

These are the perennial gifts of solitude, rich treasures whose powerful intrinsic value cannot possibly be denied. So much for the idea that solitude is merely social sleep! Now I understand how solitude works its restoration of the spirit—and how much more it can be than simply restoration. Solitude is most propitious, in itself, for achieving Freedom, Attunement to Self, Attunement to Nature, Reflective Perspective, and Creativity: if sociality is intrinsically good, as it certainly is, solitude is also intrinsically good, and for (at least[96]) five different reasons.

In closing this celebration, what has been separated should be rejoined; for the gifts of solitude are seldom single tributaries, but on the contrary ever flowing through each other. One such gathered feeling in solitude is *serenity,* the holistic state of calm imperturbability, equanimity, and peaceful comprehending acceptance. I have not called it a separate virtue of solitude because it seems to be a product of the first four gifts: secure in the sense of one's freedom of action, imagination, and reflection, attuned to the inner self and able to weave its failings with its glories into a meaningful pattern, attuned to the natural world of which one is a free-flowing part, yet able to apprehend reflectively both one's immersion in it and one's separation from it—this is the holistic experience we call serenity. Little wonder, now, that it is best found, most perfectly known, in solitude.

CHAPTER 8

The Completions of Encounter

How good it is to remember the gifts of solitude, to float in warm reveries of solitary times, recollected now in tranquillity. Yet in all remembrance there is a hidden danger, the danger of forgetting contexts and elements and antecedents and consequents which made that vanished time itself. I do not doubt that we are guilty now of a partial forgetfulness, a forgetfulness of the ways in which these very values of solitude just celebrated can find completions in propitious moments of engaged encounter. Let me pursue this suspicion.

1. Freedom

Yes, most true, the time of solitude is the time of greatest freedom—to do the works of solitude. But there are other actions, social actions, which solitude does not give us greater freedom to perform, which are indeed precluded by solitude: think of singing duets, making love, teaching a skill, ministering, playing tennis, telling jokes, not to mention organizing a day-care center or inducing a government agency to enforce environmental standards. These valued activities demand direct engagement with other people; consequently there are freedoms of encounter, just as there are freedoms of solitude.[1]

How are these two sorts of freedoms related to each other? On the psychological level, alternation and balance seem to be necessary for almost everyone (although the precise nature of the mixture is a very individual matter). Without a certain balancing by free encounters, the freedom of solitude tends to sicken into the free fall of loneliness; without solitude, the self becomes stuck to its personae. But what about the inner nature of the two experiences of freedom: are they, ultimately, one and the same, or must we speak of two essentially different kinds of freedom?

There is one underlying freedom, I suggest, with the same felt character: the difference between solitary and social freedom inheres, accordingly, in the objects with which each freedom works. For about thirty years philosophers have been finding it useful to use the concept of object when analyzing actions, emotions, desires, and thoughts (though the idea traces back through Brentano to Hume, indeed to Aristotle); definitions of that notion have differed,[2] but probably the best way to put the idea is this: the object of an action, emotion, or thought is its attentional focus, that which one is centrally attending to while acting, feeling, or thinking. Thus the object of your anger at an insult is the impudent person (or in some analyses, his words[3]), the object of the action of blowing a kiss at a friend is the friend, the object of a recollection of the dreary day in Paris is Paris. Using this notion of object, the free activities of solitude and encounter seem to differ in their objects, but not in the felt sense of the freedom: the free creative pretending of young Rilke alone with his outfits before the mirror, the free creation of a story you are telling to a group of friends, each involves the same sense of absence of interference, the same unmonitored directness, the same spontaneity.

If this is so, then the fullest experience of human freedom would have to include both free engagement and free disengagement. And this conclusion leads me to think of each freedom as, in one sense, incomplete without the other. This is not to say that young Rilke would have felt, in his pretending before the mirror, incomplete; rather it is to say that if he only freely pretended alone he would have very incompletely explored the scope and range of the underlying freedom he treasured. It would be like thrilling to the color of paintings, but never of sunsets, like admiring the landscape but never the cloudscape, like appreciating instrumental music but never vocal. How odd, how sad, how . . . incomplete.

A very different completion which engagement can bestow upon the freedoms of solitude becomes visible when you consider what people freely *do* alone: very often, their actions are pointed towards other people. Boethius, Petrarch, Montaigne, Thoreau, Muir, Sarton, Koller, and the others *wrote books:* writing is something done best in solitude, yet aimed beyond it; and if the words find their mark, an indirect encounter occurs which completes the solitary free creation. Of course few solitaries write books, but many write letters. Rilke complained about how people pestered him in his solitude, about the letters he felt compelled to write—112 in a few short months! Georgia O'Keeffe and Alfred Stieglitz wrote each other almost every day during Georgia's solitary summers. Emily Dickinson wrote 1,045 letters by the time she was fifty-six.[4]

Personally, I am behind in my correspondence. Yet I know well that odd state of being alone, at once self-absorbed and other-focused—all the while anticipating the completion of the process by the other. I tidy up the garden, so that each group of flowers stands to its best. For whom? Am I expecting anyone? No, but still it ought to be tidy—in case someone comes unexpectedly.

Writing, gardening, cleaning, chopping, you love to just think your own thoughts freely in solitude; but are they not often thoughts of other people, rehashings and rehearsings, analyses and diagnoses, bestowals and resolutions? Henry Bugbee even goes so far as to speak of this free activity as *the work* of solitude:

> I think solitude is essentially a bringing to consciousness of the manner of our being in the world with other beings and of engagement in the working out of the import continually and cumulatively borne upon us of this participation. It therefore assumes the character of a reckoning, a coming to terms with one's very life, with our disposition with regard to beings as formed in lived relation with them.[5]

I cannot go this far with him, mindful of the other virtues of solitude, but other-directed "reckoning" is certainly a profound work of solitude. And does it not implicitly anticipate a future in later encounters? Bugbee believes so: "the burden of solitude miscarries if it does not issue in a more decided participation with the beings of the world."[6] Again overstated, there is a point here: we expect the hours of free reflection upon the others to have consequences, to nourish and inform future engagements, though not in any direct correspondence. Insofar as this occurs, free solitary reflections find a completion in encounter, their blossoms becoming, in the fullness of time, fruit.

2. Attunement to Self

It is possible to collect the many objects of our emotions, desires, intuitions, and reflections into three rough groups:

1. the self
2. other people
3. the world.

Attunement to self, accordingly, involves the free flow into awareness of feelings towards oneself, but also of feelings towards others and towards the world: it will welcome, for example, my doubts about my own creativity,[7] my suspicions regarding your compliments, and my sense, before the setting sun, of something far more deeply interfused. Complete attunement to self must bring before us feelings of all three kinds.

It is true that attunement to self-focused emotions (desires, appraisals, etc.) and to world-focused emotions (etc.) is easier to achieve in solitude than while engaged, as sections 2 and 3 of the last chapter revealed. And even with regard to those emotions whose objects are other people, the mechanisms of defense often inhibit attunement in the moment of engagement: often it is only *after* an angry encounter that one can really let go, the anger now exploding that was previously restrained. But even so, this slightly dated anger cannot be the fullest attunement to the angry self: rather, what would be required would be the free-flowing towards the other of the anger you feel *right now in his presence,* the uncensored emotion pouncing on its living victim. And what more direct engagement is there than that?

In short, the most complete attunement to self requires attunement to all three types of emotional objects; and attunement to the second type, feelings towards other people, finds its completion in freely expressive encounters. This is one way in which encounter is involved in the completion of a virtue of solitude.

A second way emerges if we ask: what follows hard upon these experiences of attunement, what do they provoke us to want to do next? Very often, though certainly not always, there is a great urge to tell the experience. Reminiscing alone on the deck late one night, I suddenly felt an overwhelming feeling of pride in my son—something I seldom permit myself to enjoy before people, disliking, as I do, parents who brag about their children. It wanted to be said aloud, said to everyone and especially to him. The feeling was so strong—I did it: said aloud in the silence, "I'm *so proud* of you!" A substitute-engagement, was it not?

Feeling the pride itself was an exciting release, feeling now clearly what had been struggling underneath all the while. Such attuning to self, all alone, is good in itself: I do not seek such moments of attunement *in order to* better communicate with my friends or my son; unmarked and unspoken, their value rests secure within themselves. Still, there dwells in the heart of the experience a desire to be told. Of course, it probably can not be told: I really do dislike parental bragging, and besides he is so touchy about pride, and words would be so difficult to find because it's not really pride exactly, anyway not pride over any particular thing, and besides isn't pride one of those emotions we're not supposed to feel anymore?—on it goes. All true, but I sat there that night feeling that the thinnest net had fallen over the pride, limiting its exuberance. A slight sadness of incompleteness.

So I wrote the pride into my journal and wondered, is not a journal a substitutive telling?[8] Not just at the first, when you have to learn how to write for yourself in the journal and stop concocting false "entries" the way you think someone's journal ought to read, but at the last and always.

3. Attunement to Nature

Clear perception of nature, symbolic perception of its representations, and fusion with its totality are all best accomplished alone, I believe. But upon reflection all three are equally profound experiences of other people, who are, after all, also parts of nature, no inconsiderable part of the nature we daily confront. It is exhilarating to feel the wind's turbulence as my turbulence, to be together with it driven by a deeper animating force; but it is equally exhilarating to see my passion reflected in your eyes, to feel it swirling through us in one wild gale.

Remembering Muir's description of the dripping forest, compare this description from Nadine Gordimer's *A World of Strangers:*

> He was a tall, thin man, with a long waist and a small round head. He was the pleasant, light colour of polished wood and his hair was like wool embroidery. His eyes were far away, burnt-out; he had a small, delicately-made nose, from whose characteristically flattened tip the nostrils curled back, and the gathered-together

bones of his face gave prominence to his large mouth. When he smiled, charmingly, at Anna, he showed a battleground of gaps and fine broken teeth.[9]

Remembering Thoreau's expressions of symbolic perception, compare the way Susan perceives Jinny in Virginia Woolf's *The Waves:*

> There is Jinny. She stands in the door. Everything seems stayed. The waiter stops. The diners at the table by the door look. She seems to centre everything; round her tables, lines of doors, windows, ceilings, ray themselves, like rays round the star in the middle of a smashed window-pane. She brings things to a point, to order. Now she sees us and moves, and all the rays ripple and flow and waver over us, bringing in new tides of sensation. . . . Rhoda sees her with surprise, as if on some far horizon a fire blazed. And I, though I pile my mind with damp grass, with wet fields, with the sound of rain on the roof and the gusts of wind that batter at the house in winter and so protect my soul against her, feel her derision steal round me, feel her laughter curl its tongues of fire round me and light up unsparingly my shabby dress . . . [10]

Remembering Werther's sense of merging with the teeming valley and the torrential water, imagine how young Cathy must have felt with Heathcliff at Wuthering Heights, must often have felt if she could later share this confidence with her servant:

> What were the use of my creation if I were entirely contained here? My great miseries in this world have been Heathcliff's miseries, and I watched and felt each from the beginning; my great thought in living is himself. If all else perished, and he remained, I should still continue to be; and if all else remained, and he were annihilated, the Universe would turn to a mighty stranger. I should not seem a part of it. My love for Linton is like the foliage in the woods. Time will change it, I'm well aware, as winter changes the trees—my love for Heathcliff resembles the eternal rocks beneath—a source of little visible delight, but necessary. Nelly, I am Heathcliff—he's always in my mind—not as a pleasure, any more than I am always a pleasure to myself—but, as my own being—so, don't talk of our separation again . . . [11]

The point of these comparisons is similar to the point made above regarding Freedom: there are modes of attunement to other people paralleling attunements to nature, common underlying processes which focus now upon *Echinopanax horridum,* now upon the lovely patterns of lines around those ancient eyes.[12] Human beings are part of the natural world, an absorbing part and a lovely part. Accordingly, the quest for attunement to nature that ignored them would manifest a grave incompleteness: how sad if one delighted in the wildflowers but not the surrounding grasses, the grasses but not the tangled shrubs, the tangled shrubs but not the rabbits peering softly out, the rabbits but not the children napping on the blanket, the strong sunlight revealing the incredible fineness of their hair.

4. Reflective Perspective

Musing, Recollection, Reflection, Contemplation, each of these joys of solitude is in fact a complex state involving what we might call a *cognitive* dimension and an *affective* dimension. Regarding the latter, it is partly because musing is a light, unencumbered, happy activity that we call it a virtue/gift of solitude; just so, there is a sweetness and a satisfaction to recollection and reflection, and a wondrous awe in contemplation. But there is also the cognitive dimension: each of these experiences aims at, and then believes itself to have seized upon, Truth. The point is obvious with contemplation and reflection, but holds for musing as well: Katz would no doubt agree that he had only expressed a personal perspective on dogs, but would insist nonetheless that it was a true perspective, though perhaps only one of many true perspectives. Likewise with recollection, the experience is valued for the truth about the past it returns to us, and not merely for its pleasantness. This is shown by the fact that we value even grim recollections if they recall the truth, and by the fact that pleasant recollections are utterly spoiled if we are shown that "things never really happened that way."

This cognitive element in the virtues of reflective perspective, their concern for truth, involves other people in the completion of this value in two ways, one manifested in the felt sense of intersubjectivity of truth-claims, the other springing from our desire to verify those claims. Regarding the first point, some remarks by H. Tristram Engelhardt, Jr., are suggestive:

> To claim knowledge is to make a claim concerning other possible knowers, that they, too, can in principle share the knowledge. The objectivity of knowledge is its intersubjectivity . . .

> The project of knowing will succeed only if being a knower is an anonymous act, one which belongs to us all. Consequently, the world as an object of true knowledge cannot be a private possession. If it were, it would be a fantasy world.

[Brief reference to Kant] Even while knowing alone, in solitude, one does an intersubjective act; one appeals implicitly to others . . .

The intersubjective character of knowledge is a hidden bond with other men, but in independence of an explicit social structure. Even when alone in the enterprise of knowing, one is, in this sense, with others.[13]

One may feel that Engelhardt glides illegitimately here between the logical analysis of knowing and the phenomenology of the experience; after all, the logical presuppositions of a mode of consciousness are not always there explicitly in the experience itself. Surely the "hidden bond with other men" he speaks of is hidden from experience? Surely the revelations of solitary reflection feel complete within themselves?

An old story, however, alerts me to an experiential truth in Engelhardt's observations. Midas, the foolish king who asked Bacchus for a touch of gold and then had to beg him to take it back again, did another foolish thing: he agreed to judge a music contest between Apollo and Pan, and unwisely chose the flute of the minor god over the lyre of the more powerful. In revenge, Apollo changed his ears to ass's ears, observing that he was "merely giving to ears so dull and dense the proper shape":

Midas hid them under a cap especially made for that purpose, but the servant who cut his hair was obliged to see them. He swore a solemn oath never to tell, but the secrecy so weighed on the man that he finally dug a hole in a field and spoke softly into it, "King Midas has ass's ears." Then he felt relieved, and filled the hole up. But in the spring reeds grew up there, and when stirred by the wind they whispered those buried words—and revealed [the truth] to men . . . [14]

Again and again I have felt a similar desire to tell the secret truths that solitude has revealed, have listened to the revelations of solitaries too busy to write books. Truth, it seems, wants to be *told*—though only to a worthy listener, only to one prepared to understand and revere the insight. The sense that these conditions cannot be met is a powerful motive for keeping solitary visions secret. Yet even in the secrecy of solitude this feature of the truth-experience is discernable: observations are recorded in a journal with a sense of the importance of the recording, a sense I detect in Thoreau's journals, in Anne Frank's diary, in many other solitary tellings. What is that importance? Is it not the feeling that truth, as truth, should be recognized, recognized by all knowers? But if this is so, in that recognition would lie the final completion of the truth-experience: the cognitive side of reflective perspective in solitude, accordingly, reflects outwards towards other people. When that reflection is caught in another eye, a kind of completion of this gift of solitude occurs.

A second completion encounter can bring arises from the need to verify the truth of one's solitary reflections. Profound visions arrive in solitude—but so do grand delusions. The processes of reflection are always liable to honest error, and when we add the skewing powers of self-hatred and self-love, as well as the convoluted machinations of self-deception, the potential for mis-seeing the truth looms large. Therein lies another motive for going public with the reflections of solitude: "What do you think of this?" we begin, anxious to obtain something from the listener which will complete the exhilarating dawning moment in solitude.

Descartes provides a fine illustration of the workings of this epistemic drive towards engagement. A particularly solitary person, he lived in fourteen different houses in Holland, no doubt partly to avoid the prying of religious authorities, but largely to avoid visitors.[15] He liked to stay late in bed reading and writing, and probably composed the *Discourse on Method* and the *Meditations* thus ensconced. In the latter work, he reports the conclusions of his solitary reflections on the foundations of human knowledge: knowledge can be set on sure foundations by a skeptical "descent" through the accumulated strata of opinion towards the self, and then upwards from the foundational certainty of the self's own clear and distinct ideas towards the certainty of God's existence and veracity, and thenceforward towards the certainty of certain restricted kinds of human knowledge. No one, probably, could arrive at such a comprehensive vision and refrain from reporting it, certainly not Descartes; he worried about the best way to get his manuscripts past the religious authorities (even publishing the *Discourse* anonymously), but when it was safe he published,

> since there is nothing more to be desired than either to protest the certainty of my opinions, as it may haply be if, after distinguished men have examined them, no error is discovered in them, or else that I should be shown my errors in order that I may correct them.[16]

In order to ensure consideration of his thoughts by "distinguished men," Descartes permitted his correspondent and literary agent, Father Mersenne, to circulate manuscript copies of the *Meditations* among leading thinkers of the day, soliciting objections which would be published together with his replies as an appendix to the book. The objections were sometimes blunt. One set came from Thomas Hobbes, who was chafing under a temporary exile in Paris. His general appraisal of Descartes is recorded by his biographer Aubrey:

> Mr. Hobbes was wont to say that had Des Cartes kept himself wholy to Geometrie that he had been the best Geometer in the world but that his head did not lye for Philosophy.[17]

Hobbes's objections began with a snide complaint:

> But since Plato and other ancient Philosophers have talked about this want of certitude in matters of sense, and since the difficulty in distinguishing the waking state from dreams is a matter of common observation, I should have been glad if our author, so distinguished in the handling of modern speculations, had refrained from publishing those matters of ancient lore.[18]

Descartes was no doubt infuriated by the implication,[19] but answered moderately that he claimed no originality for this part of the argument, which merely set the problem of the book. Then he proceeded to the refutation of Hobbes's other fifteen objections, replying carefully but also permitting himself some retaliation:

> I cannot see on what pretext the imputation here of doubt and obscurity rests.

> I can see nothing here that needs an answer.

> For the rest, I am tired of repeating how it is that we can have an idea of God. There is nothing in these objections that invalidates my demonstrations.[20]

Altogether the Objections and Replies were six times as long as the *Meditations* to which they were appended, a nice illustration of the way in which solitary reflective visions yearn to find completion in encounter.

Nor is this merely a feature of narrowly logical/scientific reflection; poetic interpretations, moral appraisals, and personal introspective narratives all yearn for similar completing moments in intersubjective validation. Of course, there are many complexities which arise in these cases: reflective interpretations of such obscure texts as the modern self cannot be held to any simple verificationism. Yet there are standards of success, and accordingly room for failure: if it is true that

> a man is always a teller of tales, he lives surrounded by his stories and the stories of others, he sees everything that happens to him through them; and he tries to live his own life as if he were telling a story. (Jean-Paul Sartre, *Nausea*)[21]

it is equally true that some tellings are better—more coherent, more perceptive, more honest—than others, and that (more generous) principles of verification still operate here. Even Kafka, the most private of storytellers, sought this validation, albeit with much trepidation.

I do not wish to say that the proclaiming-need and the verification-need are equally important in each of the experiences of reflective perspective: indeed the distinction between musing and reflection resides largely in the differential strength of these feelings. Moreover, with regard to mystical experiences of enlightenment, one might wonder whether these two needs are felt at all: certainly the need to verify the revealed truth seems to be absent, all feelings of doubt and confusion having vanished in the unitive visionary moment. Yet the other element, the need to publicize the truth of the enlightenment, does seem to emerge commonly from the experience, though it is cautiously constrained by the sense of the holiness of the vision. As evidence I will cite two facts: firstly, so many contemplatives have taught of enlightenment—from Lao Tzu to the guardians of the Eleusinian mysteries to Buddha to the author of the book of Revelations to Gregory the Great to St. Catherine of Sienna to Krishnamurti. True: human words are poor dumb beasts before "the bright corruscations of the boundless light," but they can be harnessed to draw us deeper into the brilliance. I note that Zen masters take students. I remember that St. Augustine, who insisted: "Do not go abroad. Return within yourself. In the inward man dwells the truth."—returned from within himself to write the *Confessions.* The second fact that strikes me is the frequency with which even those mystics who have bound themselves to silence like to live together—in groves outside the towns, in the *celia* of the deserts, in monasteries, and more recently in communes. Is it misguided to see here one expression of an urge to intersubjective corroboration within enlightenment itself?

"Corroboration" puts the urge too dryly, though; for the truth wants not just to be told but to be celebrated. Feelings of satisfaction, delight, and wonder overflow the boundaries of the solitary self. When Archimedes discovered the principle of displacement while bathing, he jumped up and ran naked through the streets shouting "Eureka!" ("I've found it!"). Children are forever yelling, "Mommy, Mommy! Come see what I've found!" Thoreau wanted "to hear what was in the wind, to hear and carry it express!" and "watching from the observatory of some cliff or tree, to telegraph any new arrival." Trappist monks devoted to the silent life meet seven or eight times a day to sing together praises to the creator of their solitudes. Before Lao Tzu left civilization forever, he left the 5000 words to tell what could be told of solitary enlightenment; listen to the tone of celebration:

> Existence is beyond the power of words
> To define:
> Terms may be used
> But are none of them absolute. . . .

> If name be needed, wonder names them both:
> From wonder into wonder
> Existence opens.[22]

5. Creativity

All honor to the solitary creative act—but why perform it? We forget that, as Anthony Storr once put it, "art is communication . . . implicitly or explicitly, the work which [the artist] produces in solitude is aimed at somebody."[23] We forget how embedded creativity is in the social world of viewers, teachers, students, critics, buyers, and future generations. The creative act finds its balance and completion in the receptive act of the viewer, a reception that acknowledges and values both the work and the artist. May Sarton expresses this sense of validation that the audience brings the artist:

> It has been a happy week because I felt useful and because so many people came to tell me, "I have read everything you have written." It always amazes me that anyone has ever read anything of mine, so it is exceedingly heartening now to discover that somehow, little by little, the work is getting through.[24]

Communicating the work was Sarton's intention, of course, and so the need for social completion is indisputable. But is this always true? Surely Sarton writes some poems just for herself, just for her private journal? I know that reclusive people often devise ingenious inventions for their homesteads, sources of daily delight for their eyes only. I have a secret set of drawings (architectural, not erotic) that you will never see. There are these exceptions, but their importance should not be overestimated. The great bulk of creative work produced in solitude is aimed at an audience; and when it is not, I believe that the point made above regarding the felt need to celebrate the truth is apropos. I can recall a number of visits to solitary homesteads in which the lone inventor proudly showed me contrivance after contrivance fashioned out of old thrown-away stuff; they figured in schemes for raising pond water and lowering humidity, preserving bread and fermenting grapes, keeping heat in and flies out. Together we shared an appreciative recognition of the ingenious solution. And sometimes alone I have stood back from just such an invention in solitude and said to myself proudly, "This ought to be seen!"

Showing/publishing the creative work is generally a somewhat indirect form of engagement—except in the performing arts—but it does establish a communicative bond between artist and audience. May Sarton captures the uncertainty of the communication while nonetheless conveying its importance:

> once more to see the work itself stand alone and make its way, heart by heart, as it is discovered by a few people with all the excitement of a person who finds a wildflower in the woods that *he* has discovered on his own. From my isolation to the isolation of someone somewhere who will find my work there exists true communion.[25]

For Annie Dillard, the refusal to seek this communion is both immoral and self-defeating:

> the impulse to keep to yourself what you have learned is not only shameful, it is destructive. Anything you do not give freely and abundantly becomes lost to you. You open your safe and find ashes.[26]

Thus it is that, in a variety of different ways, the virtues of solitude find their completion in encounter. They are subtle ways, not deficiencies that throb in the experiences themselves, or at least not usually. Untold and unrecorded, the joys of solitude are indeed joys, and there are none greater. Yet a rounding out occurs when, at another time, they are more fully explored and celebrated in propitious moments of engagement; and I have found a sense of this possibility of completion emerging confusedly in the very experiences themselves, though more often in the solitary aftermath, alone with the diary or waiting for a letter. I am anxious to get the proportions right in this analysis, to do justice both to solitude and to the social completions that have appeared. Solitude *is solitude,* different from encounter even as it gestures towards that other moment; the values of solitude are different from the values of encounter. But not so different as one might have thought, and not completely detached. On the level of value, just as on the level of consciousness, solitude and encounter address each other.

Of course, even if my reflections in this chapter are acceptable, they only prove half the case: to complete the argument, one would need to identify the distinctive virtues of encounter and then show that they also find parallel modes of completion in times of solitude. I am not going to do this, however: it would take far too long, and I have much more to say about solitude. Besides, it must now be pretty clear how I would argue the matter. Still, a few brief illustrations are probably owed the reader.

On any list of the virtues of encounter, one item will certainly appear: Caring. It is good in itself to care for another and it is equally good to be truly cared for. The feelings themselves, as well as the effects of their diffusion through a life, are too well known to require description here.[27] What may escape notice, however, is the importance of caring for things other than people: caring seems, in this way, to be like freedom, an underlying attitude of commitment and nurturance which can take as its object not only people but also animals, gardens, houses, even systems of ideas. Mary Belenky et al. identify this kind of caring with the highest level of epistemological development, a stage they call Constructed Knowledge:

> For women at this position, attentive caring is important in understanding not only people but also the written work, ideas, even impersonal objects. Constructivists establish a communion with what they are trying to understand. They use the language of intimacy to describe the relationship between the knower and the known.
>
> Barbara McClintock, whose important work on the genetics of corn plants won her a Nobel prize, used the language of intimacy in describing her way of doing science. She told her biographer, Evelyn Fox Keller, that you had to have the patience "to hear what [the corn] has to say to you" and the openness to let it come to you." McClintock could write the biography of each of her corn plants. As she said, "I know them intimately, and I find it a great pleasure to know them."[28]

Belenky et al. are most interested in women's experiences, but this one is certainly familiar to men. Living alone in a country house for many years, I have cared for its sagging steps and squeaking hinges, polished its windows clean each spring and fall, weeded its gardens and cut overhanging overshading limbs, stood out in the field and admired it lovingly, as I used to admire my sleeping child. In return it has cared for me, nurtured me, protected me, and selflessly inscribed itself upon years of thought. I can say literally to it what we say metaphorically to caring people, "You have made a place for me in the world." This caring has been, as I suspect McClintock's was, a work of solitude, the completing balance to my care for other people.[29]

Moreover, our care for other people finds another completion in solitude, as I have always known intuitively but never understood explicitly until I read Bugbee's words, "Solitude is that distance on beings from which they register with such power."[30] We need this distance to feel the full extent of our caring for another, need to stand alone and behold the other from the distance of disengagement if they are to be to us all that they can be. There is a peculiar kind of wonder possible in this disengagement, the rapt sense you feel standing in the field looking at your house, or standing by the bookshelf looking at a favorite book, or standing by the bedside of your sleeping child. Speaking for myself, but surely for many others, only the space of solitude in nature is vast enough to feel the full power of this caring: as far as my eyes can see, out across the sea and up to the high dome of blue air, streaming outwards in every direction to the farthest limit, *this* finally is enough space for the feeling I have.

A space as great is required by grief: trees whose tallness simultaneously express height and depth, hills which rise and plunge in dull green sorrow, clouds which silently watch over the aching empty place. That was how John Burroughs lived the great loss of his wife in his eightieth year, traveling by ship around Cuba:

> I have no heart to go [with the exploring party], but crave a little solitude on the near-by hills. At 11 A.M. the launch puts me ashore and I walk up on the ridge overlooking the sea. Even Nature in her harsher aspects in the tropics soothes and heals. I stand and loiter long on the breezy ridge and look north upon the great blue crescent of the sea. I have but one thought, and am glad to be alone with it on the hills.

> [Two days later, aboard ship] As I walk the deck I look off yearningly toward the green and brown hills where I walked with my sorrow on the 8th. I left something of myself on those hills. I lived in that solitude one hour of intensified life. No

other point in the horizon so attracts me now. Thoughts of my poor lost one consecrate those hills. Oh, if she could only know how my heart went out to her that day![31]

Thus a life together, so often enriched through explorations of nature alone, was once again affirmed in solitary grief.

In time, the crushing grief lightens, moistened by many damp mornings of rising mist until the bittersweet longing of nostalgia becomes the enduring presence of the beloved. To be absorbed into that presence again, to enter its bright place beyond time and death, we set out over the hills alone.

CHAPTER 9

The Place of Solitude: The Arguments Apriori

Yet, in the sea of life enisled,
With echoing straits between us thrown,
Dotting the shoreless watery wild,
We mortal millions live alone.

—MATTHEW ARNOLD, "TO MARGUERITE"

There are those philosophers, and they are not few, who claim that we are closer to the core of human reality in solitude than we are in encounter: being alone, they insist, is "how it really is" for us. The image of a place is conjured with, a metaphysical place in which the self stands firmly rooted in Being, undisturbed by the shifting winds of encounter. To these thinkers, there is something cacophonous, distanced, illusory about all human encounter. In keeping with such metaphysics, solitude becomes the place of Knowledge: as a native shaman insisted to the arctic explorer Rasmussen, "The only true wisdom lives far from mankind, out in the great loneliness."[1] John Cowper Powys said the same thing more loquaciously in *A Philosophy of Solitude:*

> There is that in the world that throws up a cloud of dust, of fog, of thick wisps of cloying wool, between the soul's creative receptivity and the primordial elements of the universe. This dust, this fog, this heat-wave, this woolly vapour, hot, sticky, adhesive, is the gregarious projection of the herd-mind.
> Only when the soul is alone can the magic of the universe flow through it. It needs the silence for the murmur of the long centuries to grow audible, for the mystery of the cosmic procession to make itself felt.[2]

Here are metaphysics and epistemology leading us out into solitude, following the wagon tracks of old Lao Tzu.

But can this be right? After all, many profound minds have come to the opposite conclusion, that the road into the desert leads only to shifting dunes and mirages. D. H. Lawrence insisted, recall, "I am part of the great whole and I can never escape."[3] Heinz Kohut wrote late in his career that

> Self psychology holds that self-selfobject relationships form the essence of psychological life from birth to death, that a move from dependence (symbiosis) to independence (autonomy) in the psychological sphere is no more possible, let alone desirable, than a corresponding move from a life dependent on oxygen to a life independent of it in the biological sphere.[4]

And on loftier plains, the "existential-ontological" primacy of encounter was claimed by Heidegger: "Even Dasein's Being-alone is Being-with in the world. . . . Being-alone is a deficient mode of Being-with."[5]

Can this be right *either?* Perhaps both primacy views are wrong; perhaps the place of solitude is simply a matter of cultural permission and personal taste, solitude providing the contact with reality for some that encounter provides for others, neither state being in any defensible sense primary. Or maybe both are equally primary, as I have been suggesting all along.

Well, neither camp is going to accept any such easy tolerance: for among their stirring vagaries and trenchant metaphors, so interwoven as to be almost inextricable, arguments are to be found. I have been collecting them for years, and am intent upon showing my collection. Actually, only half of the collection, for I have a plan: since I am a partisan of solitude, honesty demands that I scrutinize first and most fiercely the arguments for the primacy of solitude; however, in showing (as I aim to do) how they all fail, it will become sufficiently clear how I would refute the alleged primacy of encounter. Accordingly, rather than taking time to elaborate all the encounterists' arguments and their deficiencies, I will take the equal primacy of solitude and encounter in human existence as established, and move on to other topics. Incomplete, but efficient.

Individual Differences

Any assessment of the place of solitude in human existence must acknowledge the fact that, with regard to the amounts of solitude actually desired and lived, individual differences are vast.[6] Some people have a deep and ever-flowing need for it, cherish it, exhilarate in it:

> My mind to me a kingdom is
> Such perfect joy therein I find,
> That it excels all other bliss
> That earth affords or grows by kind
>
> —Sir Edward Dyer (1543–1607), "My Mind to Me a Kingdom Is"[7]

> Society is all but rude
> To this delicious solitude. . . .

> Such was that happy garden state,
> While man there walked without a mate.
> After a place so pure and sweet,
> What other help could yet be meet?
> But 'twas beyond a mortal's share
> To wander solitary there:
> Two paradises 'twere in one
> To live in paradise alone.
>
> —Andrew Marvel (1621–1678), "The Garden"[8]

Shelley wrote,

> I love all waste
> And solitary places; where we taste
> The pleasure of believing what we see
> Is boundless, as we wish our souls to be.
>
> —"Julian and Maddalo"[9]

Byron's praise is equally famous:

> There is a pleasure in the pathless woods,
> There is a rapture on the lonely shore,
> There is society, where none intrudes,
> By the deep sea and music in its roar;
> I love not man the less, but Nature more
>
> —*Childe Harold*, Canto IV[10]

Wordsworth's poetic corpus is in large part the exploration and celebration of the landscapes of solitude, "recollected in tranquility," from the youthful joys of "Tintern Abbey"

> . . . For nature then
> (The coarser pleasures of my boyish days,
> And their glad animal movements all gone by)
> To me was all in all.—I cannot paint
> What then I was. The sounding cataract
> Haunted me like a passion: the tall rock
> The mountain, and the deep and gloomy wood,
> Their colors and their forms, were then to me
> An appetite; a feeling and a love."[11]

to the more spiritual intuitions of the "Prelude,"

> . . . the soul—
> Remembering how she felt, but what she felt
> Remembering not—retains an obscure sense
> Of possible sublimity, at which
> With growing faculties she doth aspire,
> With faculties still growing, feeling still
> That whatsoever point they gain, they still
> Have something to pursue.[12]

It was no romantic poet, however, that wrote

> Always alone among people, I return home to dream by myself, and submit to the liveliness of my own Melancholy.

but Napoleon Bonaparte![13]

It must be acknowledged, however, that a great many people find solitude unappealing, and would exclaim with William Cowper

> Oh Solitude! where are thy charms,
> That sages have seen in thy face?
> Better dwell in the midst of alarms,
> Than reign in this horrible place.

> —"Lines Supposed to Have Been Written by
> Alexander Selkirk"[14]

or at least echo his gentler pronouncement on the subject

> How sweet, how passing sweet, is solitude!
> But grant me still a friend in my retreat,
> Whom I may whisper—solitude is sweet.[15]

Byron said out of the other side of his mouth that "Quiet to quick bosoms is a Hell" (*Childe Harold,* Canto III, line 370), and even Wordsworth occasionally had misgivings:

> Farewell, farewell the heart that lives alone,
> Housed in a dream, at distance from the Kind!
> Such happiness, wherever it be known,
> Is to be pitied; for 'tis surely blind.
>
> —"Elegiac Stanzas"[16]

And is it even happiness? Pablo Neruda, I think it was, who felt, in one solitude, "Condemned to gnaw on the husks that the silence assembles."

Tastes for solitude certainly differ, then, and it is worth a few moments to speculate as to why this might be so. Age may well be an important factor. Adolescents, their sexuality awakened and hungry, are on that score less inclined towards solitude than they will be at later stages of development. However there is more to human development than hormones, and perhaps Octavio Paz is right to find in solitude one of the defining revelations of adolescence:

> All of us, at some moment, have had a vision of our existence as something unique, untransferable and very precious. This revelation almost always takes place during adolescence. Self-discovery is above all the realization that we are alone: it is the opening of an impalpable, transparent wall—that of our consciousness—between the world and ourselves. It is true that we sense our aloneness almost as soon as we are born, but children and adults can transcend their solitude and forget themselves in games or work. The adolescent, however, vacillates between infancy and youth, halting for a moment before the infinite richness of the world. He is astonished at the fact of his being, and this astonishment leads to reflection: as he leans over the river of his consciousness, he asks himself if the face that appears there, disfigured by the water, is his own. The singularity of his being, which is pure sensation in children, becomes a problem and a question.[17]

Early adulthood is in general not particularly inclined towards solitude: its dominating desires—to reproduce, to raise a family, to achieve standing in the social order—embroil it deeply in engagement. Later, though, the balance of desire seems to shift again during the "third period" of life, as Anthony Storr has called it:

> At the beginning of life, survival depends upon 'object-relationships'. The human infant cannot care for itself, and is dependent upon the care of others throughout many long years of childhood. Toward the end of life, the opposite condition obtains. Although illness or injury may make the elderly physically dependent, emotional dependence tends to decline. The old often show less interest in interpersonal relationships, are more content to be alone, and become more preoccupied with their own, internal concerns . . .
>
> [This] may also be a merciful provision of Nature, designed to lessen the pain of the inevitable parting from loved ones which death brings in train. Man is the only creature who can see his own death coming; and, when he does, it concentrates his mind wonderfully. He prepares for death by freeing himself from mundane goals and attachments, and turns instead to the cultivation of his own interior garden.[18]

Cultural variables also affect the experience of solitude—the opportunities for finding it, the forms it can take and the meanings available for its comprehension. To take an obvious example, a woman living in a traditional culture which assigns her unremitting life-long responsibility for children and the elderly will not likely assign to solitude the same reality-status as would a modern single male Canadian naturalist. As a non-obvious example, consider linguistic variations. Although we were able quite readily above to distinguish five to ten English words referring to different types of aloneness, Japanese has approximately fifty such terms. One ideograph represents a roof with nothing beneath it, another an orphan, another dogs biting each other—none exactly coordinate with our English terms.[19] Since the conceptual structure given in a language determines the experiences of those who live in that language, moments of what we call solitude will be interpreted somewhat differently by the Japanese, just as the question of the metaphysical/epistemological place of such experiences will need some translation.

Religions have also varied in their appreciation of solitude. The Desert Fathers fled from the worldliness and distractions of the early church, but the Bishops saw things differently and were often in conflict with the hermits over the social mandate of Christianity. My favorite illustration of this difference comes from *The Sayings of the Fathers:*

Blessed Archbishop Theophilus, accompanied by a magistrate, came one day to find Abba Arsenius. He questioned the old man, to hear a word from him. After a short silence the old man answered him, "Will you put into practice what I say to you?" They promised him this. "If you hear that Arsenius is anywhere, do not go there."[20]

Zen Buddhism emphasizes solitary meditation and quiet individual work, but Calvinism emphasizes church attendance and public works as proof of personal election. And although one can sit in the back of a large cathedral and feel very disengaged from the rest of those hearing the Mass, a Southern Baptist service is a very communal affair.

Modern psychiatry also manifests striking differences of opinion as to the centrality of solitude—both in normal human experience and in therapeutic practice. The elaborate interpersonal world of Freudian psychotherapy, with its convoluted dynamics of transference and counter-transference, makes the "talking cure" a very engaged affair indeed. Jungian analysis, on the other hand, tends to emphasize solitary personal exploration, with the therapist serving as a compassionate outside consultant.[21] And even the consultant vanishes in Morita Therapy.

Philosophers' Universal Claims

Yet in spite of all these individual and cultural differences, philosophers have been moved to make claims of a universal order. St. Augustine was counselling everyone when he wrote, "Do not go abroad. Return within yourself. In the inward man dwells the truth,"[22] and Montaigne, Wordsworth, and Thoreau directed their claims for solitude to the general readers of their days. In recent years, the claims have multiplied.[23] Gliding freely between loneliness and solitude, writers have insisted upon our "essential loneliness," "authentic loneliness," "inescapable solitude"; and this aloneness is not merely the aberrant state of a few persons or cultures, but rather "the profoundest fact of the human condition" (Octavio Paz). What is revealed to us in this aloneness, Martin Buber wrote, "cannot be reached by psychological concepts, it is something ontic."[24] Something ontic means something revelatory of the deep structure of human reality, and that is just what many writers have claimed for solitude.

From among the host, I have chosen the following for their forceful-ness:

> Mijuskovic (philosopher): "Man is essentially alone and irredeemably lost."[25]

> Powys (philosopher): "Every human being is alone in the core of the mind. When we are born we cry; and that cry is the cry of loneliness. . . . No day, no night should pass without gathering together of the inmost core of our being with its defiant cry: 'Alone with the universe! Alone against the universe!' "[26]

> Koller (philosopher): "You begin marking out your line of travel [towards finding/creating your true self] in the instant you recognize the extent to which you are alone: thoroughly, unremittingly, without other human beings. I call it 'being alone elementally': as an element, unconnected. It is the essential human condition."[27]

> Moustakas (psychologist): "Man is ultimately and forever lonely . . ."[28]

> Tillich (theologian): ". . . the terrifying experience of ultimate loneliness. In such moments [men] break through the surface of their average life into the depth of man's predicament."[29]

> Parkinson (literary critic): "Loneliness begins with the recognition of one's singularity—the fact that a deep communication of one's self and recognition by others of its legitimacy is not fully possible."[30]

And of course,

> Proust: "Notwithstanding the illusion by which we would fain be cheated and with which, out of friendship, politeness, deference and duty, we cheat other people, we exist alone. Man is the creature who cannot escape himself, who knows other people only in himself, and when he asserts the contrary he is lying."[31]

It is true that none of the above statements contain the word 'solitude,' so a few words of coordination are in order. Each of these authors wants to insist upon the ultimate aloneness of human existence, the separateness of each of us from all others even in what appear to be moments of encounter. This separateness from others is seen as the core fact. Additionally, that core has a negative valence for most of these authors: clear awareness of our aloneness, they think, automatically produces loneliness, although they sometimes allow that we can learn to accept our separateness, turning it into a solitude that is "fruitful" (Tillich), or at least bearable (Mijuskovic). Loneliness, then, is consequent upon the realization of the ultimate aloneness, although these separate ideas are usually run together.

There are thus two parts to these philosophies of place, and they raise two corresponding questions: are we more alone, in any ultimate sense, than we are engaged? and is that state of aloneness inherently lonely? I intend to pursue the first question in the succeeding pages, since my answer to the second question has already been given: no, aloneness is most certainly not inherently lonely. From time to time it will be useful to point out how various authors glide illicitly from "alone" or "solitary" to "lonely," forgetting solitude altogether, but in the main I want to concentrate upon the first question.

If aloneness is the core fact about us, then solitude, the state of disengagement from other people in thought, feeling, perception and action would indeed seem to be the truest way of being. If all engagements are to some extent illusory (Proust) or unsuccessful (Parkinson), then the varieties of aloneness would seem to have ontic pride of place; and of those experiences, loneliness and alienation would seem somewhat tainted, since they involve a longing for something that is ultimately a mirage. In solitude, on the other hand, disengaged from the unattainable other, one has all that really can be had. In this view, Thoreau walking alone around the pond exemplifies our final plight and best hope: true, the desire to unite with another may well up painfully at times, but this is a tragic motion in the heart; for in reality we are forever condemned to walk alone.

Now sympathetic as one must be to these cries from the heart— who has not made them himself?—calmer reflection wants to protest that their great truth is only half the truth, that men and women are not always or necessarily alone, that engaged encounter with others is as fully real, as "ultimate" a place as separateness, that in their lostness sometimes people find each other. Are any arguments advanced by these thinkers for their dark claims?

There are arguments, but before the arguments come the metaphors, images so powerful as to hold reflection in a spell. Let yourself feel their grip, for a moment:

> Proust: "I might, if I chose, take Albertine upon my knee, take her head in my hands; I might caress her, passing my hands slowly over her, but, just as if I had been handling a stone which encloses the salt of immemorial oceans or the light

of a star, I felt that I was touching no more than the sealed envelope of a person who inwardly reached to infinity."[32]

Howard: "The flesh-colored cage"[33]

Huxley: "The most intimate contact is only of surfaces, and we couple, as I have seen the condemned prisoners at Newgate coupling with their trulls, between the bars of our cages."[34]

Pirandello: ". . . this horrible thing, which really drives one mad: that if you were beside another and looking into his eyes—as I one day looked into somebody's eyes—you might as well be a beggar before a door never to be opened to you; for he who does enter there will never be you, but someone unknown to you with his own different and impenetrable world."[35]

Parkinson: "The sense of being a voice in a void—speaking in a vacuum . . . the buried genuine self . . ."[36]

Mijuskovic: "a solitary atom of consciousness, forsaken to existence among the limitless expanses of dark space and time"[37]

Sealed envelopes, stones, sea-wrecks, encaged prisoners, beggars at unopenable doors, buried alive in our bodies, mere atoms in dark space—the images almost convince us of themselves before the explicit arguments are launched.

But then come the arguments, attempts to make articulate and rational what the metaphors say to our anxious hearts. I intend now to disentangle these arguments, clarify their claims and assess their value. This chapter focuses on the more abstract arguments developed from general considerations about the nature of Being, Knowledge, and Consciousness; the next examines inferences from some striking facts about lived experience. Given my growing conviction that solitude and encounter mutually bound and interpenetrate each other, the reader will not be surprised to learn that none of these arguments strike me as successful: the most that any of them succeed in establishing is the basic and inescapable importance of aloneness as *one* of the primal features of human existence, not as *the most primary* feature: that title it shares equally with encounter. When this is seen clearly, the metaphors no longer cast a spell, though the power of their partial truth remains.

The investigation is made easier by the fact that, with minor variations, the same arguments for the primacy of aloneness can be found recurring in writer after writer. On the other hand, the task is made difficult by two general tendencies: first, different lines of argument are run together in a brief passage, with a few metaphors thrown in, making it difficult to disentangle the strands of thought (rhetoricians like the "multiplier effect"); second, there is all too often a careless gliding among terms, leaving one uncertain as to what exactly is being argued, and whether one is really being fair to the author. However, "Courage my mind, and press on mightily!" (St. Augustine).

The Metaphysical Arguments

The first line of argument often appears as a jumble of claims about our physical location in a single distinct body and the nature of individuation itself. Listen to these words of Paul Tillich:

> He was there, "alone"—so are we. Man is alone, because he is man! In some way every creature is alone. In majestic isolation each star travels through the darkness of endless space. Every tree grows according to its own law, fulfilling its unique possibilities. Animals live, fight, and die for themselves, caught in the limits of their bodies. Certainly, they appear as male and female, in families, in flocks. Some of them are gregarious. But all of them are alone! Being alive means being in a body—a body separated from all other bodies. And being separated means being alone.[38]

Nor is the last statement intended as an empty tautology: in his next paragraph, Tillich insists that the mere awareness of this aloneness produces anguish:

> He is not only alone; he also *knows* that he is alone. Aware of what he is, he therefore asks the question of his aloneness. He asks why he is alone and how he can overcome his being alone. He cannot stand it; but he cannot escape it either. It is his destiny to be alone and to be aware of it.

In these passages, being metaphysically separate becomes being alone, and that becomes, abruptly, loneliness ("he cannot stand it"). There is, in short, an argument from metaphysical individuation to phenomenal feeling-experience, indeed to a very specific kind of feeling-experience. And it is a bad argument. As for the first inference step, what would we think of the claim that an electric fuse, screwed tightly into its socket next to the other fuses, is *alone* because it is a separable entity? The separate-to-alone slide is illegitimate. As for the second leg, from alone to lonely, the gathering weight of my book's reflections is that being alone, feeling alone, and feeling lonely are distinguishable, *and often distinct,* states. The last two are experiential states but the first one is not: even if one were alone, one might not be aware that one was, and so not feel alone; and in any case feeling alone is not yet feeling lonely. (It is hard to decide whether in this passage Tillich is arguing or simply asserting; in either case he is mistaken.)

So the argument from metaphysical individuation to the primacy of experiential aloneness—whether in loneliness or solitude, the pain or the glory of being alone in Tillich's words—fails on two counts: it ignores the (metaphysical) truth that individuation is quite consistent with relationship, and it involves an illicit category-shift from metaphysics to experience. Still, it is a seductive argument; it convinced as great a thinker as Tillich, and he is by no means the only one: watch how the same shifts occur—with equal rapidity—in this passage from Mijuskovic:

> Nevertheless, whether we stipulate a consciousness which is productive of relations, negations, or both, the important consideration remains that these dual functions are unified, or synthesized, by one consciousness and hence only individual consciousnesses exist. And man is alone and lonely.[39]

Mijuskovic has many other arguments for the primacy of loneliness, but I hope we can now press on mightily past this one.

I cannot leave the subject of metaphysical "proofs" of our ultimate aloneness, however, without remarking upon the metaphysical system of the great seventeenth-century polymath, Gottfried Wilhelm von Leibniz (1646–1714); for misunderstandings of his system have often figured in lonely philosophies, and the oft-chosen epithet for solitaries, 'monad,' was Leibniz's coinage. Famous for his discovery, independently of Newton but at about the same time, of the infinitesimal calculus (including the notation still used today), his philosophical fame rests upon the ingenuity with which he was able to construct elegantly interlocking systems of paradoxical claims, supported by crisply logical proofs: this is the philosopher who set out to prove by rigorous deductive arguments the astounding proposition that this is the best of all possible worlds! There are other elements of his system, however, that have seemed particularly suggestive to lonely imaginations, for reasons that can be made readily apparent. According to Leibniz, the universe is populated by individual substances, which he calls "monads." You and I are monads, at least in so far as we are minds or spirits, and the objects we perceive about us are aggregates of monads. Each monad is simple, not composed of parts, but yet admits of modifications, as a simple mirror changes when different people walk before it. Surprisingly, though, the changes which monads undergo are all contained within themselves, and not caused by other substances as common sense might think:

> There is no way of explaining how a monad can be altered or changed in its inner being by any other creature, for nothing can be transposed within it, nor can we conceive in it any internal movement that can be excited, directed, augmented or diminished within it, as we can in composites, where there may be change among the parts. The monads have no windows through which anything can enter or depart. . . . neither substance nor accident can enter a monad from outside.[40]

Then how does change occur in a monad, how does its life unfold? Out of its own completeness, somewhat as a seed unfolds from its early stage:

> there was always in the soul of Alexander [The Great] marks of all that had happened to him and evidences of all that would happen to him and traces even of everything which occurs in the universe, although God alone could recognize all of them.[41]

Each of us, then, unfolds through time unaffected by any other being (except God), yet perfectly synchronized with every other substance according to a "pre-established harmony" which God, in his perfection, has produced in the universe. To illustrate, when I feel pain at the slap of your hand, the pain is caused not by your hand but by the unfolding of my own substance's "internal program" which was designed by God to feel pain at exactly the moment in which, according to another part of His design, your hand should contact my face: "What we call causes are in metaphysical rigor only concomitant requisites."

The pre-established harmony of simple individuals is compared by Leibniz to the collection of all of the different points of view of a single object—that object being, in this case, the universe. Somewhat as a

simple dewdrop reflects the rich variety of the surrounding forest from
its unique point of view,

> each simple substance has relations which express all the others, and, conse-
> quently, it is a perpetual living mirror of the universe.

> And as the same city viewed from different sides appears entirely different, and
> is as if multiplied *perspectively,* so also it happens that, because of the infinite
> multitude of simple substances, there are as it were so many different universes,
> which are nevertheless only the perspectives of a single one, according to the
> different *points of view* of each monad.[42]

One might imagine, here, a vast collection of small mirroring raindrops[43] in a forest, hanging from every blade of grass and every branch
tip, each mirroring drop reflecting the world from the neighboring
blade of grass out to the farthest star in its polished spherical surface.
Only, this raindrop has an impenetrable shell: admitting no intrusions
and sending no messages, it is condemned to reflect forever without
engaging, eternally sealed within itself. And when we then learn from
Leibniz that the human soul is a monad, our terrible destiny seems
clear: what more lonely vision of the universe could there be?

But as careful readers of Leibniz know, these claims about the
nature of the monads had nothing at all to do with loneliness or any
other variety of experience alone. Leibniz had his eyes upon logic,
metaphysics, and theology, not upon the phenomenological nature of
human experience. Why did he assert that monads were simple,
without parts? Not because he experienced himself as simple and
unambiguous, but for the metaphysical reason that "there must be
simple substances, since there are composites; for the composite is
only a collection or aggregate of simple substances" (*Monadology,*
para. 2). Why must Alexander contain traces of all he has been and will
be within himself? Because Leibniz's analysis of the nature of truth
holds that all truths are either identities (such as "A is A") or reducible
to identities by the analysis of concepts. Therefore the analysis of the
concept of Alexander must yield all truths about him, past, present, and
future, and "every true predicate has some basis in the nature of
things." Why is each monad's point of view different from every
other's? Not because Leibniz had unusually severe problems understanding people, but because "this is the way to obtain as great a variety
as possible, but with the greatest possible order; that is, it is the way to
obtain as much perfection as possible" (*Monadology,* para. 58). And

the reason why there must be the greatest amount of perfection possible is that the universe was created by God, whose perfection is provable by analyzing the very concept of God. And so forth.

Moreover, a little reflection upon Leibniz's system reveals that one is neither more nor less in touch with reality when alone than when with other people; the pond and the trees Thoreau surveyed were fully as much perceptions of his own soul-monad as any interloper would have been.

> We may say, therefore, that God is for us the only immediate external object, and that we see things through him. For example, when we see the sun or the stars, it is God who gives to us and preserves in us the ideas, and whenever our senses are affected according to his own laws in a certain manner, it is he, who by his continual concurrence, determines our thinking.[44]

Complete withdrawal from the world of perception into the realm of pure philosophical thought might seem to be particularly expressive of the soul-monad's plight, but Leibniz would never have endorsed such an escape from the life of Christian duty. A remarkably engaged philosopher, he was constantly involved in political negotiations, economic planning, the design of military fortifications—all the while maintaining a voluminous correspondence. Metaphysics was, for him, most closely bound to explanation in the physical sciences and in theology, and not to the clarification of our felt experience of the world. As a final proof of this, I note that in spite of the infinite diversity in monadic points of view, Leibniz championed the development of a universally intelligible and decisive logical language, through which disputants on any subject could resolve their differences by sitting down and calculating together. "Man is a lonely isolated monad" is not something the great Monadologist would have said.

The Embodiment Argument

Sometimes reasons for the primacy of aloneness are so fleetingly mentioned that it seems improper to dignify them with the name "argument." Charity might urge us to pass over them in silence, were it not that these hurried claims can appear to lend weight to other arguments. Tillich finds it relevant to mention that "being alive means being in a body—a body separated from all other bodies. And being separated means being alone."[45] Is it the separateness, or the embodiment that he finds important?

Here is another version of this line of argument, from James Howard:

> No matter how closely we make a contact with another person, we do not occupy a single skin, share a nervous system, or achieve identity in structure, function, or sensation [with another] . . .
>
> Each of us exists within his unique epidermal envelope as separate *thing*. No other person can enter that envelope, nor can any of us escape from it. We were born in that enclosure, exist within it, and will wear it as our funeral shroud.[46]

One also recalls Huxley's words, "but again, propinquity is never fusion. The most intimate contact is only of surfaces."[47]

Interestingly, Mijuskovic sees clearly the flaw in this line of thinking though missing the parallel fault in his own earlier argument: "it is philosophically unsound to argue that psychological solitude is constituted by bodily isolation."[48] Being embodied does not itself foreclose engagement—indeed it is a most wonderful facilitator of encounter, which is, after all, for us humans, the interaction between embodied selves. Lusty sex is an absorbing engagement of psyches as well as bodies—the former hardly handicapped by the latter! Disembodied engagement is perhaps conceivable, but, as the ghost stories of all cultures attest, thin and unsatisfying.

By the way, Howard's supposedly purely factual description of our state really contains a phenomenological bias towards buried Cartesian egos: for instead of saying that I am encaged within my body, why not simply say that I *am* my body?[49]

The Epistemological Arguments

Arguments for the ultimacy of aloneness based upon the nature, the possibilities and the limits of knowing other people may be roughly divided into two sorts, which we might call the Radical and the Practical, since the first insists upon the strict *impossibility* of knowing other people whereas the second insists only upon the *difficulty* of that enterprise.

The radical argument traces back to Descartes. In the *Meditations on First Philosophy* there occurs a separation of the human person into two elements, a thinking soul and an extended body. The impetus for this separation came from his attempt to set all human knowledge upon a firm foundation by applying a method of doubt to his pre-philosophical beliefs: since it was possible to doubt whether his hands, eyes, legs—even his whole body—existed but impossible to doubt his own existence as a thinking thing, he concluded that body and self must be different items:

> Accordingly, simply from knowing that I exist, and that, meantime, I do not observe any other thing as evidently pertaining to my nature, i.e. to my essence, except this only, that I am a thinking thing, I rightly conclude that my essence consists in this alone, that I am a thinking thing (i.e., a substance, the whole nature or essence of which consists in thinking). And although possibly (or rather certainly, as I shall shortly be declaring) I have a body with which I am very closely conjoined, yet since on the one hand I have a clear and distinct idea of myself, in so far as I am only a thinking unextended thing, and on the other hand a distinct idea of the body, in so far as it is only an extended unthinking thing, it is certain that I am truly distinct from my body, and can exist without it.[50]

This thinking thing, this mind, the essential Descartes, had direct and immediate access to its own ideas and perceptions; its thoughts, feelings, imaginings, and sensations were held to be immediately transparently present to scrutiny: should a person wish to know, for example, whether he feared another, he need only look within to know infallibly the answer. But the body itself is present to one only via the ideas and perceptions which it causes to appear in the immaterial, unextended mind, and thus can only be perceived mediately; it can only be known by a process of inference from mental perception to physical cause, an inference which might go astray as in the case, mentioned by Descartes, of phantom limb pains in amputees. The upshot was that the perceiving thinking self was not *in* its body, but in a sense isolated from it. Or so his arguments seemed to show: Descartes was not, however, very comfortable with the picture that emerged, honestly confessing his dissatisfaction: "I am not present in my body merely as a pilot is present in a ship; I am most tightly bound to it, and as it were mixed up with it, so that I and it form a unit."[51]

Still, the separation of mind and body appeared to him logically unassailable, particularly when it came to other people. In the Second Meditation, trying to ascertain whether external objects such as balls of wax are known by perception, imagination, or purely mental apprehension, Descartes reminds himself that

> when looking from a window at beings passing by on the street below, I similarly say that it is men I am seeing, just as I say that I am seeing the wax. What do I see from the window beyond hats and cloaks, which might cover automatic machines? Yet I judge those to be men. In analogous fashion, what I have been supposing myself to see with the eyes I am comprehending solely with the faculty of judgement, a faculty proper not to my eyes but to my mind.[52]

What the contents of other minds might be, indeed whether there are other minds at all, can in Descartes's view only be known by inference from the behavior of other bodies: other minds themselves are not directly perceivable. And as for the inference involved, how do we know that it is reliable? Descartes wondered whether it wasn't possible that instead of the benevolent God of common belief there might not be an evil genius who devoted himself to deceiving us about such things. If that were so, then since bodies without minds are merely automatic machines and not persons, our "knowledge" of (and hence engagement with) other people would be an illusion. This was so worrisome a possibility that after ascertaining the indubitability of his own existence Descartes set at once to proving that God could not be a deceiver, and that the inference from behavior to other minds could be defended.

Thus was born (in its modern form, at any rate) the Problem of Other Minds. Subsequent philosophers recognized that Descartes had raised formidable difficulties concerning knowledge of other people, but invariably found his solutions unsatisfactory. The problem is a thorny one indeed, once one accepts Descartes's claim that knowledge of other people is inferential, since the only means of knowing what—or that—other people think and feel seems to be logically wanting. As a point of logic, we validate inferences, e.g. from smoke to fire, by directly observing the causal connection in some cases; yet on Descartes's view we are never able even in principle to observe the mental fire which causes the bodily smoke. Descartes was able to convince himself with a version of the argument from analogy (roughly: I have a body which produces mental states in my mind; but other bodies behave exactly like mine; therefore it is probable that those other bodily behaviors also produce mental states), but the dubiousness of that argument was already apparent to his contemporaries (in addition to the point just made about verification, the argument seems to generalize far too broadly on a single case).[53] Worse still, the more one reflects upon the Cartesian situation, the more it seems to lead us logically into solipsism, the view that only my own mind and its states are real (since everything else is an unknown, dangling at the end of an uncheckable inference). Now that is real aloneness!

No one, of course, believes that this is so—except possibly the woman who heard Bertrand Russell lecture on solipsism and subsequently wrote to him that it was such a wonderful philosophy she thought *everyone* should adopt it! Yet where exactly Cartesian dualism goes astray is perhaps the largest question of the last 300 years of European philosophy. I can hardly solve it here. What can be done is to note that the vast weight of our actual knowledge-experiences do not cohere with Cartesianism, and that therefore a refutation must be possible, regardless of its particular details.[54] For in ordinary daily life, the reality and knowability of other people is quite immediate, not the result of a string of inferences. As Wittgenstein remarked,

> But just try to keep hold of this idea [that the people around you lack consciousness and are, therefore, purely physical bodies] in the midst of your ordinary intercourse with others, in the street say! Say to yourself, for example: "The children over there are mere automata; all their liveliness is mere automatism." And you will either find these words becoming quite meaningless, or you will produce in yourself some kind of uncanny feeling.[55]

Sartre captures the immediate experiential reality of the Other in his brilliant discussion of the Look:

> Let us imagine that moved by jealousy, curiosity, or vice I have just glued my ear to the door and looked through a keyhole. I am alone . . . But all of a sudden I hear footsteps in the hall. Someone is looking at me! What does this mean? . . . First of all, I now exist as *myself* . . . I see *myself* because *somebody* sees me. [Moreover the shame I feel] reveals to me the Other's look and myself at the end of that look.[56]

This shame, this sense of being revealed to the Other, is so powerful that even the possibility of the Other's catching me alters my experiential world utterly:

> Here I am bent over the keyhole; suddenly I hear a footstep. I shudder as a wave of shame sweeps over me. Somebody has seen me. I straighten up. My eyes run over the deserted corridor. It was a false alarm. I breathe a sigh of relief. [but] Is it

actually my being-as-object for the Other which has been revealed as an error? By no means. The Other's existence is so far from being placed in doubt that this false alarm can very well result in making me give up my enterprise. If, on the other hand, I persevere in it, I shall feel my heart beat fast, and I shall detect the slightest noise, the slightest creaking of the stairs. Far from disappearing with my first alarm, the Other is present everywhere, below me, above me, in the neighboring rooms, and I continue to feel profoundly my being-for-others. . . . Better yet, if I tremble at the slightest noise, if each creak announces to me a look, this is because I am already in the state of being-looked-at.[57]

Experientially, then, our contact with other people is as real, immediate, certain, and powerful as our contact with the natural objects surveyed in solitude.

Moreover, the same kinds of inferential gaps which plague Cartesian attempts to know other people also open between us and the physical world (a point seized by Berkeley). Seeing a tree consists, for Descartes, of an immediate awareness of some ideas in the mind, together with an (automatic) inference that those ideas are causally produced by objects in the world; the causality by extramental reality, however, is not immediately perceivable, and so some kind of argument for its existence is philosophically required. The upshot is that on Cartesian principles we are no more directly knowing a tree in solitude than we are directly apprehending a person in encounter. Whatever the fate of Descartes's arguments then, they do not confer primacy upon solitude.

Finally, Descartes seems to have been mistaken, from a phenomenological point of view, in maintaining that the contents of our own minds are always known more immediately and infallibly than those of others: taking the emotions, the hot anger from which your crackling words issue can be more immediate, indubitable, and clear than my own confused response. Knowledge of one's own self—especially of its lower depths—appears to be inferential too, confirming what Wittgenstein and Sartre forced philosophers to remember: Immediate Self and Distant Other is not how we actually experience our world knowingly.

All except solipsists may, then, pass by on the side of the radical epistemological argument for our ultimate aloneness. There are, however, other arguments for the primacy of solitude that might be called epistemological because they emphasize the difficulty of really or fully or completely knowing another person, as compared to the directness and ease of knowing ourselves. These arguments purport to derive from common experience, rather than abstract speculations. I leave them until the next chapter.

Arguments from the Nature of Consciousness

The most sustained and comprehensive attempt to argue the ontological primacy of human aloneness is Professor Ben Lazare Mijuskovic's *Loneliness in Philosophy, Psychology, and Literature*. It is a boldly written book, one upon which any student of solitude will want to test his wits. Mijuskovic tells us in his introduction that, as the result of prior studies of the metaphysics and phenomenology of consciousness,

> That man *feels* himself to be absolutely alone became undeniably certain to me. Further, that the *meaning* of man is structured by a constant futile struggle which protests against his isolated state of conscious existence was equally manifest to me. But *why* man is—or senses himself to be—alone was not at all clear. Consequently, in [this book], I have tried to develop a theory of consciousness, a philosophy of mind, which alone can account—on various levels, metaphysical, ontological, epistemological, phenomenological, existential, psychological, passional, etc.—*why* man is condemned to despairing solitude and just how he feels himself to be so sentenced.[58]

That is a great many levels, and indeed almost every argument anyone has ever used for the primacy of lonely isolation appears somewhere between his covers. Kant, Fichte, Hegel, Bergson, Husserl, Sartre, Freud are marshalled, as well as dozens of literary sources. However, apriori arguments based upon the analysis of the nature of consciousness are his specialty, and it is these lines of reasoning that I now wish to examine. Admittedly, the going gets rough: the arguments are abstract, abstruse, and couched in an intimidating philosophical jargon. So why bother, since I think the arguments all fail? Well, my sense of philosophical obligation, inspired by Bertrand Russell, compels me: I think a great deal of the book is bad philosophy, the sort of philosophy that tends to bamboozle rather than enlighten, and Russell taught us that it is part of every philosopher's duty to expose such thinking. And there is some payoff: in Mijuskovic's work one sees the mischief caused by gliding from term to term when thinking about aloneness—and one sees that even professional philosophers can be guilty. One also sees how phenomenologists can selectively ignore phenomena which speak against their bold theses. But finally, on a kinder note, one sees more clearly how aloneness is one—though not the only—primary fact of human existence.

Mijuskovic's central thesis is as uncompromising as it is extreme: the loneliness of man is "the original primordial fact," "the primary transcendental ground of human existence: "we are, he claims, "essentially alone and irredeemably lost." As though this were not bad enough, Mijuskovic also holds the (avowedly reductionistic) motivational thesis that "loneliness, more correctly the drive to avoid a sense of isolation, actually constitutes the dominant psychic force underlying all human consciousness and conduct."[59] Since every human being is inexorably driven to try to escape a condition which is nonetheless essential and inescapable, human life is futile and tragic.[60]

His arguments for the central thesis, our essential loneliness, can be divided—though hardly neatly, since he sometimes runs them together—into those for the loneliness of self-consciousness and those for the loneliness of consciousness of others. I begin with the former.

"Loneliness thus constitutes the inevitable structure of self-awareness" (p. 13). On what grounds is this claimed? On the grounds that a consciousness itself is a "reflexive nothingness." Avowedley Cartesian, his theory goes like this: "Consciousness, as a diaphanous 'medium', is a reflexive and 'existential' nothingness, 'through' or 'before' which material objects parade their presence" (p. 16). However, additionally, "thought is . . . able to 'curl back on itself', *self*-consciously, reflexively" (p. 16):

> When thought achieves this 'inward turn', then it may be said that the subject (knower) and the object (known) have fused or merged into a perfect unity, which yet preserves the duality of the original distinction within itself. (p. 16)

Having thus turned inward upon itself, the enquiring self finds as its object—itself—the nothingness of consciousness, a nothingness:

> [self-consciousness] is the absence of an awareness of any *thing* or *sensation;* it *is* a nothingness. When a human being successfully "reflects" on his self, reflexively captures his own intrinsically unique situation, he grasps (self-consciously) the nothingness of his existence as a "transcendental condition"—universal, necessary (a priori)—structuring his entire conscious—being/in/the/world. This ordinary level of recognition is the ground-source for his acute senso-cognitive awareness of loneliness. (pp. 17–18)

In short, when the mind introflects completely and successfully

> it becomes aware of a unified nothingness, it becomes reflexively conscious of its internal emptiness, and this directly results in the feeling of abandonment, emptiness, lack, in short, loneliness. (p. 20)

I pause here for some critical observations.

(1) The very possibility of this sort of pure introflection is much in doubt. As Hume famously remarked, "I never can catch *myself* at any time without a perception, and never can observe anything but the perception."[61]

(2) But granting that I can introflect/introspect and find only nothingness there, it does not follow that I feel lonely. The awareness of a nothingness is not itself loneliness,[62] and it does not necessarily produce loneliness: my own attempts to "catch myself" have produced a variety of emotions, including amusement at the difficulty of the undertaking and a calm, peaceful, open feeling. Those mystics who follow the Via Negativa do not seem to find loneliness to be a stumbling block. Descartes seems to grow more puzzled and perplexed as he focuses more and more upon himself, but there is no suggestion of loneliness. In short, if we attend to the phenomena of introflection, we do not find the inescapable loneliness of self-awareness insisted upon by Mijuskovic.

(3) Finally, even if it were true that introflection is inescapably lonely, unless there were some reason for calling introflection *primary,* more ultimate or real than extrospection, we would have no reason for calling loneliness the primary reality of human existence. The situation would just be that a person is capable of being with self in consciousness, which is lonely, or being with others extroflectively, which is not. And surely phenomenological attention to human consciousness does not reveal introflection to be its primary form: to the contrary, it is a rare and highly developed skill. The vast bulk of consciousness is intentionally directed outwards towards objects, whether things or other people, as Husserl, the patriarch of phenomenology, insisted.

Mijuskovic is certainly aware of extroflection, and characteristically, in acknowledging it, he manages to give it a lonely spin:

> Thought essentially "blows outwardly" (as well as inwardly); it posits an other than itself; and in so doing it recognizes the other as related to itself. Thus, simple, monadic consciousness, intrinsically unrelated, through freedom posits relations and/or the "other" as a means of escape from its solipsistic prison . . ." (p. 18)

Note the puzzling term 'posit' here: Mijuskovic is drawing on a theory of the origin of self-consciousness devised by the German idealist Johann Fichte (1762–1814):

> the ego (unconsciously) posits itself; next it thetically posits the 'other', or non-ego, as a sphere in opposition to itself; and finally (with the foregoing conditions being fulfilled), it is then able to return to itself, self-consciously. (Mijuskovic's account of Fichte, p. 16)

The original ego, as yet unconscious, is the primary source for both consciousness of self and consciousness of other, each of which develops out of it and in some sense comes "later"; it is all-encompassing and undifferentiated:

> At 'first'—logically, psychologically, genetically, temporally—the self is (a) simple; (b) objective; and (c) an absolute existence; it just is and it is everything because consciousness and being are identical. The other, by contrast, is reached by the transcending mechanism of free negativity, negation intrinsically generates otherness, difference . . . The other, as a meaning is generated . . . He exists only insofar as I exist and posit him. (pp. 77–78)

That an unconscious Everything, without differentiation, can do such things as "positing"—whatever exactly that is[63]—is very hard to grasp[64]; and how it can give away so much as to end up as (according to Mijuskovic's earlier doctrine) a "reflexive nothingness" is even more obscure. However let us see how the argument for our "transcendental loneliness" proceeds.

> loneliness is likewise an *a priori* synthetic pattern in which the monadic ego may be seen to posit the existence—possible or actual—of an other, a different, an alien consciousness in antithetic, but nevertheless essential, relation to its own existence. This is what I mean when I say that loneliness serves as the primary transcendental ground of human existence. (p. 73)

> As Fichte suggests, the lone ego is posited (structurally) prior to the other. (p. 49)

The objections to make here are two, and they both spring from Mijuskovic's tendency to shift back and forth between Fichte's primary (unconscious) ego and later self-conscious ego as suits his purposes.[65] As for the "lone ego" that Fichte actually holds to be prior to consciousness of the other, *it is simply unintelligible to call it lonely:* loneliness is a feeling, a conscious experience, whereas the primary ego is unconscious.[66] Moreover, whatever else it may involve, loneliness already involves the consciousness of other people, so that an undifferentiated plentitude of mental being could not feel the particular thing which is properly called loneliness.[67]

If we turn, however, to the self-conscious ego, the sort of entity that actually could in some intelligible sense feel loneliness, one notes that Mijuskovic's own account of Fichte has it coming "third," after other-consciousness ("finally, with the foregoing conditions being fulfilled, it is then able to return to itself, self-consciously"); hence on Fichte's view it would appear to be other-consciousness that has primacy of place over self-consciousness!

In fact, it makes a great deal more sense, logically, psychologically, and—why not?—"transcendentally," to hold that self-consciousness and consciousness-of-other develop together. Indeed, in another chapter, Mijuskovic insists (again with apparent inconsistency) on this very view:

> As Hegel expresses it, "self-consciousness exits in itself and for itself, in that, and by the fact that it exists for another self-consciousness"; that is to say, it *is* only by being acknowledged or "recognized" . . . We may conclude that in order to exist as a particular self-consciousness, the consciousness of the infant must be "recognized" by the alter-ego, the mother. (p. 75)

Self and other now appear to be mutually constitutive of each other. Furthermore, the actual development of the self is acknowledged by Mijuskovic to be psychologically dependent upon another:

> . . . once burgeoning infant consciousness has transcended its indistinct identification with the "oceanic feeling," it soon discovers that its own ego is genetically constituted by, and develops along with, the ego of a primary other. This other is, in most cases, the mother who, as an opposite center of consciousness and freedom, generally aids the infant's ego toward an awareness of its self. (p. 63)

From the very beginning of our being as a recognizable human self, then, we develop and define ourselves in relation to other people: right there, at the origin of consciousness and self, is . . . Mom.[68] Whence loneliness?

Let us turn now to Mijuskovic's claims about the essential nature of consciousness-of-others. Here he attempts to argue that loneliness is necessarily inescapable, that there is something inherent in encounter that renders it incapable of easing our loneliness—and not merely that such easing is rare and difficult. (Actually, he also argues the latter view—inconsistently—but I leave those arguments until the next chapter.)

Recall that Mijuskovic has claimed that the ego "posits" the other, an action which in some of his phrasings sounds like a creativo ex nihilo ("He exists only insofar as I exist and posit him."—p. 78). Mother, of course, is hardly created by baby, and even in baby consciousness it seems better to say that mother is "found," or better still, "assembled." However, even if one granted this act of creative positing, it would not follow that the other was unreal or unable to satisfy the need for companionship (as obviously Mothers do in fact do for many infants). Suppose a hiker is lost in the woods and, needing a shelter, builds (posits) one: now built, that shelter is fully real, and if the builder is even halfway skillful it really will shelter her. Mijuskovic needs more argument to move us from positing to loneliness.

It comes partly by gliding from one term to a different, more heavily loaded one. Consider the following:

> loneliness is likewise an *a priori* synthetic pattern in which the monadic ego may be seen to posit the existence—possible or actual—of an other, a different, an alien consciousness in antithetic, but nevertheless essential, relation to its own existence. This is what I mean when I say that loneliness serves as the primary transcendental ground of human existence. (p. 73)

Notice how "other" becomes "different" becomes "alien" becomes "antithetic" in this single sentence.[69] Note the same slide in the following version:

> Thus, the monadic, at first unrelated, point of consciousness strives to negate its restricted, empty unity by positing an other in relation to itself, an other which may be either a spatial object or an alien locus of consciousness . . . (p. 73)

Again, almost unnoticed, "other" has become "alien." But this is an illicit move: for "other" is by no means necessarily "alien." As Dilman observes in *Love and Human Separateness,* gratitude, which is a feeling of warm connection with another—certainly no form of loneliness!—inherently involves the awareness that an *other* has freely done us an important service. And the same holds true of all the other positive interpersonal emotions: love, admiration, amusement, etc. In short, the other is not logically the alien,[70] and indeed a great body of normal human experience denies this equation. How, then, can Mijuskovic justify his depressing view?

He attempts to do so by arguing that human interaction is inherently conflictual (and hence lonely):

conflict is necessary and eternal, i.e. it is an *a priori* synthetic structure or condition of being human . . . since this dual recognition [of one another] exists within a framework of combat, it follows, once again, that the ego is forced to regard himself as alone and lonely. (p. 79)

On what grounds is this claimed? Two, so far as I can tell. The first is a derivative of Hegel's famous analysis of the Master-Slave relationship:

> That each of us is alone is a tragedy. But when we attempt to reach the other, because no one wishes to be alone, we at once discover ourselves struggling against the other for domination, a supremacy which demands that the other *recognize* our own reflexivity while entirely subordinating his self-consciousness and freedom to us. We endeavor to force our antagonist to consciously acknowledge our self-consciousness as the primary, if not sole, reality. Meanwhile, we strive to transform the self of the other into merely possessing the status of an object, a thing devoid of consciousness (Hegel, Phenomenology of Mind, Master-slave). But in doing so, paradoxically enough, we further alienate ourselves from the other in the very process of trying to secure or reach him by attempting to compel him to submit to our "masterhood" (our self-consciousness). And yet, we cannot do other wise, for it is exactly because of our reflexive aloneness, constituting as it does the inner truth of our being, that self-consciousness cries out so desperately and yearningly to be admitted, by force if necessary, by the other. (p. 28)

But this is argument by stipulation—and exaggeration! The situation between two people no doubt approaches this in psychopathological cases, such as those discussed by Gregory Zilboorg and Freida Fromm-Reichman whom Mijuskovic cites; but both of those psychologists were careful to restrict their claims to extreme and pathological cases.[71] It may also be a perceptive account of such oppressive social structures as slavery. But as a necessary and apriori account of the structure of all interpersonal relations, it is simply false[72]: in the first place, the recognition we seek from others is often freely given without struggle; and if we must struggle for recognition, in the main we are content with recognition and not "mastery," to be respected as an equal and not to have "primacy." Moreover, even struggle and conflict between people do not seem to be in themselves lonely: there are pleasures, or at least satisfactions, in the pursuance of conflict—the sense of growth and mastery, the vigor of self-expression, the quickening hope of winning. And on a more introspective plane, if loneliness is a painful awareness of the absence of the other, conflict seems to be quite different—a painful fullness with another, as it were. In sum, the idea that lonely conflict is our inescapable plight with other people seems to be, in several senses, an apriori exaggeration.[73]

And Mijuskovic really knows that it is. Speaking of the "genesis of self" in infancy, he admits that, "the mother . . . as an opposite center of consciousness and freedom, generally aids the infant's ego toward an awareness of its self (p. 63)." A moment later, he is saying that

> The presence of the other not only provides a context of "reflection" and recognition for the self, through the mediating agency of the alien other, but—and perhaps more significantly—it also serves as a guarantee that the self is not abandoned, alone, in a foreign realm of being. (pp. 63–64)

In adult life, he admits, we can transcend our lonely origins into true encounter:

> Freedom . . . although structurally conditioned by aloneness, is manifested as a groping transcendence *beyond* the reality of isolation, it is an outward reaching toward (momentary) relatedness. When, and if, this outward seizure is temporarily accomplished—and it is never successfully achieved for long—then the unity of self-consciousness is effected; and this becomes an integrated or *reflexive unity,* one which carries the "alien" other back within self-consciousness without destroying the other's subjectivity, without turning him into an inhuman lifeless object, a thing. (p. 77)

But these admissions are clearly inconsistent with the exaggerated "philosophical" claims that loneliness is "the transcendental ground" of human existence and that "conflict is necessary and eternal, i.e. it is an *a priori* synthetic structure or condition of being human": for what can be "temporarily accomplished" can be accomplished, and is not foreclosed by "a priori structure".

As the dust settles slowly on the fallen arguments of these preceeding pages, what at last remains standing on the high clear plains of Truth? Self and Other, Solitude and Encounter. If you look carefully and keep faith with logic, you see them both. Metaphysics, Epistemology, Philosophy of Consciousness, all have enlarged our awareness of the dimensions of aloneness of the human psyche, but none have managed to prove the primacy of that aloneness over engagement. Let us turn now to the arguments from everyday experience.

CHAPTER 10

The Place of Solitude: Arguments from Experience

Philosophy consists in the assembling of reminders for a purpose.
—WITTGENSTEIN

Thee are experiences which seem to point beyond themselves. A hand trembles, a stone falls, and the heavens open. The arguments now to be considered find their beginnings in such experiences, moments which seem profoundly revelatory of the human condition. But what exactly is revealed? And how good are the arguments based upon those revelations? Is the primacy of aloneness over encounter *right there* in our very experience of the world, of other people—or only a short thought-step away? This is my subject for reflection. Much of the reflection will consist in remembering kinds of experience which loneliness can make us forget.

The Argument from Mere Self-Awareness

We have already met, in Tillich and Mijuskovic, the idea that mere awareness of our separate self-existence is, or automatically produces, a kind of ontic loneliness. Recall Tillich's lament:

> And being separated means being alone . . . [Man] is not only alone; he also *knows* that he is alone. Aware of what he is, he therefore asks the question of his aloneness. He asks why he is alone and how he can overcome his being alone. He cannot stand it; but he cannot escape it either.

Well, maybe sometimes, but not always and not necessarily. Tillich is a master, it seems to me, at taking one powerful progression of the psyche and bewitching us into seeing it as *the* progression of the (honest) psyche. Thus charmed, we forget the delightful sense of aloneness where no loneliness dwells. We also forget that self-awareness, even in its acute forms, is quite compatible with direct engagement with other people—indeed the latter is often the cause of the former. Moreover, as Dilman reminds us, the "distance" which awareness of separateness involves is in fact necessary for some of our most meaningful engagements:

> Just as my left hand cannot take what my right hand is giving, or my right hand give it to my left hand, so equally I cannot really love someone with whom I have identified myself to the extent that I do not feel her to have an identity apart from mine. The wonder of friendship and the magic of love depend on the separateness of friends and lovers; it is this which makes their response to one another a gift, something they can treasure. Without it, where the other person becomes a mere shadow or extension of one, one only loves oneself in her . . . For there to be real contact each person must have an independent identity, and each must be sufficiently autonomous to allow, accept, and indeed welcome the other person's independence, his or her separateness from him . . . human separateness becomes the space in which personal bonds may be forged.[1]

In the happy self-awareness of being recognized in a crowd by *my* friend, in the scarce-believing realization that she will stay by *me* through even this, Tillich's progression is demolished.

Even if self-awareness was inherently lonely, only if such experiences were more frequent, or perhaps more powerful, than engaged awareness of others could they establish the primacy of aloneness over encounter. But the frequency and power of these moments seem to be matters of individual difference, and not of the human condition.

Arguments from the Brevity of Encounters

Tillich seems to be aware of these objections, for he immediately advances a second argument:

> But is that really so? we ask. Did not God do better than that? Is our aloneness not largely removed in the encounter of the sexes? Certainly it is for hours of communion and moments of love. The ecstasy of love can absorb one's own self in its union with the other self. Separation seems to be overcome. But after such moments the isolation of self from self is more deeply felt than before, even to the

point of repulsion. We have given too much of ourselves, and now we want to take it back.[2]

So moments of communion are vastly outweighed in our ongoing lives by longer stretches of aloneness, an aloneness which those very moments of communion render deeper and more painful. Mijuskovic expresses a similar view when confronted with the undeniable reality of some encounters: "I do not wish to suggest that man is unable *temporarily* to alleviate his sense of loneliness but rather that the relief can never be permanent or even long lasting."[3] However, let us concentrate on the great theologian.

Notice that Tillich has focused upon a very particular kind of engagement—ecstatic loving communion, whether sexual or not—which seems to be by its nature only briefly sustainable (perhaps because of some psychic law of conservation of energy, perhaps because of the importance to the self of maintaining autonomy, as I suggested earlier). There are, however, friendly loving encounters of many kinds which are, though not so intense as ecstasy, strewn more regularly through our lives. Think of love as it exists within the context of a family, how many varieties of engagement—direct and indirect, continuing and interrupted, concentrated and diffuse—there are to this web of relationship. Reflecting upon the importance of the family in all known cultures, can we accept the idea that human encounters are too brief to constitute an equal place with aloneness?

Moreover, focusing upon "the ecstasy of love" produces a misleading picture of the prevalence of encounter in another way. As Walter Kaufmann cautioned in his introduction to Buber's *I and Thou:* "The total encounter in which You is spoken with one's whole being is but one mode of I-You. And it is misleading if we assimilate all the other modes of I-You to I-It."[4] It is not uncommon in the literature on solitude and loneliness to find poignant expressions of the idea that "real," "authentic," or "meaningful" encounters with other people are rare and brief. Although there is painful truth in these cries, they also seem to me to involve an exaggerated idea of "real encounter." My discussion with my doctor concerning the cough that will not go away, the grimacing moments when her nurse takes a blood sample, the halting conversation with the hitchhiker picked up on the way to work, the encouraging words to a student depressed by the difficulty of making sense of Kant—are these not real encounters with real people? There is nothing distant, fake, sham, manipulative, alienated, or neurotic about them. Their like constitute a large part of many of our days. I think that encounter is not briefer than aloneness.

As a closing word, Tillich has again told only one conclusion to his story. Focusing on a very real and painful sequel to intimacy, he leads us to forget a different but equally powerful and, I believe, equally common development: it can happen that the caresses of a lover, even simple words at parting, suffuse whole solitary days with warm feelings of connectedness: then the isolation of the self is not more deeply felt; then we do not want back what we have given.

Arguments from Impenetrability

The passage from Tillich just considered reveals a concern over penetration: the paragraph continues on that theme, offering another argument for the ultimacy of our aloneness:

> An expression of our desire to protect our aloneness is the feeling of shame. We are ashamed if our intimate self is opened, mentally as well as bodily. We try to cover our nakedness as Adam and Eve did after they had become conscious of themselves. Man and woman remain alone even in the most intimate union. They cannot penetrate each other's innermost center.[5]

The passage seems self-contradictory—at least if we ever do feel shame; for that would, on his view, entail that we have in fact been opened to our "innermost center." The last sentence also seems inconsistent with his previous admission that ecstatic moments of loving union do occur, albeit briefly. However, let us concentrate on the idea of impenetrability. It was a feeling that obsessed Proust: Albertine was for him a sealed envelope, "a stone which encloses the salt of immemorial oceans or the light of a star."

What is the meaning of this claim about impenetrability? Obviously it is not about physical penetration. Is it a claim about our emotional experience of other people? If so, as a universal phenomenological description it is one-sided; for although any sexually experienced adult will remember Proustian moments in sexual encounter, s/he will protest that also, sometimes—gloriously!—the existential emotional penetration of the other occurs: we feel open to our core with the other and we feel their mutual openness. "Our eyes did thread upon a common beam," and so did every vivid psychic pulse.

Nor should we think of "penetrability to the core" only in terms of sexual intimacy. Werther and Charlotte fell open to each other emotionally while gazing out of a window at a party:

> We went to the window. It was still thundering in the distance; a soft rain was pouring down over the country, and filled the air around us with delicious fragrance. Charlotte leaned on her elbow; her eyes wandered over the scene; she looked up to the sky, and then turned to me; her eyes were filled with tears; she put her hand on mine and said, "Klopstock!" I remembered at once that magnificent ode of his which was in her thoughts, and felt overcome by the flood of emotion which the mention of his name called forth. It was more than I could bear. I bent over her hand, kissed it in a stream of ecstatic tears, and again looked into her eyes. Divine Klopstock! If only you could have seen your apotheosis in those eyes![6]

Ordinary daily life brings its penetrations too: the boy runs around the corner SMACK into the table you moved while cleaning: in the instant you feel the pain! You clasp the sobbing child in urgent hugs of comfort. You echo almost fiercely his cries "it hurts!" with "I know! I know!" In this immediate empathy, who remains alone? Is there not a penetration to the aching core?

So there are experiences of impenetrability and experiences of penetrability. But what are we really talking about here, since "penetration" is a metaphor? And what about the complementary metaphor, "core"? I think that Dilman is right to interpret the metaphors in terms of deception and control[7]: it is always possible for a person either to lie to you about their "innermost" thoughts and feelings or to prevent you from finding them out by controlling their natural expressions.[8] A person exercising this kind of control, whether deliberately or automatically, is impenetrable.[9] Or rather, more or less impenetrable, since obviously there are a spectrum of responses, all the way from full gushing disclosure to stony silence. The philosophers of loneliness tend to emphasize engagements towards the opaque end of the scale, forgetting those at the clear end. Or, when they do speak of the in-between cases, those in which people are engaging with others yet exercising varying degrees of control over expression, they emphasize the aspect of control and omit the aspect of disclosure. Let us, however, remember Charlotte and Werther and the little boy, and the myriad daily ways in which we decline to exercise control over the expressions of our hearts.

There is another aspect to the idea of penetration which seems important for the philosophy of aloneness, however. "Impenetrable" is a judgment we make when we want to know someone's thoughts/ feelings but are thwarted. Recall that Proust's Marcel yearned to possess (and control) Albertine's soul. Now is it the case that *in general* we are in this frustrating situation with other people? I think not. Sometimes it happens, of course, but very often we get all we want or need of another soul by merely asking, even though this falls short of everything (full disclosure of the "core self"). After all, totally open encounter is exhausting, and quite unnecessary for many of our purposes: a certain degree of opacity is very functional and very agreeable. If people are not *totally* penetrable they are *tolerably* penetrable: we can see quite enough through the windows of the monads to suit our desires. The view that others are really, ultimately impenetrable must insist that our desires for disclosure characteristically are not met; and this does not seem to be true. Even with intimacy there are limits to the desirability of disclosure, as Blake warned:

> Never seek to tell thy love,
> Love that never told can be;
> For the gentle wind doth move
> Silently, invisibly.
>
> I told my love, I told my love,
> I told her all my heart,
> Trembling, cold, in ghastly fears,
> Ah! she doth depart.
>
> Soon as she was gone from me,
> A traveler came by,
> Silently, invisibly:
> He took her with a sigh.

("Never Seek to Tell Thy Love")[10]

Arguments from the Partiality and Incompleteness of Encounters

But how much, really, do you know about someone in knowing that they read Klopstock? Was not Werther's moment of penetration woefully incomplete as a contact with Charlotte, at least if we compare it to the fullness with which we are present to ourselves while alone? Do we ever really, fully, know anyone in the way we know ourselves? After all, that would involve communicating with them, and to what extent is this really possible?

I have referred to lines of argument and common themes: lest the reader doubt that philosophies of aloneness really do cluster and repeat in these ways, let me offer a collection of expressions of the idea that communication between people is in some deep sense impossible (with the implication that all encounters are radically incomplete):

Parkinson: "Loneliness begins with the recognition of one's singularity—the fact that a deep communication of one's self and recognition by others of its legitimacy is not fully possible."[11]

Eliot: "Everyone's alone—or so it seems to me. They make noises, and think they are talking to each other, they make faces, and think they understand each other. And I'm sure that they don't. Is that a delusion?[12]

Camus: "In the extremities of solitude, no one could hope for the help of his neighbor . . . If, by chance, one of us attempted to open his heart, to communicate something of his sentiment . . . he became aware then that the person he had spoken to and he were not speaking of the same thing. He, in effect, was expressing himself from the depth of long days of rumination and suffering, and the image which he wanted to convey had matured for a long time in the fire of waiting and passion. The other, on the other hand, was imagining a conventional emotion, the pain that is sold in the market, an everyday melancholy . . . the others were unable to find the real language of the heart . . ."[13]

Howard: "We can speak to ourselves, express ourselves, delight ourselves, and delude ourselves—in our own internal language. When we seek to share that language with another person, we discover that we can only partially communicate it. Our private speech suffers a loss in translation when it is put into the private language of another."[14]

Mijuskovic: "communication is at best a momentary or comforting illusion."[15]

Landau: "Such experiences of loneliness are rooted in our humanity, in the fact of our being born and dying alone, and in the absolute impossibility of achieving 'perfect' communication with others in the absolute and irrevocable loneliness of our separate existence."[16]

A number of different ideas jostle together in this collection of quotations (some of which focus on verbal communication while others are more general); I extract them as follows:

1. the experience of the moment is not fully (really) communicable to another
2. what can be communicated is a small part of what we are, both at the moment and as a historical being
3. there is a deep self underlying what we can communicate which is itself inaccessible to communication

Are these ideas, upon reflection, true or false? Insofar as they are true, do they serve to establish the conclusion that we are, most ultimately, alone?

(1) The claim that momentary experience is not fully communicable appears false. Didn't the boy succeed in screamingly communicating his feeling to me? When a shopper whose cart you have bumped glares at you, is there any doubt what s/he is feeling? One forgets sometimes how direct and complete nonverbal communication can be. And with regard to verbal communication, I think that those who insist upon its impossibility focus upon a rather complex and special kind of communication, the attempt to verbally *describe* one's feelings, and that this leads them to ignore other ways in which we use words to *express* feelings.[17] To see the difference, contrast the following communications:

Description: "I feel a strong desire that you give me the hammer immediately!"

Expression: "Gimme the hammer!!"

In the latter case, there seems no room for doubt about what the hammer-seeker is experiencing: if you are there—and we've all been there—you know exactly. There is nothing partial, incomplete, or unsatisfactory about "Gimme the hammer!" as a mode of communication. More reflexive descriptions, on the other hand, do seem, oddly enough, to allow of more uncertainty as to the exact nature of the feeling, perhaps owing to their reliance on general emotion terms like 'desire,' 'frustration,' 'anger,' 'apprehension,' etc. In fact, the most successful descriptions of feelings seem to be those that liken the experience to another, e.g., "at that moment I felt like a cold hose had been turned on me."[18] In any case, many communications, both verbal and nonverbal, leave no doubt in our minds about what another human being is experiencing.

(2) True, what is communicated is but a small fraction of what we are; but the conclusion about our ultimate aloneness doesn't follow. What we can give of ourselves and receive from others may be only part of the whole, but it is often totally engrossing; we feel absorbed and not isolated, mutually whole and not fragmented, together "all in all." You reveal to me, let us say, a familiar desire. I know that this desire is only part of what you are through time, but right now it is fully you, you are fully in it, and I am there in it with you. It does not just wash against my side, but floods through me. If I am not connecting, in this moment, with other feelings of yours, other moments of your inner time, that does not provide a reason for claiming that I am ALONE: for I can no more have fully present to me all the elements of my own self or the full array of beauties that surround me in the forest. In all three cases, turning attention from one thing to another is necessary in order to seize the whole; hence the inability to possess the other person without turning from moment to moment cannot prove the incompleteness of encounters in contrast to experiences of the self or nature.

(3) Is it true that there is a deeper self, inaccessible to full communication? In one sense, I believe that there is, but in that sense the inference to our ultimate aloneness is invalid. It is true that sometimes one does feel, in even the fullest encounters, a sense of an unreached beyond. This profound feeling especially moved Wordsworth: he approached it again and again, always with the reverent awe which these lines from "The Prelude" convey:

> . . . the soul
> Remembering how she felt, but what she felt
> Remembering not, retains an obscure sense
> Of possible sublimity, at which
> With growing faculties she doth aspire,
> With faculties still growing, feeling still
> That whatsoever point they gain, there still
> Is something to pursue.[19]

This feeling, which one author called the voice of man's eternal unfulfillment, can rise up in you as you gaze into a person's eyes. In spite of the direct openness between you, there is a sense of something more, a deeper place within, a different realm where something more complete would be possible. I know this feeling, and I suspect that it comprises the largest part of the wonder I feel at other people. I do not doubt that something "ultimate" is revealed in such moments.

But what is revealed is not, I think, our ultimate aloneness, and for two reasons. I believe that what is felt in these moments is the unlimitedness of the human potential for experience: I am somehow aware, even in this moment of sympathetic unity, of the great variety of other feelings you and I have had, might have had, yet may have. You open out in all directions. My wonder before this folded universe of possibilities, my sense of you reposing here among them only for a brief moment is what the sense of a "deeper, farther" self really comes to. In such moments you and I are uncapturable and incommunicable because of possibility, not because of inaccessability or opacity.

Secondly, reflecting upon the bearing of this awed experience on the question of the essential aloneness of human existence, we need to recall Berkeley's maxim (which I have used before), "that which bears equally hard on two contradictory opinions can be proof against neither."[20] Or three opinions. For the kind of awed experience of the other we have been discussing has its exact parallel in solitary experiences of nature and of the self. The same uncanny feeling can overcome you as you stare at a collection of boulders, somehow aware that vast unrealized possibilities lie accidentally frozen here. Or, when the self takes the inward turn, the sense of possibility and choice can overwhelm you with the incompletability which will forever characterize your attempts to articulate yourself. Awe before the other, awe before the self, awe before the world, each of these spring from a deep encounter with their objects, none of them vitiates or diminishes those encounters.

Collecting all these observations in a summary: the ways in which communicative encounters with other people are incomplete have either been falsely exaggerated by the lonely philosophers, or, when true, do not prove that aloneness is any more ultimate a state than encounter.

Arguments from Pain and Death

David Bakan remarks in *Disease, Pain and Sacrifice,* that

> Pain is the common companion of birth and growth, disease and death, and is a phenomenon deeply intertwined with the very question of human existence. It is among the most salient of human experiences; and it often precipitates questioning the meaning of life itself . . . Pain must, in some sense, be a touchstone for ultimate concern.[21]

A few pages later he insists that "pain is essentially lonely," "utterly lonely, without words of its own to describe it." As for the loneliness of death, consider this passage from Tillich:

> Above all, this is true of the loneliness in which we have to die. We remain alone in the anticipation of our death. No communication with others can remove this loneliness, as no presence of others in the actual hour of our dying can hide the fact that it is *our* death, and *our* death *alone,* that we die. In the hour of death we are cut off from the whole universe and everything in it. We are deprived of all things in the encounter in which we forgot our being alone. Who can stand this loneliness?[22]

These remarks express a line of thought which can be put as follows:

> *Premise One: Pain and dying are the salient facts of human existence; they embody or reveal what life most truly is for us.*
> *Premise Two: These experiences are inherently lonely/solitary.*
> *Conclusion: Human existence is ultimately lonely/solitary.*

This underlying argument echoes in many writings on pain and death, although it is only rarely that an author will actually spell out both premises; more commonly, it will simply be exclaimed that "we die *alone!*"[23]

This argument from pain and death is formally valid, but are its premises true? Each of them raises very large issues, both in psychology and philosophy, and a full consideration is out of the question here. Yet I think that enough may be said in a few pages to render both premises doubtful. Taking the first premise, and thinking of dying, it does not seem that either dying or the fear of death have the overpowering salience that Tillich and others seem to attribute to them. Certainly one's dying and one's confrontation with its inexorable import are profound psychic times—only a fool would deny it. But the argument needs to claim more than this if it is to establish the ultimate solitariness of human existence: it needs to claim that dying in some sense outweighs other life-experiences, individually and cumulatively, that in the experience of dying all else stands revealed as secondary. And this does not seem acceptable, so long as we restrict ourselves to the actual experience of dying.[24]

If one were to speak more abstractly of death, not as a type of experience but as fact about human existence, the question of salience would of course have to be rethought. Socrates insisted in the *Phaedo* that the true philosopher is always preparing for death. Christian philosophers have found in death-and-resurrection the greatest "good news" about human existence. Heidegger argued that authenticity involves continual awareness of Dasein's existential-ontological structure as a being-towards-death. However, none of these profound claims seems to me to bear on the argument we are discussing. Socrates's concern was with perfecting the soul for its future life, a concern similar to that of the Christian thinkers. Heidegger's position is more complicated (and opaque), but he explicitly distinguishes the existential analysis of death from the psychology of dying, the meaning of death from its (mere) happening as a phenomenon.[25] None of these philosophers are speaking of death as an experience, but it is in this sense that we must take it in the argument under consideration; for otherwise the claims made do not engage with the second premise, which speaks of experience.

With reference to the overpowering salience of pain in human life, this is certainly a terrible contingent fact about the lives of many people, for reasons of disease, war, famine, and cruelty. However, it seems overly pessimistic (indeed politically irresponsible) to convert such tragedies—even those afflicting whole peoples—into an existential plight, the salient part of the existential condition of being human. Too much human pain is gratuitous, surplus, eliminable; and what cannot be eliminated can be mitigated. Reflecting upon the surest agency of mitigation returns me to the question of our ultimate aloneness; it strikes me that the best "existential schema" of human pain might be: Pain, Cry for Help, Help. Seen this way, pain becomes a bridge to the other, rather than a barricade for the lone self.[26]

Which takes us to the second premise of the original argument: are pain or dying inherently lonely/solitary experiences? Perhaps pain is. Bakan maintains that "the actual experience of pain is utterly lonely, without words of its own to describe it." True, we may borrow words like "dull" or "sharp" from the other sense modalities, but most basically it is expressed "in those sounds one is able to make before learning to speak, especially the sound uttered at birth, the occasion when one is ripped from union into a condition of physical individuality."[27] For another thing,

> pain differs from the other sense modalities in being considerably less informative about the external world. It does not tell us anything at all about that world's nature. The information contributed by pain is location within the body. . . . The blindness, as it were, of pain to the external world is another aspect of its utter association with the single individual.[28]

On the other hand, Bakan reminds us of "The Phenomenally Ego-Alien Nature of Pain" (his section heading), the way in which pain is experienced by the ego as an "it" separate from itself: "Phenomenally, however, pain appears to the conscious ego as not a part of itself, but as alien to it, as something happening to the ego, with the ego, as it were, the victim of external forces . . ."[29] This acute observation puts me in mind of a personal experience of pain which, as I reflect upon it, seems to cast in doubt the inherent loneliness of pain. I lay in bed for a whole day, flattened by a leaden ball of visceral pain which from time to time rolled out terrible waves of dizzying nausea. But I was lucky to have sitting with me, holding my hand, a loving friend. When a wave would begin, I would groan (uncourageously) "its coming again!", and she would hold my hand tightly and urge, "hold onto me, we'll ride through it!" And it seemed to me, as the wave engulfed me, that *we* were together *here,* as *it* was coming up over me from *down there,* as though we were together on some terrible shore, the waves breaking first over me. Feeling the great sucking force, I did not think of letting lose her grip.

Is dying inherently lonely? No doubt it is often so, but must it be? Norbert Elias's analysis in *The Loneliness of the Dying* is very insightful on this question. He points out that the frequent loneliness of dying persons in modern Western cultures is conditioned by a number of factors, including:

> (1) The repression, on both a psychological and social level of thoughts about death.

(2) The corresponding and related secrecy and privacy and hiding which these compel us to impose upon the dying.

(3) General taboos on the expression of strong spontaneous feelings, accompanied by the absence or artificiality of standard or ritualized expressions of empathy with the dying.

(4) The development of highly technical health-care systems whose complicated and aggressive treatments require a high degree of social isolation in hospitals and intensive care units, administered not by loving relatives but by technically oriented and generally busy staff.

(5) The high degree and specific pattern of individualization in our culture. The image of death in a person's memory is very closely bound up with his image of himself, of human being, prevalent in his society. In more developed societies people see themselves broadly as fundamentally independent individual beings, as windowless monads, as isolated 'subjects', to whom the whole world, including all other people, stands in the relationship of an 'external world'.[30]

Elias argues that none of these five factors are apriori givens, and indeed have not operated in all cultures at all times. Although he thinks that the psychological repression of death is probably coeval with the awareness of death in human consciousness, the "social repression" of death can be seen to be both fairly recent (it was largely absent in medieval Western society, for example) and culturally specific, as the study of contemporary tribal societies reveals. As for the third and fourth factors, both emotional expressiveness and modes of health care can be easily shown to be society-specific. Regarding the last factor, which we have been investigating throughout this book, Elias believes that the vision of the essential loneliness of the self in an isolated internal world is to a considerable extent illusory:

> Every human being lives on 'external' plants and animals, breathes 'external' air and has eyes for 'external' light and colours. He or she is born of 'external' parents and loves or hates, makes friends or enemies of 'external' people. On the level of social praxis all this is known to people as a matter of course. [However] in more detached meditation this experience is often repressed.[31]

The lesson Elias draws is that "the idea that one dies alone matches the accentuation in this period of the feeling that one lives alone." But dying can be, and often is, even in our own society, a progression into deeper engagement: it is a time of comforting, reassuring, and closeness, a reaffirmation of the meanings that have bound the dying person's life to one's own, and so a rich experience of interpersonal meaning.[32] One need not die alone, as Elias reminds us by contrasting modern technical-intensive medical treatments of the dying, which often involve reducing or preventing intimate contact between loved ones in the interests of efficiency and routine, with care in economically less developed regions and times:

> family members crowd around the stricken person, bring food, administer medicine, clean and wash the patient and perhaps, bringing some of the dirt from the street to the sickbed, tend the patient with unwashed hands. Possibly they hasten the end, for all this is not particularily hygienic. Possibly their presence delays death, for it can be one of the last great joys for dying people to be cared for by family members and friends—last proof of love, a last sign that they mean something to other people.[33]

Finally, let us remember that the deathbed has traditionally been the time for especially meaningful words between people, as this story from Chuang Tzu illustrates:

> Suddenly Master Lai grew ill. Gasping and wheezing, he lay at the point of death. His wife and children gathered round in a circle and began to cry. Master Li, who had come to ask how he was, said, "Shoo! Get Back! Don't disturb the process of change!".
>
> Then he leaned against the doorway and talked to Master Lai. "How marvelous the Creator is! What is he going to make of you next? Where is he going to send you? Will he make you into a rat's liver? Will he make you into a bug's arm?"
>
> Master Lai said, "A child, obeying his father and mother, goes wherever he is told, east or west, south or north. And the yin and yang—how much more are they to a man than father or mother! Now that they have brought me to the verge of death, if I should refuse to obey them, how perverse I would be! . . . I think of heaven and earth as a great furnace, and the Creator as a skilled smith. Where could he send me that would not be all right? I will go off to sleep peacefully, and then with a start I will wake up.[34]

These reflections on the great mysteries of pain and death are mere beginnings towards a philosophical vision, I know. Yet they seem enough to establish that those phenomena do not prove, as Tillich and others have suggested, the ultimate aloneness of human existence.

The results of these two chapters of analysis and recollection can be expressed briefly: the view that aloneness, whether as loneliness or as solitude, is the deepest, truest most ontically primary state of human being cannot be sustained by argument. Partially blinded by the awesome power of loneliness, held fast by a horde of partial metaphors, provoked thereby into careless disregard for many experiences to-hand, goaded into exaggeration[35] and impelled by a dark defiant pride, Proust and the others have taken the half of human reality for the whole.

But they have seen deeply into their half, and made its truths vivid. It would be a waste of time, therefore, to elaborate the ways in which Lawrence, Halmos, Buber, and others are equally guilty of taking their half for the whole when they insist upon the primacy of encounter in human existence; for we would find the same partial selectivity of cases, the same exaggeration, the same sliding from metaphysics to experience, the same bewitchment by metaphors—only turned inside out, as it were. However, a few brief illustrations are called for.

Consider Ignacio Gotz's argument, some years ago, that, far from being the tragic destiny of man, loneliness is the fixation on an illusion motivated by bad faith. He wrote,

> loneliness involves a distinctive realization of one's willingness to entertain the mood, one's choice or willful acceptance of the feeling of grief and depression . . . loneliness involves bad faith in the Sartrean sense. . . . If the sadness felt upon separation or upon awakened solitude endures, it is because one acquiesces in the mood, chooses its continuance, and clothes oneself in mourning.[36]

This is a choice for illusion, he argues, because, "The truth is, rather, that I am within easy reach of the other":

> Loneliness, therefore, whatever the solitary context in which it arises, always implies bad faith, that is, the awareness that it is my own offspring, that it involves a preference of my self in narcissistic infatuation, and that it can be dissipated by my own reversal of my previous choice.[37]

These assertions are based on the unacceptable premise that "mental solitude," because it is mental, must always be a matter of one's choice; they also ignore the points Mijuskovic et al. make about the ways in which we trick ourselves into thinking we have engaged with another person. The only honest thing to do during many lonely times is to accept the feelings of loneliness; for very often there simply is no one who can ease the pain (think of an elderly person, for example, whose friends are all dead and whose children live far away). When Gotz says, "I am within easy reach of the other," we are hearing the same kind of exaggeration of which Mijuskovic, Tillich, and Proust are guilty, turned the other way.

Heidegger says in *Being and Time* that "Being-alone is a deficient mode of Being-with." On what grounds? Two, so far as I can determine, one focusing upon actual experience and the other upon philosophically revealed implications. The first emerges in his discussion of the nature of everyday experience. "Proximally and for the most part Dasein is fascinated with its world," a world of objects which present themselves not as alien "external things" but as "to-hand." However, upon closer reflection,

> In our 'description' of that environment which is closest to us—the work-world of the craftsman, for example,—the outcome was that along with the equipment to be found when one is at work, those Others for whom the 'work' is destined are 'encountered too'. If this is ready-to-hand, then there lies in the kind of Being which belongs to it (that is, in its involvement) an essential assignment or reference to possible wearers, for instance, for whom it should be 'cut to the figure'. Similarly, when material is put to use, we encounter its producer or 'supplier' as one who 'serves' well or badly. When, for example, we walk along the edge of a field but 'outside it', the field shows itself as belonging to such-and-such a person, and decently kept up by him . . . The boat anchored at the shore is assigned in its Being-in-itself to an acquaintance who undertakes voyages with it; but even if it is a 'boat which is strange to us', it is still indicative of Others.[38]

Here, it seems to me, Heidegger has perceptively noticed a common though non-obvious element of solitary experience, but then exaggerated its experiential import. As a carpenter who has built five houses over twenty years, I feel qualified to speak as a craftsman. As I reflect upon the experience of building, what its brand of consciousness is like through the minutes of the hours, I do find the reference to Others of which Heidegger speaks:

> They *seem to have milled these two-by-fours carelessly.*
> *Damn:* someone *standing on the left side of this mitred joint will see a gap.*
> We *will appreciate the enduring look of this brickwork as* we *sit by the fire.*

But for me these have usually been passing thoughts, hardly "constitutive of the structure of the experience" of building; they come and go, while all the time my deeper absorption is in the materials themselves and the geometries of their concatenation. Each two-by-four becomes a distinct, individual, self-contained presence, confronting me with its peculiarities of grain and warp; it is itself, not redolent of others. So too with mitre and brickwork: one becomes absorbed in the exact angle of the mitre, applying the square and trimming fractions until a single smooth line bisects a ninety degree angle; brickwork is a world of unyielding brick and yielding mortar, now too hard, now too soft, tapped together under the unforgiving rule of LEVEL and PLUMB. If I should take a day off building to walk across the fields towards the shore, I might indeed wonder whose field I now cross, but then attention would turn to the grasses, wildflowers, birds, and insects, the green lichen on old fence posts. There is a place along the shore where an old dinghy lies rotting in the sun: I have often wondered who originally owned it, but more often followed it in imagination back to the tree, musing upon the migrations of substances. On the level of experience, then, there are *threadings* of engagement (Being-with) in solitude, as I noted in part 1, but not, therefore, a *structuring* of solitude by engagement: there is sometimes, perhaps even frequently, the "encounter" Heidegger speaks of, but not an "essential assignment or reference." Moreover, one must not ignore the complementary threadings of engagement by modes of disengagement if one is to adequately assess the import of Being-with.

If, that is, Being-with translates into engagement. The other line of argument for the deficiency of Being-alone leads me to wonder whether this translation is correct:

> Being-with is an existential characteristic of Dasein even when factically no Other is present-at-hand or perceived. Even Dasein's Being-alone is Being-with in the world. The Other can *be missing* only *in* and *for* a Being-with. Being-alone is a deficient mode of Being-with; its very possibility is the proof of this. On the other hand, factical Being-alone is not obviated by the occurrence of a second example of a human being 'beside' me, or by ten such examples. Even if these and more are present-at-hand, Dasein can still be alone.[39]

What the first sentence seems to say is that the possibility of (direct) encounter is part of the essence of man,[40] not something inferentially risky—a claim which Wittgenstein (and I) would endorse. The next two sentences appear to combine a logical and a phenomenological point: "alone" contains within its meaning, as being-alone contains within its felt experience, reference to another. The logical point can be accepted, but note that the phenomenological claim holds only if 'Being-alone' = 'loneliness'[41]; for only then is it true that the missingness of the other is right there in the experience—the key point in Heidegger's argument ("being-alone" in the ordinary sense, need not involve any thought of any other whatsoever). But then all his argument succeeds in proving is that *loneliness* is a "deficient mode of

Being-with"; solitude remains untouched, and the great values it brings to us remain underived and untarnished.[42]

What is the place of aloneness in human existence? Given the failure of arguments to the contrary, I am inclined to accord to it an equal status with encounter. Both are states of Being and Knowledge, both are full of illusions and lies.

CHAPTER 11

Objections to Solitude: Some History

And the Lord God said, It is not good that the man should be alone; I will make him an help meet for him.

GEN. 2:18

S ince the Sixth Day, objections to solitude have been gathering. From the stern warning of Ecclesiastes,

> Woe to him that is alone! For, if he falleth, there is none to raise him up (Eccles. 4:10)

to the terse medieval French proverb,

> Homme seul est viande aux loups!
> (A man alone is meat for wolves!)

to the moralizing of Dr. Johnson,

> There is a higher order of men . . . (who) ought to consider themselves as appointed the guardians of mankind: they are placed in an evil world, to exhibit public examples of good life; and may be said, when they withdraw to solitude, to desert the station which Providence assigned them.[1]

criticisms have been launched on grounds of prudence, sanity, and morality: solitude is empty, pointless, vain, foolish, lonely, and danger-ous; it is unnatural, morbid, and pathological; it is self-indulgent, selfish, escapist, and evasive of social responsibility; (more recently) it is valued only in modern alienated capitalist cultures as a relief from degradation and hostility (even there, available only to the exploiting classes); (most recently) it is a male value, redolent of male privilege and male relational incapacity, irrelevant for post-modern women. Sign of personal weakness and moral blame, sign of ill-deserved status, sign of blindness, delusion, and folly,

> O Solitude!
> Where are the charms
> That sages have seen in thy face? (Cowper)[2]

But do the charges stick? Are the "reasons" given sound? I want to probe the logic of these arguments, to dig down to their foundations and test for strength. I am particularly curious as to how the great solitaries have responded to these charges, and how their responses measure up.

Before logic, however, some history. Criticisms of solitary withdrawal belong to a long debate in Western culture, a running argument concerning the competing claims of the "Active Life" and the "Contemplative Life," as the two options were traditionally called. The conflict between these two "lives" is already discernible in the two sources of Occidentalism, Greco-Roman culture and Judeo-Christian religion. Succeeding centuries articulated and elaborated the conflict, reframing it to address their own particular concerns. It will benefit us to survey briefly some of the high points of that history, by way of providing a background for the logical investigation to come.

The preclassical origins of Greek culture must be inferred from the writings of Homer and Hesiod, each writing around the end of the eighth century BC, but perfecting traditions of poetry that were already centuries old. There is certainly little solitude in Homer: his muse sings of the battles and wanderings of princes and warriors banded together, and separation from the band—even with a Briseis or a Calypso—proves unsatisfying.[3] Hesiod, on the other hand, celebrates the sober simple life of the independent Greek farmer, whose Works and Days ought to be devoted, insists Hesiod, to frugal self-sufficiency, with no time for convivial sociality:

> Walk right on past the blacksmith's shop
> with its crowds and its gossip
> for warmth, in the winter season, when the cold
> keeps a man from working.[4]

Hesiod's farmer was no Thoreau at the pond, to be sure: he had a few hired hands, as well as a prudently chosen wife, and he valued his neighbors highly: yet all are seen through the shrewd eyes of a self-centered individual, who sees even brother and wife primarily as means to his own economic ends.[5] The picture painted conveys a sense of disengagement, though one limited by considerations of utility.

During the classical period (roughly 600–400 BC) great emphasis was placed upon the citizen's full participation in the affairs of the polis; as Pericles declaimed in the *Funeral Oration,* "a man who takes no concern for the good of the polis we hold to be good for nothing." But the philosophers also spoke for Greek culture, and they almost invariably identified the highest human good with solitary contemplation. Plato is an interesting example: *The Republic* seems to make no provision for solitude whatsoever, yet within its framework the highest life possible is that of the philosopher-king, and the animating core of their lives is the solitary contemplation of the eternal Forms. Plato no doubt intended this path to be taken by only a select few, but his beautiful descriptions of contemplation gave such experiences a much wider appeal.[6]

Aristotle incorporates both sides of the debate within his works. Man is "the animal who lives in a polis," and therefore anyone who lives alone must be "either a beast or a god." This philosopher of the polis devotes his *Nicomachean Ethics* to the investigation of moral virtue, which turns out to be "the settled disposition to choose the mean [in passion and action], relative to us, as the man of practical wisdom would determine it" (Book II).[7] The passions and actions discussed are almost entirely social—fear in battle rather than fear of growing old, generosity towards others rather than generosity towards one's own failings. The sense is of a thoroughly social animal. However, in the final chapters of Book X it is solitary contemplation that emerges as the highest good for man:

> If happiness is activity in accordance with virtue, it is reasonable that it should be in accordance with the highest virtue; and this will be that of the best thing in us. Whether it be reason or something else that is this element which is thought to be our natural ruler and guide and to take thought of things noble and divine, whether it be itself also divine or only the most divine element in us, the activity of this in accordance with its proper virtue will be perfect happiness. That this activity is contemplative we have already said.[8]

How contemplation and action are to be harmonized in the citizen's life, Aristotle does not say.

A few centuries later in Rome, the debated options became vigorous public service versus retirement to the country seat. Horace spoke for one side in the *Second Epode,* assimilating pastoral retirement to the Golden Age of mankind:

Happy the man who, far away from business cares,
Like the pristine race of mortals,
Works his ancestral acres with his steers,
From all money-lending free;
Who is not, as a soldier, roused by the wild clarion,
Nor dreads the angry sea;
He avoids the Forum and proud thresholds
Of more powerful citizens.[9]

Virgil, Pliny, and Seneca also celebrated the leisure, safety, rest, and freedom for study that solitary withdrawal provided—although the country estates they considered retreats were certainly not places of utter solitude, dependent as they were upon serfs and slaves.[10] On the other side of the debate were Scipio, Cato, and Cicero, the latter's *De Officiis* becoming a standard source for later critics of solitude:

> Since, as Plato has admirably expressed it, we are not born for ourselves alone, but our country claims a share of our being, and our friends a share; and since, as the Stoics hold, everything that the earth produces is created for man's use; and as men, too, are born for the sake of men, that they may be able mutually to help one another; in this direction we ought to follow Nature as our guide, to contribute to the general good by an interchange of acts of kindness, by giving and receiving, and thus by our skill, our industry, and our talents to cement human society more closely together, man to man.[11]

Turning to our other "original source," ancient Judaism emphasized the essential communal bonds of the chosen people, as well as the constant presence of a personal God. Yet a kind of solitude of a people is celebrated in the desert, as Sayre observes:

> the desert is the privileged place of retreat where direct communication with God is achieved, and where the persecuted Hebrew people are free from the oppressive yoke of pagan society. It is in the wilderness that God speaks to Moses from the burning bush, that the chosen people are saved from slavery in Egypt, and that Moses receives the laws which will serve as the basis for the new nation in Palestine. There also the prophets receive the word of God.[12]

The association of wilderness solitude with divine contact thus made retreat available to both individuals and communities (such as the Essenes) as a historically validated path.

New Testament Christianity preached loving service and conversion, apparently leaving little room for solitude. And yet there were the examples of John the Baptist and Christ himself, each receiving divine revelations during trials in the desert. Later the Desert Fathers would seek to replicate this pattern of trial and enlightenment in solitude, referring to themselves as athletes and warriors. They would also cite the story of Mary and Martha, which became a cornerstone in monastic defenses of the solitary life:

> As they were travelling, He entered a certain village; and a lady named Martha entertained Him at her home. And she had a sister called Mary, who, seating herself at the Lord's feet, listened to His words. But Martha was over-busy with much serving; and standing before Him she exclaimed, "Lord, is it no matter to Thee that my sister has left me to attend to things alone? Tell her then to help me." "Martha, Martha," the Lord answered her, "thou art anxious and troubled about many things, while there is need of only a few, or of only one. For Mary has chosen the good part, which shall not be taken away from her." (Luke 10:38–42)

Critics of solitary withdrawal could thus be likened to Martha, anxious and troubled about unessential things when only loving attendance upon God (in solitary prayer) was necessary. But, responded the clerics in the towns, did not St. John ask, "for he that loveth not his brother whom he hath seen, how can he love God whom he hath not seen?" (I John 4:20). And so the argument went, each side finding its sources in the Holy Book.

The period between these discussions in the first four centuries AD and Petrarch's *De Vita Solitaria* in the fourteenth century saw a breakdown of law and security in Europe so extreme as to render solitary withdrawal prohibitively dangerous: man alone *was* food for wolves, the prey also of robbers and Vikings. Within the newly triumphant church, consolidation and orthodoxy were the concerns of the day, fought out in the great councils. However the same period saw monasticism become firmly established through the organizational genius of Pachomius, St. Basil, and St. Benedict. New institutions, but the debate continued. St. Basil forbade his monks to retreat into solitude, insisting that "the life of solitude violated the divine law of love and was injurious to the soul of the solitary in nursing a sense of self-sufficiency and spiritual pride."[13] St. Benedict, on the other hand, still accorded the highest virtue to the anchorite, although he cleverly insinuated the necessity of monastic preparation:

> It is recognized that there are four kinds of monks. The first are the Cenobites: that is, those who live in a monastery under a Rule or an abbot. The second kind is that

of Anchorites, or Hermits, who not in the first fervour of conversion, but after long trial in the monastery, and already taught by the example of many others, have learnt to fight against the devil, are well prepared to go forth from the ranks of the brotherhood to the single combat of the desert. They can now, by God's help, safely fight against the vices of their flesh and against evil thoughts singly, with their own hand and arm and without the encouragement of a companion.[14]

The apparent conflict between solitary withdrawal and Christian service troubled other church fathers as well, notably St. Jerome, St. Augustine, and Gregory the Great. St. Jerome repeatedly praised withdrawal:

O desert, enamelled with the flowers of Christ. O solitude where those stones are born of which in the *Apocalypse* is built the city of the Great King! . . . how long, brother, wilt thou remain in the shadow of roofs, and in the smoky dungeon of cities? Believe me, I see more of the light.[15]

Yet he was not unaware of the objection of social irresponsibility, writing sympathetically to a friend who had returned reluctantly from solitude to the life of clerical duty,

I have passed through troubles like yours myself. Now it is a widowed sister who throws her arms around you. Now it is the slaves who cry: "To what master are you leaving us?" Now it is a nurse bowed with age, and a body servant loved only less than a Father, who exclaim: "Only wait till we die, and follow us to our graves." Perhaps, too, an aged mother, recalling the lullaby with which she once soothed you, adds her entreaties.[16]

St. Jerome insisted, however, that

the love of God and the fear of hell will easily break such bonds. . . . [the] battering ram of natural affections will recoil powerless from the wall of the Gospel.[17]

This exhortation may strike us as distinctly un-Christian in its cold lovelessness, but it carried weight with contemporary readers. Tales like the following were told with approval, and taken together they provided a body of response to one perennial objection to solitude:

When Melania lost her husband and two out of her three sons within the same week, "not a tear fell; she stood immovable, and falling at Christ's feet, as if she were laying hold on Him herself, she smiled: 'More easily can I serve Thee, O Lord, in that Thou hast relieved me of so great a burdern.'"[18]

To an intellectual Christian like St. Augustine, the call of contemplation could not be dismissed; he devoted a great deal of energy to harmonizing its claims with those of loving service, most notably in an ingenious allegorical reading of the biblical story of Jacob, Leah, and Rachel (Gen. 29–30). Jacob, journeying into "the land of the people of the east" finds an older kinsman, Laban, who has two daughters, Leah and Rachel: "Leah was tender eyed; but Rachel was beautiful and well favoured." Jacob falls in love with Rachel, and agrees to work seven years for her hand. When the time for payment comes, however, Laban deceives him, sending to the dark tent on the wedding night the older sister Leah. When Jacob discovers the trick next morning and complains, Laban insists that the younger sister cannot be married before the older; however, if Jacob will keep Leah and work seven more years, Rachel may be his. So things come to pass. St. Augustine's interpretation of the story is succinctly summarized by Jacob Zeitlin:

> Well might Jacob be in love with Rachel, for she is the more beautiful, signifying "the hope of the eternal contemplation of God, accompanied with a sure and delightful perception of truth . . . This is the beloved of every pious student, and for this he serves the grace of God . . . A man would desire, if it were possible, to obtain at once the joys of lovely and perfect wisdom, without the endurance of toil in action and suffering; but this is impossible in mortal life." Jacob is therefore compelled first to marry Leah, by whom is figured the action of our mortal human life, "in which we live by faith, doing many painful tasks without knowing what benefit may result from them to those in whom we are interested." Leah is said to have weak eyes because "the purposes of mortals are timid and our plans uncertain," but it is necessary in the discipline of man that "the toil of doing the work of righteousness should precede the delight of understanding the truth." When we find Jacob at length married to both Rachel and Leah, there can be no doubt as to the meaning of it. It is clear that "the possession of the lovely form of knowledge will be in this world accompanied by the toils of righteousness."[19]

However, opposites are not easy to harmonize, and St. Augustine's sense of a deeper conflict emerges in the following rather evasive pronouncement:

> Holy leisure is longed for by the love of truth; but it is the necessity of love to undertake requisite business. If no one imposes this burden upon us, we are free to sift and contemplate truth; but if it be laid upon us, we are necessitated for love's sake to undertake it. And yet not even in this case are we obliged to relinquish the sweets of contemplation; for were these to be withdrawn, the burden might prove more than we can bear.[20]

The basic Christian objection to solitary withdrawal, that it foreclosed the possibility of loving service, was acknowledged by Gregory the Great, who reluctantly abandoned contemplation to assume the Papacy in AD 590. Hopefully, wrote Gregory, the active and contemplative lives can be combined, but the former must take precedence if it calls: for

> Who that knows God approaches his kingdom unless he has first labored well? Without contemplation one may enter the heavenly country, if one has not failed in the performance of good works; but without the active life one may not enter.[21]

Moreover, Gregory observed, the mind can enjoy true contemplative rapture only at uncertain intervals and for a brief span of time:

> For in the active life the mind is stablished without failing, but from the contemplative, being overcome by the load of its infirmity, it faints away. For the first endures more steadfastly in proportion as it opens itself to things about it for our neighbor's weal; the latter falls away the more swiftly, in proportion as passing beyond the barriers of the flesh, it endeavors to soar up above itself. The first directs its way through level places, and therefore plants the foot of practice more strongly; but the other, as it aims at heights above itself, the sooner descends wearied of itself.[22]

Then too, not all men are fitted for contemplation, which can actually be dangerous for the ill-equipped:

> There be some, who are quite unable to behold the world above, and spiritual things, with the eye of discernment, yet enter upon the heights of contemplation, and therefore by the mistake of a perverted understanding, they fall away into the pit of misbelief . . . When thou art not qualified for the contemplative life by a fitting degree of discretion, keep more safely the active life alone [so that thou mayest] be able to enter the kingdom of heaven at least with one eye.[23]

By the time Petrarch wrote *De Vita Solitaria* in 1346, accordingly, he was able to draw upon two long traditions of (de)valuing solitude. Much of his treatment was not new. A standard way of defending a course of action was to cite famous characters who had chosen that course, and over a third of Petrarch's book is a compilation of brief case histories of famous solitaries in pagan and Christian antiquity (often dubious, as in "Of Romulus, Achilles, and Hercules, who loved solitude"). When he defends solitude by attacking the evils of city life (recall "the busy man") one thinks of Seneca and St. Jerome, and his insistence on the propitiousness of solitude for leisurely scholarship recalls Scipio. What is new in his treatment of the subject, according to his translator, Jacob Zeitlin, is "the establishment of self-cultivation as an adequate guiding motive in life."[24] In words foreshadowing Emerson, Petrarch demands that men "follow the impulse of their genius." His own choice is for solitude, but he allows that this may not be the proper path for everyone: indeed the title of one chapter announces that, "The retired life, especially to men unversed in literature, is heavier than death and seems calculated to bring on death."[25] Again and again, after making spirited universal claims, Petrarch retreats into words like the following: "But I am not so much proposing a rule for others as exposing the principles of my own mind. If it commends itself to anyone, let him follow its suggestion."[26] Our interest in this new strain of individualism is in its provision of a new way of replying to Cicero's objection that men have duties of service to state and friends, and to the Christian objection that solitude is inconsistent with the injunction to love one's neighbour. These objections merit response, but Petrarch's actual responses seem more like special pleading:

> I should not mind, I confess, to be of service to as many as possible or even, in Ovid's words, to be a bearer of health to the entire world; but the first is in the power of only a few, the last of Christ alone. I would yield so far to persons of a contrary opinion as to admit that whoever is in a place of safety sins against the law of nature if he does not offer what aid he can to the struggling. But for me, who have myself been hitherto struggling as in a great ship-wreck, it is enough to pray for the aid of him who is alone able to provide aid in our need. . . . I could wish to have everybody, or at least as many as possible, gain salvation with me. But in the end what do you expect me to say? It is enough for me, yea, a cause of great happiness, if I do not perish myself.[27]

Elsewhere he pictures the life of the solitary man as filled with prayers for charity and divine mercy towards his neighbors, thus availing himself of the traditional monastic justifications. But his spirit is not in these defenses, and he even calls them "digressions":

> Do you see how I have striven with a roundabout profusion of words to reenter into favor with the man of action? But it is now time to set a limit to these digressions. I shall return to myself and to solitude.[28]

It is self-rewarding scholarship and the freedom of rambling through nature that Petrarch loves, not pious adoration of the Divinity or anchoritic intercessive prayer:

> How much value, my father [Jesus], do you set upon these common things: to live according to your pleasure, to go where you will, to stay where you will; in the spring to repose amid purple beds of flowers, in the autumn amid heaps of fallen

leaves; to cheat the winter by basking in the sun and the summer by taking refuge in cool shades, and to feel the force of neither unless it is your choice![29]

Effectively, his treatise unlinked solitude from both Divine and social duty, though the generally accepted nobility of scholarship served to blunt charges of wicked self-indulgence.

Petrarch's individualism slowly gained sway. Janette Dillon notes in *Shakespeare and the Solitary Man* that

> The general drift in the late sixteenth century was away from the medieval idealisation of the bonds between men towards an increased reverence for the individual enclosed in his inner world, in isolation from other men . . . The inner world of the mind came to assume greater importance, the pleasures of solitude and introspection began to usurp the sense of community, and participation in society was increasingly regarded as a duty conflicting with the individual desire for privacy. Arguments in favour of solitude in the sixteenth century were framed largely in terms of pleasure and personal choice, while arguments in defence of an active social life were framed in moral terms. There was little attempt either to extol the pleasures of civil life or to justify solitude in moral terms until well into the seventeenth century.[30]

Seventeenth-century criticisms of solitude insisted upon its emptiness, unproductive futility, triviality, and melancholy. Albrecht Dürer in *Melancholia* and Robert Burton in *The Anatomy of Melancholy* argued that melancholy, stagnancy, morbidity, and even death were brought on by solitary inactivity.[31] John Donne insisted that "No man is an island, entire of it self," and castigated retirement in the strongest terms:

> At most, the greatest persons, are but great wens, and excrescences; men of wit and delightful conversation, but as moales for ornament, except they be incorporated into the body of the world, they contribute something to the sustenation of the whole.[32]

But the most merciless depiction of the life of retirement was produced by John Evelyn in his *Publick Employment and an Active Life Prefer'd to Solitude . . .* (1667). The book was a reply to George Mackenzie's *A Moral Essay, Preferring Solitude to Publick Employment* (1665), in which that author, after excoriating the hypocrisy, greed, viciousness, etc. of social life, extolled the pleasurable diversions of solitude without any particular concern for moral duty. Evelyn, in his reply, emphasized our interdependence with other people, the virtues of service and the scope for true self-fulfillment which service provides. After answering Mackenzie's charges item by item, e.g.,

[If political life stinks with corruption, still] They are the close, stagnate and cover'd Waters which stink most, and are fullest of mud and ordure, how calm and peaceable soever they seem upon the surface . . .[33]

he concludes by painting a picture:

Behold here a Sovereign sitting in his august Assembly of parliament enacting wholesome Laws: next him my Lord Chancellor and the rest of the reverend Judges and Magistrats dispensing them for the good of the People: . . . Here a General bravely Embattailing his Forces and Vanquishing an Enemy: There a Colony planting an Island, and a barbarous and solitary Nation reduced to Civility; Cities, Houses, Forts, Ships building for Society, shelter, defence and Commerce. In another Table, the poor relieved and set at work, the naked clad, the oppress'd delivered, the Malefactor punish'd, the Labourer busied, and the whole World employed for the benefit of Mankind: In a word, behold him in the neerest resemblance to his Almighty maker, always in action, and always doing good.

On the reverse now, represent to yourself, the goodliest piece of creation, sitting on a Cushion picking his teeth; His Country-Gentleman taking Tobacco, and sleeping after a gorgeous meal: There walks a Contemplator like a Ghost in a Church-yard, or sits poring on a book whiles his family starves: Here lies a Gallant at the foot of his pretty female, sighing and looking babies in her eyes, whilst she is reading the last new Romance and laughs at his folly: On yonder rock an Anchorite at his beads: There one picking daisies, another playing at push-pin, and abroad the young Potcher with his dog and kite breaking his neighbours hedges, or trampling o're his corn for a Bird not worth six-pence: This, sitts lowsing himself in the sun, that quivering in the cold: Here one drinks poyson, another hangs himself; for all these, and a thousand more seem to prefer Solitude and an inactive life as the most happy and eligible state of it . . .

The result of all is, Solitude produces ignorance, renders us barbarous, feeds revenge, disposes to envy, creates Witches, dispeoples the World, renders it a desart, and would soon dissolve it . . .[34]

The philosophers of the eighteenth-century Enlightenment tended to concur with Evelyn, associating solitude with the worst excesses of anchorism. We have already heard what Gibbon had to say about St. Antony; here is what his friend David Hume had to say on the subject:

Celibacy, fasting, penance, mortification, self-denial, humility, silence, solitude, and the whole train of monkish virtues; for what reason are they everywhere rejected by men of sense, but because they serve to no manner of purpose; neither advance a man's fortune in the world, nor render him a more valuable member of society, neither qualify him for the entertainment of company, nor increase his power of self-enjoyment? We observe, on the contrary, that they cross all these desirable ends; stupify the understanding and harden the heart, obscure the fancy and sour the temper.[35]

For the French *philosophes,* as Sayre remarks, the human being is essentially social; withdrawal from society betokens weakness rather than courage. In the great *Encyclopédie,* the author who writes on "le solitaire" remarks,

> It seems to me that in our tranquil era a truly robust virtue is one that walks firmly through obstacles, and not one that flees them. Of what merit is that weak-complexioned wisdom that cannot tolerate the open air, nor live among men without contracting the contagion of their vices, and that fears leaving an idle solitude so as to escape corruption? . . . A solitary is, in regard to the rest of mankind, like an inanimate being; his prayers and his contemplative life, which no one sees, have no influence on society, which has more need of examples of virtue before its eyes than in the forests.[36]

Towards the end of the eighteenth century, prospects for solitude brightened. As Eleanor Sickels tells us in *The Gloomy Egoist,* the solitude which had originally been the retreat of divines and scholars was appropriated by the poets. There they could experience "white melancholy," a pensive state "penetrated with a love of quiet and solitude and philosophical musing."[37] Mutability was a favorite theme of these reflections, whose appropriate retreat became the ruin or graveyard. Thomas Gray's "Elegy Writ in a Country Churchyard" (1751) is the most famous of these poems (a recent anthologizer of English Literature wrote, "If it can be said of any English poem that it is universally known, this is the one.") A few lines may serve to give the tone of Gray's pensive solitude:

> The boast of heraldry, the pomp of pow'r
> And all that beauty, all that wealth, e'er gave
> Awaits alike th' inevitable hour.
> The paths of glory lead but to the grave.

> Full many a gem of purest ray serene
> The dark unfathomed caves of ocean bear;
> Full many a flower is born to blush unseen,
> And waste its sweetness on the desert air.[38]

There emerged from this popular genre of poetry a new defense of solitude against charges of frivolity and emptiness: it came to be felt that it was virtuous and wise to meditate upon the ruined abbeys and tumbled gravestones which gave visible proof of the age-old context of human life, a sobering timescape in which

A little rule, a little sway,
A sunbeam on a winter's day,
Is all the proud and mighty have
Between the cradle and the grave.[39]

The early Romantics also escaped to solitude, but for a different reason. Rousseau and the young Goethe retreated into solitude to explore the workings of their "hearts"; and like Narcissus gazing into the pool at his own reflection, they were heedless of any demands that their solitude be justified: "I treat my heart like a sick child," wrote Werther, "and gratify its every fancy."[40] The appropriate place for solitude changed too: wild nature now, and not ruins, became its preferred haunt. As Romanticism spread into the next century, the twin fascinations with subjectivity and nature deepened and ramified: Wordsworth, Coleridge, and Shelley were particularly intrigued with the nature of imagination—how the mind "half creates and half perceives" (Wordsworth) the natural world in which it achieves poetic vision.[41] Questions of justification and defense of solitude became important again, but the objections and defenses were made on more personal and subjective grounds. Wordsworth emphasized the sober delight of feeling, through the experience of nature, "something far more deeply interfused," but Shelley reached an opposite conclusion. In "Alastor, Or the Spirit of Solitude," he allegorized the progress of the poetic spirit: at first "joyous, and tranquil, and self-possessed" in solitary contemplation of nature, a young man is "at length suddenly awakened and thirsts for intercourse with an intelligence similar to itself." Wandering through nature in search of such an intelligence, the sights that previously gave delight are now cold and empty: he sees a swan rise skyward from a stream and wanly asks

And what am I that I should linger here,
With voice far sweeter than thy dying notes,
Spirit more vast than thine, frame more attuned
To beauty, wasting these surpassing powers
In the deaf air, to the blind earth, and heaven
That echoes not my thoughts.[42]

Finally, exhausted and having searched in vain, the wanderer perishes in a lonely cave. Shelley found the lesson important enough to draw out in a preface published with the poem:

> The picture is not barren of instruction to actual men. The Poet's self-centered seclusion was avenged by the furies of an irresistible passion pursuing him to speedy ruin. . . . Among those who attempt to exist without Human sympathy, the pure and tender-hearted perish through the intensity and passion of their search after its communities, when the vacancy of their spirit suddenly makes itself felt. All else, selfish, blind, and torpid, are those unforeseeing multitudes who constitute, together with their own, the lasting misery and loneliness of the world. Those who love not their fellow-being live unfruitful lives, and prepare for their old age a miserable grave.[43]

Powerful objections to solitude, but coming now from within the sensitive soul.

Meanwhile, in America, old world fears of wilderness had combined with Puritan allegory to create a very different attitude towards solitude in wild nature than the raptures of Goethe and Rousseau. Roderick Nash tells us in *Wilderness and the American Mind* that

> When William Bradford stepped off the *Mayflower* into "a hideous and desolate wilderness" he started a tradition of repugnance. . . .
> Two components figured in the American pioneer's bias against wilderness. On the direct physical level, it constituted a formidable threat to his very survival. The transatlantic journey and subsequent western advances stripped away centuries. Successive waves of frontiersmen had to contend with wilderness as uncontrolled and terrifying as that which primitive man confronted. Safety and comfort, even necessities like food and shelter, depended on overcoming the wild environment. For the first Americans, as for medieval Europeans, the forest's darkness hid savage men, wild beasts, and still stranger creatures of the imagination. In addition civilized man faced the danger of succumbing to the wildness of his surroundings and reverting to savagery himself. The pioneer, in short, lived too close to wilderness for appreciation. Understandably, his attitude was hostile and his dominant criteria utilitarian. The *conquest* of wilderness was his major concern.[44]

These fears, combining with the Puritan mission to build, in Winthrop's words, a city on the hill, gave short shrift to solitude: frontiersmen who went alone into the great woods were, according to Crevecoeur, writing in 1782, beyond "the power of example and check of shame": having "degenerated altogether into the hunting state," having become "no better than carnivorous animals," they showed that man "cannot live in solitude, he must belong to some community bound by some ties."[45]

Does this sound like the Deerslayer? No, because by the early

1800s, as actual wilderness receded, new attitudes towards solitude in nature slowly formed: as Nash remarks, "It was [the pioneer's] children and grandchildren, removed from a wilderness condition, who began to sense its ethical and aesthetic values."[46] Now there appeared the nostalgic writing of James Fennimore Cooper, the primitivism of Philip Freneau, and the sojourns of such men as Estwick Evans:

> In the winter of 1818, Evans donned a buffalo robe trimmed with bearskin and moccasins and, in the company of two dogs, set forth on a four-thousand-mile "pedestrious tour" into the West. "I wished to acquire," he declared, "the simplicity, native feelings, and virtues of savage life; to divest myself of the factitious habits, prejudices and imperfections of civilization . . . and to find amidst the solitude and grandeur of the western wilds, more correct views of human nature and of the true interest of man."[47]

By the 1840s, Nash tells us,

> it was commonplace for literati of the major Eastern cities to make periodic excursions into the wilds, collect "impressions," and return to their desks to write descriptive essays which dripped love of scenery and solitude in the grand Romantic manner. The capacity to appreciate wilderness was, in fact, deemed one of the qualities of a gentleman.[48]

When Thoreau went to Walden Pond in 1845, therefore, he had as much work to do shedding the encrustations of stylized approaches to nature as he did shedding his social connections.

During the same period, other New England writers were reworking the old Puritan fears of what might lie in store for the solitary individual. For Nathanial Hawthorne, solitude is the great threatening gloom of the endless primal New England forests, where small isolated communities replicate, in their isolation, the inner isolation of their members. In the solitary shadows of lonely forests and old houses, Hawthorne's characters find not idle imaginative pleasure but ineradicable depravity and guilt. Solitary withdrawal within the self leads only to the intensification of morbidity and self-hatred, as with Dimmesdale in *The Scarlet Letter.* For Herman Melville, the nature which solitary man confronts is "a noncommunicative mask, concealing a blind, indifferent, possibly even a malevolent force, or, worse still, no power at all, but a sheer mechanical conscienceless force."[49] Whereas Byron found a rapture on the ocean shore, *Moby Dick's* Ishmael gazes over the water, reflects upon "the teeming horrors of sharks and the deep drowning that awaits a single miscalculation" and exclaims, "Heed it well, ye Pantheists!" In Ahab, the bright, self-possessed self reliance of

Emerson has become dark and obsessive, the solitary years in the cabin at sea having drawn him deep into blasphemous pride. He suspects that nature's "invisible spheres were formed in fright,"[50] but cannot forbear ripping open the veil. When he does so, all but one perish. Thus solitude in nature.

The twentieth century has given the perennial debate on solitude its own specific character. Although most of the traditional attacks and defenses of solitary life have been utilized, what is distinctive in modern accounts is the idea of inescapability: Proust, Camus, Tillich, for instance, conveyed the vision of an ultimate and inescapable isolation of the inner self which we explored in chapters 9 and 10 above; and what is inescapable would be absurd to try to justify. On the other hand, Marxist analyses undertook to show that our purported isolation is a fiction supporting monopoly capitalism, that in fact our social interconnections with each other are so pervasive, whether via direct social transactions or through the indirect determinations of culture, that solitude is in fact a kind of illusion. If that is so, any attempt to extol the virtues of solitude is either in bad faith or deluded or both. Sayre concludes his Marxist study of solitude in this tone:

> It can no longer convincingly be claimed that solitude contributes to the richness of individual existence, precisely because in the twentieth century that richness has been undermined . . .
>   There is a growing awareness of the contradiction between the needs of the individual and modern capitalist social relations that both impoverish the individual and cut him off from his matrix, his "species being" in the collective.[51]

But if one's species being is inescapably in the collective, what justification can there by for solitary living?[52]

These exerpts from the history of solitude do not tell the whole story, of course[53]—how could they, if the debate between Solitude and Encounter (so intimately intertwined with the debates between Contemplation and Action, Egoism and Altruism, Mysticism and Socialism) has been one of the enduring debates of Western culture? My purpose, rather, has been to enable us to better understand the origins of certain inner questions which nag at our solitude. When we sometimes feel there a vague sense of pointlessness, wondering whether hoeing the garden can really be what human life is for, it is enlightening to realize that these wonderings arise out of cultural influences so vast and diffuse that it would in fact be a wonder if we did *not* feel them. Tracing the history of these ideas (in solitude) helps to unpack such vague feelings of uneasiness, forcing the inner voices to speak clearly and declare from whence they come (St. Antony). This in turns helps the process of formulating replies, enabling one to separate the arguments against solitude from their historical contexts and to see what logical force they have in one's current personal circumstances.

Ultimately, of course, the personal defense of one's solitude must be an affair of logic, and the next chapter will be concerned with weighing arguments. But one is also in search of an image which can satisfy the imagination, as this historical survey has revealed. "Beast or god," "voice crying in the wilderness," "athlete," "warrior," "deserter," "light in the darkness," "wanderer"—these are the images that crept into the older arguments, and they are augmented by more recent writings: Thoreau refers to himself as an "observer" and a "messenger," Hesse's solitary is a "steppenwolf," Koller uses the self-imagery of a "pathfinder." How do these images condition and limit the force of the arguments, I wonder? And might the arguments actually undercut the images? I must have my image, everyone must, you can't make a self out of arguments; but the arguments ought to nuzzle up against the image, and not snap large bites away.

CHAPTER 12

Objections to Solitude: Responses

If any one imagines that this law is lax, let him keep its commandment one day.

—EMERSON

Turning from the historical to the logical consideration of the arguments against solitude, I must begin with some remarks about duration. Throughout most of the book, I have been speaking of solitude as an experience, a period of consciousness that endures for "a time," but not necessarily for a very long time. I have had my eye on experiences like Thoreau's evening walk around the pond, Rousseau's afternoon spent drifting in his small boat, or Sarton's morning at her desk by the fire. Now aside from a few fanatics, probably no one has ever seriously objected to solitudes such as these. What raises objections is the patterning of life so as to make these experiences predominant: it is the *life* of solitary withdrawal that has drawn the critic's ire, whether that withdrawal meant an isolated cabin in the woods or merely aloofness and inner preoccupation within society.

Now obviously the extent to which solitude defines a human life is a matter of degree; and, unsurprisingly, the strength of the objections which have been levelled against solitude are roughly proportional to that degree: Dr. Johnson would have found Thoreau self-indulgent, but St. Antony fanatical. What degree of solitude, then, shall we focus on as we consider objections? On the one hand, it would be silly to ponderously defend the brief period of solitude, while neglecting the life in which it plays a more extended role; on the other hand, there seems little point in laboring to defend the choice of absolute and utter seclusion, since virtually no one has ever chosen it (recall the containment of the lives of St. Antony and Thoreau).[1] The better course would be to consider attacks upon those who make solitude a central and defining fact in their lives—those who live alone, for example.

Whatever defenses work for these solitudes should work even better for the briefer sort, though they may not serve the desert hermit. What, then, are the objections, and what can solitude reply to them? What can my own reflections add to the long debate?

Objection 1: Solitude is Unnatural, Pathological, Dangerous

To begin with the weakest of these objections, that solitary living is dangerous for the solitary, the best response is to give it its due and no more. The Bible is right on this one: if you fall when alone there is none to raise you up, one slip of the chainsaw and you bleed to death. Accordingly, prudent solitaries take precautions: they keep the tools sharp, wear chainsaw pants and heavy boots, don't work when overtired, and for a dangerous job get a neighbor. Elderly persons living alone arrange to have a friend check in on them once a day, thus following a practice which traces back to the desert fathers, who visited any brother that did not appear at the weekly common service. But ordinary solitary living is not particularly dangerous. Of course, it is exciting sometimes to imagine one's solitude as dangerous, to curl up in a chair and dream of lone explorers living on the edge: besides enduring temperatures that fell to $-83°$F, Admiral Byrd was almost asphyxiated by carbon monoxide from a leaky heating stove; Haroun Tazieff, working alone on the rim of a volcano, had it erupt on him one day[2]; Steven Callahan was shipwrecked early in a solo voyage across the Atlantic and spent seventy-six fearful days alone on a small rubber life raft, distilling barely enough water to survive, narrowly escaping starvation by eating raw fish[3]; Martha Martin delivered her own baby while isolated on an Alaskan shore with a broken leg.[4] But, of course, all of these chose unusually dangerous solitudes! The idea that solitude in general is more dangerous than social living seems insupportable when one reflects upon the relative likelihood of being struck by a car versus being struck by lightning, or being attacked by a mugger versus being attacked by a bear.

The idea that the solitary is in grave danger of slipping into derangement or depravity, the image of the solitary as a crazed monster, traces back to Old Testament times. Ancient Hebrew folklore peopled the wilderness with demons and devils,[5] a tradition the gospel writer draws upon when he portrays John the Baptist wandering in the desert clothed in camel hair, living on locusts and honey. Centuries later, Nash tells us,

> the wildernesses of central and northern Europe also swarmed with supernatural beings. . . . In the Scandinavian countries, for instance, it was thought that when Lucifer and his followers were expelled from heaven, some landed in the forests and became Wood-Sprites or Trolls. Many of the medieval European monsters were lineal descendants of the man-beasts of classical mythology. Russian, Czech, and Slovak folklore spoke of a creature living in forests and mountains with the face of a woman, body of a sow, and legs of a horse. In Germany, when storms raged through the forests, it was widely believed that the ghostly Wild Huntsman was abroad with his pack of baying hounds, riding furiously and killing everything in his path. Man-eating ogres and the sinister werewolves were also identified with wild, remote regions.[6]

The man or woman who managed to survive alone in the realms of these demons was presumed to have made a pact with them, thereby acquiring a monstrous nature: anti-social hermits thus became witches and warlocks. But even when the witch fears were long past, suspicions remained. Even the sensible citizens of Concord had their questions about Thoreau's retreat: he tells us in the opening paragraphs of *Walden* that the book was an attempt to answer "very particular inquiries" by the townspeople regarding "what I got to eat; if I did not feel lonesome; if I was not afraid; and the like"—in short, how anybody in his right mind could live that way. (My favorite illustration of this incomprehension is the man who wandered into Thoreau's camp looking for a lost dog. As Thoreau gave some helpful directions, the man stared at the cabin, stared at Thoreau, and kept blankly repeating, "But what do you *do* here?")

People do not place much stock in demons now, but the idea that something is wrong with a psyche that opts for solitude is familiar enough. The propensity among professional psychologists to see the solitary as disabled, deprived, or neurotic is well documented and criticized by Storr. In response to the widespread conviction that "health and happiness entirely depend upon the maintenance of intimate personal relationships"—a view which descended from Freud to attachment theorists like Bowlby, object relations theorists like Klein, and the self-psychology of Kohut—Storr replies firstly that Freud himself insisted on the importance for psychic health of two factors, love and work; but many people find in the work that occupies their solitudes the psychic sustenance for a meaningful and satisfying life, even when intimate relations are largely absent (Storr examines in this regard the lives of Kafka, Gibbon, Kant, Kipling, Wittgenstein, among others). Secondly, our need for relationship does not demand *intimate* relationship: it may be satisfied indirectly through communicating one's work to others, even though the recipients live far removed from the solitary place of creation. Storr also reminds us that the evidence used to support charges of pathology in solitude is taken from studies of infants (Spitz and Bowlby), animals in captivity,[7] and prisoners—none of which represent adequately the condition of the sensitive adult human being who has *chosen* to live alone. Such choices are largely a matter of temperament—whether one is an introvert or extrovert (Jung), a diverger or a converger (Hudson), a patterner or a dramatist (Gardner)[8]—and the sort of temperament that opts for generous measures of solitude is simply too widely distributed to be considered pathological. To Storr's excellent discussion, here very incompletely summarized, it is only necessary to add the exclamations of joy and heightened power in solitude which the present book has been collecting: the unusually acute feelings of freedom, vision, and attunement which characteristically accompany solitude can hardly be thought of as unhealthy, and neither can the determined commitment to make them central in one's life.

That an enlarged capacity for comfortable aloneness in adulthood is in fact a salient characteristic of the most healthy personality was claimed by Abraham Maslow, whose studies of self-actualization have so influenced humanistic psychology. Determined to provide the healthy half of psychology necessary to balance the sick side which Freud had mapped, Maslow undertook to study a group of unusually healthy individuals for the marks of "full-humanness." These individuals were found to have largely satisfied the "lower" or deficiency needs—for physical existence, safety and security, belongingness and affection, self-respect—and were thus freed to pursue their inner drives towards growth, "self-actualization" as Maslow called it. Among the characteristics of self-actualizing people, he found an increased detachment and desire for privacy:

the self-actualizing individual, by definition gratified in his basic needs, is far less dependent, far less beholden, far more autonomous and self-directed. Far from needing other people, growth-motivated people may actually be hampered by them. I have already reported . . . their special liking for privacy, for detachment and for meditativeness.

Such people become far more self-sufficient and self-contained. The determinants which govern them are now primarily inner ones, rather than social or environmental.[9]

In a long discussion of the distinctive nature of "cognition of being" during peak experiences, Maslow cites many of the features we have already noticed as particularly valuable aspects of solitary experience, for example, the senses of wholeness, perfection, completion, aliveness, richness, simplicity, beauty, uniqueness, and self-sufficiency. Moreover,

any person in any of the peak experiences takes on temporarily many of the characteristics which I found in self-actualizing individuals. . . . He becomes in these episodes more truly himself, more perfectly actualizing his potentialities, closer to the core of Being, more fully human.[10]

Is solitude socio-pathological? Sociology, and more recently sociobiology, have not so much castigated solitude as ignored it. However, the few discussions we do have are not favorably inclined. Paul Halmos, for example, in *Solitude and Society,* postulates a basic bio-social drive, a "force of phylic cohesion," as "an independent biological principle of life": "Sharing of experience, close contiguity of comradeship and face-to-face co-operative effort have always been a fundamental and vital need of man."[11] If these really are bio-social needs, then someone lacking them would certainly appear to be a deviant, and so Halmos finds them—a few grudging admissions of minor roles for brief solitudes notwithstanding. The mid-century English sociologist Trotter is cited with approval:

it is quite evident that impulses derived from herd feeling will enter the mind with the value of instincts . . . The individual of a gregarious species can never be truly independent and self-sufficient. Natural selection has ensured that as an individual he must have an abiding sense of incompleteness . . .[12]

It seems to me that the autocratic law-giving of these sociologists, authorized neither by careful study nor by sympathy for the subject, can be dismissed fairly quickly. Thoreau, Byrd, Koller, Rilke, Sarton, and all the others show that the (undeniable) need in humans for companionship makes very few demands upon some people, demands which can often be met by the indirect engagements of solitude. Trotter, Halmos's own authority, acknowledges

> an abiding sense of incompleteness which, as thought develops in complexity, will come to be more and more abstractly expressed. This is the psychological germ which expresses itself in the religious feelings, in the desire for completion, for mystical union, for incorporation with the infinite.[13]

But as we have seen, these "more abstract expressions" of desire for completion can be wonderfully successful in solitude. Secondly, as a point of logic, if there are individuals who lack a need common to their genus, this only points to a statistical abnormality, and not illness or sociopathology: Sherpas, who can climb without equipment in the high Himalayas owing to their radically diminished need for oxygen, are not sociopaths. In fact, insofar as a need can be considered a constraint upon freedom, it might be argued that the relative absence of the need for companionship is in fact a strength and a virtue.[14]

It is a pleasure to recommend a zestful exception to the general denigration of solitude among sociologists, Margaret Adams's *Single Blessedness*. Adams undertook to explore (and defend) the life choice of single women who, in spite of prevailing opinions regarding the unhappiness and unfulfillment of this plight, "in practice appear to be getting on quite well." Singleness has two essential features for her: a strong sense of psychological autonomy and personal integrity, and a "consistent and purposeful resistance to succumbing to the intricately interdependent system of marriage and the nuclear family."[15] Though a minority, there are a great many such women, and "the general tenor of their lives and their obvious competence in other areas of existence indicated that they were stable, achieving, efficient and relatively happy people." True, loneliness is usually a problem to some degree, but it is preferable to the oppressive relationship that modern marriage so often becomes, and to "the alleged but unconvincing delights of having children." Adams's insights are too numerous to summarize, but a sample of her approach can be given. Reflecting upon the invasive impoliteness of the question frequently put to single people, "What happened, X, that you're not married?," she identifies the operation of three general mechanisms:

> [First, as noted by Goffman] when an individual manifests a personal characteristic or is in a social situation that carries social stigma and devaluation, he or she forfeits the right to the normal taboos safeguarding privacy; as long as comments

are made in good faith or sympathy, any stranger is at liberty to talk about the predicament with impunity. The second phenomenon has been described by Scott and Lyman and refers to the obligation that society lays upon individuals who manifest atypical and deviant social characteristics to provide satisfactory and societally acknowledged explanations for their deviance. The third relates to society's insistence that individuals whose lives are marked by conspicuous misfortune freely acknowledge this fact; if they refuse this definition of their circumstances the implication is that they are undermining the value of the attributes or situations that society has defined as fortunate. The relevance to singleness of these three societal attitudes becomes clear when I try to turn the tables and confront a happily married woman with the same question—: "What happened Martha, Eleanor, Patricia (again, names do not signify) that you got married?" tendered in a tone of voice suggesting that an explanation is clearly needed to allay my incredulousness at such an apparently strange measure. The reaction is fascinating and illuminating . . .[16]

Single men will smile also in recognition, for they, too, have heard of themselves, at third hand: "poor X, lives there all alone—I wonder what happened?" We love the silence and freedom and autonomy enough to bear with a little loneliness from time to time, that is what happened!

But now, as so often happens when one defends a thing one loves, I am understating the dangers of the path of solitude: for there are vortices in its silence that can suck you down to deep drowning. It can happen that the more solitude becomes your way, the more you crave; and that craving can lead farther and farther away from human warmth until you find yourself in a seclusion that is too great, a pit of loneliness too deep to escape.[17] Hermann Hesse's Steppenwolf comes directly to mind: prowling the streets on rainy nights like a lone wolf from the steppes, passing by the warm houses and taverns where ordinary people lived their warm involved lives, the Steppenwolf reminds himself of his independence:

> Solitude is independence. It had been my wish and with the years I had attained it. It was cold. Oh, cold enough! But it was also still, wonderfully still and vast like the cold stillness of space in which the stars revolve.[18]

But the Steppenwolf is whistling up courage in the dark: for

> It happened to him as it does to all; what he strove for with the deepest and most stubborn instinct of his being fell to his lot, but more than is good for men. . . . He achieved his aim. He was ever more independent. . . . But in the midst of the freedom he had attained Harry suddenly became aware that his freedom was a death, and that he stood alone. . . . No one came near to him. There was no link left, and no one could have had any part in his life even had anyone wished it. For

the air of lonely men surrounded him now, a still atmosphere in which the world around him slipped away, leaving him incapable of relationship, an atmosphere against which neither will nor longing availed.[19]

No one who has lived alone for an extended period of time can read this passage without shifting uncomfortably. We know what it is to be drawn too far into the silence, to wilt there before "the basilisking gaze of Nothing" (Auden).[20] There is the real danger of solitude.

Objection 2: Solitude is Self-Indulgent

This was one of the few things Emerson could find to complain of in his eulogy of Thoreau (which appeared in *The Atlantic Monthly* of August, 1862, three months after Thoreau died of tuberculosis at age forty-five):

I cannot help counting it a fault in him that he had no ambition. Wanting this, instead of engineering for all America, he was the captain of a huckleberry party. Pounding beans is good to the end of pounding empires one of these days; but if, at the end of years, it is still only beans![21]

The years Thoreau lived at the pond (1845–1847) were busy years in the humanitarian resistance to the Mexican War and to Southern slavery: how could he sit "growing like corn" in his doorway when the battles were raging?

Thoreau's defense will occupy us shortly, but first it is necessary to look more closely at the idea of self-indulgence. To begin with, it is a failing, a negative trait. But what exactly is the nature of the failing? A self-indulgent person is a person who directly, freely, and without a second thought, pursues his every desire. This is not exactly the same failing as weakness of will: in the latter case, the agent condemns the desire which pulls at him, struggles for self-control, and loses the struggle. Not so with the self-indulgent person: there is no condemnation and no struggle, he simply feels an urge to do something and does it.

But what is wrong with that? There must be something wrong, of course, since self-indulgence is a failing. What is wrong is that there is a lack of proper self-control: a desire or cluster of desires that ought to be controlled are not controlled. To illustrate, eating dinner when one is hungry is not self-indulgent, but snacking all through the evening whenever one thinks of food is. Such snacking is unseemly and imprudent, since it is bad for the teeth, the diet, and the figure, indicates a disproportionately large concern with food, and manifests an inability to control oneself. This sort of self-indulgence is harmful mainly to the self: it manifests a want of prudence (and perhaps grace).

But the harm done can also be to other people, and then self-indulgence becomes selfishness. An audience member who keeps asking questions during the brief question period after a speech is selfishly self-indulgent: s/he indulges every desire to question, but wrongly, since such monopolization of the discussion prevents others from satisfying *their* curiosity, and hence harms them. No harm, no self-indulgence: who, for example, would call smiling all through the question period self-indulgence?

In order, then, to make a charge of self-indulgence stick to solitude, one would have to show either that indulging the desire for solitude harmed the solitary or that it harmed others.[22] As for the first assertion, the virtues of solitude destroy its credibility as a general claim—though of course some people are harmed by solitude for case-specific reasons. As for the second line of attack, it would have to be shown that the solitary life harms others (a) significantly (since we cannot be expected to forego great personal goods for trivial social gains), and (b) in ways that society has a right not to be harmed. But then the objection reduces to another one, to be considered presently, that solitude is evasive of social responsibility.[23]

Objection 3: Solitude is Escapist

This charge can be found in virtually every critique of solitude since antiquity. It is there in Cicero's *De Officiis:* "men, too, are born for the sake of men," and we only "follow Nature" when we contribute to the general good. Recall, too, the lines quoted above from Diderot's *Encyclopédie:*

> It seems to me that in our tranquil era a truly robust virtue is one that walks firmly through obstacles, and not one that flees them. Of what merit is that weak-complexioned wisdom that cannot tolerate the open air, nor live among men without contracting the contagion of their vices . . .

Today, the charge of escapism is made in breezy dismissals of the solitary life as "irrelevant."

When I hear charges like this, after feeling by turns angry and ashamed, ferocious and meek, I begin to think about the idea at issue. What exactly is escapism? Like "self-indulgent," "escapism" is a negative judgment, an indictment—my anger and shame establish that. But what are the grounds of this indictment? Three factors seem salient. Firstly, escapism implies that the refuge must be more pleasant, or at least less painful, than the place from which it is an escape: no one would think of calling the departure from a warm bed in order to go to work "escapism." Secondly, the painful/evil situation escaped must be one in which the escapist has some duty to remain, whether to try to set things right or merely to endure. All of us know this point because all of us heard our parents say, as part of our moral training, something like the following: "now if anyone starts trouble you come right home!"; and if you ran home when the boys started throwing stones at windows you were not called an escapist (though maybe a chicken). Thirdly, I think there is an element of metaphysics in the charge of escapism: the world to which an escapist escapes is thought to be in some way less real, more illusory than the world from which he flees. In this respect, we think of someone who indulges in drugs or daydreams as an escapist.

These three logical points about escapism suggest ways in which solitaries can rebut the charge. Firstly, they can argue that solitude is no picnic, that it takes as much courage to live alone as it does to live amongst people. Thoreau suggests this line of defense when he rounds upon the weak neediness of the townspeople who must have "entertainments" to occupy their leisure. May Sarton also suggests it when she mentions the dark and fearful periods of her solitude:

> This is what frightens me when I am first alone again. I feel inadequate. I have made an open place, a place for meditation. What if I cannot find myself inside it?
>
> Cracking open the inner world again, writing even a couple of pages, threw me back into depression, not made easier by the weather, two gloomy days of darkness and rain. I was attacked by storms of tears, those tears that appear to be related to frustration, to buried anger, and come upon me without warning. I woke yesterday so depressed that I did not get up till after eight.
>
> It occurs to me that boredom and panic are the two devils the solitary must combat. When I lay down this afternoon, I could not rest and finally got up because I was in a sweat of panic, panic for no definable reason, a panic of solitude, I presume.[24]

The truth which emerges from honest accounts like Sarton's is that the solitary life, in its mixture of pains and pleasures, successes and frustrations, victories and failures, is no less difficult a course than communal living.

Secondly, solitaries can argue that the evils from which they are escaping are not of their own making, and are so overwhelming and horrible that the only sensible thing to do, and hence a morally justifiable thing to do, is to flee them while one is still able. This was one of the justifications used by the Desert Fathers who, in Workman's phrase, "fled not so much from the world as from the world in the Church"; even St. Basil, who was critical of solitary withdrawal, railed against the corruption that had so quickly infected the Church Triumphant:

> The doctrines of the Fathers are despised, the speculations of innovators hold sway in the Church. Men are rather contrivers of cunning systems than theologians. The wisdom of this world has the place of honour, having dispossessed the boasting of the Cross. The shepherds are driven out; in their place grievous wolves are brought in which harry the flock. Houses of prayer have none to assemble in them; the deserts are full of mourners.[25]

Said one audacious prefect of Rome, "Make me Bishop of Rome and I will forthwith become a Christian!" Epicurean and Stoic writers had earlier supported withdrawal on similar grounds: in "De Otio," Seneca allows that a man has good reason for retiring to solitude when a state is so rotten as to be beyond helping:

> If I were to discuss each [state] separately, I should not be able to find one which the wise man could endure, or which could endure the wise man. Now if such a state as we have dreamed of cannot be found on earth, it follows that leisure is necessary for every one, because the one thing which might be preferred to leisure is nowhere to be found.[26]

Petrarch mounted this same line of defense in his sketch of the life of "the busy man" which we have already seen. Complaining that "I am living in this generation, yet I would rather have been born in any other, . . ." he insists that

> all the sulphur can be more easily drawn out from the entrails of Etna and all the mud from all the swamps, than these evils, these burning crimes, these filthy customs from the dregs of cities in which is to be found the worst market-place of such wares, among which the happy man lives unhappily even though his mind has attained its full growth, and from which it is happier to be withdrawn. What then is the upshot? I return to my oft repeated advice, that we should run away

from the plagues which we are unable to drive off. And for this purpose I know only of the haven and refuge of the solitary life . . .[27]

These images of smoking dungeon-cities burning with crimes and filthy customs can be particularly powerful for frightened older people, who have retreated finally to the protective solitude of their own apartments, sometimes their own rooms, to escape the bewildering malevolence. I entered the world of that terrible vision some years ago on a sunny afternoon in a small house in a quiet university town: in a musty living room, heavily shaded against the daylight, a frantic old woman glared wildly at me and repeated hoarsely, "They're poisoning our water, they're poisoning our water!" The vision had triumphed, reducing her to paranoia. But it is not hard to approximate her fear if one reads the ecological reports in a certain frame of mind: they *are* poisoning our water, you know.

It is never hard to find great social evils worth escaping, but that does not entirely answer the charge of escapism; for the part of that charge which we are now considering can grant the evils but insist that the solitary has an obligation to stay within society and work for change. Notice, however, that here, as with self-indulgence, the charge of escapism has boiled down to a charge of evasion of social responsibility, the charge that will occupy us shortly.

With regard to the third implication of escapism, that the choice for solitude is a choice for a world of unreality, the reply is obvious: the direct encounters with Nature, Self, and The Mysterious in solitude are in fact generally acclaimed to feel more self-authenticating, more luminous with Being than most social encounters. Even the visionary experiences of solitude seem to hold an indisputable reality for their subjects, not merely at the moment but as a powerful current running onward through their lives. And as one old anchorite who lived alone on the summit of Mt. Sinai for fifty years said simply, "the man who is visited often by mortals could not often be visited by angels."

Objection 4: Solitude is Antisocial

What an odd charge! Invited to a party, you excuse yourself on grounds that you wanted to spend the evening alone, and the host objects,

"Don't be anti-social!" What is there to say? In one sense solitude *is* against sociality: here and now it rejects it, and if the solitude ramifies into a solitary life, it is a life of such rejection. And sociable people don't like this. As Anne Morrow Lindbergh remarks,

> If one sets aside time for a business appointment, a trip to the hairdresser, a social engagement, or a shopping expedition, that time is accepted as inviolable. But if one says: I cannot come because that is my hour to be alone, one is considered rude, egotistical or strange.[28]

Of course sociable people have some reason to be suspicious of rejection: many solitaries have disliked society heartily and said so bluntly. Thoreau's journal, for example, is full, of ascerbic comments:

> April 24, 1852: "It is impossible for me to be interested in what interests men generally."

> January 3, 1853: "I love nature partly *because* she is not man, but a retreat from him.

> October 19, 1855: "I said that I suspected any enterprise in which two were engaged together."

> March 4, 1856: "Two friends, each problems."

> January 7, 1857: "The man I meet with is not often so instructive as the silence he breaks."

> December 28, 1856: "One companion a week spoils the week."

> October 23, 1852: [the social virtues are] "the virtues of pigs in a litter."[29]

Yet these aspersions are not all he had to say on the subject. The journal also contains many positive reflections about friends, the importance of friends and friendship. And if he somehow sensed that friendship wasn't his strongest suit, he could plead that it was incompatible with his greater love, nature:

> April 11, 1852: "If I am too cold for human friendship, I trust I shall not soon be too cold for natural influences. It appears to be a law that you cannot have a deep sympathy with both man and nature. Those qualities which bring you near to the one estrange you from the other."

> July 26, 1852: "By my intimacy with nature I find myself withdrawn from man . . . The mind that perceives clearly any natural beauty is in that instant withdrawn from human society."[30]

Sometimes, too, he gave a kinder answer to humanity, as in this letter to Blake: "It is not that we love to be alone, but that we love to soar, and when we do soar the company grows thinner and thinner till there is none at all."[31] Here, to my mind, he speaks best for solitude. Solitaries are more absorbed in the values of solitude than they are obsessed with the evils of society; social engagement is not for them so much an evil as it is a lesser good. They will exclaim with Byron, "I love not man the less, but nature more!"

But suppose they do love man the less, and wish to absent themselves from his company? What then? Are they failing in some obligation to be social? That would have to be proven in order to make "anti-social" a charge. And can it be proven?

Objection 5: Solitude is Evasive of Social Responsibility

Pericles regarded the man who avoids public affairs "not as one who minds his own business, but as good for nothing"[32]; and Samuel Johnson likened solitaries to deserters. Robert Louis Stevenson, in a retrospective assessment of Thoreau written some twenty years after his death, chided him on similar grounds:

> To live is sometimes very difficult, but it is never meritorious in itself; and we must have a reason to allege to our own conscience why we should continue to exist upon this crowded earth . . . those who have become free of the necessity of long toil to exist, having the more liberty, have only the higher moral obligation to be up and doing in the interest of man."[33]

Women who opt for lives which elevate solitude above service to a husband and children have been especially condemned. Victorian essayists called women who chose not to marry "superfluous," and one such writer insisted that a retributive punishment descended upon their selfish refusal: spinsters are, he wrote, "wretched and deteriorating, their minds narrowing and their hearts withering, because they have nothing to do, and none to love, cherish and obey."[34]

How might a lover of solitude respond to these charges of social irresponsibility? No doubt the proper approach would be to articulate the nature and limits of social responsibility, and then locate one's solitude beyond those limits. Easily said! Even a moment's reflection reveals that the first task raises, either directly or indirectly, most of the central issues of moral and political philosophy. A comprehensive ethical theory is beyond the scope of this essay, however, (and probably beyond the powers of this essayist) so I shall not proceed along that path. What interests me is not so much how professional philosophers have responded to questions of social responsibility as how the great solitaries have responded. Accordingly, after introducing a little order into the discussion, I intend to extract and elaborate those responses, considering at last how adequate they might be.

By way of organizing the defenses of solitude against charges of social irresponsibility, it occurs to me that there are three basic options available:

(A)   Deny the social responsibility.

(B)   Accept some social responsibility, but set limits to it, locating one's solitude outside those limits.

(C)   Argue that in solitude one actually is fulfilling one's social responsibility, either

(i) by resting and preparing to serve, or

(ii) by the actual works of solitude.

Let us take them up in order, observing how some famous loners have elaborated the bare logical bones.

(A) DENY THE SOCIAL RESPONSIBILITY

The most famous proponent of this line of argument was Emerson. In "Self-Reliance" he celebrates the individual's inner calling, the particular way in which each individual uniquely embodies Man; that inner calling should be followed devotedly, while society, especially when it interferes with the unfolding of one's genius, should be ignored:

> Society everywhere is in conspiracy against the manhood of every one of its members.
> The only right is what is after my constitution; the only wrong what is against it.[35]

Constitution reveals itself in intuition, the inner voice of one's genius; these intuitions may not be consistent over time, and one should no more be bound by past selves than by other people: "a foolish consistency is the hobgoblin of little minds . . . With consistency

a great soul has simply nothing to do."[36] This laissez-faire individualism of the hour would seem inhospitable to the demands of social
responsibility, and Emerson did not mince words:

> Do not tell me . . . of my obligation to put all poor men in good situations. Are
> they *my* poor? I tell thee, thou foolish philanthropist, that I grudge the dollar, the
> dime, the cent I give to such men as do not belong to me and to whom I do not
> belong.[37]

Indeed, as Ellen Suckiel points out in "Emerson and the Virtues,"[38]
even those who did belong to Emerson did not fare better:

> I shun father and mother and wife and brother when my genius calls me. I would
> write on the lintels of the door post, *Whim*. I hope it is somewhat better than
> whim at last, but we cannot spend the day in explanation. Expect me not to show
> cause why I seek or why I exclude company.[39]

The supreme moral duty for Emerson is to oneself, to the self-reliant
courageous difficult search for the manifestation of the Oversoul within
oneself:

> You may fulfill your round of duties by clearing yourself in the *direct,* or in the
> *reflex* way. Consider whether you have satisfied your relations to father, mother,
> cousin, neighbor, town, cat and dog—whether any of these can upbraid you. But I
> may also neglect this reflex standard and absolve me to myself. I have my own
> stern claims and perfect circle. It denies the name of duty to many offices that are
> called duties. But if I can discharge its debts it enables me to dispense with the
> popular code. If any one imagines that this law is lax, let him keep its
> commandment one day.[40]

As Suckiel remarks, it is hard to imagine a society—or even a
family—of Emersonians, and probably no one would try to defend
such moral isolationism very far.[41] Probably not even Emerson believed
it—at least he failed admirably to practice what he preached: Suckiel
reminds us that he held a political office in Concord, served as a
volunteer fireman, helped to maintain a public reading room, and gave
a kindly ear to struggling young writers, most notably Thoreau.

(B) ACCEPT SOME RESPONSIBILITY, BUT SET LIMITS TO IT, LOCATING SOLITUDE OUTSIDE THOSE LIMITS

One way in which rational limits might be set to social duty is familiar
to all of us. The idea, tracing back to republican Rome, is that extensive
service to society can earn one an excuse from further duties. Perhaps
owing to the dominance of military forms of social organization among
the Romans, it came to be felt that any citizen might serve out his "tour

of duty" to the state and retire to personal life. Most famously, the emperor Diocletian, as Petrarch tells it,

> grew weary of the turbulent court and the costly encumbrance, of troops of attendants and of general servility, suddenly changed his mind and conceived a desire to be alone and poor and free, and to swim out from the sea of imperial cares into the haven of a humbler life, naked like a pilot from a great shipwreck . . . he preferred to go to his native town of Salona in Dalmatia, and not inside the city either, but to a place near his native walls where he died in a country house . . .[42]

According to legend, when an incredulous senator came to urge him to return to Rome, extolling the pomp and glory of emperorship, Diocletian nodded impatiently and interrupted, "yes, yes, but come and look at my cabbages!" The story, and the underlying thought, have a perennial appeal: enough is enough, and after great service one can be excused to solitary withdrawal. Particularly with advanced age is this defense powerful, the lifetime of service standing as a full payment of whatever the social debt might be.

Another way to set limits to one's social responsibility is to argue that although there are such obligations *in abstracto,* the rottenness of one's particular society dissolves them here and now. This, we remember, was one of Seneca's defenses of solitude, repeated by Petrarch in his fulminations against the rottenness of the cities. It was also a popular line of defense, I remember, among those who "dropped out" during the 1960s: superpower militarism, impenetrable political establishments, endemic racism, and global pollution seemed to make withdrawal to the purer homestead the only morally sane course.

Another premise is implicated in this line of defense, however: that one cannot significantly improve the rotten situation by remaining therein. The significance of the personal act appears to be endlessly arguable, as my own struggle for moral clarity during the Vietnam War revealed: it appears to be a straightforward factual matter, but the facts give way almost at once to personal philosophies of significance. Talking far into many nights with both reclusive and politically active[43] fellow students at Berkeley, the following conviction formed: temperament contributes mightily to one's assessment of the two central issues at stake. Reclusive people, by nature more introverted and less capable of social action, less immersed and so less knowledgable in the realm of political affairs, are for those reasons inclined to be skeptical of the power of the individual to make any difference, and also inclined to maximize the evils of society. Activists, generally more extroverted personalities with greater temperamental abilities for social interaction, tend to take a different perspective on the crucial questions: How bad is it? What can I do? They also tend to believe themselves more immune to the "co-option by evil" that comprises a substantial part of the moral fear of recluses. As I spoke to these very different kinds of people, I found myself repeatedly wrenched from one perspective to the other, now seeing contemporary America all around me in the crowded plaza, flawed but salvageable, now seeing it from the cabin porch as only a faint trace of foul smoke on the horizon, ineradicable but mercifully distant. My own solution to the problem, not entirely satisfactory[44] but chosen by many impure solitaries, I suspect, was to do in solitude those things which my activist friends thought might make a difference: write letters, sign petitions, vote, work issues into the syllabi of my courses, exemplify a nonviolent life. Whether all those things made a difference, I do not know; but they went as far as belief in personal efficacy would take me, and thus satisfied (though uneasily) the skeptical social morality of an introvert.

Another way to set limits to an obligation is to portray it as conflicting with a higher obligation, a tack which has been taken by both secular and religious solitaries. We hear it in Emerson's insistence that one must first and foremost satisfy the inner voices of one's genius, and in Thoreau's insistence in *Civil Disobedience* that "we should be men [following the dictates of our own consciences] first, and subjects afterwards. . . . The only obligation which I have a right to assume is to do at any time what I think right."[45] If conscience would lead one into solitude against the arguments of society, then it must be followed. The traditional monastic interpretation of the story of Mary and Martha also insists upon higher duties: Christ was reminding Martha that although there is an obligation to be "busy with much serving" there is a higher obligation to worship God.

The religious version of this defense rests, of course, on the authority of the religious doctrine, a topic I cannot pursue here. The secular version, as ennunciated by Emerson and Thoreau, has some complexity. As a purely formal point about moral obligation their view seems correct: acting as a full moral agent involves acting autonomously, according to one's own conscientious conviction; a person who abandons the dictates of her own conscience to follow some external directive has, in an important sense, ceased to be a moral being. But no easy move can be made from this formal truth to a substantive defense of solitude, since the nature of the higher obligation is left unspecified by the true injunction to follow whatever your conscience identifies as the higher obligation.[46]

Nevertheless, Emerson and Thoreau provide some guidelines for the correct use of the "higher obligation" defense of solitude. They insist that its utility is dependent upon the particular nature of one's unique genius: to use a religious term, those who have a *calling* for solitude will have a stronger case for limiting social obligations than those whom it touches more lightly. Moreover, the Transcendentalist's exaggerated sense of autonomous individuality is the exaggeration of a truth: the woman, for instance, who feels a deep-running need for solitude but always lets family duties override this need has become servile, failing in her duty to herself[47]: if other people's needs are inherently worth attention, one's own needs are equally so, and one's "genius" may lead one into solitude to satisfy them. Finally, Thoreau's celebrations of solitude remind us of its power to provide personal well-being and growth. Many social activists, I think, disbelieve that solitude could ever represent a high moral calling because they see it as idle and trivial, at best having the value of a good rest. Whereas I have been arguing throughout that solitude offers many core human values of transcendent importance, and hence beckons to (almost) everyone's genius.

Another way in which one might limit the obligations imposed upon solitude is suggested by some remarks in the famous essay "Of Suicide" by David Hume who was, ironically, rather an enemy of solitude:

> A man, who retires from life, does no harm to society. He only ceases to do good; which, if it be an injury, is of the lowest kind.
>
> All our obligations to do good to society seem to imply something reciprocal. I receive the benefits of society, and therefore ought to promote its interest. But when I withdraw myself altogether from society, can I be bound any longer?
>
> But allowing, that our obligations to do good were perpetual, they have certainly some bounds. I am not obliged to do a small good to society, at the expense of a great harm to myself.[48]

The idea of the second paragraph is neatly logical: if the ground of social obligation is alleged to be the benefits obtained from society, by minimizing those benefits one can minimize one's obligations. Those who crave a theater circle or a hockey league have obligations to support those activities that recluses do not share, and those who need a friendly ear in time of trouble have greater obligations of friendship than those who lick their wounds alone. In *Civil Disobedience,* Thoreau adopts this strategy: he continually minimizes the services which the state provides for him ("For my own part, I should not like to think that I ever rely on the protection of the state"), but then recognizes an obligation to pay for those few services it actually does provide: "I have never declined paying the highway tax, because I am as desirous of being a good neighbor as I am of being a bad subject." The word "neighbor" appears frequently in the essay, indicating the area to which Thoreau limited the social obligations he could accept. Beyond the limits of neighborly cooperation, either deeper into intimate relations or more broadly out into politics, he was reluctant to admit any social obligations:

> I am not responsible for the successful working of the machinery of society. I am not the son of the engineer.
>
> It is not a man's duty, as a matter of course, to devote himself to the eradication of any, even the most enormous, wrong; he may still properly have other concerns to engage him . . .

But then comes the great moral teaching of the essay:

> but it is his duty, at least, to wash his hands of (such evil), and, if he gives it thought no longer, not to give it practically his support. If I devote myself to other pursuits and contemplations, I must first see, at least, that I do not pursue them sitting upon another man's shoulders. I must get off him first, that he may pursue his contemplations too.[49]

Limits can be set to social duty by eschewing benefits, but we cannot evade the duties created by our own contributions to the polity's evil machinations.

Objectors to solitary living will now insist that there are always social benefits which accrue to solitaries, even in their withdrawal, and inescapable involvements in the evils of the day: Thoreau "traveled widely in Concord" on roads built and maintained by the public, protected from harm by a system of constables and courts; when Alice Koller's dogs are ill, she rushes to the veterinary clinic on public highways; when the day of solitude is long, May Sarton is grateful for the evening news on television. And don't the latter two solitaries' taxes go towards the support of military interventions and nuclear pollution?

Granted, but what follows? Here Hume's third point seems pertinent: "But allowing that our obligations to do good were perpetual, they have certainly some bounds." I observe that the vast majority of solitary people, those in whose lives solitude has come to be a central feature, have still a considerable involvement with society and its work. Like Byrd, they run a research station, or like McLintock they do important scientific research, or like Sarton they travel about reading their work and encouraging other authors, or like Thoreau they lecture and visit elderly aunts, or like Lindberg they care for a large family much of the day and much of the year, or like Merton they counsel other monks and explain the monastic life to outsiders, or they deliver meals on wheels three days a week as my father used to do. Moreover, all the while they are paying a wide variety of taxes and keeping their own corner of the polity tidy, safe, and hospitable. They try to be good neighbors, if perhaps agreeing with Aldous Huxley that the best neighbor is one seen infrequently. Moreover, there is time in the solitude remaining for researching social issues, sifting courses of action, writing off letters and checks. Surely, after all this, bounds may be set to social responsibility?

Or can they? Sometimes a solitude is troubled by voices like these: "think of all those people, think of the good you could do with your gifts!" I know the power of those voices, but I also think that Hume helps us to see that they have changed the subject. We need to distinguish, for the voices, between social obligations and benevolences: it would be a very good deed if I sold my car and gave the proceeds to Oxfam, but I have no obligation to do so; it would be a very good thing if people planted lovely flowers in front of their houses, but who thinks that they have any such obligation? Just so, solitaries who choose to withdraw from social involvement may "cease to do good" (Hume), but do not thereby fail in their obligations. Whether it can also be argued that they "do no harm," as Hume insists, is a more difficult question; but if there is harm done it is unrelated to the question of duty. Unrelated, that is, unless one accepts the principle that every possible beneficence is a duty, a principle which no one really accepts in practice, noble exhortations to the contrary. This point was made by John Stuart Mill against such rhetorical flourishes as

Robert Louis Stevenson's claim that "those who have become free of the necessity of long toil to exist, having the more liberty, have only the higher moral obligation to be up and doing in the interest of man."[50] Mill noted that this claim would have the consequence, if taken seriously, that we were all failing in our moral duties every time we enjoy ourselves in leisure; and nobody really believes that. No, the question of what good I should do is different from the question as to what obligations I have; and furthermore, the requirements of benevolence are of weaker moral force than the requirements of obligation. It is morally "open" to me whether or not to volunteer to help you shingle your roof in a way in which it is not morally open to me whether or not to keep my promise to help Smith shingle his. Each of us, solitaries included, must struggle with the call of benevolence, but its sympathetic strains should not be confused with the stern voice of duty.

Now obviously the deeper, more complete and enduring the solitude, the harder it is going to be to both accept some social obligation and place oneself beyond it—given some measure of a social conscience. And since solitaries have tended to be rather conscientious beings, some version of the next defense has usually figured in their philosophies.

(C) ARGUE THAT IN SOLITUDE ONE ACTUALLY IS FULFILLING ONE'S SOCIAL RESPONSIBILITY

This line of argument finds the fulfillment of social responsibility either in

1. resting and preparing to serve, or
2. what one is actually doing in solitude

The first alternative is served by the Restorative View of solitude that we discussed earlier, the view of those who, in Montaigne's words, "have only stepped back to take a better jump and to hurl themselves with a stronger impetus further into the crowd."[51] Although the gathering in retreat of the energies and commitments necessary for sustained service to others is not the only value of solitude, it is an important one, as the great examples of Jesus, Buddha, and Mohammed teach. More ordinary people, too, often look back to earlier

periods of solitude which were, as they now see, important preparations for their life's work. Having reviewed the virtues of solitude
earlier, we are now in a better position to understand how solitude
develops the full humanity which underlies the best kind of service to
others. As Thoreau wrote in his journal, "Just so sacred and rich as my
life is to myself, so it will be to another."[52] And solitude seems to be
particularly propitious for finding and appreciating this sacred richness.[53]

Most paradoxical of all the defenses of solitude, and correspondingly the most fascinating, is the insistence that the solitary agent
actually serves the community by his/her solitary actions, that in
solitude, disengaged from all other people, one can fulfill one's
obligations to the human community. This line of defense has been
developed by both religious and secular apologists, and there are some
intriguing similarities to be noticed.

To begin with the religious side, let us return to the *Ancrene Wisse*
and see how the author justifies the solitary withdrawal of the three
sisters. As Georgianna presents it,

> Though apparently invisible or hidden [and dead to the world], the anchoress is
> also told she is a visible model of sanctity to all Christians and a reliable and steady
> support for the whole Church. . . .
> "The night-raven under the eaves symbolizes recluses who live under the eaves
> of the church because they know that they ought to be so holy in their lives that all
> Holy Church, that is, Christian people, may lean upon them, while they hold her
> up with the holiness of their lives and their blessed prayers . . .
> "It is for this reason that an anchoress is called an anchoress, and anchored
> under a church like an anchor under the side of a ship, to hold it, so that the waves
> and storms do not pitch it over. So all Holy Church, which is called a ship, shall be
> anchored to the anchoress, and she shall hold it secure so that the puffing and
> blowing of the devil, that is, temptations, do not pitch it over."[54]

Thus the recluses serve society by setting a visible standard of religious
excellence, as well as through the (supposed) efficacy of their daily
penances and prayers.

A modern version of this defense is given by Paul Ziegler, O.S.B. In
his preface to Peter Anson's *The Call of the Desert,* he expresses some
exasperation with the question of the defensibility of solitude, pointing out that the solitary is answering a call from God, which renders
any concerns about selfishness "irrelevant." Sensing perhaps the
thinness of this reply, he closes the section by insisting

The world can do with the shining example of a few more solitaries who in their silence, powerlessness, and all-embracing poverty are witnesses for the self-sufficient and yet radiant peace which comes from love fulfilled in ever renewed generosity and sacrifice.[55]

Thomas Merton also develops this defense, writing in *The Silent Life,*

The monastery is neither a museum nor an asylum. The monk remains in the world from which he has fled, and he remains a potent, though hidden, force in that world. Beyond all the works which may accidentally attach themselves to his vocation, the monk acts on the world simply by being a monk. The presence of contemplatives is, to the world, what the presence of yeast is to dough . . .

He is not exempted from service in fighting the great battles of his age, but rather, as a soldier of Christ, he is appointed to fight these battles on a spiritual front, in mystery, by self-sacrifice and prayer.[56]

Elsewhere Merton writes that the monk is "capable of representing God in the World" by "bearing witness to the reality of the Incarnation of the Word," living "by and for a charity that keeps the *lumen Christi,* the light of Christ, burning in the darkness of an unbelieving world," dedicated to "ceaseless performance of every work of mercy, especially the spiritual works of mercy."

Through all these justificatory remarks there runs the notion that the monk can be both hidden and potent; but how so? How can the yeast work on the dough if it is sealed away in a separate container? Or to pursue Merton's other metaphor, how can the light kept burning in the desert help the darkness in the city?[57] The Medieval anchoresses were directly visible to all, but contemporary contemplative monks are not. Leaving to the side the question of the efficacy of the monk's prayers, can their social contribution be established?

It can by a line of indirection. Solitary monks nourish the church: their contemplative explorations, struggles for self-mastery, and commitments to devotion provide living examples which impress themselves upon clergy and congregation, who in turn reflect their light upon the everyday world. Even for agnostics there is a fascination and an inspiration in these religious solitudes. When outrage over world pollution is checked in the sad realization that one's own practices of consumption, multiplied a billionfold, are the real underlying problem, it is inspiring and hopeful to think of groups of people who have broken free of consumerism. Even if they do not show us how to do this on a large social scale, the knowledge that it can be done, is being done, is heartening.

Secular solitaries, it seems to me, provide exactly the same valued services. This seems to have been intentional in Thoreau's case: his retreat was close enough to Concord to call it "anchored under the wing," and Stanley Cavell thinks that the choice of locations was deliberate: Thoreau "placed himself one mile distant from his neighbors to make himself a visible saint."[58] Whether or not there was anything quite so deliberate about the original choice—after all the site at the pond was convenient on other grounds, as belonging to Emerson—very early in the "experiment" Thoreau seems to have fixed upon the idea that he would show people by example how they ought to live. Visitors were always coming to the pond—sometimes in large groups—and he was remarkably uncomplaining about these interruptions for a solitary. As for *Walden* itself, one line is repeated twice in the book (as Cavell seems to have been the first to notice): "I do not propose to write an ode to dejection, but to brag as lustily as chanticleer in the morning, standing on his roost, if only to wake my neighbors up."[59] The idea that self-improvement and solitary achievement (things to brag about) were the surest engines of social improvement was a Transcendentalist idea[60] which held a great deal of attraction in the mid-nineteenth century (though the exact process was usually left vague). Several of Thoreau's early defenders in the literary world insisted upon the service he performed for all humanity simply by living nobly at the pond alone. Lydia Maria Child, in a review of *Walden* written in 1854, defended Thoreau's solitude thus:

> The man who, with any fidelity, obeys his own genius, serves men infinitely more by so doing, becoming an encouragement, a strengthener, a fountain of inspiration to them, than if he were to turn aside from his path and exhaust his energies in striving to meet their superficial needs. . . . [living thus he will be] adding to the stock of true nobleness in the world.[61]

Charles Abbot, in a piece on Thoreau written in 1885, wrote:

> If a man of mental force would show that his brain and brawn need not come into conflict . . . would demonstrate that a day of toil in the fields can be followed by an evening of rational intellectual enjoyment, the world would quickly advance beyond the present state of agitation and unrest . . .[62]

If one can forgive the exaggeration in these passionate defenses, their central point holds now as it did then. In a dense world with too many temptations towards superficial sociality, the solitaries who pare it down to a minimum teach lessons which our sociality needs: our knowledge that they can withdraw in order to concentrate their powers encourages us to withdraw from superficial relations into more meaningful ones. Their disdain of social approval inspires us to be less dependent upon it. Their break with social forms stimulates us to imagine new ones. Indeed their mere existence produces a delightful wonder: simply knowing that there is a solitary living in the area, meeting a quiet person who keeps her own counsels, these cause me to wonder excitedly "what do you *do* there?"

There is a final way in which the works of solitude contribute to the social whole, and again it is insisted upon by both religious and secular apologists. Among the former, consider Henri Nouwen. In "Solitude and Community" he rejects the view that solitude is opposed to community, and also the restorative view that solitude is a mere instrument of community. Rather, we should see solitude and community as a "dynamic unity":

> Solitude is essential to community life because in solitude we grow closer to each other . . . We take the other with us into solitude and there the relationship grows and deepens. In solitude we discover each other in a way which physical presence makes difficult, if not impossible. There we recognize a bond with each other that does not depend on words, gestures or actions and that is deeper and stronger than our own efforts can create . . . There we grow closer to each other because there we can encounter the source of our unity.[63]

Like Tillich and Merton, Nouwen holds this deeper source to be God, "by whom we are called together in love, in whom we can rest and through whom we can enjoy and trust one another even when our ability to express ourselves to each other is limited."[64] True community, in his view, is not our own creation, for our own purposes, but rather our "obedient response to the reality of our being united" by God. The full experience of community, accordingly, requires the awareness of its source and purpose, and this awareness can only unfold in solitude. There one comes to "distinguish carefully between what can be creatively shared with others and what is best understood in the silence of our own heart."

Perhaps the reader followed the first quotation from Nouwen with the same sense of excited recognition as I did—but then felt dismayed to hear the traditional religious explanation of the nature of this strange bond which is felt more intensely in solitude. Why not, then, keep the phenomenology and throw away the theology? We would be in good company, for many secular defenses of solitude resemble very markedly this religious one—only purged of divine elements. With Nouwen fresh in mind, consider these remarks on the social value of solitude by Henry Bugbee, a contemporary American philosopher:

> I think that solitude is essentially a bringing to consciousness of the manner of our being in the world with other beings and of engagement in the working out of the import continually and cumulatively borne upon us of this participation. It therefore assumes the character of a reckoning . . . Solitude is that distance on beings from which they register with such power. . . .[65]

What happens in these moments of reckoning in solitude, when other beings "register" upon us, is that we feel "claimed in concern." This happens, Bugbee writes,

> In a twofold way: in a way bonding us with beings present to us, whether through memory, perception, or anticipation; and in a way underlying that bonding, but ever bearing on it—sponsoring, emending and renewing our concern with them, thus radically inflecting the way in which they come to mean to us, the way in which we are enabled to participate with them.[66]

The meaning I take from these vague statements is that social relationships have elements that can only be fully experienced, and a context[67] that can only be fully appreciated, in solitude; just as the fullest experience of self involves both unreflective absorption in one's projects and reflective distancing from those projects, likewise with one's engagements. Accordingly, the fullest experience of other people, the awareness of them which completes engagement and from which renewed engagement ought to flow, demands solitude. Alone on a hillside, feeling your connectedness to other people, as well as the limits which full personal being must place upon those connections, you are living out a part of the whole which is social life: part of your social responsibility is the responsibility to comprehend and appreciate social existence in these ways, and that part is best done in solitude.

All this seems true, but two questions occur to me: Is this state in which, though alone, people are "registering on me with such power" really solitude? And does not the social contribution of this state depend upon a renewing of the engagement, returning to social encounter with this fuller awareness, so that solitude once again begins to seem defensible only as an instrumentality of encounter?

Being "claimed in concern," feeling another "register with such power"—the forceful presence of the other in one's solitude does make it a lesser, or less pure, solitude. Recalling the fourfold matrix of disengagement from part 1, Bugbee is disengaged perceptually and actively from the other, but thoughtfully and feelingly absorbed there. Absorption in the orange geometry of a marigold would be a purer solitude, a disengagement from people more complete. Is Bugbee's solitude so impure that it crosses the line into encounter? As I have said, the four criteria of solitude entail that there is not one simple line to cross, nor one common grey area: when criteria conflict, as they do here, there is no clear answer to the question. However, I note that both Bugbee and Nouwen call this impure solitude a solitude, and that is my linguistic inclination as well (unless the emotional awareness of the other blots out all else and for a longer stretch of the solitude than usually happens). In any case, this impurity does not affect the argument in progress: for "pure" carries no weight of value here, a purer solitude is not, therefore, a better solitude. From the point of view of social contribution, the point of view of this chapter, the less pure solitude emerges as the better. From a pantheistic or self-creating point of view, the purer moments with the flower might be more valuable.

Does the Nouwen-Bugbee defense of solitude depend upon returning with its heightened awareness to encounter? Bugbee thinks so: he says that solitude "miscarries if it does not issue in a more decided participation with the beings of the world."[68] With this I disagree: although solitude provides a great service when its bondings flow on into continued encounter, there is a service performed even when the registering of others remains contained within itself. I think of it as the fulfilling of a covenant, though a covenant seldom articulated. The death of our loved ones brings this covenant sadly but richly to awareness: now the telling of the love must cease forever, but the love itself can continue to be lived. Alone in the twilight, as I recall the puzzled delight my parents took in my rambling life, as I consider now the locatedness which their love gave to those rambles, a poignant sensation of presence, of continuing connectedness, diffuses through me. Because they are now dead and will not again hear the grateful expressions of my love, do these solitary recollections "miscarry"? By no means: rather have I fulfilled a trust of love, the responsibility to preserve always its meaning and power in my life. It is when love does *not* continue to live thus in solitude that a responsibility has been avoided, that something has miscarried.

These, then, are the objections to the path of solitude and the defenses which have been marshalled against them. Has solitude been vindicated? I think it has—but not necessarily yours. Working alone is a great pleasure, but not advisable on your first day with a chainsaw. Solitude is not inherently self-indulgent, but it may be self-indulgent in your particular case, if you take off in the canoe again when it is someone else's turn. Solitude is not inherently misanthropic, but you may be a misanthrope, leading a bitter and unlovely life. Retiring to an island and floating around it in lovely reveries is no evasion of social responsibility if you have no one to keep, but expect criticism if you first put your five-year-old daughter into an orphanage, as Rousseau did. The more detached your solitude becomes, the longer that solitude endures, the stronger will be the objections on grounds of evasion of social responsibility; but those objections can be answered if you write what you believe and donate what you can and, most important of all, live vigorously and nobly, celebrating humanity from your lone vantage point, allowing the radiance of that life, quietly and with humility, to be seen by other people. Then you will teach Dr. Johnson that one kind of guardian of mankind can withdraw to solitude; then you will give to friends and the state the share which Cicero claims for them; then you will not waste your surpassing powers in the deaf air (Shelley). And your work, in the solitude, can have the significance of the mower's in Robert Frost's "The Tuft of Flowers":

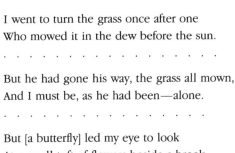

I went to turn the grass once after one
Who mowed it in the dew before the sun.

. . . .

But he had gone his way, the grass all mown,
And I must be, as he had been—alone.

. . . .

But [a butterfly] led my eye to look
At a small tuft of flowers beside a brook,
A leaping tongue of bloom the scythe had spared
Beside a reedy brook the scythe had bared.

The mower in the dew had loved them thus,
By leaving them to flourish, not for us,

Nor yet to draw one thought of ours to him,
But from sheer morning gladness at the brim.

The butterfly and I had lit upon,
Nevertheless, a message from the dawn,

That made me hear the wakening birds around,
And hear his long scythe whispering to the ground,

And feel a spirit kindred to my own;
So that henceforth I worked no more alone
. . . .[69]

CHAPTER 13

Women and Solitude

T here is an idea that runs deep through Western culture, an idea that vigorously denies the universality of the value of solitude: simply put, the idea is that solitude is not valuable for women. Solitude, it insists, has always been a male perogative, a male rite of passage, a male quest for self-knowledge and cosmic wisdom. In a woman, a passion for solitude has been thought unnatural and dangerous, contrary to her nurturant genius and tending towards evil, sad as a maiden aunt and frightening as a witch. So runs this traditional patriarchal thinking.

Contemporary feminist writings also raise some questions regarding the suitability of solitude as a value for women. As all traditional values come under critical reassessment and consequent redefinition, it is not yet clear what the fate of solitude will be. My own reading in this area causes me some concern. Firstly, solitude has not been the subject of much discussion[1]—although, as a woman remarked to me, the proportion may well be about the same as in men's writings. When solitude is mentioned, it appears more as an afterthought, a valuable item that ought to go somewhere on the list of goods but down near the bottom, as in this description by Belenky et al. of their subjects who had attained the highest level of epistemological development (on the authors' scale):

> They could be, at times, overwhelmed as they tried to balance their commitments —work, children's schedule, groceries, political action, time with their husbands or lovers, the needs of friends and parents, reading, learning, time with nature.[2]

I am also concerned that because of the association of solitude with independence and self-reliance, attributes which have been exalted for men at the cost of demeaning the traditionally female values of caring and connection, the attempt to defeat the hegemony of male values will lead to the dismissal of solitude.[3] I am convinced that this need not and ought not to follow. But what have women who have explored solitude said about it? What values have they found in it, and how does their experience differ, if it does differ, from men's experience?

First, however, I intend to examine at some length the patriarchal idea that solitude is not valuable for women. This perspective elevates some (alleged) facts to moral authority: the facts are that solitude has not been valued *in* women or *by* women, from which it is inferred that solitude *is not* valuable for women, period. Of course, the first—and most devastating—point to make against this view is a logical one: what ought to be cannot be inferred from what has been the case. "But women never *have* had the vote (reproductive freedom, freedom to travel unmolested, etc.)" is not a cogent argument for continuing these practices. This having been said, I am yet interested in the putative facts from which the patriarchal view is launched: to what extent are its truths true?

About one truth, there can be no doubt: for most of the three thousand odd years of Western culture solitude has been largely unavailable to women and considered to be a useless and dangerous passion in them.[4] While a complete history of solitude and women is out of the question here, a brief inspection of some historical attitudes is very revealing. Beginning with the ancient Middle Eastern cultures tributary to occidentalism, one scholar concluded from her survey of marital and sexual customs that

> In general, whether she was Egyptian, Babylonian or Jewish, the "free" woman—as distinct from the slave, whose lot appears to have been very little worse—was the property of her father during childhood and of her husband from adolescence on. Unless by some fortunate chance love intervened, she was to her husband essentially a mother for his children and a housekeeper, a kind of upper servant to be treated well unless she failed in her duties, in which case she could be dismissed or pensioned off according to inclination.[5]

Old Testament Judaism, for example, required every (decent) woman to be under the protective supervision of some male—whether an individual male or the "house" controlled by kindred males. The book of Deuteronomy lays down the following law regarding the disposal of widows:

> If brethren dwell together, and one of them die, and have no child, the wife of the dead shall not marry without unto a stranger: her husband's brother shall go in unto her, and take her to him to wife, and perform the duty of an husband's brother unto her.
>
> And it shall be, that the firstborn which she beareth him shall succeed in the name of his brother which is dead, that his name be not put out of Israel. (Deut. 25:5–6)

The concern of the law was not primarily the woman's happiness, but rather a patriarchal concern for the continuation of the male "name": a woman's happiness was assumed to exist in her inclusion under a male name—certainly not in any solitary autonomy.

The Book of Ruth is also instructive regarding Judaic attitudes towards female solitude. When Ruth's husband dies, she is advised by her mother-in-law Naomi to return to her mother's house, for the reason that Naomi cannot provide her with another husband. Ruth is insistent, however:

> Intreat me not to leave thee, or to return from following after thee: for whither thou goest, I will go; and where thou lodgest I will lodge: thy people shall be my people, and thy God my god:
> Where thou diest, will I die, and there will I be buried: the Lord do so to me, and more also, if ought but death part thee and me. (Ruth 1:16–17)

These are moving words to us, but not of more than passing interest to the Biblical storyteller; for the rest of the story focuses not on this deep feeling between two women, not on the personal responses of a young widow to her new aloneness, but on the urgent business of getting Ruth another husband. Mother-in-law and daughter return to Bethlehem, where Ruth asks Naomi for permission to go and glean in the fields of Boaz, a rich kinsman "in whose sight I shall find grace." The plan is successful: he notices her and speaks encouragingly. That evening, upon Naomi's instructions, Ruth goes late to the threshing floor and lays herself at his feet, asking him to accept her as a handmaid and kinswoman. Fortunately Boaz is an honorable man: they spend the night together chastely, and the next day he buys out another kinsman's rights to her. "So Boaz took Ruth, and she was his wife: and when he went in unto her, the Lord gave her conception, and she bare a son" (Ruth 4:13). The lone woman is re-absorbed into the clan; all is well.

Classical Greek attitudes towards the solitude of women can be inferred from a characterization made by Demosthenes in his legal argument, "Against Neaera": "Mistresses we keep for the sake of pleasure, concubines for the daily care of our persons, but wives to bear us legitimate children and to be faithful guardians of our households."[6] The kind of autonomy which we think of as providing the opportunity for sustained solitude, as well as the precondition for fruitful solitude, was not available to women; they were ever under the watchful authority of some male, an authority whose extent is strikingly delineated by Michel Foucault:

> For his part, the husband was bound by a certain number of obligations toward his wife (one of Solon's laws required the husband to have sexual relations with his wife at least three times a month if she was an "heiress"). But having sexual relations only with his lawful wife did not by any means form a part of his obligations. It is true that every man, whoever he might be, married or not, had to respect a married woman (or a girl under parental control); but this was because she was under someone else's authority; it was not his own status that prevented him, but that of the girl or woman who was the object of his attack. His offense was essentially against the man who held authority over the woman; this was why, if he was an Athenian, he would be punished less severely if he committed rape, overcome by the voracity of his desire, than if he deliberately and artfully seduced a woman. . . . The rapist violated only the woman's body, while the seducer violated the husband's authority.[7]

Women under such control were not considered aspirants for an ennobling solitude; if they spent some time alone, as probably seldom happened since they were generally confined to the women's quarters with other women and female children, nothing was expected to come of it.

Eighteen hundred years later in medieval Austria, a complex mixture of popular superstitions and learned doctrines congealed in the cultural nightmare of witchcraft, which spread throughout Europe a terror of the works of solitude—especially those of women. The canonical document here is the *Malleus Maleficarum* ("Hammer of Witches"), written by two Dominican inquisitors in 1486 to serve both as a theoretical treatise and as a practical guide for the detection and punishment of witches. Although a witch could be of either sex, the Latin title uses the feminine gender. Nor is this accidental, since the text contains an explicit discussion of why women are especially prone to witchcraft. In a section entitled "Why Superstition is chiefly found in Women," the authors retail the standard body of misogynist beliefs accumulated since antiquity, citing Ecclesiastes, Proverbs, Corinthians, Cicero, Seneca, St. Jerome, St. John Chrysostom, etc., and ending with the observation, "When a woman thinks alone, she thinks evil."[8]

During the three centuries that followed, over 100,000 witch trials were held in Europe, roughly 85 percent of which accused women.[9] The number of executions is not known, but appears to have been appallingly large. Important for our purposes is the fact that the stereotypical witch of medieval demonology was a solitary. This stereotype both determined and was determined by prosecutions: E. William Monter, who has studied trial records of the period, concludes that

> It is almost certain that fewer than half of all women accused of witchcraft were married at the time of their accusation. It is no accident that the typical witch of folklore should be an old woman dwelling off by herself in the woods.[10]

The lessons concerning female solitude taught by the persecutions of witches, generally condoned by both men and women for over three hundred years, were two: first, women alone are evil and dangerous, a menace both to others and to their own eternal salvation. Second, solitude is a burning offense: as Monter remarks, "The significance of witchcraft for the history of women lies in the simple but eloquent fact that it was the most important capital crime for women in early modern Europe."[11] These lessons regarding the evil and danger of women's solitude sank deep into the Western psyche, too deep to be very much affected by the passing of the superstitions which had given rise to them.

The early colonial period in the New World manifested its own obsession with witches, but also produced many milder condemnations of women's solitude. As Patricia O'Brien notes in *The Woman Alone,* a woman who was unmarried by age twenty in the colonies was called a "stale maid." The colonists also coined the term "spinster," used to refer to a single woman who was permitted to live with relatives on condition that she earn her keep by spinning cloth. Even when thus productive, however, she remained something of a monster, and the term probably incorporated both meanings.

The position of women during the Victorian era has been widely discussed, but never more interestingly than by doctors Pat Jallard and John Hooper, whose *Women from Birth to Death* collects excerpts from Victorian medical texts and lectures on Hygiene.[12] The prospects of solitude for a (proper) Victorian woman were dismal. E. J. Stilts, for example, in his treatise *Elements of Health and Principles of Female Hygiene* (1852) notes that

> woman, on the contrary [to man], ripening earlier into perfection, with the domestic hearth for her chief field of action, the affections of the heart for ever engrossing the chief portion of her energies, generally settles in marriage between 21 and 28 years of age . . .[13]

If "ripening" automatically turned her energies to marriage and family nurturance, the same was not true of the male: indeed

> The general aim of English wives is practically to convince their husbands how much happier they are married than when living in bachelor solitude, or when vainly roaming after happiness; for except domestic happiness, what does man gain by marriage? A great increase of expenses, of duties and of cares, it is true; but his experience is not augmented, nor his importance in society. Woman, on the contrary, acquires a social importance she could not otherwise attain . . .[14]

The social imperative to avoid solitary living is underscored in an article entitled "Old Maids" appearing in *Blackwood's Edinburgh Magazine* in July of 1872: the author observes that

> to be married is, with perhaps the majority of women, the entrance into life, the point they assume for carrying out their ideas and aims . . . If such a clear-sighted maiden refuses a pretender to her hand because he does not reach her social standard, she does so alive to the alternative of a future—a life which offers her few honours and small gratitude, in return for the sacrifice she makes to social obligations.[15]

Of course, things sometimes went wrong: having followed the social imperative into marriage, a woman might fail in the duties of her station. In *The Functions and Disorders of the Reproductive Organs* (1865), W. Acton discusses sanguinely what must have been a common occurrence:

> The French say that an Englishwoman makes a better mother than she does a wife, and they have some reason for so saying; as we often see, after the first year of married life, a woman becomes a slave to the nursery duties and neglects her husband and her personal appearance; and, in fact, sinking the duties of wife into those of the mother, and often regarding the husband as an incumbrance instead of treating him as the *chief,* the real, the only one requiring her care and love.[16]

Slave to the nursery or servant of the "chief, the real, the only one," these (or some combination thereof) appear to have been the options available to the Victorian wife, options which left little time and less approval for solitude.

Such were Victorian men's views of a woman's field of action. The few recorded female lecturers and writers of the time generally concurred, however, though discarding the images of slave and servant in favor of celebrations of the glories of motherhood. Frances Cobbe, in *The Duties of Women. A Course of Lectures* (1881), used the all-absorbing demands of "the great Profession of a Matron" as an argument against work or public service for mothers:

So *immense* are the claims on a Mother, physical claims on her bodily and brain vigour, and moral claims on her heart and thoughts, that she cannot, I believe, meet them all, and find any large margin beyond for other cares and work. She serves the community in the very best and highest way it is possible to do, by giving birth to healthy children, whose physical strength has not been defrauded, and to whose moral and mental nurture she can give the whole of her thoughts. This is her *Function,* Public and Private, at once,—the *Profession* which she has adopted.[17]

Immense claims, demanding "the whole of her thoughts," where would be the time for solitude? And what decent woman would refuse to serve her community "in the very best and highest way it is possible to do"?

Throughout these twenty-five hundred or so years of cultural history, misogynist ideas about women were also frequently used to underscore the threat women posed to *male* solitude. Their reputed quarrelsome nature and sexual allures were the subject of frequent jibes by the Romans: said one orator, "the man who does not quarrel is a celibate."[18] Virgil laments the distraction that women can cause, spoiling perfectly delightful solitudes:

With two fair eyes his mistress burns his breast;

He looks and languishes, and leaves his rest;

Forsakes his food, and, pining for the lass,

Is joyless of the grove, and spurns the growing grass.[19]

The Desert Fathers, with their eyes more on St. Paul's admonishments regarding celibacy ("It is good not to touch a woman" [1 Cor. 7:1], "For I would that all men were (celibate) even as I myself" [1 Cor. 7:7]) than Christ's example of compassionate interest in women, regarded women as a major threat to spiritual progress. Workman recounts several of the more extreme legends:

a pious girl of Alexandria, on discovering that it was her bright eyes that led a youth to pester her with his base offers of love, took up a weaver's shuttle and dug them out.

an abbess [said] to a monk who, when he met her, turned out of his way: "If you were a true monk," she replied, "you would not know whether we were women or not."

Of another monk we read that when he found it needful on a journey to carry his aged mother over a stream, he carefully wrapped her up in his cloak, lest by touching this "fire" the remembrance of other women should return."[20]

Petrarch repeated these themes with vigor, perhaps because he was tormented at Vaucluse with desires for the lover he was ostensibly escaping. Warming up with the story of Adam,

> that general parent of the human race, than whom, as long as he was alone, no man was happier, but as soon as he received a companion, none more wretched. Alone he stood up, with his companion he fell. Alone he was citizen of a happy land, with his companion he was a wanderer in unhappy exile. Alone he lived in peace and joy, with his companion in labor and much sorrow. Alone he had been immortal, as soon as he is joined with woman he becomes mortal. Behold herein a clear and conspicuous token of what posterity may hope from the companionship of women . . .[21]

he proceeds a few pages later, in a chapter entitled "No Poison is so destructive or so obnoxious to the life of solitude, as the company of women," to quote Virgil and Juvenal in support of the following advice: "Whoever you are that desire peace, keep away from woman."[22]

In modern times, the idea that women spoil solitude is conveyed in a poem by Rupert Brooke, "The Voice":

Safe in the magic of my woods
I lay, and watched the dying light.
Faint in the pale high solitudes,
And washed with rain and veiled by night,
Silver and blue and green were showing.
And the dark woods grew darker still;
And birds were hushed; and peace was growing
And quietness crept up the hill;
And no wind was blowing.

And I knew
That this was the hour of knowing
And the night and the woods and you
Were one together, and I should find
Soon in the silence the hidden key
Of all that had hurt and puzzled me—
Why you were you, and the night was kind,
And the woods were part of the heart of me.

And there I waited breathlessly,
Alone; and slowly the holy three,

The three that I loved, together grew
One, in the hour of knowing,
Night, and the woods, and you—
And suddenly
There was an uproar in my woods,

The noise of a fool in mock distress,
Crashing and laughing and blindly going,
Of ignorant feet and a swishing dress,
And a Voice profaning the solitudes.

The spell was broken, the key denied me
And at length your flat clear voice beside me
Mouthed cheerful clear flat platitudes.

You came and quacked beside me in the wood.
You said, "The view from here is very good!"
You said, "It's nice to be alone a bit!"
And, "How the days are drawing out!" you said.
You said, "The sunset's pretty, isn't it?"

. . . .

By God! I wish that you were dead.[23]

Solitude profaned by a quacking voice: no doubt most of us, men and women both, have had the experience, perhaps feeling momentarily the "urge to kill" which Brooke is honest enough to admit. Yet the violator of solitude in his poem is a woman, and the use of stereotypical images of flat superficiality, ignorance, and heedless emotionality ("crashing and laughing and blindly going") do intimate the idea that women are incapable of solitude: if they belong there at all, the poem suggests, it is as objects of male contemplation, and not as subjects.

In addition to these negative reasons for dissociating solitude and women, a "kinder" one was offered by the patriarchal tradition: women were wonderfully gifted by nature to fulfill an essential human role, that of nurturer. In caring for their husbands, in nurturing their children, in caring for the sick and the elderly, women made their great moral contribution to humanity. Solitude, with its emphasis on philosophical reflection and self-exploration, was irrelevant and unnecessary for these crucial activities. Besides, with the omnipresent demands of children, husband, sick relations, and elderly parents, where could a woman possibly find time for solitude? Whether in the brief escape from duty in an afternoon's solitude, or in the great escape which single living announced, traditionalists saw, and encouraged women to feel, a dereliction of duty. They were, on the whole, successful: even now, even among strongly independent women, the vague sense of selfishness permeates many solitudes. As Eileen Manion warns in "All Alone Feeling Blue? Women's Experience of Solitude," "The solitary woman must constantly combat the idea that she is not living 'as she should,' that she is not a true woman, a good woman because she is not caring for others."[24]

The upshot of these historical investigations is that part of the patriarchal claim is true: solitude has not been traditionally valued in/for women; and owing to the ability of male culture to enforce its vision of reality, solitude has not been very highly valued by women either.

There have always been exceptions, however. It may come as a surprise to learn that many early Christian women also fled to the deserts for "solitary combat with the Enemy." The *Sayings of the Desert Fathers* records the words of three Mothers—Theodora, Sara, and Syncletica—and they were not lacking in zeal: "It was said concerning [Sara] that for sixty years she lived beside a river and never lifted her eyes to look at it."[25] When Pachomius organized groups of anchorites into the first monastic communities early in the fourth century, he established twelve communities of women—apparently at his sister's urging.[26] About the same time Schenoudi is said to have had under his care "nearly four thousand monks and nuns."[27] Some of these had been great and powerful women, most famously the Roman Paula, a friend of St. Jerome's:

> Paula, a descendant of the Gracchi and of Scipio, was urged by her children not to leave them for the desert, [but] "she raised dry eyes to heaven, and overcame her love of her children by her love of God. She knew herself no longer a mother."[28]

A chilling story to our modern ears, but very inspiring to many early Christians.

There were also the great Mothers of monasticism. St. Benedict had a twin sister, Scholastica, who organized a convent along the lines of her brother's order. (Conscious of possible polluting influences, brother and sister allowed themselves only one reunion a year at the foot of Monte Cassino.[29]) About seven hundred years later, St. Francis of Assisi's dear friend Clare Favarone founded the "Second Order" of Franciscans, now known as the Poor Clares. St. Clare outlived St. Francis by many years, becoming a powerful figure in her own right whose counsels were sought by several Popes.[30] Also influential, through their writings on personal mystical experiences and the theological consequences implied therein, were Julien of Norwich (1343–1418) and St. Teresa of Avila (1515–1582).

Among literary solitaries, one could mention Aphra Behn, a seventeenth-century Englishwoman who chose to remain alone and childless after the early death of her husband, making her living writing plays, poems, and stories which enjoyed some popularity at court. One might also cite Louisa May Alcott; Manion remarks that this familiar writer

> who may, in *Little Women,* have done more than anyone else to idealise family life for generations of little girls, alternated as an adult between living alone and staying with her parents. She could do neither for long comfortably, nor with self-acceptance, but she courageously defended spinsterhood as an option for women in an era when unmarried women were casually referred to as "superfluous."[31]

George Sand, Emily Dickinson, and Beatrix Potter also come to mind, as do May Sarton and Alice Koller.

For the exemplification of courage and resourcefulness in solitary confinement, Dr. Edith Bone and Nien Cheng certainly rank as equals with Boethius and Burney and the Birdman of Alcatraz. Dr. Bone was a British linguist of Hungarian descent, active in the communist party during the 1930s and 1940s. Interested in the workings of a communist regime, she accepted work as a translator in Hungary in 1948; but shortly after her arrival in Budapest she was arrested on charges of spying for the British, and was imprisoned for seven years in solitary confinement. Although sixty and suffering from arthritis, Dr. Bone maintained her defiant attitude even when sent to a basement cell she called "The Black Hole":

> It was quite dark in there. There was no means of ventilation and no natural light at all, only electric light. In the cell itself the mortar was crumbling from the ceiling, spiders' webs hung in festoons, and on one side the wall had a sort of fur coat of fungus. On the other side, for some reason, there was no fungus but to

make up for this, there was water seeping down the wall. This water later froze into a thin coat of ice. My bed was attached to this wall and I could not pull it away; so I was in cold storage, so to speak, on ice. There was not only no heating but no means of heating at all. There was, on the other hand, a lot of very nasty dirt, human and rat droppings, and a perfectly infernal sink.[32]

In order to preserve her mental alertness in these terrible conditions, Dr. Bone recited poetry, translating freely between the six languages she spoke. Sometimes she composed and memorized her own verses:

Under the blanket of the dark I lie,
It is a warm blanket, soft as down.
It shields me from the jailer's spying eye,
And laps me in its folds as in a gown.[33]

Nien Cheng, a professional woman in Shanghai, was arrested during the frenzy of the Cultural Revolution in 1966 and held in solitary confinement for six years. Enduring terrible living conditions, brainwashing, and torture, Cheng survived partly through her ability to attune to the small bits of natural process still unfolding in her cell. The following episode reminds one of Robert Stroud and his first birds:

One day, in the early afternoon, when my eyes were too tired to distinguish the printed words, I lifted them from the book to gaze at the window. A small spider crawled into view, climbing up one of the rust-eroded bars. The little creature was no bigger than a good-sized pea; I would not have seen it if the wooden frame nailed to the wall outside to cover the lower half of the window hadn't been painted black. I watched it crawl slowly but steadily to the top of the iron bar, quite a long walk for such a tiny thing, I thought. When it reached the top, suddenly it swung out and descended on a thin silken thread spun from one end of its body. With a leap and swing, it secured the end of the thread to another bar. The small spider then crawled back along the silken thread to where it had started and swung out in another direction on a similar thread. I watched the tiny creature at work with increasing fascination . . . the spider proceeded to weave a web that was intricately beautiful and absolutely perfect, with all the strands of thread evenly spaced. When the web was complete, the spider went to its centre and settled there.
    Whether God had made the spider or not, I thanked Him for what I had just seen. A miracle of life had been shown me. It helped me to see that God was in control. Mao Tze-tung and his Revolutionaries seemed much less menacing. I felt a renewal of hope and confidence.[34]

Personifying the spider also helped to fortify Cheng:

I became very attached to the little creature after watching its activities and gaining an understanding of its habits. First thing in the morning, throughout the day and last thing at night, I would look at it and feel reassured when I saw that it was still there. The tiny spider became my companion. My spirits lightened. The depressing feeling of complete isolation was broken by having another living thing near me, even though it was so tiny and incapable of response.[35]

Women have also survived ordeals alone in nature, marshalling courage and ingenuity as remarkable as Admiral Byrd's. Christianne Ritter provides a case in point. Tempted by her husband's glowing descriptions of the Arctic hunting grounds of Spitsbergen, Ritter left her comfortable home in Germany to spend a year in a hunter's hut on the stony northern shore of the peninsula. Initially, she was shocked: arriving by steamer,

> I slowly discern in the distance a bleak, grey, long-drawn strip of coast and on it something that looks like a tiny box thrown up by the sea, which must be our hut. All the passengers come on deck and stare with the same gaping repulsion at the coast . . .
> It's a ghastly country, I think to myself. Nothing but water, fog and rain.[36]

Becoming by degrees acclimatized to living in the 10' × 10' hut with two men—her husband had neglected to tell her beforehand that he had invited a Norwegian hunter to spend the winter with them!—Ritter took great satisfaction in the "room of one's own" the men added on for her, though it was only 4' × 6'. She was not prepared, however, for the fury of an Arctic storm: the first one broke over the hut while the men were gone hunting for thirteen days.

> The gale was still increasing in violence. The hollow roaring undertone had swelled into unintermittent thunder. Now and again I could hear the first dull rumbling blows of the approaching storm at sea beating on the cliffs. It was cheerless in the hut . . . my hands were stiff with cold and black with soot. To add to it all my little lamp went out. So there I was in darkness, in the midst of that diabolic scene . . . The fire burned down quickly, and what could I do, in order not to burn still more precious fuel, but go to sleep? I felt my way into my little room. It was ice-cold, and I crept fully clothed into my little bunk. But it was easier to think of sleeping than to fall asleep, for here the noise if anything was still greater. To the crashing thunder of the storm was added the knocking and rapping of all the boards and posts leaning against the east wall. The wind was howling in the stovepipe, and on the roof the frozen corpses of skinned foxes, left up there for heaven knows what reason, were tapping and knocking.
> And the storm was still rising. Soon it was impossible to distinguish one noise from another. All were fused into a deafening roar. . . . Could a storm like this lift the hut from the ground, I wondered? If not, why should all these huts be weighted down with great logs?[37]

Ritter survived days of physical and emotional battling with the storm until, quite suddenly,

> the storm ceases, and a new experience makes an even more violent and terrible impact on my excited mind than the days of furious storm.
> For the first time I realize that in the solitude of an all-too-powerful nature things have a different meaning from that we attribute to them in our world of constant reciprocal relations between man and man. It dawns on me that in many cases it may be more difficult for a man to retain his ordinary humanity in the Arctic than to sustain his life in battle with the elements.[38]

More remarkable still is the story of Martha Martin, a gold prospector's wife who was left isolated on an Alaskan shore for several winter months sometime during the 1920s (her diary is not dated). Separated from her husband by a storm which stranded him and loosed an avalanche upon her, causing a broken arm and leg, Martin bravely splinted up her limbs and prepared to deliver her own child.

> I killed a sea otter today. I actually did kill a sea otter. I killed him with the ax, dragged him home, and skinned him. I took his liver out, and ate part of it. I'm going to eat the rest of it, and his heart, too. His liver was quite large, bigger than a deer's, and it had more lobes to it. It was very good liver, and I enjoyed it.
> Most of today was devoted to the sea otter; getting the hide off was a real task. It's a lovely skin, the softest, silkiest, thickest fur I have ever seen. I am going to make a robe for my baby out of the beautiful fur. My darling child may be born in a lowly cabin but she shall be wrapped in one of the earth's most costly furs.[39]

As the temperature dropped, Martin accelerated her preparations for the birth.

> The wind still howls, swirls, and rages. It's awful cold, maybe ten below . . . While I was out in the cold, my breasts ached. They drew up and the nipples stuck out firm, and they ached . . . Soon my child will be here, and I am not yet ready to receive her. So much to do and so little time . . .

> I have decided to burn the floor.

> I always think of the child as a girl. What if it's a boy? Oh, it couldn't be . . .

The child was born, after two days of labor, and it was a girl. Martin christened her Donna: "My darling little girl-child, after such a long and troublesome waiting I now have you in my arms. I am alone no more. I have my baby." A whole month was to elapse before she and the child were rescued. The native fishermen who discovered them were amazed:

There was a consultation in Siwash.
"Not dead?"
"No, not dead."

These exceptional women of whom we have been speaking provide striking counterexamples to the idea that women cannot handle solitude. But another thought occurs to me. These women excelled in solitude lived alone, the predominant male pattern of solitude. But what if there were distinct women's strategies of disengagement which did not involve living alone? If solitude is as important a human value as I have been arguing, one would expect to find that women have devised ways of obtaining it even when "confined" to the home and the family circle. And in fact this is just what we do find, solitudes distinguished from historically typical male solitudes in two important aspects, their *places* and their *works*.

When life is lived out largely within the confines of the house, special places must be found and secured for solitude. The bedroom has often been such a place. As Storr remarks,

> The Victorian lady used regularly to retire for a "rest" in the afternoon. She needed to do so because convention demanded that she should constantly be empathically alert to the needs of others without regard to any needs of her own. Her afternoon rest allowed her to recuperate from the social role of dutiful listener and ministering angel; a role which allowed no scope for self-expression. Even Florence Nightingale, who was far from being merely a ministering angel, found that the only way in which she could study and write was to develop a neurotic illness which released her from the burden of household duties and enabled her to retire to the solitude of the bedroom.[40]

For a somewhat more extended example of solitude within the home, consider the life of Emily Dickinson. An unusually intense and intelligent girl, she was not at first so emotionally different from other girls of her age:

> Like most young girls she rhapsodized about marriage and sentimentally effused about the great happiness and mystery of the union. Undoubtedly the meretricious presentation of love in popular books inspired some of these enthusiasms. One in particular, Ik Marvel's *Reveries of a Bachelor,* so impressed Emily that her disgruntled father denounced it and all similar modern books as being ridiculous. . . . [However] Marvel's vapid portrait of the languishing young girl established a cult of little girl mannerisms which Emily often imitated. She began signing her name "Emilie" and wrote to [her Brother] Austin that she hoped that they would never have to grow up.[41]

However, the intensity of her maturing personality began to render human relationships increasingly fraught with anxiety. Frequent bouts of illness forced—or enabled[42]—her to construct an emotionally more bearable world within the family house. By twenty-one she was running home after church to avoid meetings and begging off outside social engagements. She communicated with the world more and more through letters, devoting larger measures of her time at home to her poetry. Then broke the storm: around thirty (1860) she fell overpoweringly in love: "I cannot find my channel. The Creek becomes Sea."[43] At home, alone, she struggled desperately for control of the internal upheaval, striking off poem after poem—366 in 1862, and 400 in the next two years. The identity of this mysterious love, called "Master" in the poems, is not known to scholars and, given the ambiguity of Dickinson's letters, may not have even been known to the Master. Finally, in 1862, the unattainability of the object of her passion became undeniable, and she began the painful task of disengagement, withdrawing ever more deeply within herself through the poetry. The same year another fateful event occurred, no doubt connected to the first: Emily sent a batch of her poems, until then kept private, to a literary figure for advice. He replied encouragingly, but urged her to delay publication until certain "weaknesses" in her style could be overcome. For reasons which will always remain obscure, upon hearing this advice Dickinson decided almost immediately, and irrevocably, to remain a private poet. Writing at the time, "I find I need more veil," she strengthened the barriers around her, refusing even to come down to see guests at the house. With the shock of her father's death in 1874, the seclusion became complete: she saw no one face to face, communicated with her dear sister-in-law who lived across the street by letter and received visitors while sitting on a chair behind a half-open door. Thus she lived until her death in 1886.

No doubt this was an unusually solitary life for a woman of those times, but many elements of that life in the house are suggestive more generally regarding women's solitude. Jean Mudge has argued in *Emily Dickinson and the Image of Home* that, "Emily Dickinson's image of house or home, touching the poet's tangible and imaginative worlds at once, is perhaps the most penetrating and comprehensive figure she employs."[44] Consider, for example, the following two characterizations of solitude:

The Soul selects her own Society—
Then—shuts the Door—
To her divine Majority—
Present no more—

There is a solitude of space
A solitude of sea
A solitude of death, but these
Society shall be
Compared with that profounder site
That polar privacy
A soul admitted to itself—
Finite Infinity.[45]

Here is the solitude of a room ("shuts the door," "admitted to"), of a soul who burrows deeper within the house to find solitude, rather than rambling in the woods or climbing a mountain (Petrarch, Wordsworth, Thoreau).[46] Within this house-scape, the endless daily examination of each part of the dwelling reveals its own sacred groves and secret powers. Mudge believes that Dickinson "selected the hearth, front doorstep, her room, and the garden as indirect expressions of her identity."[47] The room, with its small desk and inkstand, was the inner sanctum of retreat from guests and family responsibilities, a cozy private place for the writing that was so much her life. There she could rise regally above the rejected social world, writing to her sister-in-law on a snowy Sunday morning when Church had been cancelled, "as I sit here, Susie, alone with the winds and you, I have the old *king feeling* even more than before, for I know not even the cracker man will invade *this* solitude, this sweet Sabbath of our's."[48] As for the front doorstep, the limit of her secluded world, it was there she stood to glimpse the great Mysteries that Shelley and Byron went to the Sea for:

> Dear Susie, I don't forget you a moment of the hour, and when my work is finished, and I have got the tea, I slip thro' the little entry, and out at the front door, and stand and watch the West . . . and the great, silent Eternity, for ever folded there . . .[49]

Perhaps nothing more movingly expresses her feeling for the house than the directions she left for her funeral: she asked, a friend recounted, "to be carried out the back door, around through the garden, through the opened barn from front to back, and then through the grassy fields to the family plot, always in sight of the house."[50]

The second distinctive feature of women's solitude has lain in its work: for what women often did, safe in their own rooms, was to write, and moreover a particular kind of writing. The world of publishing was largely closed to them—open just a crack to receive maudlin celebrations of the status quo. But that did not prevent, indeed no doubt encouraged, private writing in diaries and letters. Mary Jane Moffat and Charlotte Paynter, examining extant women's diaries written during the last two hundred years, discovered "a literature by women about their personal feelings that is so vast and varied that many shelves of anthologies would not exhaust the subject."[51] Under constant demands from the "public" family, and discouraged from any bold individuality in discussions with visiting males, the need for a private place to speak in a voice all one's own must have been insistent, and the diary form lent itself to this purpose. Moffat observes that

> The form has been an important outlet for women partly because it is an analogue to their lives: emotional, fragmentary, interrupted, modest, not to be taken seriously, private, restricted, daily, trivial, formless, concerned with self, as endless as their tasks.[52]

The striking thing about this literary form is its ubiquity: Moffat relates the remark of a student in one of her courses, "I never before realized I was part of a literary tradition." I remember, as a child in the 1940s, the kindly expectation that my sister would want to keep a diary—it was something girls did. I was certainly not discouraged from keeping one, but the expectation was not there. Writing in a diary was a "permission for solitude" given to girls who could not go off fishing at dawn alone as I used to do.

These diaries were understood to be private works, jealously protected from all eyes, but a few have nevertheless become public. One remembers the poignant liveliness of the diaries of Anne Frank:

> I haven't written for a few days, because I wanted first of all to think about my diary. It's an odd idea for someone like me to keep a diary; not only because I have never done so before, but because it seems to me that neither I—nor for that matter anyone else—will be interested in the unbosomings of a thirteen-year-old schoolgirl. Still, what does that matter? I want to write, but more than that, I want to bring out all kinds of things that lie buried deep in my heart.
>   . . . Yes, there is no doubt that paper is patient and as I don't intend to show this cardboard-covered notebook . . . to anyone, unless I find a real friend, boy or girl,

probably nobody cares. And now I come to the root of the matter, the reason for my diary: it is that I have no such real friend . . .[53]

Almost as famous (though very different indeed!) are the diaries of Anais Nin. These five volumes are, of course, extraordinary, the work of a very unusual woman; yet one of her primary motives would be recognized by any diary-keeper:

> The false person I had created for the enjoyment of my friends, the gaiety, the buoyant, the receptive, the healing person, always on call, always ready with sympathy, had to have its existence somewhere. In the diary I could re-establish the balance. Here I could be depressed, angry, disparaging, discouraged. I could let out my demons.[54]

Moffat emphasizes the moral growth which this process can produce:

> the courage required to acknowledge one's demons and the slow labor of bringing individuality to the fuller consciousness that honest and regular self-examination implies, are not only attributes of persons of character, they form character.[55]

If keeping a diary is a solitary work normally intended to remain private, the letter is clearly in a different category. The intensity of felt contact with the letter's recipient is often so powerful that the experience may seem more an encounter than a solitude (the ambiguous quality of the experience is succinctly captured in Dickinson's line to Susie, "alone with the winds and you"). On the other hand, the near environment of writing (and reading) letters is solitary detachment, and it is a detachment from the surrounding home that women have found particularly useful, just as its engagement function has been crucial for them when domestic duties prevented travel. Dickinson's case is again instructive, extreme as it certainly was. Christopher Benfey remarks,

> Today, when letter writing has disappeared, or is practiced as a faded art, it is hard to conceive of the importance of private letters in the nineteenth century, especially among literate women . . . [Her more than one thousand extant letters] show, among other things, how seriously Dickinson, her siblings, and her adult friends took the art of letter writing. It was an art that was learned, with rules and forms, and practiced constantly.[56]

No doubt Dickinson's use of the form was extreme: she sometimes hid when guests arrived, afterwards writing an apologetic letter insisting upon how good it was to hear their voices rising up through the house; she wrote daily letters to her sister-in-law who lived across the street; her contact with the man who captured her heart was largely via letters; at her death, an intimate confidant of many years had never seen her face. Yet who would not smile in recognition at this poetic account of receiving a letter?

> The Way I read a Letter's—this—
> 'Tis first—I lock the Door—
> And push it with my fingers—next—
> For transport it be sure—
>
> And then I go the furthest off
> To counteract a knock—
> Then draw my little Letter forth
> And slowly pick the lock—[57]

In thus serving women's needs to unburden themselves, to attune to their own inner experience and to express their creativity, diaries and letters provided crucial works of solitude. Moreover, family acceptance of the legitimacy of this work constitutes the most significant recognition of the validity of solitude for women during the last two centuries.

So much for history and tradition. What emerges is that, although severely limited in its scope, solitude has in fact been a value for women to a greater extent than patriarchal traditionalists have acknowledged. But now, leaving the level of factual claims about what has been the case, let us ascend to the evaluative plain: *Is* solitude an important value for women? *Ought* it to be recognized as such?

I must confess that these questions are hard for me to take seriously. Without doubt, solitude is of great value for women: the values that it bears—Freedom, Attunement to Self, Attunement to Nature, Reflective Perspective, Creativity—are not male values or female values but human values. As I have read women's writings on solitude, my overwhelming impression has been of a common experience. What women have found in solitude, considered abstractly as this study has attempted to do, men have found in solitude: the writings of St. Teresa,

Sand, Dickinson, Woolf, Sarton, Koller, Manion, Moffat, and others contain expressions of the same joys expressed by Eckhardt, Petrarch, Thoreau, Rilke, and Byrd. However, in the light of the historical truths just presented and the implication in some contemporary feminist writing that solitude is inconsequential as a value, some closing endorsements of solitude by women are in order.

Margaret Adams's researches convinced her of "the enduring validity of the singleness principle or, to express it more concretely, the overmastering desire of some individuals for psychological and social independence."[58] "This compelling intent to maintain territorial integrity of the spirit" leads towards solitude and single living, but does not imply withdrawn isolation:

> this parthenogenetic identity and its social correlate of psychological autonomy do not disqualify single people from making, sustaining, and enjoying significant interpersonal relationships . . . [which] do contribute to the personal growth and social development of many single people.[59]

However, psychological autonomy ought to come first:

> it is only possible to negotiate equality of status in relationships from a position of emotional and social independence. Psychological autonomy is, therefore, a protection against the preordained social obligations and emotional dependency that are inherent in many intimate relationships between the sexes.[60]

Moreover, as her book emphasizes, there are goods which this autonomy, and the solitary living which expresses it, offer which are undeniably attractive: privacy, freedom to travel, freedom to devote oneself unstintingly to one's work, and freedom to follow "the preoccupation many single people have with the world of ideas and the drive they manifest for expanding their living experiences, philosophical insights, and imaginative conception of life."[61] The last theme is repeated by Eileen Manion:

> There are joys to celebrate—moments of intense, ecstatic contemplation, exultation, a kind of grace. "Ordinary life does not interest me. I seek only the high moments." For anyone who agrees with Anais Nin, solitude is a rational choice. In solitude, 'ordinary life' can be reduced to a minimum; inner life can expand as far as it will go.[62]

With regard to "ordinary life," it is sometimes forgotten that a substantial number of women live alone, whether out of pure choice or because divorced or widowed: according to the U.S. census of 1987,

39.5 percent of all women over eighteen were single (although this figure is not an accurate guide to the proportion of women living completely alone, since it includes cohabiting couples and unmarried women living with children, relatives, and friends).[63] In Canada, the 1991 census revealed that 23 percent of women over fifteen years of age were single and never-married.[64] This last designation is particularly interesting for our purposes, since these women are more likely to actually live alone than other such surveyed groups, and hence likely to have the most extensive experience of solitude. How do they find it?

Ten years ago Nancy Peterson published her interview study of eighty never-married women, ages twenty to seventy-eight. Her summary of findings regarding self-perception and self-esteem is especially interesting:

> self-esteem of never-married women appears to be quite high . . . Their pride, their sense of self-respect and well-being came through. They felt good about themselves; they were happy with their lives. True, they sometimes talked of problems, heartaches, disappointments, and hurdles they had not been able to overcome. But defeat, "downness," and depression were rarely the tone of our encounters. Most often I heard about assessing, coping, drawing on internal strengths and external resources, setting goals and attaining them. They were proud to relate the story of their lives . . .
>
> When I was finished, I knew I had listened to a group of healthy, whole women, and I remembered Bruno Bettelheim's model of mental health: self-mastery and wholeness, autonomy. These women had those qualities in abundance.[65]

Peterson found the responses of her oldest interviewees particularly encouraging:

> How improbable the stereotype of the elderly spinster now seems—the notion of the sad and forlorn figure spending out her years bitter and alone. As a group, the older never-married women seem quite the opposite—vigorous, in control, happy and satisfied with their lives.[66]

The same impression of fruitful solitude emerges from the following interview with the actress Helen Hayes, who found in old age and widowhood the first opportunity for tasting its joys.

> There were many times in my life, until I was left alone, that I wished for solitude. I now find that I love solitude. I never had the blessed gift of being alone until the last of my loved ones was wrested from me. Now I can go sometimes for days and days without seeing anyone. I'm not entirely alone, because I listen to the radio and read the newspapers. I love to read. That is my greatest new luxury, having the time to read. And oh, the little things I find to do that make the days, as I say, much too short.
>
> Solitude—walking alone, doing things alone—is the most blessed thing in the

world. The mind relaxes and thoughts begin to flow and I think that I am beginning to find myself a little bit.[67]

In her philosophical autobiography, *The Stations of Solitude,* Alice Koller emphasizes the crucial role of solitude in self-creation:

> You begin marking out your line of travel in the instant you recognize the extent to which you are alone: thoroughly, unremittingly, without other human beings. I call it "being alone elementally": as an element, unconnected. It is the essential human condition.[68]

Here, and only here, writes Koller, you finally enter yourself; if you can bear that terrible aloneness, you will learn two things:

> The first is that you are a ragtag assembly of relationships and of memories of events and hopes for the future, that their accretion is something you have more or less stumbled onto over the years, that you have patched together a life from the leavings of others. . . .
> The second thing you will learn in that place is that your life is entirely within your own hands: to shape to you, to make fit you, as only you know how best to do, how to do at all.[69]

Then, she writes, you are ready to begin a true solitude, "your unending creation of the life you can choose to live":

> Being solitary is being alone well: being alone luxuriously immersed in doings of your own choice, aware of the fullness of your own presence rather than of the absence of others. Because solitude is an achievement. It is your distinctive way of embodying the purposes you have chosen for your life, deciding on these rather than others after deliberately observing and reflecting on your own doings and inclinings, then committing yourself to them for precisely these reasons.[70]

It is a difficult undertaking, and Koller is not modest about her success:

> I have succeeded in an undertaking few men have even attempted: I have become myself.
>
> I knew precisely what person I was and exactly how I wanted to live.[71]

The way of that self she calls "singling":

> It is a single life I live, in many senses. Single in being without other human beings, not a member of a group, unaffiliated. Single in being individual, of my own design, unalike. Single is being unmarried. But also single is being integrated into an unbroken whole, unified.[72]

The last achievement seems especially fortunate, considering that most people feel more or less conflict and ambivalence in the face of their commitments to self, work, and other people. Koller, however, finds that singleness in all these forms enables her to "wind together into a single cord the two strands of my work and my life in the country."[73] There she can live fully her commitments to her dogs and to the kind of philosophical writing she believes in, "living with no demarcation between them, as much one as I can make them":

> Persisting in unifying my life holds no religious significance for me. It is, rather, a moral and an intellectual pursuit. Moral, in being about the kind of person one is or can become. Intellectual, in being unceasingly concerned to clarify and to bring together into one consistent whole what would otherwise be the erratically joined parts of my mind and my actions, each within each, each to each. The philosopher I am is inextricably entwined with the person I am.[74]

Emily Dickinson, Louisa May Alcott, Virginia Woolf, Margaret Adams, May Sarton, Nien Cheng, Christianne Ritter, Eileen Manion, Nancy Peterson, Helen Hayes, Alice Koller, and the other women quoted throughout these reflections claim for solitude values and ideals of attainment to which any sensitive human being must bow with respect. They are not "masculine" values, opposed to "feminine" values, but human values. The solitudes they irradiate are, in their essential nature, not different from the solitudes of men.

However, discussions with a number of women who love and seek solitude has brought home to me the severity of two obstacles to the attainment of fruitful solitude for women. The first is mentioned by Manion above: so long as women are socialized to take primary responsibility for the care of others it will be correspondingly difficult to disengage consciousness from other people in the way that solitude requires. As Manion remarks,

> The woman who wants to integrate work or even just some independent activity of her own into her caring for others must constantly struggle for time for herself. That struggle may exhaust her so that it becomes difficult to use her time [in solitude] productively.[75]

Moreover, even if an afternoon a week might be found away from children and husband and aging parents, mental disengagement from their omnipresence can be extremely difficult: when I asked a friend if, given her expressed desire for solitude, she couldn't get away on a regular basis she replied sadly, "What would be the point?"

The other obstacle to women's solitude is particularly disturbing: violence against women. The North American statistics are appalling: they differ slightly from year to year, from source to source, from Canada to the United States, but the following are characteristic:

At least one in four Canadian women will be sexually assaulted at some time in their lives, half before age 17.

A recent study of reports collected from 13 police departments between 1988 and 1991 indicates that sexual assault is heavily directed at girls and young women, and that the younger the victim the more likely an assault will be sexual.

Of the aboriginal women surveyed by the Ontario Native Women's Association, 80% had been assaulted or abused.

Of the women who were born with a disability surveyed in another study, 53% had been raped, abused or assaulted.

Fear of sexual assault limits women's participation in city life. 56% of Canadian women living in cities feel unsafe walking alone after dark in their own neighbourhoods.[76]

The last statistic makes the connection between this violence and women's solitude brutally clear: solitary men may wander the streets or the parks or the beaches at night but more than half of all women are afraid to do so. In the daytime the fears are still there, in marked contrast with the typical male experience. Men experience mainly irritation when a solitary walk on a deserted beach is disturbed by the appearance of a figure in the distance; but for very many women, that irritation would be compounded by apprehension. Even when no figure appears, a general sense of watchfulness and vulnerability pervades many women's solitudes in nature—hardly emotions liable to increase one's enjoyment of freedom, attunement to nature, or any of the other values of solitude.

The inherent value of solitude for women documented in this chapter makes the two obstacles just described especially repugnant. The socialization of women to take primary responsibility for everyone must cease. The violence must stop.

CHAPTER 14

A Universal Value?

Solitude . . . is not an exclusively Mexican characteristic.

—OCTAVIO PAZ

I s solitude of universal human value? The reflections of these chapters, ranging over many centuries, social conditions, philosophical persuasions and character types have inclined me towards that opinion. Of course, I am well aware that not all societies have placed a high value upon solitude: as a culture values the five virtues of solitude so will it value solitude, and there certainly are historical peoples that have placed little value upon those virtues—the Golden Horde of Genghis Khan and the Toltecs of fifteenth-century Mexico come to mind. Moreover, for long historical periods the subsistence needs of both individuals and societies were too pressing to allow much time for the pursuit of solitude, as Famine, Pestilence, and War herded men and women close together for survival. What these cases really show, however, is only that brutality and hardship can reduce human existence below the level where many true values can be realized. But as levels of peace and health rise, the virtues of solitude come more and more into their own. Moreover, I have been struck by the appearance of testaments to solitude even in the darkest times: the lives of the Desert Fathers, the first monastics, and Boethius stand out sharply against the destructions of the last years of the Roman Empire, just as Victor Frankl's stolen solitudes recreate humanity among the horrors of Auschwitz.

But there are those who find even this qualified a universalism naive. They argue that solitude as we understand it, a time in which the individual disengages from society in order to express individual freedom, attune to individual nature, bring the spirit into harmony with nature, engage in individual reflections and explore individual creativity, is not commensurable with historically earlier forms of aloneness because of radical differences in the experience of individuality. It is claimed that the *individual,* as we conceptualize that creature, only emerged from group-consciousness around the time of the Renaissance, becoming more strikingly and painfully separated from the social substance as capitalism developed in the early modern period. Preindustrial and primitive societies, in this view, consist of "individuals" who are completely group-identified: they do not think of themselves as separate individuals in the way that we do, so that the self-exploration and self-attunement we regard as key virtues of solitude are neither possible nor meaningful to them. Indeed, it is sometimes claimed that group dependence and group definition make such people instinctively hate and fear solitude.

Sayre seems, with some qualifications, to take this view, at least with regard to classical Greece before the fifth century and with regard to the medieval period. He argues that solitude was primarily, for the early Greeks, a place of exile from one's city—whether into the wilderness or into another foreign city—and that to be thus exiled was "one of the worst fates for a Greek citizen," since "to the Greek mind one is truly alive only within the context of one's city."[1] As evidence he cites Medea's anguished cry to the women of Corinth that she is "lone, cityless, and outraged . . . Mother nor brother have I, kinsman none, for port of refuge from calamity."[2] Electra, "an outcast from the polis because of her hostility to Aegisthus," is still not completely alone, since "she does not think of herself as existing apart from her lineage," and the same is true of Antigone, whose defiant action places loyalty to her clan above loyalty to King Creon:

> Thus Antigone and Electra, while they feel destitute of family support in a hostile city, are in a more fundamental way united with all of their family. For their entire being is defined by its participation in a lineage. They have no individuality except as an expression of the larger group's destiny.[3]

Sayre believes that individual existence began to change in the sixth century BC, owing to "the growth of a new economy based on commerce and exchange":

> the individual—free to make, buy and sell on his own account—began for the first time in human history to exist with relative autonomy from the social group. Yet strong solidarities—social and religious—continued to enclose and protect this individual. He was not yet, and would not be for many centuries, a monad isolated within the human community.[4]

That the "emergence into individuality" did not occur until the Renaissance was famously argued by Jacob Burckhardt in *The Civilization of the Renaissance in Italy*. There he wrote,

> In the Middle Ages both sides of human consciousness—that which was turned within and that which was turned without—lay dreaming or half awake beneath a common veil. The veil was woven of faith, illusion, and childish prepossession, through which the world and history were seen clad in strange hues. Man was conscious of himself only as a member of a race, people, party, family, or corporation—only through some general category. In Italy this veil first melted into air; an *objective* treatment of the State and of all the things of this world became possible. The *subjective* side at the same time asserted itself with corresponding emphasis; man became a spiritual *individual,* and recognized himself as such.[5]

Weber, Tawney, Durkheim, and others then traced the growth of individualism to such factors as the Protestant work ethic, the growing division of labor, and the new possibilities for separation within the family dwelling.

There is certainly erudition behind these claims, and yet something seems wrong: for the consequence of these general views, taken literally, would be that Achilles, Medea, St. Antony, Peter Abelard, and Petrarch were not individuals, which is absurd. Perhaps the problem is one of words: "self," "individual," "individuality," "self-conscious" are all susceptible to varying interpretations. I had better begin with terminology, then, if I am to respond to these learned doubts about the pre-Renaissance existence of individuality (enough individuality, that is, for the valuing of solitude). Here are some interesting etymological observations by Jim Swan (one of the doubters):

> "Individuality," in fact, did not make its first recorded appearance until the early seventeenth century, apparently in response to the new development in the meaning of "individual." The history of this latter word is remarkable; it underwent almost a complete reversal of meaning. For "individual" as an adjective, two related meanings, first recorded in Middle English, became obsolete during the last half of the seventeenth century: (1) "One in substance or essence, indivisible"; (2) "inseparable." Then two modern meanings were introduced during the seventeenth century: (3) "Existing as a separate indivisible entity; numerically one, single, particular, special"; (4) "Distinguished from others by attributes of its own." The change from the second to the third and fourth meanings, from being inseparable to being separate and distinct, is a radical one. It describes the transition to the modern experience of identity.[6]

Granting these linguistic developments, and granting the important growth in individuality which they betoken, I think we have to insist that Sayre, Burckhardt, Swan, et al. have considerably overstated their case. No doubt Medea and Electra are strongly family-identified, more so than Thoreau and Sarton (though doubtfully more so than Dickinson or Lindberg), but they stand out to us, as they did to the Greeks whom they fascinated, as individuals in both senses (3) and (4)—the "modern" senses. Medea is fiercely aware of the wrong done, not to her clan or her lineage, but to herself personally: in her own eyes, she is certainly "distinguished from others by attributes of her own" (sense 4). Moreover, in refusing Jason's offer of a place with "old friends that dwell on foreign shores, who will entreat thee well" she refuses the sort of absorption into the group which became Ruth's fate. True, a woman must have a city, and she does arrange a place of sanctuary with Aegeus, King of Athens; but there is no suggestion of desire for inclusion in the active life of that polis. Moreover, her negotiations for sanctuary are straightforwardly individualistic, a quid pro quo: if Aegeus gives her a place she will use her sorcery to cure his impotence. In her own eyes, certainly, she "existed as a separate indivisible entity" (sense 3). As for Electra and Antigone, the separable individuality of each is highlighted by the behavior of their sisters who are too timid to break free of traditional social roles. And when Ismene finally does take courage, late in *Antigone,* and seeks to immerse herself in her sister's guilt, as we would expect a family-defined character to do, Antigone scornfully insists that she acted alone:

> *Ismene:* I'll say the deed was mine, if she consents:
> My share of the blame I bear, and do not shrink.
> *Antigone:* Justice forbids thy claim: neither didst thou
> Agree, nor I admit thee to my counsels.
> *Ismene:* I am not ashamed, in thine extremity,
> To make myself companion of thy fate.
> *Antigone:* Whose was the deed, know Hades and the dead . . .[7]

The complicated forces of family guilt and atonement in which the Greeks believed are undeniably essential elements in the mentality of these women; yet equally undeniable is the individuality of each protagonist's struggle with her situation. It only remains to point out that Medea, Antigone, and Electra each settled on their courses of action in solitude.[8]

Burckhardt remarks that in the Middle Ages "Man was conscious of himself only as a member of a race, people, party, family, or corporation—only through some general category."[9] Again, I must complain of exaggeration, at least if it is meant that the medieval individual did not ponder his/her individual relationship to the race, people, and so on, the sort of pondering that solitude would be propitious for. Not to speak of exceptional cases such as the *inclusi,* one remembers the solitary vigil a squire was expected to keep the night before receiving his arms as a knight, a vigil intended to include reflection upon a knight's obligations and his own worthiness. One also recalls medieval treatises on courtly love, which emphasized the need for soul-searching on the part of both lady and lover. The dialogues in Andreas Capellanus's *The Art of Courtly Love* (written around 1185), for example, reveal a clear awareness of individual differences, personal attributes which make a lover suitable/unsuitable, attributes upon which both man and woman surely reflected long during the extensive periods of separation that characterized this unique form of relationship. Moreover, although the practice of courtly love was restricted to the upper classes, Capellanus discusses the proper way for a man or woman of the "middle class" (the class of tradespeople) to proceed, and the following retort by a woman of that station to a noble suitor demonstrates a marked sense of individuality:

> I am greatly pleased by the interpretation of your words by which you allow me to consider which lover I should select as preferable [rather than feeling bound to choose a man of my own social class], because I guard that gate of Love's palace which neither refuses to let anybody into the palace nor permits everybody to enter who asks, but admits only the man who gets in on the strength of his own good character after we have consulted long and deliberated carefully. Therefore after I have thought the matter over and carefully weighed the considerations, I shall try to admit the better man.[10]

There appear, then, to have been individuality enough and work enough for solitude during the Medieval period.

In the remarks quoted above, Jim Swan locates the arrival of the modern concept of individuality in the seventeenth century. Storr cites another interesting study:

> [Peter Abbs] points out that, according to the *Oxford English Dictionary,* it was not until 1674 that the word 'self' took on its modern meaning of 'a permanent subject of successive and varying states of consciousness'. He goes on to list a number of instances of 'self' forming compounds with other words which all entered the language at roughly the same time. Self-sufficient (1598), self-knowledge (1613), self-made (1615), self-seeker (1632), selfish (1640), self-examination (1647),

selfhood (1649), self-interest (1649), self-knowing (1667), self-deception (1677), self-determination (1683), self-conscious (1687).[11]

Caution is advisable, however, in drawing inferences regarding the state of mind of people who preceeded this time, as the misadventures of a sixteenth-century Italian miller, masterfully reconstructed by Carlo Ginzburg from the records of several heresy trials, reveal. Domenico Scandella, called Menocchio, was born in 1532 in a small town in the hills near Venice. A miller by trade, he was a talkative fellow who got on well with everyone, even serving as a minor official in the local government. Unfortunately for him, his favorite subject of conversation was theology, an area in which he had some very eccentric opinions. As a neighbor said later, "He is always arguing with somebody about the faith just for the sake of arguing—even with the priest," and not just arguing, but "preaching and dogmatizing shamelessly."[12] This behavior finally reached the ears of the Holy Office of the Inquisition, and he was arrested and examined for heresy. Although counselled by a local vicar to simply answer questions in a humble way and "try not to talk too much," Menocchio could not resist the temptation to try out his theories on the learned judges. Here is some of what they heard:

> I have said that in my opinion, all was chaos, that is, earth, air, water, and fire were mixed together; and out of that bulk a mass formed—just as cheese is made out of milk—and worms appeared in it, and these were the angels. The most holy majesty decreed that these should be God and the angels, and among that number of angels, there was also God, he too having been created out of that mass at the same time, and he was made lord, with four captains, Lucifer, Michael, Gabriel, and Raphael.[13]

For four long months of interrogation Menocchio poured out heresies such as these, leaving the judges no alternative but to convict him. He was sentenced to life imprisonment, but after serving two years appealed for pardon, and because of his apparent contrition was released on terms of confinement to his own village, with orders not to discuss theology. Working at a variety of jobs—schoolteacher, guitar player at festivals, minor official—many years passed safely; but in the end he could not keep silent, and word of his relapse into disputatiousness reached the Holy Office, which promptly had him arrested. Now an old man, he was interrogated, tortured, and finally executed.

Ginzburg emphasizes the individuality and self-determination of this unsimple miller. Throughout lengthy interrogations, "Menocchio showed himself ready, almost insolently, to exercise his freedom of judgement, and his right to assume an independent stand": when the judges demanded to know who had taught him these heresies, he insisted, "My opinions came out of my head." Menocchio was well aware of the danger involved in holding original ideas, and tried to effect obedient orthodoxy; but in the end he could not contain his pride: "I have never associated with anyone who was a heretic, but I have an artful mind, and I have wanted to seek out higher things about which I did not know."[14] The judges must have found this exasperating in an ordinary miller: in their condemnation at the sentencing session, they complained loudly of his audacity and obstinacy: "thus pertinacious in these heresies . . . you persevered with an obdurate heart . . . with diabolical mind you affirmed . . . you contrived this most wicked thing."[15] During the second trial fifteen years later, Menocchio was threatened with torture if he would not reveal his accomplices. He insisted that he had none, and persevered in this insistence even when shown the instruments of torture: "They prepared him for the strappado. 'Oh Lord Jesus Christ, mercy, Jesus mercy, I don't remember having spoken with anyone, may I die if I have either followers or companions, but I have read on my own, Oh Jesus Mercy!' "[16] Finally, after two stretchings, he gave them a name, but it was clearly concocted in order to end the torture.

Domenico Scandella, called Menocchio, was not a modern individual but he was certainly an individual in the modern sense of the term. This is particularly interesting because of his social rank, in the light of claims that individuality was at best an upper class phenomenon. He also displayed many of the attributes which apparently received common English designations only in the next century. How representative was the talkative Miller? It is clear that the townspeople regarded him as an eccentric, yet he got along and was several times chosen to hold a minor office—even after he was convicted of heresy. Moreover, the church's concern over unorthodox opinions among the lower classes seems to have been in part a recognition of the dangerous individuality about in the land. During this period of the Reformation, theological dispute had spread through every class, even in rural Italy. A poet of the day wrote, "The porter, the maidservant, and the bondsman dissect free will and make hash of predestination,"[17] and one of the books Menocchio read contains the following complaint:

Many fools who think themselves scholars
Speak constantly of Holy Scripture,
Barbers, smiths and tailors,
Theologizing beyond measure,
Causing people to fall into many errors,[18]

It would be quite wrong, therefore, to conceive of Menocchio as some strange goat who unaccountably wandered off from the herd into self-consciousness. No, sixteenth-century individuals were individuals, separable enough in their own minds to appreciate and utilize the solitude that was often their lot.

Anthropology has taught us to be suspicious of attributions of pan-human universals, and it has done so largely by studying preindustrial, precapitalist social groups with a tribal organization. What these studies reveal, not surprisingly, is that the valuation of solitude varies considerably from group to group. True, there are peoples like the Tarahumara Indians of the Sierra Madre in Mexico, who have, writes Professor J. Ralph Audy, "almost a cult of solitude":

A small family may live in a cave 10 miles from its neighbor and keep sheep . . . A little boy of six may take his ration of pinole [corn ground into a powder] and disappear with the sheep for one or two weeks without seeing a single other person before he returns. In the hinterland these Indians are so accustomed to leading solitary lives that they feel embarrassed and at a loss when called on to converse with others. In fact they are so shy that they may even start a conversation with their backs toward each other. The only time they seem to communicate freely—verbally, nonverbally, or sexually—is on the occasions of periodic drinking parties . . .[19]

On the other hand, there are societies like the Zuñi Indians of the American Southwest who choose to live in very densely populated villages.

However, even in apparently solitudeless societies, subtle methods of disengagement are observable. This point is well made by Clifford Geertz in a discussion of the norms and mechanisms of privacy which exist in two aboriginal societies in Indonesia. Of course, privacy is not solitude, as we have seen, but it is easy to extract some relevant lessons.

In Java people live in small bamboo-walled houses, each of which almost always contains a single nuclear family . . . The houses face the street with a cleared front yard in front of them. There are no walls or fences around them, the house walls are thinly and loosely woven, and there are commonly not even doors. Within the house people wander freely just about any place any time, and even outsiders wander in fairly freely almost any time during the day and early evening. In brief, privacy in our terms is about as close to nonexistent as it can get. . . . the Javanese have literally almost no defense against the outside world of a physical sort. The result is that their defenses are mostly psychological. Relationships even within the household are very restrained; people speak softly, hide their feelings and even in the bosom of a Javanese family you have the feeling that you are in the public square and must behave with appropriate decorum. . . . It is not, in short, that the Javanese do not wish or value privacy; but merely that because they put up no physical or social barriers against the physical ingress of outsiders into their household life they must put up psychological ones and surround themselves with social barriers of a different sort.[20]

Geertz then compares the Javanese situation to that found in nearby Bali: there

people live in houseyards surrounded by high stone walls into which you enter by a narrow, half blocked-off doorway. . . . In contrast to Java, nonkinsmen almost never enter one's houseyard. Within the yard one is in one's castle and other people know better than to push their way in (if they wish to see you they will send a child to fetch you, etc.).

In contrast to the restrained, "stuffy" interpersonal atmosphere of a Javanese house, however, the Balinese family manifests "a tremendous warmth, humor, openness, . . . [but] As soon as the Balinese steps through the doorway to the street and the public square, market and temples beyond, however, he becomes more or less like the Javanese."[21] Geertz's observations illustrate what sociologists call social distancing or avoidance rules, norms which enable individuals to protect themselves from the strains of both casual and intimate encounters. These methods of distancing, of creating a private, personal, inviolable space, are quite varied: "Restricting the flow of information about oneself in the extended household is often accomplished by covering the face, averting the eyes, going to one's mat, or facing the wall."[22] Young Vincent Van Gogh adopted such a strategy for distancing himself from the family group (within which he felt uncomfortable): his sister wrote that when eating at the table with the family he kept his eyes half-closed.[23] Such distancing behaviors sound, returning from privacy to our primary interest in solitude, like strategies for disengaging from others to be alone with oneself. They remind us that there can be solitude in a crowded thatched house on a mat in the corner. And they call to mind an ancient Chinese saying: "Greatest hermit in crowded street."[24]

The Plains Indians of nineteenth-century North America were preindustrial, precapitalist tribal peoples. Group-identified and dependent upon the group for survival in the face of other hostile tribes and hostile whites, they would appear to be an interesting test case: did solitude play any important role in their existence? According to one of them, it did. Charles Alexander Eastman (Ohiyesa) was a mixed blood Sioux, the descendant of a white artist and a Sioux chief. During the Sioux uprising of 1862, Eastman, then only four, was separated from his father, and fled with his grandmother to Canada, where he lived among his people until reunited with his father in the Dakota Territory at age fifteen. In manhood, he became one of the best-known and most highly educated Native Americans of his time, attending Dartmouth and Boston University where he earned degrees in Science and Medicine. A witness to the events that culminated in the Wounded Knee massacre, he dedicated himself to preserving the knowledge and appreciation of Native American culture, writing eleven books with the help of his wife Elaine Goodale Eastman. In *The Soul of the Indian* (first published in 1911), he undertook to portray "the religious life of the typical American Indian as it was before he knew the white man." Here are some excerpts from that account:

> The original attitude of the American Indian toward the Eternal, the "Great Mystery" that surrounds and embraces us, was as simple as it was exalted. To him it was the supreme conception, bringing with it the fullest measure of joy and satisfaction possible in this life.
> The worship of the "Great Mystery" was silent, solitary, free from all self-seeking. It was silent, because all speech is of necessity feeble and imperfect; therefore the souls of my ancestors ascended to God in wordless adoration. It was solitary, because they believed that He is nearer to us in solitude, and there were no priests authorized to come between a man and his Maker.[25]

The Sioux, like the Hopi to the Southwest, sent the ripening young man out upon a vision quest:

> The first *bambeday*, or religious retreat, marked an epoch in the life of the youth, which may be compared to that of confirmation or conversion in Christian experience. Having first prepared himself by means of the purifying vapor-bath, and casting off as far as possible all human or fleshly influences, the young man sought out the noblest height, the most commanding summit in all the surrounding region. Knowing that God sets no value upon material things, he took with him no offerings or sacrifices other than symbolic objects, such as paints and

tobacco. Wishing to appear before Him in all humility, he wore no clothing save his moccasins and breech-clout. At the solemn hour of sunrise or sunset he took up his position, overlooking the glories of earth and facing the "Great Mystery," and there he remained, naked, erect, silent, and motionless, exposed to the elements and forces of His arming, for a night and a day to two days and nights, but rarely longer. . . . In this holy trance or ecstasy the Indian mystic found his highest happiness and the motive power of his existence. . . . Of the vision or sign vouchsafed to him he did not speak, unless it had included some commission which must be publicly fulfilled. Sometimes an old man, standing upon the brink of eternity, might reveal to a chosen few the oracle of his long-past youth.[26]

Eastman also emphasized the role of solitude in daily life:

His daily devotions were more necessary to him than daily food. He wakes at daybreak, puts on his moccasins and steps down to the water's edge. Here he throws handfuls of clear, cold water into his face, or plunges in bodily. After the bath, he stands erect before the advancing dawn, facing the sun as it advances upon the horizon, and offers his unspoken orison. His mate may precede or follow him in his devotions, but never accompanies him. Each soul must meet the morning sun, the new sweet earth and the Great Silence alone![27]

Speaking of mates, what role did solitude play in the life of a Sioux woman? Discussing the religious dimensions of mothering, Eastman writes:

it was supposed by us that the mother's spiritual influence counted for most. Her attitude and secret meditations must be such as to instill into the receptive soul of the unborn child the love of the "Great Mystery" and a sense of brotherhood with all creation. Silence and isolation are the rule of life for the expectant mother. She wanders prayerful in the stillness of the great woods, or on the bosom of the untrodden prairie, . . .

And when the day of days in her life dawns—the day in which there is to be a new life, the miracle of whose making has been intrusted to her, she seeks no human aid. She has been trained and prepared in body and mind for this her holiest duty, ever since she can remember. The ordeal is best met alone, where no curious or pitying eyes embarrass her; where all nature says to her spirit: "'T is love! 't is love! the fulfilling of life!" When a sacred voice comes to her out of the silence, and a pair of eyes open upon her in the wilderness, she knows with joy that she has borne well her part in the great song of creation![28]

No doubt Eastman somewhat exalted the life of the Sioux in the preinvasion period—he was writing, after all, largely to combat the image of the Indian as "savage." But even allowing for some exaggeration, the importance of solitude in this way of life is clear; moreover the values it contributed to that way of life appear to be very much the ones celebrated throughout this book.

Of course there are cases and cases,[29] and I have neither the space nor the expertise for an exhaustive cross-cultural study. My aim, rather, has been to attempt to shift the burden of proof to those who hold that solitude has *not* been an important value, generally, in human culture. How, in the few remaining pages, can I weight that burden most heavily? Obviously, by picking a culture dramatically different from our own.[30] What about an Eastern culture, what about an ancient precapitalist preindustrial culture, what about China during the Warring States Period, approximately 700–200 BC? This would be a good test of the ubiquity of the valuing of solitude, since, as Herlee Creel remarks,

> Until around the beginning of the Christian Era, Chinese civilization was probably more isolated than any other great culture . . . The student of Western philosophy who studies Indian thought finds much that is new, but by no means everything is totally unfamiliar. The metaphysical subtleties to which he is accustomed are there—if anything, in forms of even greater complexity. But the Western philosopher who studies early Chinese thought may be inclined to deny that it is philosophy at all. Certainly one has to admit that it is a very different kind of philosophy, which usually stays very close to the ground of human life here and now and to human problems.[31]

The tumultuous and unsettled years of the Warring States Period resemble in some ways our own early middle ages; around 771 BC a strong coalition of feudal lords broke the power of the Chou king, and then fell to fighting among themselves for the right to rule all of China. As Creel remarks,

> In general, it may be said that at this time "law and order" scarcely existed, for there was no strong central authority to enforce them. Since the king was powerless, states fought among themselves constantly. By the sixth century B.C., in which Confucius was born, there were four large states of pre-eminent power on the periphery of the Chinese world and a number of smaller states in the center. The large states customarily met to fight their battles in the territory of the central states; sometimes they did this annually, for as much as ten years without intermission.[32]

This political turmoil was a fertile seedbed for philosophy, producing a host of competing thinkers and schools. Two, however, came to have the greatest impact upon the development and distinctive nature of Chinese culture, Confucianism and Taoism (even today a scholar remarks that every Chinese is a Confucian in society and a Taoist alone[33]).

Confucius (559–471 BC) was primarily a moralist, seeking the best ways for men to achieve happiness together. Combining principles of what we would call courtesy and morality, he exhorted his disciples to infuse the traditional rites of sacrifice and duties of office with moral regard for other people. His great desire (like Plato) was to be given the guidance of a state, a desire that was frustrated, though many of his disciples came to occupy positions of power. His fearless devotion to principles of justice and humanity inspired his students to risk death in the attempt to moralize the violent conniving ministers and rulers of the day.

Radically different from, and in many ways opposed to this humane, sensible, socially oriented, moralistic philosophy there arose, somewhere in the fourth century BC, a view of life that came to be called Taoism (although Confucius also used the term 'tao,' which means "the way"). Describing a philosophy that repudiates all descriptions is not an easy task, but perhaps "a nature mysticism" is protean enough to begin with. It was expressed in two books, the *Tao Teh Ching* (The Canon of The Way and of Virtue) and the *Chuang Tzu*. The *Tao Teh Ching* was supposed to have been authored around the time of Confucius by a sage named Lao Tzu (which translates as "Old Master"), about whom fanciful stories abound: "Immaculately conceived to a shooting star, carried in his mother's womb for sixty-two years and born, it is said, white haired . . ."[34] he served for many years as keeper of the royal archives at Loyang; becoming at length disgusted with the depravity of court society, he disappeared into the wilderness on a black ox, pausing only to dictate to a gatekeeper the five thousand characters of the *Tao Teh Ching*. Scholars are doubtful of the immaculate conception, and generally agree that the book is a composite of writings by several different authors (Creel locates its actual composition in the fourth century BC). Yet there is a remarkably consistent voice to the book that gives it a distinctive philosophico-poetic power: mystical and metaphysical, humble and earthy, it is like no other book.

The *Chuang Tzu,* probably written about a generation later, does seem to have been authored by a man named Chuang Tzu (Master Chuang) who lived in Honan province and died around 300 BC.[35] In tone, the book is very different from the *Tao Teh Ching:* Chuang Tzu loves paradox, fable, myth, philosophical questions without answers, wordplay, word-distortion, irony, under- and overstatement—and sometimes shock:

Master Tung-kuo asked Chuang Tzu, "This thing called the Way,—where does it exist?"
   Chuang Tzu said, "There's no place it doesn't exist."
   "Come," said Master Tung-kuo, "you must be more specific!"
   "It is in the ant."
   "As low a thing as that?"
   "It is in the panic grass."
   "But that's lower still!"
   "It is in the tiles and shards."
   "How can it be so low?"
   "It is in the piss and shit." (ch. 22[36])

I wish now to make some claims about the importance of solitude in these Taoist classics.[37] What an undertaking! First I think of Chuang Tzu's playful attitude towards all verbal claims:

> Now I am going to make a statement here. I don't know whether it fits into the category of other people's statements or not. But whether it fits into their category or whether it doesn't, it obviously fits into some category. So in that respect it is no different from their statements. However, let me try making my statement. (ch. 2)

Then I think of the differences between the nine translations of the *Tao Teh Ching* which I have read. Ancient Chinese is notoriously ambiguous, and different translations often produce very different meanings. Consider, for instance the difference between the following translations of the closing lines of chapter 39:

> *Witter Bynner:*
> Who will prefer the jingle of jade pendants if
> He once has heard stone growing in a cliff![38]

> *Arthur Waley:*
> They did not want themselves to tinkle like jade-bells,
> while others resounded like stone-chimes.[39]

> *Gia-Fu Feng and Jane English:*
> Do not tinkle like jade
> Or clatter like stone chimes.[40]

The first translation, and possibly the third, seem to guide one towards solitude whereas the second does not. However, for all the paradox and playfulness, for all the complexity and ambiguity,[41] one thing stands clear, at least to my eyes: the central importance of solitude in ancient Taoism. So let me try making my statement.

Certainly a sense of solitude pervades the Taoist writings:

> Look, it cannot be seen—it is beyond form.
> Listen, it cannot be heard—it is beyond sound.
> Grasp, it cannot be held—it is intangible.
>
> (*Tao Teh Ching*, ch. 14)

Yet it is not so easy to articulate the precise nature of this solitude. For one thing, when one thinks of solitude there is a tendency to think of an hermitic existence apart from other people; yet there are relatively few references to hermits to be found in either book.[42] On the contrary, the *Tao Teh Ching* says, "A Sound man's heart is not shut within itself But is open to other people's hearts," (ch. 49)[43] and the parables of the *Chuang Tzu* are full of teachers arguing with disciples, friends mourning at funerals, hopeful advisors discussing strategy, and so on. Indeed, both Chuang Tzu and another (perhaps fictional) Taoist sage, Lieh Tzu, had wives! Can there be a solitude among people?

There can, and our previous analysis of disengaged consciousness enables us now to comprehend it. To begin with the *Tao Teh Ching*, unclear as it is (must be!) precisely what Tao is—primal substance, metaphysical form, living structure, dynamic energy?—the central teaching of the book is that one must attempt to bring one's whole nature into harmonious union with Tao:

> Though there can be no name for it [Tao],
> I have called it 'the way of life,'
> Perhaps I should have called it 'the fullness of life,'
> Since fullness implies widening into space,
> Implies still further widening,
> Implies widening until the circle is Whole.
> In this sense
> The way of life is fulfilled,
> Heaven is fulfilled,
> Earth fulfilled
> And a fit man also is fulfilled (ch. 25)

"Widening" into "the fullness of life" is accomplished by opening oneself to all things in an accepting noninterfering way:

> Be utterly humble,
> And you shall hold to the foundation of peace.
> Be at one with all these living things which, having
> arisen and flourished,
> Return to the quiet whence they came,
> Like a healthy growth of vegetation
> Falling back upon the root.
> Acceptance of this return to the root has been
> called "quietism' (ch. 16)

This return to the root is essentially a solitary process for Lao Tzu, for a number of reasons. First there is his repudiation of words—the naming, assertive, argumentative discourses we share with other people. From the famous opening pronouncement

> Existence is beyond the power of words
> To define:
> Terms may be used,
> But are none of them absolute (ch. 1)[44]

to the warning

> Those who know do not tell,
> Those who tell do not know. (ch. 56)

to the final chapter's admonition

> Since those who argue prove nothing,
> A sensible man does not argue (ch. 81)

all naming and articulate verbal knowledge are rejected; for language presupposes distinctions, distinctions which artificially break the organic wholeness of Tao. "End the nuisance of saying yes to this and perhaps to that, distinctions with how little difference!" (ch. 20) Thus language can only becloud Tao; and since language is the medium of our interactions with other people, it is futile to seek Tao through them.

Secondly, Lao Tzu finds humankind alone, among all of the parts of creation, out of tune with Tao. Filled with individuating desires and emotions, foolishly striving against the true ways of existence, unquiet in body and spirit—these ordinary human creatures are certainly not gateways for the sage seeking the Tao. Far better to let them be and seek Tao on your own—better for you and actually better for them too:

> If I keep from meddling with people, they take care of themselves,
> If I keep from commanding people, they behave themselves,
> If I keep from preaching at people, they improve themselves,
> If I keep from imposing on people, they become themselves. (ch. 57)

Thirdly, people—the self as well as others—occupy no special place in Lao Tzu's universe. What arrogance and chauvinism he would have found in the humanist idea that "the proper study of man is man." Other people are but a tiny part of the vast ever-changing universe which the Tao informs; and really, "Who will prefer the jingle of jade pendants if he once has heard stone growing in a cliff!" (ch. 39)

For all these reasons, "the sensible man prefers the inner to the outer eye" (ch. 12):

> Knowledge studies others,
> Wisdom is self-known (ch. 33)

> There is no need to run outside
> For better seeing,
> Nor to peer from a window. Rather abide
> At the center of your being;
> For the more you leave it, the less you learn.
> (ch. 47)

How is it that knowledge of Tao can be obtained within the self? Because Tao is already prefigured there: "The wholeness of life has, from of old, been made manifest in the part" (ch. 39). Man

> Is in himself an image of the world
> And, being an image of the world,
> Is continuously, endlessly
> The dwelling of creation. (ch. 28)

Each of us is a microcosm of the macrocosmic universe, a cell whose DNA encodes the whole body. What need have we, then, to consult with other cells?

The passages just cited convey the idea of the fullness with Tao of the individual self, but numerous other passages insist that this fullness is in fact acquired by emptying oneself, by becoming "the valley of the world" (ch. 28), letting all the ten thousand things flow into and through oneself so that one is as ever-full and ever-emptying as Tao itself (ch. 5). In this state, the active, assertive, determinate self, so much a part of normal human interactions, has been abandoned; there is no longer a distinct self to engage with the other, but only a receptive emptiness. As before, thus, normal human intercourse is not the way to Tao.

So other people, in the *Tao Teh Ching,* are seen at worst as obstacles and babbling diversions from the Tao, and at best as one sort of curious objects among countless others flowing past us. Should one live apart from them, then? Yes, in the sense of solitary disengagement, no, in the sense of hermitic isolation. Other people are a part—though only a part—of the great whole of creation, and so one should let them flow through without hindrance as do all the other parts; but one should practice *wu wei,* "inaction," towards them as towards everything else. *Wu wei* is a notoriously difficult idea in Taoism, but one interpretation of the teaching can be made in terms of the disengagement which I have called the essence of solitude. If we eliminate from our experience of the other all striving to affect him and engage with him (whether to help or to harm), if we eliminate all the passions and desires which imply such striving and engagement, if we perceive and think of the other only in a detached, non-desiring, non-striving way, we have achieved what I understand as *wu wei.* But this could be Thoreau at Walden Pond completely detached from the men harvesting ice at the far end, thinking his own thoughts: it is a solitude.

One might object that there are passages in Lao Tzu which certainly seem to preach engagement with others. In the realm of feelings for example:

> A sound man's heart is not shut within itself
> But is open to other people's hearts:
>
> .   .   .   .
>
> .   .   .   .
>
> I feel the heart beats of others above my own
> If I am enough of a father,
> Enough of a son. (ch. 49)

But, in fact, it is possible to render these passages consistent with the foregoing interpretation. A sound man's heart is open to others because it seeks to open itself to every particle and aspect of reality; it is not self-contained, selfish, self-centered in the normal senses of those terms. But it is merely open to these others, a valley they may flow through just as all existence may flow through: there is no suggestion of active involvement. Similarly, it is possible to read the last three lines of the chapter not as a plea for altruism but as endorsing an openness to all other beings in the world, the abandonment of narrow self-consciousness and self-interestedness on the way towards forgetfulness of self in union with the Tao.

Turning now to the *Chuang Tzu,* in spite of numerous differences of both style and substance[45] from the *Tao Teh Ching,* one finds basically the same conception of Tao and the same directions for harmonizing with it. Tao is not to be obtained from other people. This is in part owing to their overexcited, strife-and-striving way of living, but more deeply owing to the incommunicability of Tao through "discriminating" language: "The Great Way is not named; the Great Discriminations are not spoken; . . . If the Way is made clear, it is not the Way" (ch. 2). In story after story, Chuang Tzu insists that the discriminations we actually share with other people are illusory or arbitrary. Again and again he exhorts us to forget knowledge, rules, etiquette: all of these are attempts to separate things which are in themselves hopelessly jumbled and intertwined, and all of them involve the illegitimate move of setting up one of the innumerable perspectives on the world as the only true one.

> In the northern darkness there is a fish and his name is K'un. The K'un is so huge I don't know how many thousand li he measures. He changes and becomes a bird whose name is P'eng. The back of the P'eng measures I don't know how many thousand li across and, when he rises up and flies off, his wings are like clouds all over the sky. . . . When the P'eng journeys to the southern darkness the waters are roiled for three thousand li. He beats the whirlwind and rises ninety thousand li, setting off on the sixth-month gale. (ch. 1)

The cicada and the little dove laugh at the very idea that great P'eng can fly ninety thousand li to the south, and the little quail adds "I never get more than ten or twelve yards . . . and that's the best kind of flying anyway! Where does he think He's going?" (ch. 1); but they merely make us laugh at the relativism of their judgments, and lead us to wonder if all distinguishing judgments may not be similarly arbitrary. Especially if a K'un can suddenly become a P'eng.

Abandoning the illusions of order, knowledge, and interpersonal objectivity, the sage steers by "the torch of chaos and doubt" on his solitary voyage: he

> leans on the sun and moon, tucks the universe under his arm, merges himself with things, leaves the confusion and muddle as it is, and looks on slaves as exalted. Ordinary men strain and struggle; the sage is stupid and blockish. He takes part in the ten thousand ages and achieves simplicity in oneness. For him, all the ten thousand things are what they are, and thus they enfold each other. (ch. 2)

Yen Hui wins Confucius's approval by forgetting benevolence and righteousness, more encouragement when he has forgotten rites and music, and finally startled admiration when he can sit down and "forget everything":

> I smash up my limbs and body, drive out perception and intellect, cast off form, do away with understanding, and make myself identical with the Great Thoroughfare. This is what I mean by sitting down and forgetting everything. (ch. 6)

Yet however necessary disengaged solitude may be for Free and Easy Wandering in the Tao, there is a profound awareness in the *Chuang Tzu* that the human condition situates us inextricably "In the World of Men" (the title of chapter 4). You feel this first in the sense of human presence that pervades the book; whereas the poetically mysterious teachings of the *Tao Teh Ching* seem sometimes like disembodied words heard in rustling leaves, in river water rushing over boulders, the *Chuang Tzu*'s truths about the Tao are almost always spoken by one easily imaginable person to another.

Our original condition of social embeddedness, the initial position from which we struggle towards Tao, is of course partly a matter of bio-social origins, but more importantly is owing to what a Christian might have called our "fallen" nature: "The true Man breathes with his heels; the mass of men breathe with their throats . . . Deep in their passions and desires, they are shallow in the workings of Heaven" (ch. 6) The desire and passion which tie us to other people are impediments to Tao: they are conditions to be transcended by the sage. But they *are* our condition, and we never escape them permanently:

> What use does (the sage) have for men? He has the form of a man but not the feelings of a man. Since he has the form of a man, he bands together with other

men. Since he doesn't have the feelings of a man, right and wrong cannot get at him. Puny and small, he sticks with the rest of men. Massive and great, he perfects his Heaven alone. (ch. 5)

But no one is always massive and great: even Chuang Tzu mourned at his wife's funeral.

There is a sad realization, too, of our vulnerability and need for each other,[46] complemented by our instinct to care for each other: "When the springs dry up and the fish are left stranded on the ground, they spew each other with moisture and wet each other down with spit—but it would be much better if they could forget each other in the rivers and lakes" (ch. 6). It would be much better if—but it isn't: we are linked with humanity.

A crucial problem for ancient Taoism thus emerges: how, inextricably situated in the world of men, can one find the disengaged solitude necessary for attaining Tao? What is the life of transcendence actually like for a social being? To my mind, it is a great virtue of these texts that while a variety of solutions to the problem are recorded, no single one is given clear endorsement over all the others. Here, from the *Chuang Tzu*, are four different paths:

> (1) T'ien Ken was wandering on the sunny side of Yin Mountain. When he reached the banks of the Liao River, he happened to meet a Nameless Man. He questioned the man, saying, "Please may I ask how to rule the world?"
>
> The Nameless Man said, "Get away from me, you peasant! What kind of a dreary question is that! I'm just about to set off with the Creator. And if I get bored with that, then I'll ride on the Light-and-Lissome Bird out beyond the six directions, wandering in the village of Not-Even-Anything and living in the Broad and Borderless field. What business do you have coming with this talk of governing the world and disturbing my mind?" (ch. 7)[47]

> (2) After this, Lieh Tzu concluded that he had never really begun to learn anything. He went home and for three years did not go out. He replaced his wife at the stove, fed the pigs as though he were feeding people, and showed no preferences in the things he did. He got rid of the carving and polishing and returned to plainness, letting his body stand alone like a clod. In the midst of entanglement he remained sealed, and in this oneness he ended his life. (ch. 7)[48]

> (3) Tzu-Ch'i of South Wall sat leaning on his armrest, staring up at the sky and breathing—vacant and far away, as though he'd lost his companion. Yen Ch'eng Tzu-yu, who was standing by his side in attendance, said, "What is this? Can you really make the body like a withered tree and the mind like dead ashes? The man leaning on the armrest now is not the one who leaned on it before!"
>
> Tzu-Ch'i said, "You do well to ask the question, Yen. Now I have lost myself. Do you understand that? You hear the piping of men, but you haven't heard the piping

of earth. Or if you've heard the piping of earth, you haven't heard the Piping of Heaven!" (ch. 2)

(4) Master Ssu, Master Yu, Master Li and Master Lai were all four talking together, "Who can look upon nonbeing as his head, on life as his back, and on death as his rump?" they said. "Who knows that life and death, existence and annihilation, are all a single body? I will be his friend!"

The four men looked at each other and smiled. There was no disagreement in their hearts and so the four of them became friends.

Suddenly Master Lai grew ill. Gasping and wheezing, he lay at the point of death. His wife and children gathered round in a circle and began to cry. Master Li, who had come to ask how he was, said, "Shoo! Get Back! Don't disturb the process of change!" (ch. 6)[49]

Nameless Man's strategy is the withdrawal of the hermit, true; but notice first that he is not entirely successful—intruders like T'ien Ken keep turning up—and second that his strategy is only one of the variety elaborated. Lieh Tzu remains with his family, but seems to have achieved a kind of total and permanent disengagement from them. Tzu-Chi contacts the Tao through the total disengagement of trance meditation, but is quite willing to discuss the resulting insights with a student. Master Li, finding a man who agrees with him about the Tao of human life and death, actually becomes his friend; he inquires after the friend's health and stays to talk in a kindly way just as any other kind friend might do—though with a detachment that is certainly distinctive of Taoism.

If I am right that the central life-project for Lao Tzu and Chuang Tzu is the achievment of Free and Easy Wandering of the spirit in Tao while situated In the World of Men, the relevance of their works as life philosophies for the late twentieth century increases dramatically over that which is usually accorded them. When the texts are read solely as guides to an isolated personal transcendence, no matter how moving and how profound the teachings, there is an aura of unreality about them. For very few people are hermetically isolated: the hermit's life has never been a popular option, and today it is virtually impossible to achieve—most impossible in China, the birthplace of Taoism! Inescapably situated in social and intimate nexes, yet touched by some dim sense of the nourishing and fulfilling power of solitary spiritual transcendence—this is the common human plight. The human Way, accordingly, leads not towards denial of either human relationship or inner transcendence, but along a road which winds through both territories. So it was for Lao Tzu and Chuang Tzu during the Warring States Period, so it was for Seneca in imperial Rome, so it was for St. Antony in the crowded Egyptian desert, so it was for Menocchio in Renaissance Italy, so it was for the Sioux hunter on the vast American plains, so it is for Octavio Paz in modern Mexico; and what has been so for twenty-five centuries will perhaps not change.

EPILOGUE

Here, but only for now, these reflections on solitude find their limit. Solitude has been the great silent half of my rich life. Half! I have been pondering this fact for over thirty years. Has that half of life been a sad abberation, a dazed fearful turning from vibrant social living towards the Dead Lands? These reflections have brought to explicit knowledge the answer I have known inarticulately all the while:

> He is no fugitive—escaped, escaping.
> No one has seen him stumble looking back.
> His fear is not behind him but beside him
> On either hand to make his course perhaps
> A crooked straightness yet no less a straightness.
> He runs face forward.

> (Robert Frost)[1]

Solitude is the luminous silent space of freedom, of self and nature, of reflection and creative power. There we feel and see and contemplate with a freshness scarcely to be believed; there, in the Free and Easy Wandering of the spirit, in the startling exhilaration of a creative vision, we make hash of predestination. There is nothing better for a human person, though there are loving things as good.

It is in the nature of a half, however, that it yearns to be a whole. I have watched the human halves working within each other in the phenomena of engaged disengagement, as solitude and encounter thread their ways through what might at first have seemed whole cloth: solitude ambles among warm reservoirs of personal meaning, with a dim sense of containment in a chosen community; encounter finds itself now flowing through people into image-worlds of its own, now giving greatly of itself with a sense of autonomous power found in solitary self-appropriation. In these many ways, solitude and encounter, though definitionally opposed to each other, nevertheless reveal a surprising companionship.

In the silent hours near dawn when people wander through your thoughts, in the bright noise of almost-absorbing encounters when you suddenly glimpse, over a shoulder, a quiet place that wants you alone, a vision forms and draws you in: it is a vision of wholeness, of a life in which solitude and encounter, lived to their full intensity, find harmony and true balance. These reflections have striven to show the philosophical coherence of that vision, to insist that Proust and Lawrence are both wrong, that solitude and encounter can coexist in a life without delusion or self-deception or betrayal, without denaturing life into a watery compromise. Such a life may be difficult to achieve, but it is possible: there can be a love that brings the fruits of its solitude to the togetherness, a togetherness that fashions out of itself the materials and the strength to send forth the lovers into fruitful solitude. As Rilke expressed it,[2] there can be

> the love that consists in this:
> that two solitudes protect,
>   and limit,
>   and embrace each other.

NOTES

INTRODUCTION

1. The story is told by Robert Gregg in the introduction to his translation of Athanasius's *Life of Antony* (New York: Paulist Press, 1980).

2. Franz Kafka, *Letters to Felice*, trans. James Stern and Elisabeth Duckworth (London: Penguin, 1974), p. 156. Anthony Storr discusses the psychological connections between Kafka's solitude and his writing in *Solitude* (New York: Free Press, 1988), chap. 7.

3. Richard Byrd, *Alone* (Los Angeles: J. P. Tarcher, Inc., 1966), p. 14.

4. Emily Carr, *Hundreds and Thousands* (Toronto: Clare, Irwin & Co.; 1966), pp. 64, 260, respectively.

5. Byron, *Childe Harold*, Canto III, Stanzas 842–43.

6. Francesco Petrarch, *De Vita Solitaria*, trans. Jacob Zeitlin (Westport: Hyperion Press, 1978), p. 288. Compare this line from Milton's *Paradise Lost* (Book IX, line 249): "For Solitude, sometimes is best society." Edward Gibbon expressed the same feeling: "I was never less alone than while by myself" (*Memoirs, I*).

7. Marcel Proust, *Remembrance of Things Past* (Paris: Pleiade, 1954), vol. III, p. 459.

8. Cited in Paul Halmos, *Solitude and Privacy* (New York: Greenwood Press, 1953), p. v.

9. Proust, op. cit., p. 393.

10. Byrd, op. cit., p. 4.

11. Holmes Welch, *Taoism* (Boston: Beacon Press, 1957), p. 2.

12. Prof. Tang Yi-jie of Beijing University suggested to me an answer to this question. See ch. 14, n. 44.

13. Petrarch, op. cit., p. 108.

14. Quoted from Thucydides in I. F. Stone's *The Trial of Socrates* (New York: Doubleday, 1988), p. 99.

15. From *The Adventurer*, no. 126, reprinted in *The Yale Edition of the Works of Samuel Johnson*, vol. II, *The Idler and the Adventurer*, ed. W. Bate, J. Bullitt, and L. Powell (New Haven: Yale University Press, 1963), pp. 475–76.

16. Plato's *Phaedrus* line 230d, from *The Collected Dialogs of Plato*, ed. Edith Hamilton and Huntington Cairns (New York: Pantheon Books, 1961), p. 479.

17. Aristotle, *Nicomachean Ethics*, trans. W. D. Ross, book IX, ch. 9, 1169b, 18–19.

18. Aristotle, op. cit., book X, ch. 7, 1177a.

CHAPTER ONE: *Dimensions*

1. Henry David Thoreau, *Walden* and *Civil Disobedience*, ed. Sherman Paul (Cambridge: Riverside Press Cambridge, 1960), p. 89.

2. Burton Watson, trans., *The Complete Works of Chuang Tzu* (New York: Cornell University Press, 1968), ch. 2. (Since various translations of this work are current, and since each chapter is quite short, I will cite passages by chapter.)

3. Thoreau, op. cit., pp. 89 and 91, respectively.

4. Richard Triumpho, *No Richer Gift* (Fort Atkinson: Hoard & Sons Co., 1979), p. 24.

5. Oliver Morgan, "Music for the Dance: Some Meanings of Solitude," *Journal of Religion and Health* 25, no. 1 (Spring 1986): 21.

6. Viktor Frankl, *Man's Search for Meaning* (New York: Washington Square Press, 1968), p. 81.

7. Thomas Gaddis, *The Birdman of Alcatraz* (New York: Aeonian Press, 1955), pp. 24–25.

8. Ibid., pp. 59–60.

9. It is not the painful, fearful nature of these experiences that renders the term 'solitude' inappropriate; for there are dark, evil solitudes, times when disengaged thought finds only sorrow and misery to feed upon. One must not romanticize the solitude of prisoners, as Sue Halpern reminds us in her pungent *Migrations to Solitude* (New York: Pantheon Books, 1992). Writing out of curiosity to a prisoner in solitary confinement, she asks, "What is the best thing about solitary confinement?" The prisoner responds, "I can't think of anything" (p. 53). She dug up another eloquent assessment of enforced solitude:
> "Do you find it difficult to endure solitude?" Alexis de Tocqueville and Gustave de Beaumont asked a prisoner in solitary in the course of their research for *On the Penitentiary System in the United States and Its Application in France*. "Ah, sir, it is the most horrible punishment that can be imagined!" (p. 55)

10. Quoted in Edgar Collard, ed., *The Art of Contentment* (Toronto: Doubleday Canada, 1974), p. 103.

11. Quoted in Collard, op. cit., p. 166.

12. Morgan, op. cit., p. 19.

13. Alice Koller, *The Stations of Solitude* (New York: William Morrow and Co., 1990), p. 23.

14. Charles Alexander Eastman, *The Soul of the Indian* (Lincoln: University of Nebraska Press, 1911/80), p. 89. Compare these lines from the *Book of Chuang Tzu*, written around AD 280

> When water is still it is a perfect Level and the greatest artificer takes his rule from it. Such is the clearness of still water, and how much greater is that of the human Spirit! The still mind of the sage is the mirror of heaven and earth, the glass of all things. Vacancy, stillness, placidity, tastelessness, quietude, silence and non-action; this is the Level of heaven and earth, and the perfection of the Tao . . .

15. Bernard Dauenhauer's recent phenomenological study, *Silence: The Phenomenon and Its Ontological Significance* (Bloomington: Indiana University Press, 1980) adds more dimensions of complexity. In this intriguing, original, and obscure work, Dauenhauer develops the view that silence is "an active performance," on grounds that "silence necessarily involves conscious activity" (p. 4). The activity involved is (at least) "an abstaining from some previously engaged-in stream of experience . . . the severing or detaching from some specific set of performances" (p. 60). Dauenhauer speaks of these severings of silence as "cuts"; the first cut "segments the pregiven whole of spontaneous, pre-predicative experience, rendering each theme determinate"; the second cut "interrupts the self's thematizing activity and acknowledges that there are other selves who thematize" (p. 63)—thus opening up the sociality of experience. The final cut, which "opens the way for signifying performances or discourse properly so called" involves suspending the stream of perceptual experience, creating "space for mediating perceptual experience through symbols and signs" (p. 63). Although silences might be assigned to each of the first two cuts, "at least the third cut is unquestionably an occurrence of silence" (p. 64). Thus silence and discourse are "intimately intertwined" (p. 64), an intertwining whose unraveling occupies much of the book.

Particularly interesting, both in their own right and in their suggestiveness for the understanding of solitude, are Dauenhauer's reflections upon the motivations which lead us to cut or break the stream of perception and action:

> On the one hand, the suspension is motivated by the recognition of the finitude of any set of particular performances intending determinate objects of any specific sort. On the other hand, the suspension is motivated by the recognition that whatever determinate stream of performances I am in fact living in is not the only stream in which I can live. The awareness of my capacity to suspend or interrupt the present stream in which I am living for the sake of a not yet determinate different stream, together with my awareness of the capacity of others to do likewise is the awareness of awe in the face of the wide but limited range and scope of possible human performances. (p. 80)

Deciding whether the suspensions are motivated by these recognitions as Dauenhauer maintains, or whether, as I am more inclined to believe, the recognitions crystallize out of the suspensions themselves would take us beyond the scope of the present inquiry. But Dauenhauer has certainly pointed the way towards a more complex understanding of the profound sense of awe-in-the-face-of-one's-finitude which so powerfully colors many solitudes.

For a more chilling study of silence, see M. Belenky et al., *Women's Ways of Knowing* (Boston: Basic Books, 1986), part I, ch. 1. The authors chose the term 'silence' to refer to the most impoverished level of women's perspectives on knowing, "a position in which women experience themselves as mindless and voiceless and subject to the whims of external authority" (p. 15). Among the youngest and most socially, economically, and educationally deprived of the women the authors interviewed, raised in profound isolation and the most demeaning circumstances, these women failed to develop the powers of linguistic representational communication which make possible both the effective voicing of autonomous concerns and the inner speech of self-examination.

They felt 'deaf' because they assumed they could not learn from the words of others, 'dumb' because they felt so voiceless. . . . Words were perceived as weapons . . . used to separate and diminish people, not to connect and empower them. (p. 24)

Describing the self was a difficult task for all of the women we interviewed, but it was almost impossible for the silent ones. . . . these women believe that the source of self-knowledge is lodged in others—not in the self. (p. 31)

16. William Wordsworth, "Ode: Intimations of Immortality," lines 1–5. Robert Sayre asserts that

In its earliest meaning, solitude designates a location: areas beyond the bounds of the societies of men. Forests, wastelands, deserted islands, open seas—the *eremia* of Greek literature is dangerous and forlorn. [*Solitude In Society* (Cambridge: Harvard University Press, 1978), p. 13]

17. Thoreau, op. cit., p. 77.

18. May Sarton, *Journal of a Solitude* (New York: Norton & Co., 1973), p. 54.

19. Many contemporary writers on time adopt some version of this distinction, though the versions differ significantly in their details. I have followed Hans Meyerhoff's articulation in *Time in Literature* (Berkeley: The University of California Press, 1968); although he prefers to refer to "time in experience" vs. "time in nature," he says of the former, "Time so defined is private, personal, subjective or, as is often said, psychological." (pp. 4–5). An excellent anthology of writings on time, through which a variety of subjective-objective distinctions thread, is Charles Sherover's *The Human Experience of Time* (New York: New York University Press, 1975).

20. Henri Bergson, *Duration and Simultaneity*, trans. Leon Jacobson, cited in Sherover, op. cit., pp. 218–19.

21. Alfred Schutz and Thomas Luckerman, *The Structures of the Life-World*, trans. R. Zaner and H. Engelhardt (Evanston: Northwestern University Press, 1973), p. 47.

22. Erazim Kohák, *The Embers and the Stars* (Chicago: University of Chicago Press, 1984), p. 29.

23. See especially pp. 16–19 and 205–10. He also argues that neither the psycho-subjective nor the biological models of time are able to explain a crucial part of our experience of time in solitude, the experience of eternity. On the last matter, see Meyerhoff's discussion in *Time in Literature* (op. cit.), pp. 54–64.

24. Joseph Conrad, *Heart of Darkness* (London: Dent & Sons, 1974), p. 93.

25. I do not say "external givens" because even bodily feelings can be approached more subjectively or more objectively—arthritic pain, for example, as felt in the night and as assessed the next day in the doctor's office. In both cases, though, the pains are (sadly) independently resistant to our construal; they are, in their own way, The Other.

Kohák reminds us that object and attending subject exist within "the matrix of nature's rhythm which establishes personal yet nonarbitrary reference points: when I have rested, when I grow weary, when the shadows lengthen, when life draws to a close" (op. cit., p. 16).

26. Collard, op. cit., p. 79.

27. George Lakoff and Mark Johnson, *Metaphors We Live By* (Chicago: University of Chicago Press, 1980), p. 56.

28. Richard Zaner has articulated the complex set of relationships that together constitute the gestalt "complexure" of a simple triangle of three points, and his analysis seems very promising for unravelling more fully than I have time for now the experiential nature of seeing an object in the presence of another person. If we consider a triangular arrangement of points, 1, 2, and 3,

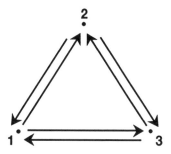

(a) 1 makes a simple direct reference to 2 and to 3, but also (b) an indirect reference to each of these via its reference to the other; i.e. 1 — 2 (direct) and 1 — 3 — 2 (indirect). But since these references are all symetrical, each point is (c) itself doubly referenced by the others, which are (d) cross-referenced to each other. Finally, each point is characterized by (e) self-reference, since it refers to points which refer back to it, a self-reference which can be either direct or indirect. Thus, says Zaner,

> the intrinsic functional significance of a constituent is formed of (a) simple reference, (b) complex reference, (c) double reference, (d) multiple cross-reference, and (e) simple, complex, and multiple self-reference. . . . the configuration itself is neither more nor less than this system of intrinsic references. [*The Context of Self* (Athens: Ohio University Press, 1981), pp. 82–84.]

I leave it to the reader to work out the references involved when the gestalt is composed of the self and the Intruder and the trillium.

29. Part III, ch. 1, part IV.

30. Professor Graeme Hunter has raised with me the question whether it is the presence of perception and subjectivity that is salient here, or whether it is the peculiar kind of subjectivity that makes a locus of perception a *person*. Would the intrusion of a racoon or a dog or a bear produce the same reconstitution of space as the intrusion of a person? Or is it the demand for recognition which a person makes—royal member in the Realm of Ends!—that causes the disturbance? I am unsure how to answer. In my own experience, racoons and rabbits and dogs and skunks (never met a bear) have the same kind of coordinating power; however, this may well be owing to an overdeveloped personifying mechanism in my brain.

31. Cited in Collard, op. cit., p. 191.

32. For an obscure but suggestive discussion of experienced spatiality, see Martin Heidegger's discussion in *Being and Time* (trans. John Macquarrie and Edward Robinson [New York: Harper and Row, 1962]), pp. 135–49.

CHAPTER TWO: *Near Relations: Loneliness, Isolation, Privacy, Alienation*

1. Charles Brownfield, *Isolation: Clinical and Experimental Approaches* (New York: Random House, 1965), pp. 126–27.

2. Halmos, op. cit., p. 102.

3. Rubin Gotesky, "Aloneness, Loneliness, Isolation, Solitude" in *An Invitation to Phenomenology*, ed. J. Edie (Chicago: Quadrangle Books, 1965), p. 236. This fine study first alerted me to the important distinctions between these varieties of aloneness.

4. Thomas Parkinson, "Loneliness of the Poet" in *The Anatomy of Loneliness*, ed. Joseph Hartog et al. (New York: International Universities Press, 1980), p. 468.

5. Ralph Harper, *The Seventh Solitude* (Baltimore: Johns Hopkins Press, 1965), p. 5.

6. John Cowper Powys, *A Philosophy of Solitude* (New York: Simon and Schuster, 1930), pp. 37–38.

7. Nicolas Berdyaev, *Solitude and Society* (New York: Charles Scribner's Sons, 1938).

8. From Paul Tillich, "Loneliness and Solitude" in J. Hartog, op. cit., p. 547. This piece is an excerpt from Tillich's *The Eternal Now* (New York: Charles Scribner's Sons, 1957).

9. Clark Moustakas, *Loneliness* (New York: Prentice Hall, 1961), p. 2.

10. Ben Lazare Mijuskovic, *Loneliness in Philosophy, Psychology and Literature* (Assen: Van Gorcum, 1979), p. 9.

11. I defend this intuitive idea against seven lines of counter-argument in "Emotion and Bodily Feeling," *Dialogue* 26 (1987): 59–75.

12. Albert Camus, *The Myth of Sisyphus and Other Essays* (New York: Vintage Books, 1955), p. 8.

13. The definition, as well as many of the remarks to come, appeared in my paper "Loneliness without Objects" (*Southern Journal of Philosophy* 21, no. 2 [1983]: 193–209).

14. Tillich, op. cit., p. 549. It may be, though, that the original German terms carry these implications.

15. Gotesky, op. cit., p. 237

16. Reprinted in the Penguin Books paperback edition of *The Life and Adventures of Robinson Crusoe* by Daniel Defoe (London: Penguin Books, 1965), p. 23.

17. Ibid., p. 80.

18. Ibid., p. 80.

19. Ibid., p. 80.

20. Quoted in Frank Ellis, ed., *Twentieth Century Interpretations of Robinson Crusoe* (Englewood Cliffs: Prentice Hall, 1969), p. 22.

21. Ibid., p. 193.

22. Ibid., p. 185.

23. R. Megroz tells us in *The Real Robinson Crusoe* (London: Cresset Press, no date given) that although Defoe's prototype differed considerably in some particulars from the fictional Crusoe, the sequence of adjustment to the isolation was accurate.

> The terror that overwhelmed him at first was not any fear of starvation on that island, but the very real fear of solitude which in an unimaginative man might not have come so promptly and distressingly as it did to the young Fife sailor. . . . in his initial despair at being marooned alone, nothing less than the force of hunger compelled him to rouse himself to do anything.
>
> During the first eighteen months, a period of hopeless dejection, he exerted himself as little as possible, but began to read his Bible and pray; and then good health, youth, and his religious faith acted together in a beneficent recovery of his spirits and he began to enjoy his peaceful and healthy life. Companionship with his tamed cats and kids seems to have afforded him consolation for the loss of human society, which he probably could dispense with more easily than less self-centered men. (pp. 84–85)

Defoe mentions ways in which Crusoe's pets became a nuisance when they overpopulated the cave, but in this case it seems to be the novelist that understates the reality: Megroz quotes an early biographer of Selkirk, Woodes Rogers, who wrote:

> He was at first much pester'd with Cats and Rats, that had bred in great numbers from some of each Species which had got ashore from Ships that put in there to wood and water. The Rats gnaw'd his Feet and Clothes while asleep, which oblig'd him to cherish the Cats with his Goats-flesh; by which many of them became so tame that they would lie about him in hundreds, and soon deliver'd him from the Rats. (p. 95)

Hundreds of cats? Selkirk must have thanked Providence for the sandy beaches.

24. Christianne Ritter, *A Woman in the Polar Night* (London: Allen and Unwin, 1954). For more on her experiences, see chapter 13.

25. Halpern, op. cit., p. xiii. She writes in an introductory note that her interest is in "[the] experience of solitude, not as an existential dilemma but as a physical fact. And I wanted to know . . . about privacy as a quality of life, rather than as a vague, contested, and often rhetorical legal concept, privacy as a matter of rights." (p.vii)

26. Halpern, op. cit., p. 21.

27. Halpern mentions the notion of a right to privacy, dismissing it as a "limited distinctly American invention" which "queers our relationship to the thing itself" (p. vii). Some support for her view is found in H. J. McCloskey's thorough review of conceptions of privacy, "Privacy and the Right To Privacy" (*Philosophy*, no. 55, [January 1980]: 17–38); after a brief survey of the liberal tradition running through Locke, Rousseau, Kant, and Mill, none of whom emphasized privacy, he writes: "It is the lawyers of the USA, through criminal and civil law, and through the interpretation of the Constitution, who have

contributed most to the development of the political ideal of privacy." (p. 18) I have been reflecting upon "the thing itself" here, suggesting that the very feeling of privacy may have the sense of entitlement built in, regardless of how the legal/political question of a general right to privacy may be settled. To see this, imagine a thief who is surprised in his mountain hideout by the police: raging at "the intrusions and observations of others" (Halpern), he would hardly complain that his privacy was being violated—unless, perhaps, he owned the cabin.

28. In *Privacy and Freedom* (New York: Atheneum, 1967) A. F. Westin identified four types of experience of privacy: solitude, intimacy, anonymity, and reserve. One notes that the last three entail a social context.

29. McCloskey, with characteristic scope, surveys nine definitions which have been proposed for 'privacy'—and finds deficiencies in each. The list is interesting for showing the wide range of ideas which lie about in the countryside of solitude, and I shall reproduce it here.
Privacy has been variously construed as:
(1) being let alone
(2) the right to selective disclosure of personal information
(3) the absence of publicity
(4) secrecy
(5) exclusive access to a realm of one's own
(6) respect for personal autonomy
(7) part of the idea of respect for persons
(8) protection from the appropriation or exploitation of one's affairs
(9) that which, when made known, causes feelings of shame, humiliation, etc.
(10) the personal, the inviolate personality

30. Sayre, op. cit., p. 1.

31. Richard Schacht, *Alienation* (Garden City: Anchor Books, 1971), p. 3.

32. Schacht, op. cit., p. 9. The other quotations in this paragraph are taken from pp. 9–11.

33. Schacht, op. cit., pp. 43–44.

34. Indeed, as Prof. Peter Trnka reminds me, Hegel may have believed solitude as I define it—consciousness disengaged from others—to be impossible: "self-consciousness exists in itself and for itself, in that, and by the fact that it exists for another self-consciousness" (G. Hegel, *The Phenomenology of Spirit*, cited in Mijuskovic, op. cit., p. 80). For more discussion of these matters, see chapter 10 below.

35. Karl Marx, *A Contribution to the Theory of Political Economy*, trans. N. I. Stone (Chicago, n.p., 1904), p. 268.

36. Bertell Ollman, *Alienation* (Cambridge: Cambridge University Press, 1971), pp. 133–34.

37. Walter Kaufmann's "Introductory Essay" in Schacht, op. cit., p. xvi.

38. Cited in Gotesky, op. cit., p. 211.

39. Robert Weiss, *Loneliness* (Cambridge: MIT Press, 1974), p. 4.

40. Our discussion of alienation began with the intuition that it is something by nature evil and unpleasant, and the definition we derived from the historical survey mirrored this point. But is that true? Kaufmann, in an essay entitled "The Inevitability of Alientation" which introduces Schacht's book, appears to challenge this truth. Pursuing a line of thought developed in Schiller and Hegel, he argues that "self-consciousness involves a sense of what is other—*alienum* in Latin. If anyone literally found nothing human alien to himself, he would be totally lacking in any sense of selfhood" (p. xxiv). Moreover, "It is hard to see in perspective and comprehend what is very close to us: Comprehension requires some distance and consists in a triumph over distance. . . . when a play, a painting or a piece of music is exceedingly familiar to us, we lack distance and must become alienated if we would comprehend it" (p. xxv). Further, "Plato and Aristotle remarked that philosophy begins in wonder or perplexity. We could also say that it begins when something suddenly strikes us as strange—or that philosophy is born of estrangement" (p. xxvii).

Finally, the individuation of the maturing child requires alienation: "the adolescent who gains a sense of distance experiences a gulf between himself and all sorts of things and people, and he feels estranged. . . . Estrangement from nature, society, ones fellow men, and oneself is part of growing up. One has to detach oneself from the womb of one's environment in order to become a person" (p. xliv). I do not find his reasoning persuasive, however. He refers to the feelings of of otherness, distance, unfamiliarity, strangeness, and detachment, but none of these are yet alienation. Both Lao Tzu and Wordsworth wondered at the strangeness of nature, but neither were alienated from it. As for philosophical wondering, it is just too paradoxical to call this gripping experience alienation. And the claim that one needs to feel painfully separated from one's parents and society in order to mature seems to elevate a widespread contemporary friction into a human universal.

41. H. Tristam Engelhardt, "Solitude and Sociality," *Humanitas* 10, no. 3 (Nov. 1974): 278.

42. Kohák errs in the opposite direction by over-externalizing solitude's focus of attention: "Solitude is the condition of being alone in the presence of a living, familiar world, willing to listen to it, to see and to understand it in *Einfuhlung* and *Eindeutung*, sharing in its feel and meaning" (op. cit., p. 39).

43. Peter Munz, *Relationship and Solitude* (Middletown: Wesleyan University Press, 1965), pp. 28–29.

44. Halmos, op. cit., p. 102.

45. Halmos, op. cit., p. 168.

46. Ways in which willed loneliness might be regenerative in some other area are conceivable, but Halmos does not develop his remark along any such lines. What he has in mind are the restorative powers of solitude which are so often celebrated, powers which crucially depend upon *avoiding* loneliness during the time of aloneness.

47. Sayre, op. cit., p. 200.

48. Ralph Harper, op. cit. Subtitles can be instructive: the last word in Halmos's

subtitle to *Solitude and Privacy* tells us what he really thinks of both states: "A Study of Social Isolation, Its Causes and Therapy."

CHAPTER THREE: *Disengagement*

1. Hardly an unusual or modern experience. Sayre reminds us of the importance of this presence-in-absence to the poets of courtly love such as Petrarch, who felt his beloved Laura as a constant presence in the retreat at Vaucluse in the Alps: "In fact, the farther Petrarch is from Laura, the closer he is to her. As he wanders *solo y pensoso* over mountains, woods, and open country, he holds continual conversation with Amor." (Sayre, op. cit., p. 36)

2. Henry Bugbee, "Loneliness, Solitude, and the Twofold Way in Which Concern Seems to Be Claimed", in *Humanitas*, op. cit., p. 317.

3. Franz Kafka, *Letters to Felice*, op. cit., letter of 6/26/13.

4. Franz Kafka, "The Judgment" in *Selected Short Stories of Franz Kafka* (New York: Modern Library, 1952), pp. 13–14.

5. Craig Eisendrath observes that:
Writing served Kafka as a simulacrum for the processes of life, much as chess can serve those in power as a prototype of politico-military strategy. Writing gave Kafka an area of activity removed from immediate connections and casual [causal?] contingencies, one in which he could pick and choose possibilities and strike on a particular path. Writing thus formed a pattern for decision making that Kafka could continuously perfect through the years. . . ." ("In Search of the Self: The Case of Franz Kafka" in P. Young-Eisendrath and J. Hall, eds.: *The Book of the Self* [New York: New York University Press, 1987], p. 155)
Eisendrath is surely right to emphasize the degree to which Kafka doubted the usefulness to others of his work, considering it rather "the artifact of a private struggle, and with few exceptions, to be burnt and buried with the life with which it was intimately and hermetically bound" (p. 156). For another vivid and perceptive study of the role of the writing in Kafka's life, see Ernst Pawel's fine biography, *The Nightmare of Reason* (New York: Farrar, Strauss, Giroux, 1984)

6. Thomas Merton, *The Silent Life* (New York: Farrar, Straus & Cudahy, 1957), p. 150.

7. Fyodor Dostoevsky, *Crime and Punishment*, trans. Constance Garnett (New York: Harper, 1951), p. 71.

8. From Witter Bynner's translation of the *Tao Teh Ching, The Way of Life according to Lao Tzu* (New York: Perigee Books, 1944), ch. 21.

CHAPTER FOUR: *Engaged Disengagement*

1. Marcel Proust, *Swann's Way* (New York: Vintage, 1970), p. 34.

2. Ibid.

3. Eleanor Sickels, *The Gloomy Egoist* (New York: Octagon Books, 1969).

4. Philip Larkin, "Churchgoing," collected in *20th Century Poetry and Poetics,* ed. Gary Geddes (Toronto: Oxford University Press, 1985), p. 230.

5. Lakoff and Johnson, op. cit., p. 3.

6. Ibid.

7. Lakoff and Johnson, op. cit., p. 4.

8. Lakoff and Johnson, op. cit., pp. 117–18.

9. A psychological experiment, whose reference I have now lost, had subjects observe colored dots moved about on a screen. Invariably, the subjects described the movement of the dots in human terms, e.g. "the green dot is making a pass at the red dot," "the dots are ganging up on the yellow dot," etc.
Zaner endorses the theory, propounded originally by Max Scheler in *The Nature of Sympathy,* that

> our conviction of the existence of other selves is *deeper and earlier* than that of natural things. . . . .'Animism' or 'panvitalism', it could be said, are not first of all or primarily theories or even myths; *they are first of all concrete stages of human life.* (Zaner, op. cit., p. 210)

Zaner is interested in the stages of infancy through which an explicit sense of self and other emerge, but Scheler himself found the same mechanisms operating during the childhood of the species:

> In the case of the primitive, so well described by Levy-Bruhl, we might perhaps go further and say that everything whatsoever is given, for him, as 'expression' and that what we call development through learning is not a subsequent addition of mental elements to an already-given inanimate world of material objects, but a continuous process of disenchantment, in that only a proportion of sensory appearances retain their function as vehicles of expression, while others do not. Learning, in this sense, is not *animation,* but a continual *'deanimation'*. (*The Nature of Sympathy,* trans. P. Heath [New Haven: Yale University Press, 1954], pp. 239–40).

10. Defoe, op. cit., pp. 185–86.

11. Alice Koller, op. cit., pp. 115–16.

12. Koller takes up explicitly at many points the question of the personhood of her animals. After reporting how one led her across a room to the location of a hidden playball, she remarks that

> The extraordinary element is the reasoning Logos displayed. His problem was to get me to understand not only that his ball was under the cabinet but also that he wanted me to retrieve it. His solution made use of facts known to him:
> (1) When the teething bone connected us, he could lead me where he wanted to go.
> (2) But the teething bone was absent
> (3) But my hand, the part of my body he most closely associated with our game, was present. Therefore, he would now lead me to the ball by connecting directly to my hand.
> I do not say that he actually followed these steps, marshalled the data in just this way, then drew his conclusion. I say that these premises are logically required for his conclusion. But even when human beings reason, we rarely move step-wise from premises to conclusion. All that is required is that the reasoning follows (logically, not temporally) an accepted pattern of inference.
> Logos had abstracted a broadly applicable principle from his understanding of a specific situation, and he had applied it to an appropriate new situation. These are two widely accepted criteria for intelligence when the beings displaying it are human beings. (pp. 205–6)

Logos also manifested, in Koller's experience, many other attributes that cause us to love human partners: he knew how to pretend and to invent games; he was capable of a wide range of emotions and able to exercise self-control; he trusted Alice completely.

13. Quoted in Lawrence Cunningham and Dennis Stock, *Saint Francis of Assisi* (San Francisco: Harper and Row, 1981), p. 62.

14. Cited in Herbert Workman, *The Evolution of the Monastic Ideal* (Boston: Beacon Press, 1962), p. 306. He remarks that, paradoxically, "that Monasticism which began with an almost Gnostic hatred of the created world, as the medium of temptation and the abode of sin, oft-times ended in the identification of the man with nature itself" (p. 305).

15. Athanasius, *Life of Antony*, op. cit., p.33.

16. Ibid., p. 34.

17. For a study of prevailing attitudes towards blacks in St. Antony's day, see F. M. Snowden, *Blacks in Antiquity: Ethiopians in the Greco-Roman Experience* (Cambridge: Harvard University Press, 1970). Characterizing the devil as a boy perhaps expressed fears of homosexual indulgence that seem to have been sometimes well-founded. Sister Ward discusses the issue briefly in her translation of the *Sayings of the Fathers* (Kalamazoo: Cistercian Publications, 1975), referring to the words of Isaac of The Cells, who admonished his fellow hermits, "Do not bring young boys here. Four churches in Scetis are deserted because of boys" (p. 100). Sister Ward writes:

> the theme of homosexual temptations . . . is noticeably absent from the first generation in Scetis; it appears as part of the decline in monastic standards after the devastations. There is in these sayings a nostalgia for the virtues and austerities of the early days which mark them as belonging to the third generation. (p.99)

18. Athanasius, op. cit., pp. 33–35.

19. Ibid., pp. 38–39.

20. Workman reminds us that Antony's belief in demons was the common view of the time—a fact that partly explained the immediate success of Athanasius's biography.

> In reality the *Life of Antony* was produced at the psychological moment. With consummate art it presented Monasticism as the one adequate solution of the difficulties of life. We must not forget that everywhere men lived in dread of the powers of evil; superstition was triumphant. In the *Historia Lausiac* of Palladius nearly all the ills of life are attributed to the agency of demons. The Devil and his angels were regarded as foes almost omnipotent, certainly omnipresent. The powers of darkness "filled the atmosphere which extends between earth and heaven" (Cassian). (Workman, op. cit., p. 97)

This vision of a world crammed with demons, attacking on every side, explains the importance ordinary citizens in the middle ages attributed to the unceasing prayers and "contests" of the hermit-monks.

21. Linda Georgianna, *The Solitary Self* (Cambridge: Harvard University Press, 1981), p. 131.

22. Ibid., p. 132.

23. Ibid., p. 138.

24. From *The Decline and Fall of the Roman Empire*, quoted in Peter Anson, *The Call of the Desert* (London: SPCK, 1964), p. 14.

25. Storr reveals this in the introduction of his *Solitude* (New York: Free Press, 1988).

26. All of these quotations are from the "Solitude" chapter of *Walden*, op. cit.

27. Thoreau, op. cit., p. 93.

28. Martin Buber, *I and Thou* (New York: Charles Scribner's Sons; 1970), p. 58.

29. My account in this section must omit the role of personification in the solitary work of scientific researchers, owing to my own lack of familiarity with that realm of experience. For an interesting discussion of this matter, specifically the ways in which some contemporary female scientists have developed a "personal-relational model of subject-object relations" in their research, see Lorraine Code's *What Can She Know?* (Ithaca: Cornell University Press, 1991), especially pp. 150–54. I find equally provocative Donna Haraway's suggestion that

> Ecofeminists have perhaps been most insistent on some version of the world as active subject, not as resource to be mapped and appropriated in bourgeois, Marxist, or masculinist projects. Acknowledging the agency of the world in knowledge makes room for some unsettling possibilities, including a sense of the world's independent sense of Humor. (Donna Haraway, "Situated Knowledges," in *Feminist Studies* 14 (Fall 1988): 593)

30. Sarton, op. cit., p. 25.

31. Anson, op. cit., p. 18. Sister Ward writes that,

> By AD 400 Egypt was a land of hermits and monks. There were three main types of monastic experiment there, corresponding very roughly to three geographical locations. (xvii)

Lower Egypt was the stronghold of the hermits, of whom Antony is the prototype. Upper Egypt, almost from the beginning, developed an organized monasticism under the direction of Pachomius (AD 290–347).
Furthest to the North, in the deserts of Nitria and Scetis, "there evolved a third form of monastic life in the 'lavra' or 'skete' where several monks lived together, often as disciples of an 'abba' " (xvii). Christian monarchism took somewhat different forms in Syria, which emphasized inhuman asceticism, in Asia Minor where a more learned and liturgical monasticism was developed by Saint Basil The Great (AD 330–379), and Palestine which combined Egyptian models with older practices of the Essenes." (op. cit., xii–xv)
As for the numbers involved, they seem to have been large. A contemporary observer, Rufinus, no doubt exaggerated when he wrote that "the number of monks in the deserts equals the population of the cities" (from his *Historia Monachorum in Aegypto*), but Workman tells us that according to Palladius, another contemporary source, "Pachomius ruled over three thousand monks, while in the Nitria there were five thousand dwelling in fifty lauras. Schenoudi, also, is said to have had under his care nearly four thousand monks and nuns." (Workman, op. cit. p.111)

32. Ward, op. cit., p. 3.

33. Cited in Anson, op. cit., p. 21. Anson tells another story which conjures up for me the monastic ideal of "community in isolation." Since before the ninth century there has been a monastery at Montserrat, built on precipitous slopes above a gorge. Higher still, accessible to the monastery only via a steep staircase cut into the rocky slopes, some cells

were long ago cut out of the rock to house thirteen solitaries. After a seven year trial period, during which they could descend to the monastery for services, the solitaries graduated into permanent anchorites, never to leave their cells except for one communal meal on the feast day of St. Benedict. It is their awakening ritual that interests me: "At 1:45 AM, summer and winter, one of them rang the bell of his chapel, and it was soon answered by the bells of his bretheren." (Anson, p. 65)

34. Ward, op. cit., p. xxiv.

35. Workman, op. cit., p. 23. Rufinus Tyrannius mentions a different kind of rivalry among the desert hermits.

> Quiet are they and gentle. They have, indeed, a great rivalry among them—it is who shall be more merciful than his brother, kinder, humbler, more patient. If any be more learned than the rest, he carries himself so commonplace . . . (so as to seem) the least among them . . . (from the *Historia Monachorum*, cited in Anson, op. cit., p. 20)

36. Workman, op. cit., pp. 45–46.

37. Workman, op. cit., p. 42.

38. Why did any of these desert fathers and mothers choose the ascetic path? Workman mentions the influence of the Stoic ideal of apathea, the perfect domination over all the inclinations of nature, and the neo-platonic philosophy of Origen:

> So the monk fled into the desert that he might the more fully in the university of its solitudes pursue the knowledge of himself. But this self-knowledge, as the better school of the Neoplatonist claimed—for we may ignore the school which relied on magic—can only be won by a self-discipline the chief feature of which is its asceticism. Only by a holy abstinence can a man rise clear of the entanglements of matter into a purer existence where he can contemplate and hold communion with the absolute. As Origen bluntly puts it: "All evil which reigns in the body is due to the five senses." The gospel of Neoplatonism was the gospel of salvation by release from a world of sense. (op. cit., p. 29)

And of course the ascetic path was taught by holy examples. Anson notes the stories of the old testament prophets and their solitudes, such as Elijah, who

> set out on a journey of his own devising . . . (eventually leaving) his servant to wait there, while he himself went on, a whole day's journey into the desert. Betaking himself there, and sitting down under a juniper tree, he prayed to have done with life. [But roused and exhorted by an angel] he rose up, and ate and drank; strengthened by the food he went on for forty days and forty nights till he reached god's own mountain Horeb. There he made his lodging in a cave. . . . (I Kings 19:4–9)

For exemplars in the New Testament, one could cite John the Baptist, the "voice crying in the wilderness," who lived on locusts and honey. And of course there was Christ himself: the gospel of Luke relates that

> "Jesus, being full of the Holy Ghost, returned from Jordan, and was led by the Spirit into the wilderness,
>
> Being forty days tempted of the devil. And in those days he did eat nothing: and when they were ended, he afterward hungered.
>
> And the devil said unto him, If thou be the Son of God, command this stone that it be made bread.
>
> And Jesus answered him, saying, "It is written, That man shall not live by bread alone, but by every word of God." (Luke 4: 1–4)

39. Anson, op. cit., p. 170.

40. Although there were hermits living out in the wilds away from the towns, the

"desert calling" was more frequently followed in the towns during this period. A number of factors operated to produce this situation, but one which Georgianna emphasizes is particularily interesting:

> The enormous expansion of society in the eleventh and twelfth centuries and the resulting myriad of new towns all over Europe made the practical requirements of remoteness difficult to achieve. In England especially, where one historian notes that by the twelfth century no spot in the country was more than half a day's walk from the nearest village or town, the desert cry of the new breed of solitaries seems somewhat futile . . . though the new monasteries were self-consciously called deserts, physical solitude was in fact rare. And in one of the few places in England where it was actually created—Revesby—it was, as one historian wryly notes, "at the expense of destroying three small towns." (Georgianna, op. cit., p. 36)

Although immurement became the socially dominant form at this time, it was not a new thing. Workman mentions fourth century *inclusi*

> who spent their lives shut up in a cave or cell, some of them for more than eighty years. One of the earliest of these was the harlot Thais (c. AD 350) who was fed through a window by the nuns of a neighboring convent. Day and night she sobbed aloud, "O my Creator, have mercy upon me." (Workman, op. cit., pp. 49–50)

41. From the *Ancrene Wisse*, cited in Georgianna, op. cit., p. 52.

42. From the *Ancrene Wisse*, quoted in Anson, op. cit., p. 171.

43. Georgianna, op. cit., p. 66.

44. From the *Ancrene Wisse*, cited in Georgianna, p. 70.

45. Ibid., p. 71.

46. From the *Ancrene Wisse*, cited in Georgianna, op. cit., p. 72.

47. Georgianna, op. cit., p. 73.

48. Koller, op. cit., p. 104.

CHAPTER FIVE: *The Symmetry of Engagement and Disengagement*

1. Cited without reference by Halmos, op. cit., p. v.

2. Martin Heidegger, *Being and Time*, op. cit., pp. 156–57. I thank Prof. Peter Trnka for bringing this passage to my attention.

3. Heidegger, op. cit., p. 184.

4. Ashley Montagu, *On Being Human* (New York: Hawthorn Books, 1966), p. 77.

5. Roberto Unger expresses similar suspicions:

And a metaphysic, while pretending to derive conclusions about human nature from allegedly fundamental truths about the world, typically does the very opposite: it projects a view of subjectivity and intersubjectivity into a picture of ultimate reality and then pretends to derive from this projection the very image of man that had originally inspired the metaphysical account. Thus, the modernist metaphysicians of the twentieth century (e.g. Heidegger, Sartre) sometimes tried to rededuce a modernist anthropology from an ultra-metaphysical story about the nature of being. (from his *Passion* [New York: The Free Press, 1984] p. 82)

6. I offer a more direct response more to Heidegger in chapter 9, however.

7. "Primary," and not "only." For on the one hand, what distinguishes the permissible impersonal relations from *using* is surely the recognition throughout the interaction of the personhood of the utensil. And, on the other hand, personal relations may coherently contain some instrumentality, as when we draw on a friend's insights to solve a problem. Then there are the borderline cases, so puzzling for their mixture of the personal and the impersonal: a salesperson speaks so honestly to you that you feel personally involved with them; a friend seems more interested in getting a lift home than in talking to you. Some acts are typically impersonal, e.g. filling a tooth, some are typically personal, e.g. making love, and each of these is very strange indeed when performed in the other mode.

For a fuller discussion of these matters, see my paper "Emotional Ambivalence," *Philosophy and Phenomenological Research* 48, no. 2 (December 1987).

8. Lawrence Blum, "Deceiving, Hurting and Using," collected in Alan Montefiori, ed., *Philosophy and Personal Relations* (Montreal: McGill Queens University Press, 1973).

9. From his introduction to Martin Buber's *I and Thou*, op. cit., pp. 16–17.

10. From "Lover's Bodies," in Joyce Carol Oates, *Angel Fire* (Baton Rouge: Louisiana State University Press, 1973).

11. Lakoff and Johnson, op. cit., pp. 46–67.

12. Perhaps, though, objectification becomes less operative as the level of personal involvement deepens? Perhaps, although this is not obvious to me—unless lack of objectification is made the criterion of depth, which I of course find a bad idea. For our assimilation of objects to cherished persons is visible in the expression of some of our most powerful feelings towards them:

But soft! what light through yonder window breaks?
It is the east, and Juliet is the sun!
Arise, fair sun, and kill the envious moon,
Who is already sick and pale with grief,
That thou her maid art far more fair than she;
(Romeo and Juliet)

Not all loving expressions are as elaborately worked out, of course, but almost everyone seems to have some object-metaphor of endearment for their beloved: sunshine, rock, bean-pole, sweetie pie, tulip, button, little violet, and so on. There are also those unflattering objectifications of our intimate wrath: blockhead! birdbrain! get out of bed you great lump!

13. Quoted in Margaret Furse, *Mysticism* (Nashville: Abingdon Press, 1977), p. 105.

14. Buber, op. cit., p. 59.

15. Ibid., pp. 68–69.

16. D. H. Lawrence, *The Rainbow*, ch. 1.

17. This has been denied by Peter Munz in *Relationship and Solitude* (op. cit.). However, his argument relies upon exaggeration and somewhat eccentric definitions, and so I shall not consider it here.

18. For a vision even darker than Buber's—perhaps equally poetic—see Roberto Unger's *Passion*. In the dynamic between engagement and disengagement Unger sees a

conflict between two "root projects." Engagement is imperative for providing the indispensable means of survival and identity, but beneath even these rolls an inchoate longing:

> The boundlessness of our need for the other person comes down to this: that everything we get from other people, or that they give to us, or that they represent for us by the mere fact of their present or past existence seems like an advance on a spiritual transaction that we are unable to complete. The unrestricted character of the need is confirmed by our inability to specify just what it would take to fulfill it. (p. 96)

But there is a complementary and unlimited fear: in the quest for survival and identity

> . . . you can never have enough security. No defense against exploitation and no hoarding of acquired advantage can guarantee you against a later defeat and decline in your experiments with the uses of contract, community and domination. No endured vulnerability to others can give you unbreakable promises of reconciliation in society and of corrigibility in character. You fear the others both for what they can deny you and for what, even under the best of circumstances, they cannot give you, and your fear of them knows no bounds. (p. 100)

If the containing sense I have spoken of translates roughly as the voice of this longing, the autonomous sense expresses the fear. Because of the boundless character of our mutual longing and mutual jeopardy, neither solitude nor encounter can endure free of the other; and in neither alone can we find peace.

Unger believes, however, that an empowering resolution of this conflict is possible: granting the boundlessness of the need and the fear, one slowly learns that "the failure of control is not the imminence of annihilation":

> The consequence of all this endured vulnerability is therefore not the annihilation of your self—your enslavement to the powers and opinions of other people—but rather the discovery that you can exist uniquely and, at some ultimate level, safely in a world of increasingly dense relations with other people. (p. 108)
>
> Your longing for the other person therefore culminates in an experience of mutual confirmation in self-possession. Your primitive horror of the other person becomes your strengthened acknowledgement of apartness. (p. 117)

If his remarks I quoted earlier are not exaggerated, however, the senses of mutual confirmation and comfortable acknowledgement of apartness must be inherently unstable. But in fact they are exaggerated, as I will argue in chapter 10.

CHAPTER SIX: *Images of Solitude*

1. From "The Love Song of J. Alfred Prufrock" in *British Literature from Blake to the Present Day,* ed. Spencer, Houghton, and Barrows (Boston: D.C. Heath and Co., 1952), p. 914.

2. From "I Saw in Louisiana a Live-Oak Growing" in *The Portable Walt Whitman,* ed. Mark Van Doren (New York: Viking Press, 1945), p. 248.

3. Empedocles (DK, 31B fr. 17).

CHAPTER SEVEN: *The Virtues of Solitude*

1. Petrarch, op. cit., pp. 107–8.

2. Ibid., p. 109.

3. Ibid., p. 120.

4. Kohák, op. cit., p. 42. Kohák does not himself think that restoration is the central meaning of solitude (see pp. 42–46).

5. Robert Sayre reminds us that the idea of a retreat from society has a long and complicated history, stretching from Pliny, Seneca, and the early Christian hermits to Montaigne and Pascal, Rousseau and Werther, Flaubert and Anatole France:

> As the balance of social forces changes, and as these changes are reflected in the predominance of one class or another in the major authors of the period, the theme passes from one group to another and is altered by its particular class perspective; but a basic continuity makes the theme a cross-class phenomenon.
>
> Why does such a continuity exist? Recalling the many manifestations of the theme, both in classical antiquity and "ancien regime" France, we might view the unifying principle of solitary retreat as a revolt against the conditions of a new social order—the early market economy, the beginnings of industrialism, and, in the sixteenth century, the full advent of capitalist organisation. The theme is an expression of early revolt in the prehistory and early history of capitalism. . . . Country solitude is always a retreat from a society based on competition, antagonism, self-interest. (*Solitude in Society*, op. cit., p. 45)

Particularly interesting is his contention that as capitalism develops during the nineteenth century the retreat of solitude becomes more and more a retreat within oneself while remaining in the now more and more alienating society: "Solitude has been transformed from a place outside society to a universal state of mind within society, and an aristocratic, feudal vision of the world has given way to a wholly bourgeois vision." (p. 87)

6. Michel de Montaigne, "Of Solitude" in *The Essays of Montaigne* (London: Oxford University Press, 1927), p. 238.

7. Ilsa Veith, "Hermits and Recluses: Healing Aspects of Voluntary Withdrawal from Society", in Hartog, op. cit., pp. 537–46. After this period of bed-rest, the patient is encouraged to work in the garden surrounding the hospital, thus re-establishing an emotional connection with nature through the processes of attunement discussed later in this chapter.

8. Montaigne, op. cit., p. 242. He uses the image to characterize Pliny and Cicero who foolishly devoted their solitude to writings which they hoped would earn them immortal fame. Such men, he scolds, "have only their arms and legs out of the throng; their souls and intentions are more than ever in the thick of it." It would be better, he thinks, to abandon ambition altogether: "We should do like those animals that remove the traces of their footsteps at the entrance to their lair." (p. 245)

9. From his *Soledad*, cited on page 48 of Paul Ilie, *Unamuno* (Madison: University of Wisconsin Press, 1967). Unamuno here expresses his social and religious commitment, but also the results of a convoluted analysis of the nature of consciousness and the possibility of self-knowledge. See Ilie's study, especially chapters 1–3.

10. Halmos, op. cit., p. 168. Elsewhere he quotes with approval Montaigne's remark about going back to leap the better.

11. *Tao Teh Ching*, op. cit., ch. 39.

12. Ralph Waldo Emerson, "Friendship," collected in Brooks Atkinson, ed., *The Selected Writings of Ralph Waldo Emerson* (New York: Modern Library, 1950), p. 226.

13. Petrarch, op. cit., p. 108.

14. Francis Bacon, "Of Marriage and the Single Life," collected in Hazelton Spencer, *British Literature from Beowulf to Sheridan* (Boston: D.C. Heath and Co., 1951), pp. 405–6. Bacon's essay was written around 1612.

15. From William Hazlitt, *Table Talk* (London: Bell, 1889), ch. 19, p. 251. William Cowper (1731–1800) imagined the freedom of Alexander Selkirk—the real Robinson Crusoe—as a sense of power and dominion similar to Hazlitt's: "I am monarch of all I survey/My right there is none to dispute" (from "Verses Supposed to Be Written by Alexander Selkirk" in *The Poems of William Cowper*, vol. I, ed. John Baird and Charles Ryskamp (Oxford: Oxford University Press, 1992), p. 403.

16. Compare Byrd, op. cit., p. 103.

17. *The Book of Chuang Tzu*, op. cit., ch. 1.

18. Virginia Woolf, *To the Lighthouse* (New York: Grove Press, 1961), pp. 120–21.

19. R. D. Laing, *Knots* (New York: Vintage Books, 1970), p. 2.

20. Rainer Maria Rilke, *The Notebooks of Malte Laurids Brigge*, trans. Stephen Mitchell with an Introduction by William H. Gass (New York: Vintage Books, 1985), p. xxii.

21. Laing, op. cit., p. 20.

22. Halpern, op. cit., p. 202.

23. Rilke, op. cit., pp. 102–3.

24. Sarton, op. cit., p. 81.

25. St. Augustine, *Confessions*, book X, para. 26.

26. Christopher Burney, *Solitary Confinement* (London: Macmillan & Co., 1961), p. 28.

27. David Grayson, *Adventures in Solitude* (New York: Doubleday, 1931), pp. 72–73.

28. Koller, op. cit., p. 12. Koller mentions Kant but does not try to unravel his paradoxical doctrine of freedom as a particular kind of causality. For a clear introduction to the problems involved, by a renowned Kantian scholar, see R. P. Wolff's *The Autonomy of Reason* (New York: Harper and Row, 1973).
The distinction at issue here was discussed in a now-famous essay by Isaiah Berlin, "Two Concepts of Liberty" (in his *Four Essays on Liberty* published by Oxford University Press, 1969), where he called the two "negative liberty" and "positive liberty." The latter was the freedom Kant emphasized in the *Groundwork*, but the former was of the greatest importance in the Koenigsburger's personal life. Anthony Storr informs us that throughout his life Kant sequestered himself from even his own brothers and sisters lest they make family demands upon his time. (Storr, op. cit., p. 155)

29. Oliver Morgan, op.cit., p.19. This self-attuning process is central in Morgan's vision of solitude:
genuine solitude is a way of being of a person, an ambience of quiet and stillness, characterized

by aloneness, by self-presence, by openness to the emergence and revelation of the Self, and willingly chosen as a style for living a whole and integrated life. (p. 20)

30. Sarton, op. cit., p. 207.

31. Ibid., pp. 195–96.

32. Ibid., p. 145.

33. From the Fifth Promenade of the *Musings of a Solitary Stroller,* cited in Ann Hartle, *The Modern Self in Rousseau's Confessions* (Notre Dame: University of Notre Dame Press, 1983), p. 150. The reader interested in Rousseau's conception of the self and the roles he assigned to solitude and nature in the processes of self-discovery should not miss Hartle's insightful study (which I found more interesting than Rousseau's text).

34. Koller, op. cit., p. 2 and p. 8.

35. Anne Morrow Lindbergh, *Gift from the Sea* (New York: Pantheon Books, 1955), p. 42.

36. Merton, writing in 1957, meant, I am sure, to include women. Rolston (the next long quotation), writing in 1989, might have found more gender-neutral language.

37. Merton, op. cit., p. 167. For Merton, true solitude, interior solitude, is necessary in order to find the true self because to be a person *is* to have an incommunicable inner solitude, "an incommunicable personality that is ours, our alone and no one else's."
But when we hear Merton's account of the nature of that inner personality, one's true self, it seems to vanish into a sort of personalityless collective being in Christ/God: "Who am I? My deepest realization of who I am is—I am one loved by Christ . . . the depths of my identity are in the center of my being" (quoted in Robert Faricy, "Thomas Merton: Solitude and the True Self," *Science et Esprit* 31, no. 2 (1979): 195)
As Faricy interprets him,
> Emptying myself of the contents of the false self, I find myself as made in the image and likeness of God. In losing my false self for the sake of Jesus Christ, I find my true self hidden in him. "It is this inner self," Merton writes, "that is taken up into the mystery of Christ, by his love, by the Holy Spirit, so that in secret we live in Christ." (Faricy, op. cit., p. 195)
Paul Tillich expresses the same idea: "In moments of solitude something is done to us. The center of our being, the inner self which is the ground of our aloneness, is elevated to the divine center and taken into it. Therein we can rest without losing ourselves." (in Hartog, op. cit., p. 533) I cannot help wondering what is left of a distinct integral self in the solitude of these theologians.

38. Holmes Rolston, III, *Philosophy Gone Wild* (Buffalo: Prometheus Books, 1989), pp. 228–29. Rolston's position here is especially interesting because he argues the sociality of all consciousness. I discuss those arguments briefly in chapter 10

39. We have to do here with "topographies of the human person," in Morgan's felicitous phrase. His own researches, primarily in the field of religious psychology, turned up a repeated pattern:
> . . . a first outer layer variously described as the 'surface self,' the 'persona,' the 'false self,' or the 'everyday self.' This surface level is seen as a public face or mask we present to the world.

Here the ego holds sway with its plans, its involvements, its distractions. Here we are acted upon by our environment, our culture, our beliefs and aspirations, our fears and prejudices, our images of self and the roles or scripts we live.

Deeper within the person, according to this model, is the 'true Self,' the 'secret self,' and when framed in religious language, the 'heart.' This is the seat of our identity, the reservoir of our being and consciousness, that which truly is Me. This is the 'self' most often spoken of in Jungian thought.

And finally, deep within this Self, there is that which—for want of a better term—might be described as a door, or an opening. This door or passageway connects us to the full human and cosmic community, to the transcendent Mystery which surrounds all of life. This psychic structure might be called the 'Transpersonal Self,' the 'collective unconscious,' or more metaphorically, the 'underground river of God.' (Morgan, op. cit., pp. 21–22)

On the Jungian view, which Morgan likes, there is a dynamism inherent in the person, a striving towards the synthesis and integration of the conscious and unconscious personalities, a movement of growth towards wholeness. Solitude, for him, involves the willing acceptance of this dynamism, this "teleology" of the deeper selves; it is a willingness, not a willfulness, an openness and readiness for the emergent, a "waiting stance" before the self.

I would certainly like to believe that Jung is right in this, and many personal experiences in solitude support him. Yet others do not, and the issues are involved. Part of the problem is that the comprehensiveness of Jung's theories is partly achieved by a too-generous freedom of usage. As Redfearn has noted,

Jung used the word *self* to describe (at various times):
(1) a primary unity inseparable from a cosmic order;
(2) the totality of the individual
(3) a feeling or intimation of such a totality, an experience of "wholeness"
(4) a primary organizing force or agency outside the conscious "I"
(5) the predisposition to organize a center of consciousness
(6) subjective experiences of a personal self (J. T. Redfearn, "Terminology of Ego and Self: From Freud(ians) to Jung(ians)," collected in *The Book of the Self*, op. cit., p. 393.

40. Zaner, op. cit., p. 220.

41. Possibly this is so because I begin with an unusual preference for solitude, and so should not argue from my own case. Perhaps, too, there is a factor of gender at work: perhaps men are less inclined to seek self-attunement with others than women. Belenky et al. discuss these issues at various points throughout *Women's Ways of Knowing* (op. cit.); see especially pp. 144–46, "Real Talk," which cites Jean Elshtain and Jurgen Habermas.

42. A strong introduction to recent conceptions of the nature of the self is *The Book of the Self*, a collection of articles by twenty-three different authors (mostly psychologists) edited by Polly Young-Eisendrath and James Hall (op. cit.). To read this collection is to be reminded of the differences in the ways contemporary theorists use ordinary terms like self, myself, agent, person, and of the different ways they use technical terms like ego, personna, self-construct, and core-self. The differences in models or constructs of the self are equally striking: for Blasi and Oresick, "the self as subject is not a concept or a set of concepts but a concrete reality immediately grasped in experience" (p. 76); for Schafer, however, the self is not "a coherent experience of unity or continuity" but a narrative construction which aims at providing a coherence which is not to be found in the events themselves: "On this view, the self is a telling" (p. 7). In other writers, the self becomes an analytic construct, a shorthand for a group of psychic functions or processes.

Philosophers have been worrying the nature of the self since Plato, which explains why I can offer no simple analysis here. Particularly interesting recent writings, together with an extensive bibliography, may be found in D. Kolak and R. Martin eds., *Self and Identity* (New York: Macmillan, 1991).

43. Quoted in Gaston Bachelard, op. cit., p. 12.

44. Sarton, op. cit., p. 35.

45. Loren Eiseley, *The Immense Journey* (New York: Random House, 1946), pp. 19–20. Eiseley's many books are a great treasury of celebrations of attunement to nature.

46. From a letter to Robert Johnson, quoted in "The Creation of Yosemite National Park," *Sierra Club Bulletin* 39 (1944), p. 50. I am indebted to Roderick Nash's *Wilderness and the American Mind* (op. cit.) for the quote and many of the details of the following brief life.

47. John Muir, *The Story of My Boyhood and Youth* (Boston: Houghton Mifflin, 1913), p. 286.

48. As Nash remarks,

Muir's books were minor best-sellers, and the nation's foremost periodicals competed for his essays. The best universities tried to persuade him to join their faculties and, when unsuccessful, settled for his acceptance of honorary degrees. As a publicizer of American wilderness Muir had no equal. (Nash, op. cit., p. 122)

49. John Muir, *Travels in Alaska* (Boston: Houghton, 1915), pp. 110–11

50. There is a literature on this matter. See William Hammitt's article "Cognitive Dimensions of Wilderness Solitude" (*Environment and Behavior* 14, no. 4, [July 1982]: 478–93) for some interesting empirical research on perceptions of solitude in wilderness.

51. Quoted in Cohen, op. cit., pp. 71–72. See his interesting discussion of danger and vision, pp. 67–75.

52. Quoted from Muir's "The Earthquake" in Edwin Teale, *The Wilderness World of John Muir* (Boston: Houghton Mifflin, 1976), p. 169.

53. Cited in Michael Cohen's comprehensive study of Muir, *The Pathless Way* (Madison: University of Wisconsin Press, 1984), p. 129.

54. Muir was as symbolic a viewer as Thoreau, whose philosophy he admired:

Understandably, most of Muir's ideas were variations on the Transcendentalists' staple theme: natural objects were "the terrestrial manifestations of God." At one point he described nature as a "window opening into heaven," a mirror reflecting the Creator." Leaves, rocks, and bodies of water became "sparks of the Divine Soul." (Nash, op. cit., p. 125)

He knew the dynamic progression towards fusion, too: with a Transcendentalist's spiritual intuition, "you bathe in these spirit-beams, turning round and round, as if warming at a camp-fire. Presently you lose consciousness of your separate existence: you blend with the landscape, and become part and parcel of nature." (Nash, op. cit., p. 126)

55. Thoreau, op. cit., p. 122. Nothing reveals better the elaborativeness of Thoreau's perception—or makes a better story—than the following incident related by Geoffrey O'Brien:

Thoreau hears "a dull, dry, rushing sound, with a solid core to it, yet as if half smothered under the grasp of the luxuriant and fungus-like forest, like the shutting of a door in some distant entry of the damp and shaggy wilderness." He asks his Indian guide what it is and the latter replies simply: "Tree fall." (Geoffrey O'Brien, "Thoreau's Book of Life," *New York Review of Books* 33, no. 46 [January 15, 1987]: 29)

In spite of the verbal skill he knew he had, Thoreau regarded himself as an amateur natural observer compared to the Native Americans. As for the rest of us, he had hopes—if we would only pause to look. The next to the last entry in the journal, Nov. 3, 1861, only six months before he died, made with reference to a minute observation of the effect of a storm upon gravel, insists "All this is perfectly distinct to an observant eye, and yet could easily pass unnoticed."

56. *Walden*, "The Ponds," op. cit., pp. 128–29.

57. Thoreau's journal entry of April 19, 1854.

58. Thoreau, op. cit., p. 62.

59. O'Brien remarks, "he had taken so much from Emerson that he had finally to find out what if anything he had *not* taken from him," directing us to Robert Richardson's *Henry Thoreau: A Life of the Mind* (Berkeley: University of California Press, 1986) for a detailed study of the extent to which "Thoreau in the pre-Walden period thinks with borrowed thoughts." (p. 26)

Sherman Paul reminds us that the Concord Transcendentalists were not enthusiastic about Thoreau's proposed experiment with "the simple, fibrous life," and maintained a sullen silence during his two years at the pond (with the exceptions of Bronson Alcott and William Channing, whose happy visits are alluded to in "Winter Visitors").

60. O'Brien brought to my notice Thoreau's anxiety about seeing others and feeling their gazes (e.g. "The first pattern and prototype of all daggers must have been a glance of the eye"; "serpents alone conquer by the steadiness of their gaze"; "I have never yet met a man who was quite awake. How could I have looked him in the face?"). When introduced to some young women at a party, he wrote later that one "was said to be pretty-looking, but I rarely look people in their faces" (journal entry of Nov. 14, 1851). O'Brien connects this anxiety to the vocation of writing and to the great liberation of seeing at the pond: "The eyeball-to-eyeball confrontation of two equally enlightened beings figures as a blaze too destructively bright . . . Thoreau requires a shadowing, a distance; writing provides it. Writer and reader cannot see each other's eyes."(op. cit., p. 26)

61. All quotations are from "Solitude" in *Walden*, op. cit.

62. Of course this oversimplifies matters. Thoreau really *felt* the commonality which the next-to-be-cited passage from "Spring" expresses, but it also cohered with some Transcendental ideas he probably shared with Emerson. As Paul puts it,

Nature, Emerson had shown, was not mechanical but organic, the continuing handiwork of God; the life in Nature was the ever-present spirit of God, and her phenomena "the present expositor of the divine mind." Man, therefore, had "access to the entire mind of the Creator" because the ideas he had in his communion with Nature were Ideas, the constitutive Reality of the universe as well as the reality of his mind.

In this organically spiritualized idealism, every fact of Nature answered to a fact of consciousness in the human mind, and because of this correspondence the life of consciousness could best be pursued in Nature. Everything in Nature, the entire external world, could be taken possession of by the mind: the brute fact transformed in this experience into value, was fused with the inner and subjective and given its human-spiritual significance. Seized in this way, the fact flowered in a truth . . . (from his introduction to *Walden*, op. cit., p. xv)

63. Thoreau, op. cit., p. 210.

64. Ibid, p. 156.

65. Ibid, p. 87.

66. Thoreau, op. cit., p. 61. As Sherman Paul reminds us, while Thoreau drew from other mythologies, he was really concerned to construct—and enact—his own. One of the great discoveries at Walden Pond was that Walden was as good as Greece or Troy. See also William Byshee Stein's "Walden: The Wisdom of the Centaur," in John Vickery, ed., *Myth and Literature* (Lincoln: University of Nebraska Press, 1966): Stein believes that Thoreau "spent seven years rewriting his journals in order to give them the 'signifying' form that would recapture the mythic implications of his transformative experiences in the woods" (Vickery, p. 336).

67. Cited in William Wolf, *Thoreau: Mystic, Prophet, Ecologist* (Philadelphia: United Church Press, 1974), p. 110. Charles Anderson has seen one mythic dimension to *Walden:*
The skeleton plot of Walden is the archetypal monomyth of the hero's retreat from society, his initiation, and final return—as epitomized by Joseph Campbell: A hero ventures forth from the world of common day into a region of supernatural wonder: fabulous forces are there encountered and a decisive victory is won: the hero comes back from this mysterious adventure with the power to bestow boons on his fellow men. (*The Magic Circle of Walden* [New York: Holt, Rinehart and Winston, 1968], pp. 260–61)
John Broderick finds that going out and returning are the structural form not only for the whole book, but even for chapters and paragraphs: "Thoreau's best paragraphs, however, do not depend entirely on 'the personality of the writer' for their unity. Instead, they move as Thoreau did and as his books do—from the mundane known to the transcendent knowable and back again." ("The Movement of Thoreau's Prose" in Richard Ruland, ed., *Twentieth Century Interpretations of Walden* [Englewood Cliffs: Prentice-Hall, 1968], p. 66)
See also Reginald Cook's "Ancient Rites at Walden" in Ruland.

68. Cited in Stanley Cavell's study, *The Senses of Walden* (New York: Viking, 1972), p. 26. Things were not always so bright and joyous at the front, though. As many scholars have noted, Walden Pond was a rural environment, and when Thoreau actually got out to wilderness, the experiences were frequently aversive: descending Mount Katadn through some burned out wasteland, for example, was disturbing: "Vast, Titanic, inhuman Nature has got him at a disadvantage, caught him alone, and pilfers him of some of his divine faculty . . . She seems to say sternly, why came ye here before your time? . . . Here is no shrine, nor altar, nor any access to my ear." He could also write, "this vast, savage, howling mother of ours, Nature"
In these sentiments he was more a man of his times, as Roderick Nash reveals in *Wilderness and the American Mind* (op. cit.). The first generations of Americans brought to the wilderness of their new land 100,000 years of fear of forest wilds, Biblical execrations of it, and dark European superstitions stretching back to the Middle Ages. These first settlers called it "howling, dismal, terrible" (p. 23), and set out to subdue and conquer it in the great Morality play of the westward expansion. Living ever surrounded by wilderness

produced and reinforced a fear of it: "It remained for the children and grandchildren who grew up separated from it to develop an affection for it." By the first half of the 1800s this affection was beginning to emerge. Cooper, Bird, Freneau, Rush, Evans, and Daniel Boone celebrated primitive wilds, and the intellectuals of the cities took up the call, making excursions into the wilds to take "impressions" to be written up later back in town.

The Transcendentalist philosophy which rose out of this awakening held nature to be the Great Source and Text of the Creator's mind; but individual Transcendentalists had to contend with 100,000 years of fear. One can feel Thoreau wrestling with these primitive feelings: one of our first and sanest advocates for wilderness experience and preservation, even he was sometimes thrown by the thing in the raw. (See Eugene Hargrove, "The Historical Foundations of American Environmental Attitude," *Environmental Ethics* 1, no. 1 (1979), for a discussion of Thoreau's attitudes toward wilderness.)

69. The modern descendants of the Sturm und Drangers, the wilderness campers, have written often of moments of interfusion with nature. Recently one of them, Jay Vest, a scholar and forester, wrote a wide-ranging article on "The Philosophical Significance of Wilderness Solitude" for *Environmental Ethics*, 9 (1987): 303–30. which any student of solitude will want to read. On interfusion, he writes

> Wilderness solitude implies a "standing with," reflecting upon the presence of all things as they stand together in a felt unity. This is an "at-one-ment" wherein one is interfused with wildness in the sense of *compresence*. . . . the constatic rapture that is wildness "at-one-ment," an experience in which the critical tendencies of exclusive differentiation are severely mitigated or absolved . . . a realization of our creatureness with others in phenomenal existence;(p. 328)

Vest discusses many of the other issues we have been reflecting upon and deserves reading, although I found both his style of writing and method of argument rather obscure. For another study of solitude by an environmental philosopher, see Holmes Rolston's *Philosophy Gone Wild*, op. cit., especially the chapter on "Lake Solitude."

70. Goethe, *The Sorrows of Young Werther*, trans. Victor Lange (New York: Holt, Rinehart and Winston, 1949), pp. 53–54.

71. Op. cit., p. 111.

72. Quoted in J. Cohen and J-F. Phipps, *The Common Experience* (Los Angeles: J. P. Tarcher, 1979), pp. 31–32.

73. Richard Katz, *Solitary Life* (New York: Reynal & Co., 1959), p. 46.

74. Thoreau, op. cit., p. 91.

75. Triumpho, op. cit., p. 82.

76. Bugbee, op. cit., p. 317.

77. Cited in James Hart's excellent study, "Towards A Phenomenology of Nostalgia" (*Man and World*, 1973), p. 405. Hart finds nostalgia to be such a moment of gathering: "It is a return to the time when the wishes and hopes which constitute our present were fresh and before the wishes and hopes were battered and bruised—but which wishes and hopes still constitute our life-project" (p. 408). Proust held that such moments of "found" time constitute the highest happiness that is available to us. They produce "fragments of existence withdrawn from Time," a contemplation of the

essences of life; and though they are fleeting, "yet I was vaguely aware that the pleasure which this contemplation had, at rare intervals, given me in my life, was the only genuine and fruitful pleasure I had known" (from *The Past Recaptured,* trans. Andreas Mayor [New York: Vintage Books, 1970], p. 136).

78. René Descartes, *Discourse on Method,* part II, para. 1.

79. Perhaps also the masculine nature of its prevailing epistemological ideal. See Susan Bordo's intriguing study, *The Flight to Objectivity* (Syracuse: State University of New York Press, 1987).

80. René Descartes, *Meditations on First Philosophy,* Med. I, para. 2.

81. Plato, *Symposium,* in *The Collected Dialogues of Plato,* op. cit., pp. 562–63. One notices here, and in the famous "Allegory of the Cave" in the *Republic,* the repeated use of the language of sight—"vision," "beholding," "gazing"—to describe contemplation.

82. *The Book of Chuang Tzu,* ch. 6. In the preface to his comparative study, *The Tao of Physics,* Fritjof Capra recounts a personal experience of illumination—on the face of it very different from that of Yen Hui:

> I was sitting by the ocean one late summer afternoon, watching the waves rolling in and feeling the rhythm of my breathing, when I suddenly became aware of my whole environment as being engaged in a gigantic cosmic dance. Being a physicist, I knew that the sand, rocks, water and air around me were made of vibrating molecules and atoms, and that these consisted of particles which interacted with one another by creating and destroying other particles. I knew also that the earth's atmosphere was continually bombarded by showers of 'cosmic rays', particles of high energy undergoing multiple collisions as they penetrated the air. All this was familiar to me from my research in high-energy physics, but until that moment I had only experienced it through graphs, diagrams, and mathematical theories. As I sat on that beach my former experiences came to life; I 'saw' cascades of energy coming down from outer space, in which particles were created and destroyed in rhythmic pulses; I 'saw' the atoms of the elements and those of my body participating in this cosmic dance of energy; I felt its rhythm and I 'heard' its sound, and at that moment I knew that this was the Dance of Shiva, the Lord of Dancers worshipped by the Hindus.

Capra's moving description causes one to ponder what diverse experiences now get attributed to Taoism.

83. Quoted in Cohen and Phipps, op. cit., p. 20.

84. Gregory the Great, *Magna Moralia,* xxiv,11, cited in Sister Mary Mason's *Active Life and Contemplative Life* (Milwaukee: Marquette University Press, 1961), p. 55. Sister Mason emphasizes the visual metaphor in a footnote to this passage. She also includes Menager's observation that "*contemplum* once signified a section of the heavens *observed* or *watched* for the sake of auspices" (p. 55).

Although Gregory emphasized vison and emotion, St. Thomas Aquinas stressed the intellectual foundations of contemplation:

> The contemplative life has one act wherein it is finally complete, namely the contemplation of truth, and from this act it derives its unity. Yet it has many acts whereby it arrives at this final act. Some of these pertain to the reception of principles . . . others are concerned with deducing from principles . . . and the last and crowning act is the contemplating itself of the truth.

This is however attended with love:

> Since, then, the contemplative life consists chiefly in the contemplation of God, of which charity is the motive, . . . it follows that there is delight in the contemplative life, not only by reason of the contemplation itself, but also by reason of the divine love. . . .
>
> Both because of the operation itself and because of the excellence of the object, "the delight thereof surpasses all human delight." (Sum Theol. IIa-IIae, q.180, 3 and 7. cited in Mason, p. 85)

85. Cited in Cohen and Phipps, op. cit., p. 111.

86. Cited in Cohen and Phipps, op. cit., p. 14.

87. Annie Dillard, *The Writing Life* (New York: Harper Perennial, 1990), pp. 10–11.

88. William Carlos Williams, "Danse Russe," in *Twentieth Century Poetry and Poetics*, ed. Garry Geddes (Toronto: Oxford University Press, 1985), pp. 37–38.

89. Letter to Stieglitz, fall 1937, in Anita Politzer, *A Woman on Paper* (New York: Simon and Schuster, 1988), pp. 223–24.

90. Cited in Thomas Parkinson, op. cit., pp. 468–69. This unclear passage makes the most sense if we translate 'loneliness' as 'solitude.'

91. Cited in Politzer, op. cit., p. 250.

92. Ibid., p. 263.

93. Cited in Rolston, op. cit., p 253. Cobb's book is entitled *The Ecology of Imagination in Childhood* (New York: Columbia University Press, 1977).

94. Storr, op. cit., pp. 119, 122.

95. I learned this some years ago from Abraham Maslow's wise discussion of "Creativity in Self-Actualizing people" in *Towards a Psychology of Being* (New York: D. Van Nostrand Company, 1968), pp. 135–48. There he notes a number of differences between what he calls "special-talent creativeness" and "self-actualizing creativeness."

96. I do not assign great significance to the number five, or to my particular designations of these categories, and would be delighted to see a different systematization. All I can claim for my system of categories is that it makes a remarkably diverse set of experiences conceptually manageable without intolerable oversimplification.

I have not argued for the *moral* virtues of solitude, feeling them to be derivative from the five virtues we have explored, but other authors have placed their emphasis there. Johann Zimmerman was a case in point. Sometime physician to King George III of England, Zimmerman wrote a book on solitude, insisting that

> Society is the school of Wisdom, and Solitude the temple of Virtue. . . . How should that man discharge any part of his duty aright, who never suffers his passions to cool? and how should his passions cool, who is engaged, without interuption, in the tumults of the world? This incessant stirring may be called *the perpetual drunkenness of life* . . . Whereas he who mingles rational Retreat with worldly Affairs, remains calm, and master of himself. (*Solitude* [Boston: Joseph Burnstead, 1804], pp. 402–3)

Similar moral themes are evident in many of the quotations I have collected in these pages. See especially Erazim Kohák's evocation of "the moral sense of nature" which emerges best in solitude.

CHAPTER EIGHT: *The Completions of Encounter*

1. I am not so ungrateful as to forget the many ways in which the freedoms of solitude are causally dependent upon the services of other people. It is certainly true that my solitary afternoon in the woods with the chainsaw depends upon the services of saw and gasoline and file manufacturers, road-builders and farm lane clearers, and rests secure upon the bosom of police protection and available hospitalization. I do not discuss them because I am concerned in this book with the *experiential nature* of solitude and encounter, and not with their causality.

2. Kenney's *Action, Emotion and Will* resuscitated interest in this analytical tool in 1963, and there followed a modest duststorm of discussion in philosophical journals and books on emotion during the next ten years. Not surprisingly, I still feel that the most cogent of those studies was my own article, "Loneliness without Objects" (op. cit.); there the reader will find a survey of four different conceptions of object that were about in the literature, together with copious references.

Phenomenologists use the term "intentionality" to refer to object-directedness, tracing their analyses back to Brentano and Husserl.

3. What seem quibbles to the uninitiated can seem very important to professionals: I remember, vaguely, a philosopher insisting that the object of my feeling of dismay, should I be told by some brave student, "Your lecture was boring," would be—not the student, not his detectable statement, but the propositional fact *that my lecture was boring*. Why such contortions? The philosopher was trying to work out a comprehensive theory of objects which would be able to assign an object to every emotion, and he was struggling with emotions whose objects, to put it baldly, don't exist: what, for example, is the object of your fear that war will break out if it never does break out?

4. Cynthia Wolff, *Emily Dickinson* (New York: Alfred Knopf, 1986), p. 128. Wolff discusses Dickinson's self-image of a fox, who watches secretly and then discloses itself at the proper time, remarking that

> Dickinson's poetry apotheosizes this central human paradox: the poignant, inevitable isolation of each human being—the loneliness and the yearning to be seen, acknowledged, and known—on the one hand; on the other, the gleeful satisfaction in keeping one part of the self sequestered, sacred, uniquely powerful, and utterly inviolate—the incomparable safety in retaining a secret part of the "self" that is available to no one save self." (p.130)

Thomas Johnson, who edited her letters, wrote

> Perhaps no sentence that she wrote more aptly epitomizes her relationship with people than this, written to James Clark in 1882: 'A Letter always seemed to me like Immortality, for is it not the Mind alone, without corporeal friend?' (from Johnson's note to the twelfth series of her published letters, *The Letters of Emily Dickinson* [Cambridge: Harvard University Press 1958], p.808)

5. Bugbee, op. cit., p. 317.

6. Ibid., p. 318.

7. Of course, these are not simple matters, as readers of Sartre will be protesting. One thinks of the discussion of "bad faith" in *Being and Nothingness* where Sartre attacks sincerity as "a phenomenon of bad faith," on grounds that it attempts to freeze into a determinable *thing* that self which is, rather, a *freedom* (see, e.g., Hazel Barnes's translation [New York: Philosophical Library], part I, ch. 2, p. 63).

Ilham Dilman pursues this Sartrean theme in *Love and Human Separateness* (Oxford: Basil Blackwell, 1987), insisting that there is a clear sense in which a person can transcend his/her qualities and history: he/she "can endorse or repudiate them and thus assume responsibility for what he is."

> When a man repudiates an aspect of his character, say his greed, there is an obvious sense in which he transcends it. He does not identify himself with it, he does not act from greed; but when he does he feels ashamed.
>
> In [this] case we shall make contact with the man not so much through the greed which he fails to resist as through the shame he feels. For he is at one with his shame as he is not with his greed—the greed that is 'his' in the weak sense that the signature, for instance, on the agreement that makes him the beneficiary of a large sum of money is his signature . . . (p. 132)

8. John Burroughs, the prolific naturalist and essayist whose range of personality enabled him to establish friendships with such disparate individuals as Walt Whitman, John Muir, Teddy Roosevelt, and Henry Ford, kept notebooks and journals from the age of seventeen until his death at eighty-four. In the last journal (1921), he wrote:

> Men who write journals are usually men of certain marked traits—they are idealists; they love solitude rather than society; they are self-conscious, and they love to write . . . their Journals largely take the place of social converse. Amiel, Emerson, and Thoreau, for example, were lonely souls, lacking in social gifts, and seeking relief in the society of their own thoughts. Such men go to their Journals as other men go to their clubs. They love to be alone with themselves, and dread to be benumbed or drained of their mental force by uncongenial persons. To such a man his Journal becomes his duplicate self, and he says to it what he could not say to his nearest friend. It becomes both an altar and a confessional." (Clara Barrus, *The Heart of Burroughs' Journals* [Port Washington: Kennikat Press, 1928], p. vii)

I must agree with his editor, Clara Barrus, who remarks after this quotation, "True, but one thinks of other than 'lonely souls' that have kept Journals, or, more often, Diaries, with the vivid pictures of their days, their times, their associates, and themselves." Journals and diaries have been particularly important for women, as Mary Jane Moffat and Charlotte Paynter show in *Revelations: Diaries of Women*, a work discussed in chapter 13 below.

9. Nadine Gordimer, *A World of Strangers* (New York: Penguin Books, 1984), p. 85.

10. Virginia Woolf, *The Waves* (London: Granada Panther, 1979), p. 81.

11. Emily Bronte, *Wuthering Heights*, Hilda Marsden and Ian Jack, eds. (Oxford: Clarendon Press, 1976), pp. 101–2.

12. There are also distinctions and complexities to explore here, as John Heron shows in "The Phenomenology of Social Encounter: The Gaze" (*Philosophy and Phenomenological Research* 31 (December 1970): 243–64). There he develops a primary distinction between "perceiving the other's eyes as such (that is, as purely physical objects) and perceiving his gaze" (p. 245). The distinction is easy to verify experientially:

> You seat yourself at close range to the other, and while he gazes at you, you look exclusively at his eyes qua eyes, observing only their properties and deliberately excluding the quality of the gaze that they mediate; then at a certain point return from his eyes as purely physical entities to take up his gaze, and note the sense of reciprocal entry, contact and widening out, the experience, in short, of actual meeting (in the strict sense). This phenomenological test is quite irreducible, and provides the fundamental datum from which any discussion in this area must proceed . . . (p. 245)

The salient difference between the two cases is that "in the former case the observer is attending to the physical features of the other's eyes, in the latter to the psychical features" (p. 246). Having tried his experiment, I can attest to the uncanny "break" between the two experiences. However, there are many varieties of perceptual experience in between these two extremes—the clinical and the existential-metaphysical, we might call them—and looking lovingly at the patterns of lines around an old friend's face, seeing them now as expressive of a character, now of a life, now of the eternal war between time and substance, all these are experiences of the friend that are easy to parallel in attunements to nature. And coming at his distinction from the other side, "the three striking features of the gaze which I thus meet: its luminosity, its straming quality and its meaning" (p. 252) also find their parallels in our experiences of nature, as Buber's encounter with the tree illustrates.

13. H. Tristram Engelhardt, "Solitude and Sociality" in *Humanitas*, op. cit., pp. 279-81.

14. Edith Hamilton, *Mythology*, op. cit., pp. 412-13.

15. See, for example, Anthony Kenny's biographical notes in his study *Descartes* (New York: Random House, 1968).

16. From the Letter to Father Dinet appended to the end of the Objections and Replies which Descartes published together with the *Meditations On First Philosophy*. The quotation appears in Elizabeth Haldane and G. Ross, eds., *The Philosophical Works of Descartes* (New York: Dover Publications, 1955), Vol. 2, p. 304.

17. Quoted in Anthony Kenny, *Decartes*, op. cit., p. 9.

18. Haldane and Ross, op. cit., p. 60.

19. Ben-Ami Scharfstein has noted "the independence and originality that evidently constituted Descartes's value in his own eyes"; insistence on these qualities appears throughout the works, and threats to them provoked Descartes's most venomous responses. Here is an excerpt from a letter he wrote to Beeckman, the Dutch scholar who had befriended Descartes in his youth and now presumed to suggest that Descartes might have learned some things from him:

> I could in no way imagine that you had become so stupid and understood yourself so ill that you might in effect think that I had ever learned from you, or even that I could ever learn anything from you, if not in the way that I usually learned from everything natural, even the least ants and the smallest worms. . . . Consider, I ask you, and see if in all your life you have found or invented anything that is really worth praising? (quoted in Scharfstein's "Descartes' Dreams," in Berel Lang, ed., *Philosophical Style* [Chicago: Nelson-Hall, 1980], pp. 324–26)

20. Haldane and Ross, op. cit., pp. 65, 69, 74, respectively.

21. Jean-Paul Sartre, *Nausea*, trans. Lloyd Alexander (New York: New Directions, 1964), p. 39.

22. *Tao Teh Ching*, op. cit., ch. 1.

23. Anthony Storr, *The Integrity of Personality*, op. cit., p. 24.

24. Sarton, op. cit., p. 120.

25. Sarton, op. cit., p. 67.

26. Dillard, op. cit., p. 79.

27. Two excellent philosophical studies of caring are Milton Mayeroff's *On Caring* (New York: Harper and Row, 1971), and Nel Noddings's *Caring* (Berkeley: University of California Press, 1984).

28. Belenky et al., op. cit., pp. 143–44.

29. Is this merely a male value, this caring for nonhuman things? Surely not. Women as well as men have always cared for their houses, their tools and furniture, their gardens and their farms, now their biosphere. Children are taught by men and women to care for things, and we all think it a failure if a child—male or female—grows to adulthood deficient in this sense of care.

30. Bugbee, op. cit., p. 318.

31. From Burroughs's journal as collected in Barrus, op. cit., pp. 303–5.

CHAPTER NINE: *The Place of Solitude: The Arguments Apriori*

1. Source lost.

2. Powys, op. cit., p. 51. Often eloquent, Powys could become metaphorically overheated, as when he urged the meditative soul to begin by banishing daily cares, "these devilish worries that drain the living udders of the soul like snakes at the teats of cows" (p. 116).

3. D. H. Lawrence as cited in Halmos, op. cit.

4. Heinz Kohut, A. Goldberg, and P. Stepansky, eds., *How Does Analysis Cure?* (Chicago: University of Chicago Press, 1984), p. 47.

5. Heidegger, op. cit.

6. Storr's *Solitude* is particularily rewarding on this topic. See especially chapter 7: "Solitude and Temperament."

7. Sir Edward Dyer (1543–1607), "My Mind to Me a Kingdom Is" in *British Literature from Beowulf to Sheridan*, ed. H. Spencer (Boston: D.C. Heath and Co., 1951), p. 270.

8. Andrew Marvel (1621–1678), "The Garden" is H. Spencer, op. cit., p. 530.

9. Percy Bysshe Shelley, "Julian and Maddalo" (1818), in *The Oxford Dictionary of Quotations*, 4th ed., ed. A. Partington, (Oxford: Oxford University Press, 1992), p. 640.

10. Lord Byron, *Childe Harold*, Canto IV in Spencer, Houghton, and Barrows, op. cit., p. 242.

11. William Wordsworth, "Tintern Abbey" in Spencer, Houghton, and Barrows, op. cit., p. 48.

12. William Wordsworth, *The Prelude, 1799, 1805, 1850*, ed. J. Wordsworth, M. Abrams, and S. Gill (New York: W.W. Norton and Co., 1979), p. 82. The lines quoted are from the 1805 version, Book II, lines 334–341.

13. Quoted in Jean Clay, *Romanticism* (Secaucus: Chartwell Books, 1981), p. 8. Another military dictator, to my surprise, appeared to gesture towards solitude: Adolf Hitler entitled chapter 8 of volume 2 of *Mein Kampf*, "The Strongest Man is Mightiest Alone" (a line he stole from Schiller's *William Tell*, Act I, Scene III). Actually, though, Hitler's chapter has little to do with solitude, being a discussion of the pitfalls of forming political parties out of federations of small groups.

14. William Cowper, "Lines Supposed to Have Been Written by Alexander Selkirk," op. cit.

15. William Cowper, op. cit.

16. William Wordsworth, "Elegiac Stanzas," in Spencer, Houghton, and Barrows, op. cit., p. 65.

17. Octavio Paz, *The Labyrinth of Solitude* (New York: Grove Press, 1961), p. 9. On page 203 he writes that "solitude is a distinctive characteristic of adolescence. Narcissus, the solitary, is the very image of the adolescent . . . The vision of the adolescent as a solitary figure, closed up within himself and consumed by desire or timidity . . ."

18. Storr, op. cit., p. 168–69. In this chapter Storr studies the late works of a number of composers, finding in each case a search for new forms of unity and coherence. See also Reed Larson et al., "Being Alone versus Being with People: Disengagement in the Daily Experience of Older Adults" in *Journal of Gerontology* 40, no. 3 (1985).

19. Discussed in Hartog, op. cit., p. 8. This is a remarkable linguistic profusion in a culture so densely inhabiting a small land area; it should suffice to refute any simple notions that solitude is not a value in crowded cultures. Indeed it suggests that the reverse may be closer to the case: just as breathable air is not a valued commodity when it is effortlessly available, though it is a necessity of existence, so it may be with solitude.

Linguistic problems of translation suggest themselves to me in this remark from Paz's *The Labyrinth of Solitude*: "Popular language reflects this dualism by identifying solitude with suffering . . . solitude is both a sentence and an expiation" (p. 196). This identification is certainly not in the English language, if Paz is indeed right about Spanish.

20. Ward, op. cit., p. 10.

21. See Storr's discussion, op. cit., pp. 190–94.

22. St. Augustine, *Of the True Religion*, section xxxix.

23. Sayre's social history of solitude is interesting on the origins of some of these views in western culture: see part 1 of *Solitude*, especially chapter 2. Sayre attributes the rise of literary interest in "solitude in society" to developments in late-modern capitalism. Whether he is right about this or not, there certainly has been a resuscitation of interest in loneliness during the last twenty years—perhaps betokening a cultural resignation to the fact that alienation is here to stay, our only option being to try to find what we can in it.

24. Quoted in Hartog, op. cit., p. 559.

25. Mijuskovic, op. cit., p. 6.

26. Powys, op. cit., pp. 37, 41.

27. Koller, op. cit., p. 3.

28. Moustakas, op. cit., p. 3.

29. Tillich, op. cit., p. 550.

30. In Hartog, op. cit., p. 467.

31. Proust, op. cit., p. 459.

32. Marcel Proust, *Remembrance of Things Past*, op. cit.

33. J. Howard, *The Flesh Colored Cage*, cited in Mijuskovic, op. cit., p. 81.

34. Aldous Huxley, *After Many a Summer* (London: Chatto, 1950).

35. Luigi Pirandello, *Henry IV* (London: Eyre; Methuen, 1979).

36. Parkinson, op. cit.

37. Mijuskovic, op. cit., p. 27.

38. Tillich, op. cit., p. 547.

39. Mijuskovic, op. cit., p. 94. There is also the suggestion of an argument based on separation in the following passage from Octavio Paz:
> All men, at some moment in their lives, feel themselves to be alone. And they are. To live is to be separated from what we were in order to approach what we are going to be in the mysterious future. Solitude is the profoundest fact of the human condition. (*The Labyrinth of Solitude*, op. cit., p. 195)

40. Gottfried Wilhelm von Leibniz, *Monadology*, para. 7. All references are taken from the translations collected by M. C. Beardsley in *The European Philosophers from Descartes to Nietzsche* (New York: Modern Library, 1960). Since these are all short works, often with section numbers, and since they are now available in many translations, I cite the work and section rather than the page in Beardsley.

41. Leibniz, *Discourse on Metaphysics*, section VIII. Compare this passage from section XIV:
> In fact nothing can happen to us except thoughts and perceptions, and all our thoughts and perceptions are but the consequence, contingent it is true, of our precedent thoughts and perceptions, in such a way that were I able to consider directly all that happens or appears to me at the present time, I should be able to see all that will happen to me or that will ever happen to me.

42. *Monadology*, paras. 56 and 57.

43. The mirroring dewdrop is the closest I can come to a clear illustrative example of a Leibnizian monad, but even this is inaccurate: strictly speaking, a raindrop is an *aggregate* of substances, a pond and not a fish (see *Monadology*, 67).

44. *Discourse on Metaphysics*, section XXVIII.

45. Tillich, op. cit., p. 547.

46. Quoted in Mijuskovic, op. cit., p. 81.

47. Cited in Dilman, op. cit., p. 73.

48. Mijuskovic, op. cit., p. 81.

49. Howard rests his case on more than mere embodiment, insisting that our sensations and the language we devise to express ourselves are inescapably internal and personal. I will consider views such as this in the next chapter, wishing here only to insist that mere embodiment itself is not an argument for the primacy of aloneness.

50. René Descartes, *Meditations on First Philosophy,* Meditation VI (from Beardsley, op. cit.).

51. Ibid.

52. Ibid., Meditation II.

53. See Norman Malcolm's now-classical modern discussion, "The Argument from Analogy," collected in V. C. Chappell, *The Philosophy of Mind* (Englewood Cliffs: Prentice-Hall, 1962). Chappell's introduction contains an excellent overview of mid-century attempts to resolve the problems raised by Descartes.

54. The line of response to Descartes which I favor is developed by Ilham Dilman in two recent works, building critically on the work of Wittgenstein. Dilman writes:

> For Wittgenstein it is the notion of *the person* that is the primary notion. We do not understand that in terms of any prior concepts of mind and body. For it is the flesh and blood person who has feelings, desires, intentions and thoughts, not some disembodied mind; it is the sentient, conscious person who behaves, acts, moves his limbs voluntarily, not a body operated by a mind.
>
> Thus when one meets another person one does not see a certain kind of behavior from which one then infers a particular "state of mind" . . . No, the feelings, the intentions are *in* the behavior, even though a person can, of course, keep these to himself . . . It is because we see it as human behaviour in the first place that we may wonder what he is up to when his feelings and intentions are opaque to us. (*Love and Human Separateness,* op. cit., p. 29)

Elements of behavior, smiles, frowns, dances, fist-shakings do not occur as mere separate elements, but in ensemble connect provoking circumstances and future actions to form patterns which repeatedly recur in our lives. "Mental terms" like joy and sorrow refer to these complex patterns, and not merely to inner unobservable events:

> Hence anger or joy is not only what a person feels when he is angry or joyful and says so, but also what we see when he is angry or feels joy and does not hide it. What he feels and what we see are thus *one and the same thing;* they form part of the same conception. . . . To see the pattern is to see his soul. (ibid., pp. 33–34)

It is true that feelings can be hidden and we can be deceived. But we need to remember that one must learn how to conceal feelings — largely through the acquisition of language.

> The child does not learn to express his feelings. For his feelings do not, in the first place, exist in separation from his responses. . . . Concealing one's anger is thus logically a more sophisticated form of behavior than giving vent to it or displaying it. To express it, all he has to do is to let go, to abandon himself to natural impulse. Whereas to hide one's feelings may require effort and renunciation, and it may call for cleverness and subterfuge. (ibid, p. 50)

If these observations, which certainly ring true, can be combined with satisfying diagnoses of the erroneous reasonings which originally led Descartes astray, we will have the solution to The Problem of Other Minds. All this I must leave, however, to the epistemologists.

For a provocative psycho-cultural analysis of Descartes's system, the reader might consult Susan Bordo's recent work, *The Flight to Objectivity* (Albany: State University of

New York Press, 1987). There she identifies a "flight from the feminine" world-view of medieval culture, a masculinization of thought which reconstructed knowledge and consciousness of self to maximize autonomy, separation, and distance—exactly the features we have been considering here. Bordo's complex study resists summary statement, but her intriguing application of Freudian analysis to epistemological constructions can be exemplified. After detailing the feminine (especially maternal) aspects of the medieval world-view and the general anxiety felt as that view began to crumble under the weight of developments in nascent science, religious heterodoxy, and contact with non-European cultures, Bordo cites Freud's analysis of an odd game developed by a little boy whose mother had to leave him occasionally: the boy would throw small objects away from himself into inaccessible corners, expressing great satisfaction—a behavior which Freud interpreted as a re-enacting of the mother's disappearance, only now controlled by the sufferer. Bordo then writes,

> Within the context of the cultural separation anxiety described in this study, Descartes' masculine 'rebirthing' of the world and self as decisively separate appears, not merely as the articulation of a positive new epistemological ideal, but as a reaction-formation to the loss of 'being-one-with-the-world' brought about by the disintegration of the organic, centered, female cosmos of the Middle Ages and Renaissance. The Cartesian reconstruction of the world is a 'fort-da' game [Freud's name for the little boy's game]—a defiant gesture of independence from the female cosmos, a gesture which is at the same time compensation for a profound loss. (*The Flight to Objectivity* [Albany: State University of New York Press, 1987], p. 106)

55. Ludwig Wittgenstein, *Philosophical Investigations* (London: Blackwell, 1963), section 420.

56. Sartre, Jean-Paul: *Being and Nothingness*, trans. Hazel Barnes (New York: Philosophical Library, 1961), pp. 259–61.

57. Ibid., p. 277.

58. Mijuskovic, op. cit., p. 3.

59. Ibid., p. 11.

60. The book ends by offering us permission to do what we can to forget our plight through

> genuine and intimate friendship, . . . amusements, tasks, travel, sports, sex, scholarship, philanthropy, etc., all falling under the genus of extro-reflective activities which successfully promote forgetfulness. . . .
> Much—but certainly not everything—is fair in the pursuit of individual happiness and the flight from loneliness. And so we may all be permitted, and forgiven, if we indulge in some sophistry and self-deception on ourselves." (p. 100)

61. *A Treatise of Human Nature*, ed. L.A. Selby-Bigge (Oxford: Clarendon Press, 1896), I, i, 6.

62. For an interesting discussion of experiences of nothingness, see Michael Novak's *The Experience of Nothingness* (New York: Harper Colophon Books, 1970).

63. Sometimes positing seems to be a logical operation, sometimes a psychological process, sometimes a strange "transcendental process" which bundles the two together: "I thetically posit the existence of the alter ego as a necessary condition for my own existence, for my subjectivity, i.e., self-consciousness means consciousness for a subject" (p. 76). But compare: "For only later, genetically and 'logically', can the ego become reflexively conscious of itself as a distinct entity . . ." (p. 58).

64. Norbert Elias makes a parallel criticism of Freud's Id theory:

Freud held the view that the psychological agency that he called the 'Id', the most animalistic layer of the psyche, closest to the physis, which he treated almost as a little person, believes itself immortal. But I do not think we can accept this. On the level of the Id a person has no foresight, so no anticipatory knowledge of her or his own mortality. Without this knowledge the compensatory idea of personal immortality cannot be explained: it would have no function. Freud here attributes to the Id-impulses, which are wholly oriented to the here and now, a level of reflection inaccessible to them." (Norbert Elias, *The Loneliness of the Dying* [Oxford: Blackwell, 1985], p. 36)

It seems to me that this criticism applies equally forcefully to Freud's original narcissistic ego, and to Fichte's primary ego. They simply do not have the wherewithal to do what they are said to do. There is a sort of illogical bootstrapping at work in these authors.

65. Indeed, he moves back and forth between Fichte's two egos and his own—the self as a reflexive nothingness—which is not the same as either of Fichte's.

66. Richard Zaner does more wisely by coining a new term when discussing related matters, "aloneliness":

There is for every self that by which it is itself and is utterly alone. Subtle, elusive and often disguised, this can only be discovered *to* the self; it can never be chosen nor can it be created. For it is that whereby all choosing and creating are accomplished. The self can and does build screens for itself and before others—masks, fronts, images—but that within the self which accomplishes this is not itself constructed. On this, accordingly, what Ricoeur sees as Freud's "silence" on the self—the "self-positing" in desire—is clearly correct. The question is always: *whose* disguises are they, and thus *who* is behind their making and being lived? It is this, which I shall call "aloneliness"—as distinct from "loneliness," an essentially *social* phenomenon—that must be seized upon here.

Although self is thus an aloneliness and elusive thereby, it is not secret, not an essential hiddenness; for *it seeks to be manifest*, to be a presence, an inwardness seeking to become outwardly revealed . . . That whereby the self is itself and alone is experienced by the self as an urgency to be itself in explicitness, ultimately in fullness, as an urge for meaning, clarity and order (and as dread over their constantly possible distortion, failure, or absence). The self seeks to be this manifestly, to utter overtly and share openly with that within the actual other self whereby he or she, too, is himself or herself, alone, and has an urgency to be with the other, this self. (op. cit., pp. 151–52)

67. Here Mijuskovic appears to find another argument for loneliness, though it is hard to make out. After quoting from Fichte, Hegel, and Freud (the oceanic feeling of the original ego), he remarks that

the critical consideration in all three of these paradigms is that the stipulated 'totality' of (original) awareness constitutes a unity, a oneness, an identification of (a) the ego with itself as well as (b) being with consciousness. (It is due to this principle of unity, as we shall see, that it directly follows that the ego, in turn, is alone and lonely.) (p. 60)

How this is supposed to directly follow never gets any clearer than the following passage makes it: "the unity of the ego, the *feeling* of identity the ego exhibits within its own immanent sphere of aloneness, then, constitutes the ultimate origin of loneliness" (p. 61). My comments are that:

(1) The feeling of unity and oneness sounds like the *opposite* of the feeling of loneliness, which is a feeling of insufficiency.

(2) This primary oceanic ego cannot yet experience itself as alone, a concept which implies otherness which is not yet present in the ego's realm.

(3) And in any event, feeling alone is not feeling lonely.

68. Mijuskovic cites with approval Freud's account in *Civilization and its Discontents*

of the origin of the 'oceanic feeling'—an account which suggests that Freud was a Fichtean:

> Originally the ego includes everything, later it detaches from itself the external world. The ego-feeling we are aware of now is thus only a shrunken vestige of a far more extensive feeling—a feeling which embraced the universe and expressed an inseparable connection of the ego with the external world. If we may suppose that this primary ego-feeling has been preserved in the minds of many people—to a greater or lesser extent—it would co-exist like a sort of counterpart with the narrower and more sharply outlined ego-feeling of maturity, and the *ideational* content belonging to it would be precisely the notion of limitless extension and oneness with the universe—the same feeling as that described by my friend as "oceanic". But have we any right to assume that the original type of feeling survived alongside the latter one which has developed from it? Undoubtedly we have. (cited in Mijuskovic, p. 60)

69. In a chapter entitled "Types of Loneliness," Mijuskovic sets out to dismiss the claim that different terms for aloneness mark important differences:

> I wish to deny (1a) Professor Gotesky's claim that there are four distinguishable types of loneliness; and further (1b) that there is, as Professor Gotesky holds, a positive, or "sought after" form of aloneness. Instead, as I shall go on to argue (2) loneliness is always reducible to the one basic form of despairing isolation. (p. 50)

His argument (which rather misrepresents Gotesky's fine article) proceeds by insisting first on the marginality of non-lonely solitary experiences: "our pangs of loneliness may be intermittently, momentarily alleviated, nevertheless they cannot be avoided for long and never permanently, except by death" (pp. 52–53).

Secondly, even then "the drive to avoid the sense of abandonment continually motivates human consciousness, even when one is not consciously attending to it" (p. 53).

And when even this seems implausible, he retreats to the sort of claim we have been assessing: "all human desires and actions are ultimately grounded in the attempt to escape our sense of being condemned to loneliness" (p. 55).

My responses to his remarks in this chapter are scattered throughout the present book.

70. There is a passage in the chapter "Loneliness and Narcissism" which tries to argue alienation on the grounds of individuation:

> Thus each of us, completely alone, carves from the original fund of consciousness labeled as the 'oceanic feeling' our own peculiar, subjective, definite image of a Narcissus that reflects us individually. And the more sharply etched and determinate our image is, the more it stands in stark alienation and opposition to the 'other'. (pp. 62–63)

But this argument is blown by simply noting that if my sharply etched image is—or includes—that I am Mama's boy, or Sister's brother, or Xenobia's husband, then determinacy of self is quite compatible with interpersonal relationship.

71. Fromm-Reichman begins a famous article by distinguishing four or five kinds of normal loneliness she will *not* be discussing, and ends by insisting that: "The kind of loneliness I am discussing is nonconstructive if not disintegrative, and it shows in, or leads ultimately to, the development of psychotic states" (Frieda Fromm-Reichman, "Loneliness," in Hartog, op. cit., p. 342).

72. Even Hegel did not claim that the master-slave dialectic was insoluble: out of this encounter, he thought, *recognition* could be born.

73. Another argument in this exaggerated style appears in the same section:

> . . . the desires of the ego, desires which can only be satisfied if they are recognized outwardly by the consciousness of the other. This is necessary because by its very nature a desire is for something other than itself; no desire merely desires itself; this would lead to immobility and death.

Thus, desire desires that the other acknowledge it as a desire that demands satisfaction. Differently put, the desire strives to command as master. (p. 78)

But all this really says is that desire wants to be satisfied. And since people often freely agree to—even take pleasure in—satisfying others' desires, no conflict over mastery need occur. Even in cases which appear to fit Mijuskovic's analysis, I think his phenomenology is a little clumsy: I don't *really* want to command you as master, I'd like your free glad help.

CHAPTER TEN: *The Place of Solitude: Arguments from Experience*

1. Dilman, op.cit., pp. 105–6.

2. Tillich, op. cit., p. 548.

3. Mijuskovic, op. cit., p. 9. See also p. 77.

4. Kaufmann, in Buber, op. cit., p. 17.

5. Tillich, op. cit., p. 548.

6. Goethe, op. cit., p. 25.

7. See his chapter on Proust, op. cit., especially his discussion of Proust's views on the intervention of fantasy between self and other.

8. This is not quite true, as the case of torture reveals. See Elaine Scary's profound study, *The Body in Pain* (Oxford: Oxford University Press, 1985).

9. As for the "core" metaphor, part of the idea has to do with generality: desire to succeed is more core than desire to beat this partner at tennis today because it figures in a wider range of behaviors. Another part of the idea is enduringness over time: I gave up tennis two years ago, but the desire to succeed remains. A third part concerns vulnerability: the core self is that which triggers the greatest anxiety when approached, and the more such approach is forbidden, the more one feels inclined to speak of an impenetrable core.

10. William Blake, "Never Seek to Tell Thy Love" in Spencer, Houghton, and Barrows, op. cit., p. 21.

11. Parkinson, op. cit.

12. T. S. Eliot, *The Cocktail Party* (London: Faber and Faber, 1949), p. 118.

13. Albert Camus, *The Plague*, cited in Dilman, op. cit., p. 118.

14. Howard, cited in Mijuskovic, op. cit., p. 82.

15. Mijuskovic, op. cit., p. 82.

16. J. Landau, "Loneliness and Creativity" in Hartog, op. cit., pp. 486–505, p. 499.

17. In fairness, Howard and Mijuskovic take up the philosophy of language explicitly, each holding that we are locked within a private language which only we can fully understand, which suffers too much "loss in translation" to serve as a vehicle of true communication (see Mijuskovic's chapter, "Loneliness and the Possibility of a Private Language"). Philosophers of language now generally follow Wittgenstein in rejecting the coherence of the idea of an inherently private language, arguing that such a "language" would lack the necessary criteria of correct/incorrect use without which the use of symbols cannot count as language. But the issues are complicated, and I cannot pursue the matter here. Interested readers might begin with Norman Malcolm's review of Wittgenstein's *Philosophical Investigations* (collected in Chappell's *Philosophy of Mind*, op. cit.) That Mijuskovic has missed Wittgenstein's meaning appears in such remarks as: "For if—as Wittgenstein and Ryle contend—all sensations and feelings are inherently public, because they are all reduced to objectively determined 'meanings', then . . ." (p. 83).

18. For fuller discussions of the nature of emotional expression, see John Benson's "Emotion and Expression" (*Philosophical Review* 76 [1967]) and my own "Expressing Emotion" (*Pacific Philosophical Quarterly* 64 [1983]). Benson distinguishes between verbal and nonverbal expressions, the latter of which can be either natural or conventional. As for the former, he is particularly interested in those expressions which succeed in conveying an emotion without characterizing it by the use of an emotion-name: e.g. expressing one's fear of spiders by exclaiming "Spiders, those hairy things that eat their mates!" My article explores the way in which expressive actions symbolically capture the intentional mental states which together comprise the emotion.

19. Wordsworth, "The Prelude." See note 12 of ch. 9.

20. George Berkeley, *Three Dialogues between Hylas and Philonous* (New York: Bobbs-Merrill, 1954), p. 109.

21. David Bakan, *Disease, Pain, and Sacrifice* (Chicago: University of Chicago Press, 1968), pp. 57–58.

22. Tillich, op. cit., p. 551.

23. Notice how the loneliness of dying is inserted as a "fact" in the passage from Jacob Landau we considered in the last section.

24. I am aware of Freud's later writing on the death instinct, and its reworking in more recent writers such as Norman O. Brown (see his *Life against Death*); there it is argued that a death-instinct, *Thanatos* in Freud's terminology, operates throughout life to shape lived experience. The most these highly speculative theories seem able to render plausible, though, is the equi-potency of Thanatos with Eros, and not the superiority which our argument would demand.

25. He writes,

death as the end of Dasein is the innermost, unrelative, certain and as such indefinite, unsurpassable possibility of Dasein. As the end of Dasein, death *is* in the being of this essent toward his end. (Cited in a study to which I am indebted for much of my meager understanding of Heidegger, J. L. Mehta's *Martin Heidegger: The Way and the Vision* [Honolulu: University of Hawaii Press, 1976], p. 217)

26. I have the terrible difficulty here of addressing a vast and profound subject in a few words. Conscious of the failing, let me recommend to the reader Bakan's entire book, as well as Elaine Scary's extraordinary study, *The Body in Pain* (op. cit.).

27. Bakan, op. cit., p. 64.

28. Ibid., p. 66.

29. Ibid., p. 74. Since pain is, as we have already noticed, localized in the body, and since one is one's body, something psychologically complex must be going on here. Bakan's analysis of the strategy is intriguing:

> The ego, in managing pain, seeks to make pain distal with respect to the ego itself, if it cannot make it distal with respect to the body. . . . in this process pain gets differentiated into the 'it' as present in a certain part of the body, with the body itself becoming something 'other' to the ego. (p. 76)
> To summarize, in the normal instance there are two functions performed by making pain ego-alien; one, providing a psychological precondition for engaging in acts of rectification; and, two, preparing to sacrifice the affected part. But, these are clearly in conflict. (p. 77)

30. Elias, op. cit., pp. 45–52.

31. Elias, op. cit., p. 56.

32. Elias has some interesting things to say about the meaning of the term "meaningful" in connection with life and death. Rather impatient with "metaphysical meaning [which] can at best be the subject of philosophical speculation" producing "arbitrary inventions" (p. 63), he offers a social-functional conception of meaning:

> If something has such a function for the life of a person and an event furthers or reinforces it, we say it has meaning for her or for him. Conversely, when something that has such a function for a person or group ceases to exist, becomes unrealizable or is destroyed, we speak of a loss of meaning (pp. 63–64)

> 'Meaning' is a social category; the subject corresponding to it is a plurality of interconnected people . . . (p. 54)

> The meaning of a person's words and the meaning of a person's life have in common that the meaning associated with them by that person cannot be separated from that associated with them by other persons. The attempt to discover in a person's life a meaning that is independent of what this life means for other people is quite futile. In the praxis of social life the connection between a person's feeling and the awareness that it has meaning for other human beings, and that others have a meaning for that life, is easy enough to discover. (p. 55)

As a lover of solitude, I cannot agree with this excessively social analysis; solitaries seem to be remarkably able to separate the meanings of their lives from those "associated with them by other persons."

33. Elias, op. cit., p. 87.

34. *The Book of Chuang Tzu*, op. cit., ch 6.

35. There are two kinds of exaggeration that strike one in these writings. The first

converts a strange face into a Stranger, and then into an Alien. In Hegel and Freud and Mijuskovic, the desire for recognition becomes the desire for dominance, personal autonomy demands Masters and Slaves, and power becomes omnipotence.

The second kind of exaggeration relates to the states of encounter/engagement which we are said to seek: Proust wants to possess Albertine *totally*, and when this turns out to be impossible he laments that he has *nothing* of her; Tillich will have us either penetrating to the "innermost center" or alone, and Freud/Mijuskovic think of all engagements as vain attempts to recreate an "original narcissism . . . in which the childish ego enjoyed *total* self-sufficiency." In short, if there is not oceanic fusion, there is no engagement at all.

Besides exaggeration, there is a very partial selection of cases in these arguments. Parkinson actually acknowledges this at the end of his attempt to argue that "in a sense the only subject of poetry is human loneliness"; he writes, "One of the difficulties and challenges of writing about the poet's loneliness has been to make a narrow, arbitrary channel through the immense diversity of poetic literature" (op. cit., p. 485). From a logical point of view, what an odd remark!

Mijuskovic, on the other hand, shows an outstanding blindness to that which does not suit his purposes—I can find no other words to describe an author who actually quotes Catherine's famous "I *am* Heathcliff" in a chapter that argues the essential aloneness of all persons. He is also able to cite in evidence the loneliness of Silas Marner while forgetting how the story turns out—ignoring, as his exaggerated thesis must do, one of the most beautiful expressions of human salvation in our literature:

> In old days there were angels who came and took men by the hand and led them away from the city of destruction. We see no white-winged angels now. But yet men are led away from threatening destruction; a hand is put into theirs, which leads them forth gently towards a calm and bright land, so that they look no more backward; and the hand may be a little child's. (George Eliot, *Silas Marner*, ch. xiv)

Finally, one cannot help noting the theological motivation of Tillich's exaggerated claims; the more hopeless human communion becomes on its own, the more desperately we will need a divine facilitator—and in fact this is exactly Tillich's position:

> How can communion grow out of solitude? we have seen that we can never reach the innermost center of another being. We always are alone, each for himself. But we can reach it in a movement which rises first to God and then returns from him to the other self. In this way man's aloneness is not removed but taken into the community with that in which the centers of all beings are resting and so into a community with all of them. (op. cit., 553)

36. Ignacio Gotz, "Loneliness," in *Humanitas* 10, no. 3 (1974): 292–93.

37. Ibid, p. 297.

38. Heidegger, op. cit., pp. 153–54 (the chapter entitled "Being-in-the-World as Being-With and Being-One's-Self).

39. Ibid., pp. 156–57.

40. Heidegger says in the opening lines of the chapter that in the investigation to follow "we shall be led to certain structures of Dasein which are equiprimordial with Being-in-the-world: *Being-with* and *Dasein-with*" (op. cit., p. 149).

Being equiprimordial is not being solely primordial, however, and many of Heidegger's descriptions of the *presence* of being, a presence which seems to me best felt in solitude, argue convincingly for the equiprimordial status of human aloneness. As he says elsewhere, and as solitaries have always felt, "Proximally and for the most part Dasein is fascinated with its world."

41. Here is J. Mehta's gloss on Heidegger's argument:

That man's being-in-the-world is intrinsically constituted by his being-with is an existenzial and ontological feature of man, even though ontically, in a particular case, there may not be anybody else in fact there with him. Being-with determines Dasein existenzially even when actually another Dasein is not present or to be seen. Even Dasein's being alone is being-with in the world: loneliness being a privative mode of the latter, its very possibility is evidence of being-with. (Mehta, op. cit., p. 139)

Here is the equation of Being-alone and loneliness is made explicit. Mehta does not use the same equation in glossing the rest of the Heidegger passage: "Conversely, the fact of my being alone cannot be removed by the mere presence of one or many other men in my vicinity" (ibid).

But he should have done so: for "factical Being-alone" (Heidegger's words) *is* removed ("obviated") by the presence of other people if the phrase means just being in fact alone—though not if the phrase means being in fact lonely.

42. In fact many passages from Heidegger could be cited in support of the virtues of solitude, for example

A painting by Van Gogh. A pair of rough peasant shoes, nothing else. Actually the painting represents nothing. But as to what *is* in that picture, you are immediately alone with it as though you yourself were making your way wearily homeward with your hoe on an evening in late fall after the last potato fires have died down.

This "existential presentness of the painting . . . its existence which reaches into *our* being" (Steiner, op. cit., pp. 45–46) can scarcely be imagined to unfold in company.

CHAPTER ELEVEN: *Objections to Solitude: Some History*

1. Johnson, *The Adventurer*, No. 126, op. cit.

2. Cowper, op. cit.

3. Petrarch argues that Homer, of whose life he grants that we know nothing, must have loved solitude to have written as he did:

What shall I say of Homer. . . . ? Homer has so well described the lonely places not only of Greece but of Italy, that what, according to Cicero, he did not himself see (for tradition makes him blind) he has made visible to us, so that we behold the painting, it were, of his genius and not the poetry. But shall we believe that he would have been able to do this if he had not before growing blind carefully observed those palaces and faithfully retained the memory? (op. cit., p. 271)

Later he writes, "We read that Achilles learned in solitude what soon made him terrible in the cities of Asia and famous in those of Greece" (ibid, p. 286). But where can he have read this—not in the *Iliad*, certainly.

4. Hesiod, *The Works and Days*, trans. Richmond Lattimore (Ann Arbor: University of Michigan Press, 1959), p. 77 (lines 494–495).

5. See especially lines 372–375, 405–410, 443, 695–705.

6. Plato himself, in Zeitlin's happy phrase, "harnesses the ideal to the service of the actual":

It is the duty of us, the founders, then, said I, to compel the best natures to attain the knowledge which we pronounced the greatest, and to win the vision of the good, to scale that ascent, and when they have reached the heights and taken an adequate view, we must not allow what is now permitted. . . . that they should linger there and refuse to go down again among those bondsmen and share their labors and honors . . . (*Republic* VII, p. 519)

> the law is not concerned with the special happiness of any class in the state, but is trying to produce this condition in the city as a whole, harmonizing and adapting the citizens to one another by persuasion and compulsion, and requiring them to impart to one another any benefit which they are severally able to bestow upon the community . . . (ibid., p. 520)

Note, however, the proportion assigned to the contemplative life a few lines further on:

> Will our alumni, then, disobey us when we tell them this, and will they refuse to share in the labors of state each in his turn while permitted to dwell most of the time with one another in that purer world? (ibid.)

    7. Aristotle, op. cit., 1107a.

    8. *Nicomachean Ethics*, book X, ch. 7. (1177a, 12–18). In tension with this conclusion, however, are the opening remarks of book I, which identify Politics as the "master art" (since it uses all the other sciences and "legislates what we are to do") and sets its end as "the good for man":

> For even if the end is the same for a single man and for a state, that of the state seems at all events something greater and more complete whether to attain or to preserve; though it is worth while to attain the end merely for one man, it is finer and more godlike to attain it for a nation or for city-states. (book I, ch. 2 [1094b, 8–10])

But it is *moral* virtue and its implicated *practical* reason that political science requires, not the philosophic wisdom sought in contemplation. Aristotle seems to have been of two minds about the value of solitary contemplation.

    9. Cited in Saryre, op. cit., p. 22.

    10. See Sayre's discussion of solitude as treated by Roman writers, op. cit., pp. 20–25.

    11. Cicero: *De Officiis*, I, vii, 22.

    12. Sayre, op. cit., p. 18.

    13. Zeitlin, op. cit., p. 39.

    14. *The Rule of St. Benedict*, trans. Cardinal Gasquet (New York: Cooper Square Publishers, 1966), pp. 7, 8. Of the other two types of monks, the Sarabites "who have not been tried under any Rule nor schooled by an experienced master," and the Gyrovagi (wanderers), Benedict heartily disapproved. For the development of cenobitism out of eremitism, both in the East and the West, see Workman's comprehensive discussion in *The Evolution of the Monastic Ideal*, especially chapters 2 and 3. While emphasizing the great and continuing influence of the individual exploits of St. Antony and St. Martin, he argues that their influence was secondary to that of St. Pachomius, a contemporary of Athanasius who, after a brief period of eremetical withdrawal, gathered together the hermits of the Thebaid in upper Egypt into "a well-organized self-supporting community of nine monasteries." Workman remarks,

> Monasticism, in fact, almost as soon as it was born, passed through its first transition; monachism gave place to cenobitism, at first the loose organization of the laura or cluster of cells around

some common center, later the stricter rule of a monastery. Thus, by three stages of development, the 'monk' becomes the brother of the common life, the mark of whose life is not so much his isolation as his socialism. (pp. 124–25)

15. Cited in Workman, op. cit., pp. 31–32.

16. Ibid., p. 118.

17. Ibid., p. 119.

18. Ibid., p. 60.

19. Zeitlin, op. cit., pp. 42–43. Augstine's words are taken from his *Reply to Faustus*, book XXII, sections 52–53.

20. *City of God*, pp. xix, 19. Sister Mason finds guidance in resolving the practical problem of conflict between the two lives in these words of Augustine, but it is hard for me to see the direction indicated. However for more on Augustine resolution of the conflict through an ingenious interpretation of the story of Jacob's relations to his two wives Leah and Rachel, see her discussion and Zeitlin's (op. cit., pp. 42–43n).

21. Cited in Zeitlin, p. 48.

22. Ibid., p. 49.

23. Ibid., p. 50.

24. Zeitlin, op. cit., p. 87.

25. Petrarch, op. cit., book I, tractate 4, ch. 1.

26. Ibid., p. 130.

27. Ibid., p. 130.

28. Ibid., p. 140.

29. Ibid., p. 149.

30. Janette Dillon, *Shakespeare and the Solitary Man* (Totowa: Rowan and Littlefield, 1981), p. xiii. Dillon identifies a cult of solitude, which reached its peak in the 1590s. By the second quarter of the next century, solitude had become so respectable as to no longer be noteworthy (see chapter 2, "The Cult of Solitude").

31. See Brian Vickers's discussion in *Public and Private Life in the Seventeenth Century: The Mackenzie-Evelyn Debate* (New York: Delmar, 1986) p. xviii. In two early poems, John Milton (1608–1674) compared The Lively Man, "L'Allegro," with The Contemplative Man, "Il Penseroso." The former poem begins, "Hence, loathed Melancholy,/Of Cerberus and blackest Midnight born," but "Il Penseroso" exclaims, "Hail, divinest Melancholy!/ Whose saintly visage is too bright/ To hit the sense of human sight." (Both poems are found in Spencer, op. cit., pp. 556–60)

32. Cited in Vickers, op. cit., p. xiv.

33. Ibid., p. 174.

34. Ibid., pp. 251–54.

35. David Hume, *An Enquiry Concerning the Principles of Morals* section IX, part I, para. 3. Even Hume, however, betrays some ambivalence about solitude. In the conclusion to volume I of his *Treatise of Human Nature* he describes the skeptical solipsism in which his arguments have landed him in negative terms: "I am first affrighted and confounded with that forlorn solitude in which I am placed in my philosophy, and fancy myself some strange uncouth monster, who, not being able to mingle and unite in society, has been expelled all human commerce, and left utterly abandoned and disconsolate." (book I, Conclusion, para. 2) Two pages later he refers to the realms into which his principles lead him as "dreary solitudes." Yet there is obvious approval of some solitudes, and in fact the pleasure of solitary reflection is later called "the origin of my philosophy." See John Sitter's interesting discussion of Hume in *Literary Loneliness in Mid-Eighteenth-Century England* (Ithaca: Cornell University Press, 1982), ch. 1.

36. Cited in Sayre, op. cit., p. 49.

37. From Eleanor Sickels's classic work, *The Gloomy Egoist* (New York: Octagon Books, 1969), p. 11.

38. Quoted from *British Literature: Beowulf to Sheridan*, ed. Hazelton Spencer, op. cit., pp. 838–39. The remark is Spencer's, who also quotes the following appraisal of Gray by Dr. Johnson—certainly no friend of solitary brooding: "In the character of his *Elegy* I rejoice to concur with the common reader . . . The *Churchyard* abounds with images which find a mirror in every mind, and with sentiments to which every bosom returns an echo. . . . Had Gray written often thus, it had been vain to blame and useless to praise him" (p. 838).

39. Sickels, op. cit., p. 12. Of course there were better and worse expressions of this melancholy: in the latter camp, consider these lines by John Clare: ". . . the wistful train/of dripping poultry, whom the broad leaves/Shelter no more." (Cited in Sickels, p. 248)

40. Goethe, op. cit., p. 5.

41. The literature on the romantics is vast. However, a useful beginning can be made with Halstead's *Romanticism*. For the more ambitious, M. H. Abrams's work, especially *The Mirror and the Lamp*, is widely recognized as setting a standard of excellence. With regard to solitude, I have found the following useful:
Jay Macpherson, *The Spirit of Solitude*
R. D. Havens, *The Mind of A Poet*
C. Salvesen, *The Landscape of Memory*
E. Hirsch, *Wordsworth and Schelling*
M. Rader, *Wordsworth*

42. Percy Bysshe Shelley, "Alastor, Or the Spirit of Solitude," lines 285–290, in Thomas Hutchinson, ed., *Shelley. Poetical Works* (London: Oxford University Press, 1967).

43. Preface to "Alastor," op. cit.

44. Nash, op. cit., p. 24.

45. Cited in Nash, op. cit., p. 30. Joseph Conrad developed the same theme late in the century in *Heart of Darkness* (London: Dent & Sons, 1974). The narrator tells us that, having found the self-exiled Mr. Kurtz in the Congo wilderness,

> I tried to break the spell—the heavy mute spell of the wilderness—that seemed to draw him to its pitiless breast by the awakening of forgotten and brutal instincts, by the memory of gratified and monstrous passions . . . But his soul was mad. Being alone in the wilderness, it had looked within itself, and, by heavens! I tell you, it had gone mad. (pp. 144–45).

46. Ibid., p. 43.

47. Ibid., p. 56.

48. Ibid., p. 60.

49. Wilson Clough, *The Necessary Earth*, (Austin: University of Texas Press, 1964), p. 128.

50. Clough, op. cit., p. 130.

51. Sayre, op. cit., pp. 200–201.

52. The answer to this question which Sayre gives is characteristically Marxist in its brevity and vagueness:

> Thus the transcendence of the condition of solitude in society in no way implies the abolition of individual being as it has developed historically or the return to a primitive communalism. On the contrary, the modern individual necessarily would transform, enrich, carry to a higher level the meaning of community. At the same time, the individual's being would be similarly transcended if reintegrated into an authentic modern community. (op. cit., p. 200)

53. See, for instance, Frances Ferguson's *Solitude and the Sublime* (New York: Routledge, 1992) which studies the aesthetics of the sublime in Kant and Burke. One of the issues arising concerns the necessity of solitude for apprehending the sublime (as opposed to the beautiful, which appears a more social category).

TWELVE: *Objections to Solitude: Responses*

1. Of course, there have always been a few extreme hermits. One such in our century was Sylvan Hart, who set off into the Idaho wilderness as a young man to live a life of total self-sufficiency. When Harold Peterson journeyed up the River of No Return to talk with the hermit, he found a thriving homestead where "the year is 1844 forever." Growing his own vegetables, hunting deer with rifles and homemade ammunition, eating on utensils whose copper he mined and smelted himself, wearing buckskin clothing and making his pie crust out of bear-fat, Hart made only very infrequent trips to the distant town of Burgdorf ("pop. summer 6, winter 0") for powder, books, and Darjeeling tea. As a concession to the twentieth century, the hermit had blasted himself a large bomb-shelter in rocky hillside near his cabin; and in a cranky but endearing way, he made it large enough to accommodate any visitors or neighbors who might come begging. (His story is told in H. Roskolenko, ed., *Solo* [Chicago: Playboy Press, 1973], pp. 123–32.)

2. Ibid., pp. 89–94.

3. Steven Callahan, *Adrift* (Boston: Houghton Mifflin Co., 1986). The reader interested in this genre of adventure tales might consult Chichester's travel journals, or Chay Blyth, *The Impossible Voyage* (London: Pan Books, 1973), or Robin Graham, *Dove* (New York: Bantam, 1973).

4. See chapter 13 for more details.

5. See Nash's discussion and references, op. cit., p. 15.

6. Nash, op. cit., p. 12.

7. An example of a (relatively cautious) inference from animal behavior to our own is J. Ralph Audy's article, "Man the Lonely Animal: Biological Roots of Loneliness" (in Hartog, op. cit.) He writes, for example,

> In short, normal functioning of the mind seems to depend on a sufficient level *and variety* of incoming stimuli to keep one in constant contact with the outside world and reality. In the primate laboratories at Yerke and elsewhere, apes brought up in sensorially rich environments have been compared with others reared in sensory isolation. Not only do the latter become deranged, but it soon becomes obvious that an isolated chimpanzee simply is not a whole chimpanzee. Individual minds seem to be at least in part the products of minds in association. (p. 117)

The last claim about "minds in association" is not supported by the evidence cited regarding "sensory isolation," however.

8. See Storr's discussion in chapter 7 of *Solitude*.

9. Abraham Maslow, *Toward a Psychology of Being* (New York: van Nostrand Co., 1968), pp. 34–35.

10. Maslow, op. cit 97. The characteristics of B-cognition are listed on page 83.

11. Halmos, op. cit., p. 1. The two preceeding remarks appear on pages 8 and 10 respectively. Although Halmos is largely concerned with the unwanted and dehumanizing isolation of contemporary society, his statements often reach beyond their evidence to tarnish solitude.

12. Quoted from Trotter's *Instincts of the Herd in Peace and War* (London, 1947), p. 52.

13. Ibid.

14. Halmos's bio-sociology anticipates socio-biology in the following passage:

> Hence individuation is as essential to life as sense-organs are essential to a human being: yet the total functioning of all sense-organs is a good deal less than life itself. Individuation is as indispensable to the species as sense-organs are to the human being: thus individuation is a tool of the species and not its purpose. (p. 12)

Whether this is social Darwinism or genetic fascism I am not sure, being very unclear about what would constitute the purpose of a species. I think I am out of my element here. However, insofar as I understand Halmos's remarks, they seem to bear with equal force against the view that communitarianism is "the purpose" of the species; for that would violate the "essentiality" of individuation.

15. Margaret Adams, *Single Blessedness* (New York: Penguin Books, 1976), p. 19.

16. Ibid., pp. 61–62.

17. Even the heroes of solitude are vulnerable here: Clough has dug out of Emerson's journal this entry (October 27, 1851) made after a conversation with Thoreau: "We stated over again, to sadness almost, the eternal loneliness. . . . How insular and sadly pathetically solitary are all the people we know" (Clough, op. cit., pp. 116–17).

18. Hermann Hesse, *Steppenwolf,* trans. Basil Creighton (New York: Bantam Books, 1972), p. 43.

19. Ibid., pp. 53–54.

20. Compare these remarks by Christianne Ritter, alone for nine days in a hut in northern Norway while her husband is away hunting:

> Out of doors the country lies white, rigid and absolutely quiet. There is not a breath of wind. . . . for humans this stillness is horrible. It is days since I have been outside the hut. Gradually I have become fearful of seeing the deadness of the land. . . . I do not want to have my mind free for a moment to think, a moment in which to become aware of the nothingness outside. . . . I have an inkling, or rather I know with certainty, that it was this, this terror of nothingness, which over the past centuries has been responsible for the death of some hundreds of men here in Spitsbergen. (Ritter, op. cit., p. 145)

See also Kohák's description of an experience of "the terror of sheer nothing," op. cit., pp. 61–62.

21. Cited in Wendell Glick, *The Recognition of Walden* (Ann Arbor: University of Michigan Press, 1969), p. 32.

22. This is a little oversimplified. Not just harm but a tendency towards (or predictable outcome of) harm are probably enough to make a charge. Someone who indulges their eating desires may not be directly harming themselves, but we think that this sort of giving-in will lead to worse things over time.

23. Rolston writes in *Philosophy Gone Wild,*

> We think that a person is narrow and selfish who cultivates intrinsic worth and withdraws from seeking any instrumental value in the community. A person's intrinsic worth—for example, creative ability—is not separable from the power to confer a benefit on others. Excellence does not consist in what a thing is merely for itself, but in what it is for others. This is true of persons, animals and plants. Excellence is not a matter of encapsulated being, but of fittedness into a pervasive whole. (op. cit., p. 133)

This radical reversal of Kantian humanism seems well suited to the ecological holism Rolston recommends ("Bios is intrinsically symbiosis" [p. 224]), and it may be finally the only consistent position an informed holism can occupy. However, there is quite a leap from ordinary moral intuition to this position, a gap which Rolston disguises with the opening sentence in the passage. When I think of John Muir exploring the Sierras alone, and imagine away his writings on the subject, I do not find a charge of selfishness coming to mind and I doubt that many others would either; a pity, perhaps, but hardly a moral failing. Selfishness implies taking more than one's share of something, but what was Muir taking more than his share of? The wilderness? His own abilities?

24. Sarton, op. cit., pp. 12, 13, and 94, respectively. On page 57 she confesses, "Here in Nelson I have been close to suicide more than once . . ."

25. Workman, op. cit., p. 9.

26. Cited in Zeitlin, p. 33, to whom I owe these observations. Elsewhere Seneca remarked, "As oft as I have been among men I have returned home less a man than I was before" (Epistle 7, quoted by Thomas a Kempis and by Workman, op. cit., p. 32).

27. Petrarch, op. cit., p. 184. Compare Montaigne,

> . . . let us boldly appeal to those that are in the thick of the dance; and let them cudgel their conscience and ask themselves if on the contrary those positions, those offices, and that

hurly-burly of the world are not rather sought after with a view to making private profit at the public expense. The evil means we adopt to push ourselves in these days very clearly show that the end cannot be worth much. ("Of Solitude," op. cit., p. 234)

Compare also Tennyson:

Form the world of sin and noise
And hurry I withdraw,
For the small and inward voice
I wait with humble awe.
                              (from "The Ancient Sage")

28. Lindbergh, op. cit., p. 50.

29. All quotations are found in Odell Shephard, *The Heart of Thoreau's Journals* (New York: Dover Publications, 1961)

30. Ibid.

31. Cited in Wolf, op. cit., p. 117.

32. Cited in I. F. Stone's *The Trial of Socrates* (New York: Doubleday, 1988), p. 99. Stone is critical of Socrates for "simply going home" when the Thirty Tyrants ordered him to bring in for execution an innocent man:

Was that fulfilling his civic duty against injustice? Or was he merely avoiding personal complicity and, as he expressed it, saving his soul? (p. 114)
    How does a man perfect his soul? by withdrawing from life, or plunging into it and fulfilling himself as part of the community? The classic ideal was to perfect oneself in perfecting the city. (115)

Stone's own answer to these questions is clearly the classic one.

33. Quoted in Glick, op. cit., p. 74.

34. Cited in Nina Auerbach's foreword to Laura Doan, ed., *Old Maids to Radical Spinsters* (Urbana and Chicago: University of Illinois Press, 1991), p. ix.

35. Ralph Waldo Emerson, "Self Reliance," op. cit., p. 178.

36. Ibid., p. 183.

37. Ibid., pp. 179–80.

38. Ellen Suckiel, "Emerson and the Virtues," collected in Marcus Singer, ed., *American Philosophy* (Cambridge: Cambridge University Press, 1985), pp. 135–52.

39. Emerson, "Self Reliance," op. cit., p. 179.

40. Ibid., p. 193.

41. Suckiel discusses lucidly the justification that Emerson did offer via the idea of compensation:

Emerson's position becomes, if not ultimately more justified, at least more understandable, when seen within the broader context of his metaphysics. In his famous doctrine of compensation, articulated in an address of that same name, Emerson argues that from the point of view of material benefits or misfortunes, the universe balances itself out. Every materially good event or object in one's life will be balanced by some cost, and every misfortune balanced by a benefit. Thus, there is no point to feeling responsible for those less fortunate than ourselves, no need to help the disadvantaged, since whatever evils they experience must ultimately be balanced by corresponding goods. (op. cit., p. 144)

She remarks dryly, "Emerson does not go into a concrete account or explanation of how this might be so."

42. Petrarch, op. cit., p. 284.

43. Here I must greatly oversimplify in order to make an important point stand out; but I would not wish to be held to any simple typology of political characters, and do not believe that introversion/extroversion of themselves excuse/condemn political inaction.

44. I say this not on grounds of philosophical adequacy but in recognition of the nagging feeling of "not doing enough" that pervaded those years. Curiously, however, my activist friends who were doing much more seemed to feel the same emotion even more acutely. This suggests to me again that the moral sense is more closely linked with extroversion/introversion than has generally been acknowledged.

45. Thoreau, *Civil Disobedience*, ed. Sherman Paul (Boston: Houghton Mifflin Co., 1957), p. 236.

46. Here dispute will arise between those who locate intrinsic moral value in the individual person, from which it flows out into family, society, world, and universe, and those who locate it in the collective whole, which pays value out to participating individuals according to the quality of their participation. The former party is obviously going to find a higher obligation to solitary self-development in many cases where the latter party will find it in social service, and this finding will speak with the small inner voice of conscience.

47. On this matter, see Thomas Hill's useful essay, "Servility and Self-Respect," *Monist* 57, no. 1 (January 1973): 87–104.

48. From "Of Suicide," collected in *David Hume: Essays Moral, Political and Literary*, ed. Eugene Miller (Indianapolis: Liberty Classics, 1985), p. 586.

49. Thoreau, op. cit., p. 241. But how much is required in this handwashing? Both activists and pacifists can find supporting texts in *Civil Disobedience*, as well as in Thoreau's political activities: the refusal to pay the poll tax might be construed as passive handwashing, but the many lectures he gave, as well as the publication of the essays, certainly seem to manifest a moral commitment to action which goes beyond mere hand-washing.

50. Robert Louis Stevenson, cited in Glick, op. cit., p. 74.

51. Montaigne, op. cit., p. 242.

52. David Norton has recently argued (in "The Moral Individualism of Henry David Thoreau," collected in Marcus Singer, ed. *American Philosophy* (Cambridge: Cambridge University Press, 1985), pp. 239–53) that Thoreau valued solitude primarily as a necessary preparation for moral service, that solitude was for him "a purely instrumental value, not an intrinsic one": it was "instrumental to the self-discovery that he takes to be the responsibility of every person," a self-discovery which would be the true preparation for service to society. Solitude is the necessary setting for self-discovery because our innate and unique genius has been masked by the overlays of value and definition which family, friends, and neighbors have unthinkingly plastered over us. However, in solitude "Let us settle ourselves, and work and wedge our feet downward through the mud and

slush of opinion, and prejudice, and tradition, and delusion, and appearance . . . til we come to a hard bottom" (from the conclusion to *Walden*)

This "hard bottom" is our genius, which sets for each of us the moral work that is, according to Thoreau, our first responsibility—"the work of progressively actualizing our distinctive potential worth." When Thoreau says, "Let everyone mind his own business, and endeavor to be what he was made," it is this primary moral business that he is referring to (p. 244).

It is not easy business, as the other famous "hard bottom" story from *Walden* reminds us:

> We read that a traveler asked the boy if the swamp before him had a hard bottom. The boy replied that it had. But presently the traveller's horse sank in up to the girths, and he observed to the boy, "I thought you said this bog has a hard bottom." "So it has," answered the latter, "but you have not got half way to it yet."

Still, "There is a solid bottom everywhere," and once found it will give us the archimedean fixed place to lever virtue into the world: Norton writes,

> [This primary moral business of self-discovery] is by no means a selfish business for by attending to it we actualize in the world objective worth, which is to say it will be of worth, not alone or primarily to the person who actualizes it, but to others as well. "Just so sacred and rich as my life is to myself," Thoreau says, "so it will be to another." Indeed, Thoreau identifies the life lived according to its genius as the foundational form of gift-giving, and says, "Be sure that you give men *the best* of your wares, though they be poor enough, and the gods will help you lay up better store for the future." [both Thoreau quotes are from his journal]

According to Norton, "We begin to understand Thoreau's 'independence' aright when we recognize that, having achieved it, he uses it to re-establish relations with everything he has divorced himself from, but in new terms."

Norton's Thoreau is certainly there in the writings, but it is not the only Thoreau, indeed I think not the dominant Thoreau. The sustained feeling of *Walden*, rising often to a passion, is that solitude, or self-discovery in solitude, is *for itself* not for ultimate service to society. Regarding society, Thoreau is ever the bemused outsider, hectoring the strange creatures *over there* who seem as different from him as the "hindoos." As for the relative importance of service to others in the scale of things, his dominant feeling is well represented by the journal entry of March 28, 1853, when he was living in the large house in Concord with his mother and aunt:

> My Aunt Maria asked me to read the life of Dr. Chalmers, which, however, I did not promise to do. Yesterday, Sunday, she was heard through the partition shouting to my Aunt Jane, who is deaf, "Think of it! He stood half an hour today to hear the frogs croak, and he wouldn't read the life of Chalmers." (quoted in Shephard, op. cit.)

53. Tillich assigns a different preparatory role to solitude:

> We have seen that we can never reach the innermost center of another being. We always are alone, each for himself. But we can reach it in a movement which rises first to God and then returns from him to the other self. In this way man's aloneness is not removed but taken into the community with that in which the centers of all beings are resting and so into a community with all of them. . . . only in solitude are those who are alone able to reach those from whom they are separated. Only the presence of the eternal can break through the walls which isolate the temporal from the temporal. In one hour of solitude we may be nearer to those we love than in many hours of communication. (op. cit., p. 553)

Solitude is here identified as the only pathway to communion with others, a pathway that leads first away from them into solitude, then through the solitude towards God and through Him towards the other. Solitude thus becomes implicated in the Christian project to serve in loving communion.

54. Georgianna, op. cit., p. 52.

55. Preface to Anson, op. cit., p. xiii.

56. Merton, op. cit., pp. 173–74. There is also a more mystical defense of solitude which Merton offers, one which traces back to Peter Damian's "Disputed Questions." In true solitude, he claims, one realizes that "he has entered into a solitude that is really shared by everyone" and is thus one with their perils and anguish. What exactly can this mean? Merton finds the explanation in the following lines from Damian:

> The Church of Christ is so connected in its members, united by charity with one another, that in many she is one, and in each individual she is mysteriously present as a whole. Thus the whole Church is rightly called one Spouse of Christ, and each single soul, by virtue of the mystery of the sacrament, is rightly believed to be the whole Church. (Merton, op. cit., p. 151)

Through this mystical integration of part and whole, the solitary hermit becomes (in this sense) the whole church; and "The fact that this mystical integration in the whole Christ is increased by solitude is the theological justification for the ermitical life." (ibid.)

Taken as theological-metaphysics, this strains ascetic intelligibility, but taken as an expression of feeling I think we can make some sense of it. For just as one can feel a mystic identification with all nature in solitude, so can one feel an identification with all other people. I confess to feeling, in solitudes of my own, an uncanny sense of the presence of the great solitaries—as though we are all hauntingly together here in the windy countryside, just over the hills from each other. Then I feel, Merton might say, the mystical integration of my own church.

57. In the last talk he gave before his untimely death in Asia, Merton used another analogy to defend solitude: "If you want to pull a drowning man out of the water, you have to have some support yourself. Supposing somebody is drowning and you are standing on a rock, you can do it" (*The Asian Journal of Thomas Merton*, ed. N. Burton et al. [New York: New Directions, 1975], p. 341).

The solitary Christian hermit, alone before God, is on rock. But can he reach us in the water, if his rock has unassailable cliffs?

58. Stanley Cavell, *The Senses of Walden* (New York: Viking Press, 1972), p. 11. Cavell believes that *Walden* was to be an American Heroic epic with its author as hero, a scripture for America in which Thoreau would be Jerermiah and Ezekiel (p. 19).

59. Ibid., p. 35.

60. That self-improvement would more or less automatically produce social improvement was a generally held view of the Transcendentalists. Harding and Meyer, in *The New Thoreau Handbook*, quote with approval Alexander Kern's conceptual summary of Transcendentalism:

> (1) an intuitive idealism which accepted ideas as ultimates; (2) a view of the imagination or intuition (in their language Reason) giving a direct apprehension of reality which the logical faculties (the Understanding) could not furnish; (3) the concept of an organic universe in which Nature, suffused by an immanent God, corresponded with spirit in such a way that the connections and indeed the whole could be grasped by contemplation and intuition; (4) a living religion in which miracles seem natural; (5) the divinity of man, who consequently did not need salvation; (6) a concept of Genius which could produce works of art by recording its intuitions through the use of nature's symbols; (7) a freedom and spontaneity in art to permit the creation of works liberated from the artificialities produced by talent or mechanical rules alone; (8) an individual moral insight which should supercede the dollar as the standard of conduct; (9) self-improvement as the primary avenue of

social improvement; (10) individualism, i.e. reliance on God, rather than conformity to the will of a political or social majority; (11) an optimism about the potentialities of individual lives and the universe. (from Kern's *The Rise of Transcendentalism, 1815–1860*, quoted in Harding and Meyer, pp. 250–51)
In Harding and Meyer's opinion, "If we are willing to grant Thoreau the broad margin he always demanded, it is accurate to say that he subscribed to these Transcendental concepts" (p. 123).

61. Cited in Glick, op. cit., p. 10.

62. Ibid., p. 127.

63. Henri Nouwen, "Solitude and Community," *Worship 52*, (January 1978): 18.

64. Ibid.

65. Bugbee, op. cit., pp. 317–18. Bugbee appears to be a theist of sorts himself (see pp. 323–26), but the comments I have quoted seem intended to stand on their own.

66. Bugbee, op. cit., pp. 317–19. There Bugbee adds another social justification for solitude: "As we are sustained in our selfhood the more understandingly, so we are the more able to address others as selves" (p. 319).

67. For the role of solitary experiences of the Sublime in our sense of the context of our being-with-others, see Bugbee's essay, "The Philosophic Significance of the Sublime," in *A Series of Essays, 1958–1974* (Missoula: University of Montana Press, 1974).

68. Ibid.

69. Robert Frost, "The Tuft of Flowers" in *The Poetry of Robert Frost*, ed. Edward Lathem (New York: Holt, Rinehart and Winston, 1969), pp. 22–23.

CHAPTER THIRTEEN: *Women and Solitude*

1. The situation has improved somewhat since 1981, but this is what Nancy Peterson had to say then about the state of affairs she confronted when beginning her study of one group of women for whom solitude is a central fact of life, the never-married:
     The women's movement might be the place to deal with what Friedan called "the problem that has no name," but for some illusive reason, the movement shared with my friends and me a curious reticence to address the life-style and circumstances of never-married women . . . The failure to even acknowledge the concerns of ever-single women were particularly striking because of the extraordinary degree of participation of single women in the Movement. (*Our Lives for Ourselves* [New York: G.P. Putnam's Sons, 1981], pp. 18–19).
Turning to a standard review and annotated bibliography of studies concerning women, she found that only 10 of the 3600 inclusions concerned spinsters or single women (p. 20). My own computer searches through the National Library data banks two years ago were equally disappointing on women's writings on solitude. Delese Wear's new volume, "The Center of the Web: Women and Solitude" (Albany: State University of New York Press, 1993), is thus a most welcome addition to the literature. Unfortunately, it has reached me just as my own work is going to press, so I am prevented from discussing it.

2. Belenky et al., op. cit., p. 151. Compare Christine Downing, writing in *The Goddess* (New York: Crossroad, 1984):
     We seek images that affirm that the love women receive from women, from mother, sister,

daughter, lover, friend, reaches as deeply and is as trustworthy, necessary, and sustaining as is the love symbolized by father, brother, son, or husband. We long for images which name as authentically feminine courage, creativity, loyalty, and self-confidence, resilience and steadfastness, capacity for clear insight, inclination for solitude, and the intensity of passion. (p. 5)

3. Nel Noddings's relational ethics of caring worries me in this way. In *Women and Evil* (Berkeley: University of California Press, 1989) she writes:

An ethic of caring is based on a relational ontology; that is, it takes as a basic assumption that all human beings—not just women—are defined in relation. It is not just that *I* as a preformed continuous individual enter *into* relations; rather, the *I* of which we speak so easily is itself a relational entity. *I* really am defined by the set of relations into which my physical self has been thrown. (p. 237)

This ethic, and its ontological assumption, lead her to dismiss contemplation (done best, I have argued, in solitude) as a response to evil:

Is it really necessary (or even possible) to define 'the True, the Good and the Beautiful,' or might this very project maintain some forms of evil? Do we require a sense 'of intimacy with the cosmic process'? Or do we need to recognize that our recourse stands beside us in the form of other human beings through whom we really do live and define our being? (pp. 31–32)

For other philosophers' worries that Noddings's ethic of caring will preclude the self-explorations which (I have maintained) proceed best in solitude, see Rosemarie Tong's discussion in *Feminine and Feminist Ethics* (Belmont: Wadsworth Publishing Co., 1993), pp. 123–34.

4. There are of course a few exceptions to this generalization: in addition to the ones I will be discussing shortly, one should remember Greek priestesses such as the Delphic oracle, the sibyls of Roman antiquity, the Vestal Virgins, Christian girls who were permitted (before the flight to the desert in the fourth century) to remain sequestered virgins in the home, etc.

5. Reay Tannahill, *Sex in History* (New York: Stein and Day, 1982), p. 64.

6. Quoted in Michel Foucault, *The Uses of Pleasure*, trans. Robert Hurley (New York: Pantheon Books, 1985), p. 143. In his discussion of the accuracy of this aphorism, Foucault comments

it would be a mistake to interpret this text as offering a definition of three distinct roles; it is more in the nature of a cumulative enumeration, to be read as follows: pleasure is the only thing a courtesan can give; as for the concubine, she is capable of providing the satisfactions of everyday life besides; but only the wife can exercise a certain function that is owing to her special status: she can bear legitimate children and ensure the continuity of the family institution. . . . The radical separation between marriage and the play of pleasures and passions is doubtless not an adequate formula for characterizing marital life in antiquity. (pp. 150–51)

Tannahill reminds us that Demosthenes's remark is slightly misleading, omitting as it does the highest class of courtesans, the *hetairai*, who operated among men as equals. Knowledgeable in classical literature as well as in the arts of love, shrewd business women and sometimes influential political forces,

They were, in fact, pioneers—the first group of women in recorded history to achieve detente with men. The *naditu* priestesses of Babylon had been accepted because of the quality of their minds; protitutes in all countries for their bodies. But the hetairai used both and were admired for both. (op. cit., p. 105)

Still, it was a very small class of women, and their equality was probably limited in general to their short working life.

7. Foucault, op. cit., p. 146.

8. From *The Malleus Maleficarum of Heinrich Kramer and James Springer,* trans. Rev. Montague Summers (New York: Dover Publications, 1971), part I, question VI.

9. E. William Monter, "Pedestal and Stake: Courtly Love and Witchcraft" in R. Bridenthal and C. Koonz, eds., *Becoming Visible: Women in European History* (Boston: Houghton Mifflin Co., 1977), p. 129.

10. Monter, op. cit., p. 134. Monter notes that although courtly love, the other great social invention of the period affecting women, was an upper class phenomenon, "witchcraft was almost completely restricted to the lower classes." Accordingly, historians look to developments in the peasant class to understand why witchcraft arose at just this time. Monter mentions two possible explanations:

> An important argument advanced [by H. Midelfort] recently says that the changing European marriage pattern, the shift to a system that delayed marriages and left a sizable minority of women permanently unmarried, first becomes visible in the sixteenth century, about the time when the first great witch hunts began. If witch trials were primarily projections of general social fears onto atypical women (those who lived apart, without husbands or fathers to rule them), then the sudden growth of spinsters and an increased number of widows who did not remarry automatically provided a much larger range of witchcraft suspects than before.
>
> [Another theory, by E. Ladurie] suggests that women were unusually defenseless during the time of the great witch trials because the social gap between men and women in rural villages was larger then than before or afterward. . . . the poverty gap and the literacy gap between rural men and women were especially great during the centuries of witchcraft trials, thus aggravating the vulnerability of women (particularly isolated women, widows, or spinsters) to charges of witchcraft. (pp. 133–34)

11. Monter, op. cit., p. 133.

12. An excellent companion piece here would be Sheila Jeffreys, *The Spinster and Her Enemies: Feminism and Sexuality, 1880–1930* (London: Pandora, 1985). For more on these exceptions to the nineteenth-century pattern, see also: Laura Doan, *Old Maids to Radical Spinsters* (Urbana: University of Illinois Press, 1991); Nina Auerbach, *Woman and the Demon: The Life of a Victorian Myth* (Cambridge: Harvard University Press, 1982); Dorothy Yost Deegan, *The Stereotype of the Single Woman in American Novels* (New York: Octagon Books, 1969); Martha Vincus, *Independent Women: Work and Community for Single Women, 1850–1920* (Chicago: University of Chicago Press, 1985).

13. Dr. Pat Jallard and Dr. John Hooper, *Women from Birth to Death* (Sussex: Harvest Press, 1986), p. 124.

14. Ibid.

15. Ibid., p. 126.

16. Ibid., p. 125.

17. Ibid., p. 127.

18. Cited by Petrarch, op. cit., p. 206.

19. Virgil, *Georgics,* iii, 215–16 (Dryden's translation).

20. Workman, op. cit., pp. 61–62.

21. Petrarch, op. cit. pp. 195–96.

22. Ibid., p. 205.

23. From *The Collected Poems of Rupert Brooke* (London: Sidgwick & Jackson, 1924), pp. 103–4.

24. Eileen Manion, "All Alone Feeling Blue? Women's Experience of Solitude" in *Women and Men* (Markham: Fitzhenry and Whiteside, 1987), p. 309. Manion wonders if there is a deeper guilt operating here, a guilt springing from "the sense that in choosing solitude, a woman at some level rejects her mother. . . . To live alone is not only to refuse the social role of mother, but is also to reject the internalized mother, and perhaps to feel rejected by her in turn, since any separation provokes fears of abandonment" (p. 310). Yet, Manion reflects, "Paradoxically, of course, to live alone is not only to reject this internalized mother, but also to become her, to become one's own mother, both the 'good' Mother' who takes care, and the 'bad' one who prescribes Duty" (p. 319).

25. Ward, op. cit., p. 230.

26. Workman, op. cit., p. 89.

27. Ibid., p. 111.

28. Workman, op. cit., p. 60. The quotation is from Jerome's *Letters*.

29. Workman, op. cit., p. 143.

30. Dennis Stock and Lawrence Cunningham, *Saint Francis of Assissi* (San Francisco: Harper and Row, 1981), p. 30.

31. Manion, op. cit., pp. 318–19. I learned of Aphra Behn from Manion's essay.

32. Edith Bone, *Seven Years Solitary* (New York: Harcourt, Brace and Co., 1957), p. 106.

33. Ibid., p. 123.

34. Nien Cheng, *Life and Death in Shanghai* (New York: Grove Press, 1987), pp. 130–31.

35. Ibid., pp. 131–32.

36. Christianne Ritter, op. cit., pp. 22–23.

37. Ibid., pp. 77–78.

38. Ibid., p. 83.

39. Quoted in Jane Moffat and Charlotte Paynter, eds., *Revelations: Diaries of Women* (New York: Random House, 1974), p. 302. These and the following quotations are excerpts from Martin's diary as arranged by Moffat and Paynter, pp. 301–13.

40. Storr, op. cit., p. 94.

41. John Pickard, *Emily Dickinson* (New York: Holt Rinehart and Winston, 1967), p. 20.

42. John Cody discusses the motivations for her withdrawal at great length in *After*

Great Pain: The Inner Life of Emily Dickinson (Cambridge: Harvard University Press, 1971). He writes,

> Many practical or commonsense explanations for Emily Dickinson's seclusion from the world have been based on the assumption that she possessed an essentially 'healthy' personality. Thus, she is said to have retreated:
> (1) because of a frustrated love affair;
> (2) to conserve energy and have time to write;
> (3) to ponder 'a metaphysical quandry';
> (4) as a stratagem to dramatize a drab existence;
> (5) to protect her vulnerability to overstimulation;
> (6) as a social protest and to avoid conformity;
> (7) to control and regulate her personal relationships;
> (8) as a reaction to her repressive schooling;
> (9) to spite her father or because of his dependence on her;
> (10) because of her plain looks.
> In contrast, it is the hypothesis of this study that both the failure of Emily Dickinson to achieve complete fulfillment socially and sexually and the anxiety and ambivalence which subverted her ambition to reach the reading public she merited are ultimately traceable to psychological determinants rooted in her [unsatisfactory] transactions with her mother. (pp. 414–42)

This very full list of reasons for seclusion does, however, omit a very important item: a woman who sought solitude in the mid-nineteenth century simply *could not* go out to the woods to "live deliberately"; deliberate living had somehow to be engineered in and around the home.

43. Cited in Cody, op. cit., p. 285.

44. Jean Mudge, *Emily Dickinson and the Image of Home* (Amherst: University of Massachusetts Press, 1975), p. 1.

45. From *The Complete Poems of Emily Dickinson*, ed. Thomas Johnson (Boston: Little Brown and Co., 1960). The first four lines quoted are from Poem #303 (p. 143); the last eight lines are from Poem #1695 (p. 691).

46. Interestingly, during a recent CBC radio interview with Peter Gzowski two women seized upon and repeated the image of solitude as *being in a closet*. Said one woman with children, "I get up a half hour earlier just to have some solitude. And I take long baths. The bathroom is my closet."

47. Mudge, op. cit., p. 53. Mudge mobilizes Freud and Erikson to explore these identifications.

48. Ibid., p. 51.

49. Ibid., p. 50.

50. Quoted in Christopher Benfey, ed., *Emily Dickinson: Lives of a Poet* (New York: George Brasiller, 1986), p. 30. Dickinson's obssession with death is well known, but her use of images of house and room in its description is noticed only by Mudge. Here is Emily writing to a friend at age sixteen: "The grave will be my last home."

51. Moffat and Paynter, op. cit., p. 4.

52. Ibid., p. 5.

53. Quoted in Moffat and Paynter, op. cit., p. 15.

54. Moffat and Paynter, op. cit., p. 6.

55. Ibid., p. 7.

56. Benfey, op. cit., p. 59.

57. Cited by Benfey, op. cit., p. 60.

58. Adams, op. cit., p. 195.

59. Ibid., p. 191.

60. Ibid.

61. Ibid., p. 202.

62. Manion, op. cit., p. 320.

63. The statistics are from the U.S. census as cited in Bryan Strong and Christine DeVault, *The Marriage and Family Experience* (St. Paul: West, 1989), p. 151.

64. See *Statistics Canada*, "1991 Census of Canada," Catalogs 93–310 and 93–312.

65. Peterson, op. cit., pp. 254–55.

66. Ibid., p. 245.

67. Quoted in Patricia O'Brien, *The Woman Alone* (New York: Quadrangle Books, 1973), p. 232.

68. Koller, op. cit., p. 3.

69. Ibid., p. 5.

70. Ibid., p. 4.

71. Ibid., pp. 198 and 123, respectively.

72. Ibid., p. 185.

73. Ibid., p. 185. The words quoted in the next sentence are from her p. 223.

74. Ibid., pp. 223–24.

75. Manion, op. cit., p. 320.

76. From a condensation of a report by the National Action Committee on the Status of Women, *Review of the Situation of Women in Canada 1992*, which appeared in *Common Ground* 11, no. 4 (August 1992).

CHAPTER FOURTEEN: *A Universal Value?*

1. Sayre, op. cit., pp. 13–14.

2. Ibid., p. 14.

3. Ibid., p. 15.

4. Ibid., p. 15.

5. Quoted in Storr, op. cit., p. 77.

6. Jim Swan, "Difference and Silence; John Milton and the Question of Gender," in *The (M)other Tongue*, ed. S. Nelson Garner, C. Kahane, M. Sprengnether (Ithaca: Cornell University Press, 1985), p. 159.

7. Sophocles, *Antigone*, trans. Robert Whitelaw, collected in Lane Cooper, ed., *Fifteen Greek Plays* (New York: Oxford University Press, 1960), p. 227.

8. Even if we go back to the *Iliad*, individuality in senses (3) and (4) is apparent: Achilles certainly "exists as a separate indivisible entity," "distinguished from others by attributes of his own"—to himself, to the Achaeans and to the Trojans. And Hesiod's *Works and Days* portrays a shrewd individual who is perfectly recognizable to modern eyes.

9. Burckhardt, as quoted in Storr, op. cit.

10. Andreas Capellanus, *The Art of Courtly Love*, trans. John Parry (New York: Columbia University Press, 1990), p. 67.

11. Storr, op. cit., pp. 79–80. The reference is to an unpublished dissertation by Peter Abbs, "The Development of Autobiography in Western Culture: From Augustine to Rousseau" (University of Sussex, 1986).

12. Testimony recorded in his heresy trial, selected by Carlo Ginzburg in *The Cheese and the Worms* (Baltimore: Johns Hopkins University Press, 1980), p. 2.

13. Ibid., p. 6.

14. Ibid., p. 12.

15. Ibid., p. 92.

16. Ibid., p. 111.

17. Ibid., p. 20.

18. Ibid., p. 25. Ginzburg has read all of the books Menocchio confessed to reading, and comments: "Any attempt to consider these books as 'sources' in the mechanical sense of the term collapses before the aggressive originality of Menocchio's reading." (p. 33)

19. J. R. Audy, "Man the Lonely Animal," in Hartog, op. cit., p. 119.

20. Clifford Geertz, quoted in A. F. Westin, *Privacy and Freedom* (New York: Atheneum, 1967), pp. 15–16.

21. Ibid., pp. 16–17.

22. Ibid., p. 17.

23. Noted in Albert Lubin's "Loneliness, Creativity and van Gogh" in Hartog, op. cit., p. 524.

24. I owe this apothegm to Prof. Zhong Zhaopeng of the Religion Institute, Chinese

Academy of Social Sciences, Beijing. I am also grateful to him for helpful guidance on some of the later parts of this chapter.

25. Charles A. Eastman, *The Soul of the Indian* (Lincoln: The University of Nebraska Press, 1980), pp. 3–4.

26. Ibid., pp. 7–9.

27. Ibid., pp. 45–46.

28. Ibid., pp. 29–30.

29. Storr cites one:

> Pre-industrial societies have little notion of a person as a separate entity. A Nigerian psychiatrist told me that, when a psychiatric clinic was first set up in a rural district of Nigeria to treat the mentally ill, the family invariably accompanied the sufferer and insisted upon being present at the patient's interview with the psychiatrist. The idea that the patient might exist as an individual apart from the family, or that he might have personal problems which he did not want to share with them, did not occur to Nigerians who were still living a traditional village life. (op. cit., p. 78)

The case is interesting, and certainly suggests a low valuation of solitude among these traditional Nigerians, although one would like to know much more about their distancing strategies, rites of passage, etc. In any event, Storr's initial statement is far too strong in the light of the examples cited in this chapter.

30. Of course, uncanny similarities are always to be found. The following complaint sounds as though it comes from Thoreau, although in fact it appears in the third Taoist classic, the book of *Lieh Tzu* (perhaps a forgery), where it is attributed to a precurser of the taoists, Yang Chu:

> Do we live for the sake of being now cowed into submission by the fear of the law and its penalties, now spurred to frenzied action by the promise of a reward or fame? We waste ourselves in a mad scramble, seeking to snatch the hollow praise of an hour, scheming to contrive that somehow some remnant of reputation shall outlast our lives. We move through the world in a narrow groove, pre-occupied with the petty things we see and hear, brooding over our prejudices, passing by the joys of life without even knowing that we have missed anything. Never for a moment do we taste the heady wine of freedom. We are as truly imprisoned as if we lay at the bottom of a dungeon, heaped with chains. (quoted in Herlee Creel, *Chinese Thought* [Chicago: University of Chicago Press, 1953], p. 96)

Had Thoreau read the Taoists? It seems likely, given his interest in oriental thought and his access to Emerson's library and the Harvard library. But then, as with all of his other reading, "I chose my texts after the sermon was written."

31. Creel, op. cit., p. 186.

32. Ibid., p. 21.

33. See Lin Tung-chi, "The Chinese Mind: Its Taoist Substratum," *Journal of the History of Ideas* 8, no. 3 (June 1947): 259–72: "The fact is, we are socially Confucian and individually Taoist. . . . Consciously we are Confucianists, but deep in the obscure subconscious we feel with alternate fear and joy the blatant Taoist in us all" (p. 259). Burton Watson remarks, in the introduction to his translation of *The Complete Works of Chuang Tzu* (op. cit.) that

> One should therefore think of Confucianism and Taoism in Han times [200BC–100AD] not as rival systems demanding a choice for one side or the other, but rather as two complementary doctrines, an ethical and political system for the conduct of public and family life, and a mystical

philosophy for the spiritual nourishment of the individual, with the methaphysical teachings of *The Book of Changes* acting as a bridge between the two. (p. 10)

34. Bynner, op. cit., p. 11.

35. The book attributed to him has thirty three chapters, but only the first seven (the Nei Peng, or "inner chapters") are probably his own, the others being the accretions of followers.

36. Burton Watson, trans., *The Book of Chuang Tzu*, op. cit. This is the sole translation used in the chapter. As before, however, since there are other translations in print, I will omit footnote references in favor of chapter numbers.

37. This section of the chapter is a revision of my article, "Solitude in Ancient Taoism," which appeared in *Diogenes*, no. 148 (1989).

38. Bynner, op. cit., p. 70.

39. Arthur Waley, *The Way and Its Power* (New York: Grove Press, 1958), p. 192.

40. Gia-fu Feng and Jane English: *Tao Te Ching* (New York: Vintage Books, 1972).

41. The ambiguity of the ancient Chinese is pervasive. Compare, for example, the following two translations of the opening lines of ch. 28:

Bynner:
 One who has a man's wings
 And a woman's also
 Is in himself a womb of the world

Lin:
 He who is aware of the Male
 But keeps to the Female
 Becomes the ravine of the world

When visiting with some Chinese scholars in Beijing several years ago, I asked a graduate student in philosophy, Mr. Huang Hua-liang, which of the two translations was more accurate. After discussion with some colleagues, he produced his own preferred translation:

 If you're a man, keep to that
 If a woman, keep to that;
 Then you flow with the river.

42. But compare Wolfgang Bauer: "Taoist philosophy in general—and that contained in *Chuang Tzu* in particular—may be called a Philosophy of eremitism; almost every paragraph of the book is interpretable along these lines." ("The Hidden Hero: Creation and Disintegration of the Ideal of Eremitism," in *Individualism and Holism: Studies in Confucian and Taoist Values*, [Ann Arbor: University of Michigan Press, 1985], p. 164). However, Bauer operates with an unconventionally broad definition of "eremitism" (see p. 161, op. cit.), and his illustrations come from the later chapters of *Chuang Tzu*, not from the Nei peng. Nevertheless his is a learned and insightful study from which I have profited greatly.

43. Witter Bynner's translation, op. cit., ch. 49. All subsequent quotations will be from this translation. Again, for ease of comparison to other versions I will cite the chapter number in the text.

Translations of the *Tao Teh Ching* are notoriously different, as we have seen, and any choice is sure to offend some scholars. Bynner's is controversial, using poetic license liberally in an attempt to capture the poetic spirit of the original. On its behalf, I may note that the renowned sinologist Herlee Creel found, after considering twenty-nine translations of the opening line of the *Tao Teh Ching*, that he was most in agreement with Bynner's version (see: H. Creel. "On the Opening Words of the Lao Tzu," *Journal of Chinese Philosophy* 10, no. 4 (1983): 315).

44. Professor Tang Yi-jie of Beijing University has pointed out to me the sense of solitude issuing from these very opening lines: not only Existence in general, but my own personal inner reality is "beyond the power of words to define." Prof. Tang reads a similar expression of the inescapability of solitude in the traditional story that Lao Tan for many years a librarian, finally left the library and indeed the whole middle kingdom: books—words—are incapable of communicating both Tao and inner self, so Lao Tzu was in no deeper solitude wandering in the wilderness than he was in the court library.

45. Prof. Zhou Gui-dian of Beijing Normal College pointed out to me the far greater concern on Lao Tzu's part with teaching rulers about Tao so that it may guide their governance—a concern with which Chuang Tzu appears to have little patience. Further, Lao Tzu's *wu wei* has an aim, the proper governance of self and mind which is intrinsically valuable; but Chuang Tzu is suspicious of the ideas of intrinsic value and usefulness: many parables teach that apparent usefulness is not useful and that apparent uselessness is useful!

46. Compare *Tao Teh Ching*, chs. 67 and 68.

47. Compare the story of Shan Ch'uan in chapter 28.

48. Compare the story of "the farmer of Stone Door" in chapter 28.

49. The general bent of the *Tao Teh Ching* is in the direction of Master Li's solution (see especially chapters 8, 13, 54, and 67). However, an advocate of any of the other three solutions could cite passages which support those solutions, at least implicitly. For example, "There is no need to run outside for better seeing . . . rather abide at the center of your being" (ch. 47) could be interpreted as underwriting the ways of Nameless Man, Lieh Tzu or T'ien Ken!

EPILOGUE

1. Robert Frost, "Escapist—Never," collected in Lathem, op. cit., p. 421.

2. Rainer Maria Rilke, from *Letters to a Young Poet*, letter of 14 May 1904, as cited in *The Oxford Dictionary of Quotations*, 3rd ed. (Oxford: Oxford University Press, 1979), p. 406. I have chosen to translate the last line using 'embrace' rather than 'greet.'

VERY SELECT BIBLIOGRAPHY

The Comprehensive Bibliography presented in the next section aims at completeness; its purpose is to make accessible to scholars the results of my five years of research on solitude. But many readers of this book, I hope, will not be scholars: their wide-ranging interests may allow time for another book or two on solitude, but not more. It is to such readers, that I offer this selection: although very different books, each of them provokes me to exclaim, "If you have time for another book on solitude, don't miss this one!" (Full bibliographical information can be found in the Comprehensive Bibliography.)

Margaret Adams: *Single Blessedness*
Athanasius: *Life of Antony*
Richard Byrd: *Alone*
Daniel Defoe: *Robinson Crusoe*
Linda Georgianna: *The Solitary Self*
Erazim Kohák: *The Embers and the Stars*
Alice Koller: *The Stations of Solitude*
Anne Morrow Lindbergh: *Gift From the Sea*
Michel de Montaigne: *Of Solitude*
Francesco Petrarch: *The Life of Solitude*
Rainer Maria Rilke: *The Notebooks of Malte Laurids Brigge*
Christianne Ritter: *Woman in the Polar Night*
May Sarton: *Journal of a Solitude*
Anthony Storr: *Solitude*
Henry David Thoreau: *Walden*

COMPREHENSIVE
BIBLIOGRAPHY

Abrams, Meyer. *The Mirror and the Lamp.* Oxford: Oxford University Press, 1953.
———. *Wordsworth.* Englewood Cliffs: Prentice Hall, 1972.
Adamowski, T. "Addie Bundren's Solitude: The Self and Others." *Review of Existential Psychology and Psychiatry* 15, no. 1 (1977).
Adams, Margaret. *Single Blessedness.* New York: Penguin Books, 1976.
Alger, William. *The Solitude of Nature and of Man.* Boston: Roberts Brothers, 1867.
Allchin, A. *Solitude and Communion.* Oxford: S.L.G. Press, 1977.
Anderson, Charles. *The Magic Circle of Walden.* New York: Holt, Rinehart and Winston, 1968.
Angel, Leonard. *The Silence of the Mystic.* Toronto: Morgan House, 1983.
Anson, Peter. *The Call of the Desert.* New York: Morehouse, 1964.
———. *The Hermit of Cat Island.* London: Burns and Oates, 1957.
Aristotle: *Nicomachean Ethics.* Trans. W. D. Ross. New York: Random House, 1941.
Athanasius. *Life of Antony.* Trans. Robert Gregg. New York: Paulist Press, 1980.
Audy, J. Ralph. "Man the Lonely Animal: Biological Roots of Loneliness." In *The Anatomy of Loneliness,* edited by Joseph Hartog et al. New York: International Universities Press, 1980.
Augustine. *The Confessions of St. Augustine.* Trans. E. Pusey. New York: E. P. Dutton and Company, 1951.
Bachelard, Gaston. *The Poetics of Reverie.* Boston: Beacon Press, 1971.
Bakan, David. *Disease, Pain and Sacrifice.* Chicago: University of Chicago Press, 1968.
———. *The Duality of Human Existence.* Boston: Beacon Press, 1966.
Barrus, Clara. *The Heart of Burrough's Journals.* Port Washington: Kennikat Press, 1928.
Bauer, Wolfgang. "The Hidden Hero: Creation and Disintegration of the Ideal of Eremetism." In *Individualism and Holism: Studies in Confucian and Taoist Values,* edited by Donald Munro. Ann Arbor: University of Michigan Press, 1985.
Belenky, Mary, et al. *Women's Ways of Knowing.* Boston: Basic Books, 1986.
Benedict. *The Rule of St. Benedict.* Trans. Cardinal Gasquet. New York: Cooper Square Publishers, 1966.
Benfey, Christopher, ed. *Emily Dickinson: Lives of a Poet.* New York: George Brasiller, 1986.
Benson, John. "Emotion and Expression." *The Philosophical Review* 76 (1967): 337–58.
Berdyaev, Nicolas. *Solitude and Society.* New York: Scribner's, 1938.
Berlin, Isaiah. *Four Essays on Liberty.* New York: Oxford University Press, 1969.
Blum, Lawrence. "Deceiving, Hurting and Using." In *Philosophy and Personal Relations,* edited by Alan Montefiore. Montreal: McGill Queens University Press, 1973.
Blyth, Chay. *The Impossible Voyage.* London: Pan Books, 1973.
Boethius. *The Consolation of Philosophy.* Trans. Richard Green. New York: Bobbs Merrill, 1962.
Bone, Edith. *Seven Years Solitary.* New York: Harcourt, Brace and Co., 1957.
Bordo, Susan. *The Flight to Objectivity.* Syracuse: State University of New York Press, 1987.
Brownfield, Charles. *Isolation: Clinical and Experimental Approaches.* New York: Random House, 1965.
Buber, Martin. *I and Thou.* Trans. Walter Kaufmann. New York: Charles Scribner's Sons, 1970.
Bugbee, Henry. "Loneliness, Solitude, and the Twofold Way in Which Concern Seems to Be Claimed." *Humanitas* 10, no. 3 (1974).
Burdick, Carol. *Woman Alone: A Farmhouse Journal.* Middlebury: P. S. Eriksson, 1989.
Burges, Tristan. *Solitude and Society Contrasted.* Providence: Carter & Wilkinson, 1797.
Burney, Christopher. *Solitary Confinement.* London: Macmillan & Co., 1961.

Byrd, Richard. *Alone*. Los Angeles: J. P. Tarcher, 1966.

Callahan, Steven. *Adrift*. Boston: Houghton Mifflin Co., 1986.

Camus, Albert. *The Myth of Sisyphus and Other Essays*. New York: Vintage Books, 1955.

Capellanus, Andreas. *The Art of Courtly Love*. Trans. John Parry. New York: Columbia University Press, 1990.

Capra, Fritjof. *The Tao of Physics*. Berkeley: Shambhala, 1975.

Carmichael, Montgomery. *The Solitaries of the Sambuca*. London: Burns, 1914.

Carnochan, W. B. *Gibbon's Solitude*. Stanford: Stanford University Press, 1987.

Carr, Emily. *Hundreds and Thousands: The Journals of Emily Carr*. Toronto: Clare, Irwin & Co., 1966.

Cashen, Richard. *Solitude in the Thought of Thomas Merton*. Kalamazoo: Cistercian Publications, 1981.

Cavell, Stanley. *The Senses of Walden*. New York: Viking Press, 1972.

Cheng, Nien. *Life and Death in Shanghai*. New York: Grove Press, 1987.

Chuang Tzu. *The Complete Works of Chuang Tzu*. Trans. Burton Watson. New York: Cornell University Press, 1968.

Clay, Jean. *Romanticism*. Secaucus: Chartwell Books, 1981.

Clay, Rotha Mary. *The Hermits and Anchorites of England*. London: Methuen, 1914.

Clough, Wilson. *The Necessary Earth: Nature and Solitude in American Literature*. Austin: University of Texas Press, 1964.

Cody, John. *After Great Pain: The Inner Life of Emily Dickinson*. Cambridge: Harvard University Press, 1971.

Cohen, J., and Phipps, J. *The Common Experience*. Los Angeles: J. P. Tarcher Inc., 1979.

Cohen, Michael. *The Pathless Way*. Madison: University of Wisconsin Press, 1984.

Collard, Edgar. *The Art of Contentment*. Toronto: Doubleday Canada, 1974.

Collins, Stephen. *Selfless Persons*. Cambridge: Cambridge University Press, 1982.

Conrad, Joseph. *The Heart of Darkness*. London: Dent & Sons, 1974.

Cox, Stephen. *"The Stranger Within Thee": Concepts of the Self in Late-Eighteenth-Century Literature*. Pittsburgh: University of Pittsburgh Press, 1980.

Creel, Herlee. *Chinese Thought*. Chicago: University of Chicago Press, 1953.

———. "On the Opening Words of the Lao Tzu." *Journal of Chinese Philosophy* 10, no. 4 (1983).

Crosby, Donald. "Religion and Solitariness." *Journal of the American Academy of Religion* 40 (1972).

Cunningham, Lawrence, and Stock, Dennis. *St. Francis of Assisi*. San Francisco: Harper and Row, 1981.

Dauenhauer, Bernard. *Silence: The Phenomenon and its Ontological Significance*. Bloomington: Indiana University Press, 1980.

Deegan, Dorothy Yost. *The Stereotype of the Single Woman in American Novels*. New York: Octagon Books, 1969.

Defoe, Daniel. *The Life and Adventures of Robinson Crusoe*. London: Penguin Books, 1965.

Descartes, René. *Meditations on First Philosophy*. In *The European Philosophers From Descartes to Nietzsche*, edited by M. C. Beardsley. New York: Modern Library, 1960.

Dillard, Annie. *Pilgrim at Tinker Creek*. New York: Harper & Row, 1974.

———. *The Writing Life*. New York: Harper Perennial, 1990.

Dillon, Janette. *Shakespeare and the Solitary Man*. Totowa: Rowman & Littlefield, 1981.

Dilman, Ilham. *Love and Human Separateness*. Oxford: Basil Blackwell, 1987.

Doan, Laura. *Old Maids to Radical Spinsters*. Chicago: University of Illinois Press, 1991.

Dombrowski, Daniel. *Thoreau the Platonist*. New York: Peter Lang, 1988.

Dostoevsky, Fyodor. *Crime and Punishment*. Trans. Constance Garnett. New York: Harper, 1951.

Druin, Francis. *The Sounding Solitude: Meditations for Religious Women*. Staten Island: Alba House, 1971.

Dunne, John S. *The Reasons of the Heart*. New York: Macmillan, 1978.

Durrant, Geoffrey. *Wordsworth and the Great System*. Cambridge: Cambridge University Press, 1970.

Eastman, Charles Alexander. *The Soul of the Indian*. Lincoln: University of Nebraska Press, 1911/1980.

Eastman, Elaine Goodale. *Sister to the Sioux*, edited by Kay Graber. Lincoln: University of Nebraska Press, 1978.

Eiseley, Loren. *The Immense Journey*. New York: Random House, 1946.

Elias, Norbert. *The Loneliness of the Dying*. Oxford: Blackwell, 1985.

Ellis, Frank, ed. *Twentieth Century Interpretations of Robinson Crusoe*. Englewood Cliffs: Prentice Hall, 1969.

Engelhardt, H. Tristram. "Solitude and Sociality." *Humanitas* 10, no. 3 (1974): 277–87.

Euripides. *Medea*. Trans. Gilbert Murray. In *Fifteen Greek Plays*, edited by Lane Cooper. New York: Oxford University Press, 1943.

Faricy, Robert. "Thomas Merton: Solitude and the True Self." *Science et Esprit* 31, no. 2 (1979): 191–98.

Festugiere, Andre-Jean. *Personal Religion Among the Greeks*. Berkeley: University of California Press, 1954.

Fisher, Seymour. *Bodily Experience in Phantasy and Behavior*. New York: Appleton-Century-Crofts, 1970.

Fisk, Emma. *A Cape Cod Journal*. New York: Norton, 1990.

Foucault, Michel. *The Uses of Pleasure*. New York: Pantheon Books, 1985.

Frankl, Victor. *Man's Search For Meaning*. New York: Washington Square Press, 1968.

Freemantle, Anne. *Desert Calling: The Life of Charles Foucauld*. London: Hollis & Carter, 1950.

French, R. M., trans. *The Way of a Pilgrim*. San Francisco: Harper, 1973.

Fromm-Reichman, Frieda. "Loneliness." In *The Anatomy of Loneliness*, edited by Joseph Hartog et al. New York: International Universities Press, 1980.

Fritz, Mary. *Take Nothing for the Journey: Solitude as the Foundation for the Non-Possessive Life*. New York: Paulist Press, 1985.

Furse, Margaret. *Mysticism*. Nashville: Abingdon Press, 1977.

Gaddis, Thomas. *The Birdman of Alcatraz*. New York: The Aeonian Press, 1955.

Geddes, Gary, ed. *Twentieth Century Poetry and Poetics*. Toronto: Oxford University Press, 1985.

Georgianna, Linda. *The Solitary Self*. Cambridge: Harvard University Press, 1981.

Gerbault, Alain. *In Quest of the Sun*. London: Hodder and Stoughton, 1930.

Ginsberg, Carlo. *The Cheese and the Worms*. Baltimore: Johns Hopkins University Press, 1980.

Girardot, Norman. "Behaving Cosmogonically in Early Taoism." In *Cosmogony and Ethical Order*, edited by Robin Lovin and Frank Reynolds. Chicago: University of Chicago Press, 1985.

Glick, Wendell, ed. *The Recognition of Henry David Thoreau*. Ann Arbor: University of Michigan Press, 1969.

Goethe, Johann Wolfgang von. *The Sorrows of Young Werther*. Trans. Victor Lange. New York: Holt, Rinehart and Winston, 1949.

Gonnaud, Maurice. *An Uneasy Solitude*. Trans. Lawrence Rosenwald. Princeton: Princeton University Press, 1987.

Gotesky, Rubin. "Aloneness, Loneliness, Isolation, Solitude." In *An Invitation to Phenomenology*, edited by James Edie. Chicago: Quadrangle Books, 1965.

Gotz, Ignacio. "Loneliness." *Humanitas* 10, no. 3 (1974): 289–99.

Graham, Angus. *Disputers of the Tao*. La Salle: Open Court, 1989.

Graham, Robin. *Dove*. New York: Bantam, 1973.

Grayson, David. *Adventures in Solitude*. New York: Doubleday, 1931.

Griffin, Susan. *Woman and Nature: The Roaring Inside Her*. New York: Harper Collins, 1979.

Hall, Edward. *The Hidden Dimension*. New York: Doubleday, 1966.

Halmos, Paul. *Solitude and Privacy*. New York: Greenwood Press, 1953.

Halpern, Sue. *Migrations to Solitude*. New York: Pantheon Books, 1992.

Hammit, William. "Cognitive Dimensions of Wilderness Solitude." *Environment and Behavior* 14, no. 4 (1982): 478–93.

Harding, Walter. *The Variorum Walden*. New York: Washington Square Press, 1963.

Harding, Walter, and Meyer, Michael. *The New Thoreau Handbook.* New York: New York University Press, 1980.

Hardy, Richard. "Solitude: A Sanjuanist Perspective." *Eglise et Theologie* 6, no. 1 (1975).

Harper, Ralph. *The Seventh Solitude.* Baltimore: Johns Hopkins Press, 1965.

Harre, Rom. *Personal Being: A Theory for Individual Psychology.* Cambridge: Harvard University Press, 1984.

Hart, James. "Towards a Phenomenology of Nostalgia." *Man and World* (1973): 397–419.

Hartog, Joseph et al. *The Anatomy of Loneliness.* New York: International Universities Press, 1980.

Havens, Raymond. *The Mind of a Poet.* Baltimore: Johns Hopkins University Press, 1941.

Heidegger, Martin. *Being and Time.* Trans. John Macquarrie and Edward Robinson. New York: Harper and Row, 1962.

Helps, Arthur. *Companions of My Solitude.* London: W. Pickering, 1851.

Heron, James. "Phenomenology of Social Encounter: The Gaze." *Philosophy and Phenomenological Research* 31 (1970).

Hesse, Hermann. *Steppenwolf.* Trans. Basil Creighton. New York: Bantam Books, 1972.

Hillesheim, James. "Action and Solitude: A Nietzschean View." *Education Theory* 19 (1969).

Hirsch, Eric. *Wordsworth and Schelling.* New Haven: Yale University Press, 1960.

Hubbell, Sue. *A Country Year.* New York: Harper and Row, 1983.

Hume, David. *Essays Moral, Political and Literary,* edited by Eugene Miller. Indianapolis: Liberty Classics, 1985.

Ilie, Paul. *Unamuno.* Madison: University of Wisconsin Press, 1967.

Isreal, Joachim. *Alienation: From Marx to Modern Sociology.* Boston: Allyn and Bacon, 1971.

Huth, Hans. *Nature and the American: Three Centuries of Changing Attitudes.* Berkeley: University of California Press, 1957.

Jallard, Pat, and Hooper, John. *Women from Birth to Death.* Sussex: Harvest Press, 1986.

Jeffreys, Sheila. *The Spinster and Her Enemies: Feminism and Sexuality, 1880–1930.* London: Pandora, 1985.

Johnson, Thomas. *The Letters of Emily Dickinson.* Cambridge: Harvard University Press, 1958.

Jones, Richard, and Daniels, Kate. *Of Solitude and Silence.* Boston: Beacon Press, 1981.

Jorgenson, Paul. *Lear's Self-Discovery.* Berkeley: University of California Press, 1967.

Jung, Carl Gustav. *Memories, Dreams, Reflection.* New York: Pantheon, 1973.

Kafka, Franz. "The Judgment" and "The Burrow." In *Selected Short Stories of Franz Kafka.* New York: Modern Library, 1971.

———. *Letters to Felice.* Trans. James Stern and Elisabeth Duckworth. New York: Penguin, 1974.

Katz, Richard. *Solitary Life.* New York: Reynal & Co. 1959.

Kingley, Charles. *The Hermits.* London: Macmillan, 1891.

Koch, Philip. "Expressing Emotion". *Pacific Philosophical Quarterly* 64 (1983).

———. "Loneliness without Objects." *The Southern Journal of Philosophy* 21, no. 2 (1983).

———. "Solitude in Ancient Taoism." *Diogenes* 148 (1989).

———. "Solitude." *The Journal of Speculative Philosophy* 4, no. 3 (1990).

Kohák, Erazim. *The Embers and the Stars.* Chicago: University of Chicago Press, 1984.

Kohut, Heinz, et al. *How Does Analysis Cure?* Chicago: University of Chicago Press, 1984.

Koller, Alice. *The Stations of Solitude.* New York: William Morrow and Co., 1990.

Kramer, Heinrich, and Spenger, James. *The Malleus Maleficarum.* Trans. Montague Summers. New York: Dover Publications, 1971.

Krutch, Joseph Wood. *Thoreau.* New York: Sloan, 1948.

Laing, R. D. *Knots.* New York: Vintage Books, 1970.

Lakoff, George, and Johnson, Mark. *Metaphors We Live By.* Chicago: University of Chicago Press, 1980.

Lao Tzu. *The Way of Life According to Lao Tzu.* Trans. Witter Bynner. New York: Perigee Books, 1944.

Larson, Reed, et. al. "Being Alone versus Being with People: Disengagement in the Daily Experience of Older Adults." *Journal of Gerontology* 40, no. 3 (1985).

Laski, Marghanita. *Ecstasy*. New York: Greenwood Press, 1968.

Lattimore, Richmond. *Hesiod*. Ann Arbor: University of Michigan Press, 1959.

Laubier, Patrick de. "Sociological Aspects of Solitude in Advanced Industrial Societies." *Labour and Society* 9, no. 1 (1984).

Leclercq, Dom Jean. *Alone with God*. Trans. Elizabeth McCabe. New York: Farrar, Straus and Cudahy, 1961.

Leibniz, Gottfried Wilhelm von. *Discourse on Metaphysics* and *Monadology*. In *The European Philosophers from Descartes to Nietzsche*, edited by M.C. Beardsley. New York: Modern Library, 1960.

Lentfoehr, Sr. Therese. "Thomas Merton: The Dimensions of Solitude." *The American Benedictine Review* 23 (1972).

Levinson, Daniel, et al. *The Seasons of a Man's Life*. New York: Ballantine Books, 1979.

Lewis, Hywel. "Solitude in Philosophy and Literature." In *Philosophy and Literature*, edited by A. Phillips Griffiths. Cambridge: Cambridge University Press, 1984.

Lewis, Richard. *The American Adam*. Chicago: University of Chicago Press, 1955.

Leyser, Henrietta. *Hermits and the New Monasticism*. New York: St Martin's Press, 1984.

Lin, Tung-chi. "The Chinese Mind: Its Taoist Substratum." *Journal of the History of Ideas* 8, no. 3 (1947)

Lindbergh, Anne Morrow. *Gift from the Sea*. New York: Pantheon Books, 1955.

Line, Francis. *Sheep, Stars and Solitude: Adventure Saga of a Wilderness Trail*. Irvine: Wide Horizons Press, 1986.

The Lives of Simeon Stylites. (No author given) Kalamazoo: Cistercian Publications, 1992.

Losa, Francisco de. *The Holy Life of Gregory Lopez* [microfilm]. Ann Arbor: University Microfilms, repr. 1977, c1675.

Lubin, Albert. "Loneliness, Creativity and van Gogh." In *The Anatomy of Loneliness*, edited by Joseph Hartog et al. New York: International Universities Press, 1980.

Mackay, Agnes Ethel. *An Anatomy of Solitude: Towards a New Interpretation of the Sources of Creative Inspiration*. Glasgow: MacLellan, 1978.

Macpherson, Jay. *The Spirit of Solitude*. New Haven: Yale University Press, 1982.

Malits, Elena. *The Solitary Explorer*. San Francisco: Harper and Row, 1980.

Manion, Eileen. " 'All Alone Feeling Blue'? Women's Experience of Solitude." *Women and Men*, edited by Greta Hofmann. Markham: Fitzhenry and Whiteside, 1987.

De la Mare, Walter. *Desert Islands and Robinson Crusoe*. London: Faber, 1930.

Marx, Karl. *A Contribution to the Theory of Political Economy*. Trans. N.I. Stone. Chicago: n.p., 1904.

Masefield, John. *Multitude and Solitude*. New York: Macmillan, 1925.

Maslow, Abraham. *Towards a Psychology of Being*. New York: D. Van Nostrand Company, 1968.

Mason, Sr. Mary. *Active Life, Contemplative Life*. Milwaukee: Marquette University Press, 1961.

Mayeroff, Milton. *On Caring*. New York: Harper and Row, 1971.

McCloskey, H. J. "Privacy and the Right to Privacy." *Philosophy* 55 (1980).

Megroz, Rodolphe. *The Real Robinson Crusoe*. London: Cresset Press, 1939.

Mehta, J. L. *Martin Heidegger: The Way and the Vision*. Honolulu: University of Hawaii Press, 1976.

Meltzer, Milton, and Harding, Walter. *A Thoreau Profile*. New York: Thomas Crowell Co., 1962.

Merton, Thomas. *The Monastic Journey*, edited by Brother Patrick Hart. Kansas City: Sheed Andrews and McMeel, 1977.

———. *The Silent Life*. New York: Farrar, Straus & Cudahy, 1957.

Meyerhoff, Hans. *Time in Literature*. Berkeley: University of California Press, 1968.

Mijuskovic, Ben Lazare. *Loneliness in Philosophy, Psychology and Literature*. Assen: Van Gorcum, 1979.

Miller, Perry. *The American Transcendentalists*. Garden City: Doubleday & Co., 1957.

Moffat, Mary Jane, and Paynter, Charlotte. *Revelations: Diaries of Women*. New York: Random House, 1974.

Montagu, Ashley. *On Being Human*. New York: Hawthorn Books, 1966.

Montaigne, Michel de. *The Essays of Montaigne*. London: Oxford University Press, 1927.

Monter, E. William. "Pedestal and Stake: Courtly Love and Witchcraft." In *Becoming Visible: Women in European History,* edited by R. Bridenthal and C. Koonz. Boston: Houghton Mifflin Co., 1977.

Moore, Hastings, and Moore, Gary, eds. *The Neighborhood of IS: Approaches to Inner Solitude: A Thematic Anthology.* Lanham: University Press of America, 1984.

Morgan, Oliver. "Music For The Dance: Some Meanings of Solitude." *Journal of Religion and Health* 25, no. 1 (Spring 1986): 18–28.

Moustakas, Clark. *Loneliness.* New York: Prentice Hall, 1961.

Mudge, Jean. *Emily Dickinson & The Image of Home.* Amherst: University of Massachusetts Press, 1975.

Muir, John. *Travels in Alaska.* Boston: Houghton, 1915.

Munro, Donald J. *Individualism and Holism: Studies in Confucian and Taoist Values.* Ann Arbor: University of Michigan Press, 1985.

Munro, Thomas. "Society and Solitude in Aesthetics." *Journal of Aesthetics and Art Criticism* 4 (1945).

Munz, Peter. *Relationship and Solitude.* London: Eyre & Spottiswoode, 1964.

Murphy, James. *Concepts of Leisure: Philosophical Implications.* Englewood Cliffs: Prentice-Hall, 1974.

Nash, Roderick. *Wilderness and the American Mind.* New Haven: Yale University Press, 1982.

Newick, Shula. "The Experience of Aloneness and the Making of Art." *The Journal of Aesthetic Education* 16 (1982).

Nicholson, Marjorie. *Mountain Gloom and Mountain Glory.* New York: Norton, 1959.

Noddings, Nel. *Caring.* Berkeley: University of California Press, 1984.

——. *Women and Evil.* Berkeley: University of California Press, 1989.

Norton, David. "The Moral Individualism of Henry David Thoreau." In *American Philosophy,* edited by Marcus Singer. Cambridge: Cambridge University Press, 1985.

Nouwen, Henri. "Solitude and Community." *Worship* 52 (1978): 15–29.

Novak, Michael. *The Experience of Nothingness.* New York: Harper Colophon Books, 1970.

O'Brien, Geoffrey. "Thoreau's Book of Life." *The New York Review of Books* 33, no. 46 (1987): 27–30.

Olman, Bertell. *Alienation.* Cambridge: Cambridge University Press, 1971.

Parsons, Howard. "A Philosophy of Wonder." *Philosophy and Phenomenological Research* 30 (1969).

Pawel, Ernst. *The Nightmare of Reason.* New York: Farrar, Straus, Giroux, 1984.

Paz, Octavio. *The Labyrinth of Solitude.* New York: Grove Press, 1961.

Peplau, L., and Perlman, D. *Loneliness: A Sourcebook of Current Theory, Research and Therapy.* New York: Wiley-Interscience, 1982.

Perkins, Jean. *The Concept of the Self in the French Enlightenment.* Geneva: Droz, 1969.

Peterson, Nancy. *Our Lives for Ourselves.* New York: G. P. Putnam's Sons, 1981.

Petrarch, Francesco. *The Life of Solitude* (De Vita Solitaria). Trans. Jacob Zeitlin. Westport: Hyperion Press Inc., 1978.

Petroff, Louis. *Solitaries and Solitarization.* Los Angeles: University of Southern California Press, 1936.

Picard, Max. *The World of Silence.* London: Harvill Press, 1952.

Pickard, John. *Emily Dickinson.* New York: Holt, Rinehart and Winston, 1967.

Plato. *The Collected Dialogs of Plato,* edited by Edith Hamilton and Huntingdon Cairns. New York: Pantheon Books, 1961.

Politzer, Anita. *A Woman On Paper.* New York: Simon and Schuster, 1988.

Powys, John Cowper. *A Philosophy of Solitude.* New York: Simon and Schuster, 1930.

Proust, Marcel. *Remembrance of Things Past.* Paris: Pleiade, 1954.

Rader, Melvin. *Wordsworth: A Philosophical Approach.* Oxford: Oxford University Press, 1967.

Richardson, Robert. *Henry Thoreau: A Life of the Mind.* Berkeley: University of California Press, 1986.

Rilke, Rainer Maria. *Letters to a Young Poet.* Trans. Stephen Mitchell. New York: Random House, 1984.

————. *The Notebooks of Malte Laurids Brigge.* Trans. Stephen Mitchell. New York: Vintage Books, 1985.

Ritter, Christianne. *A Woman in the Polar Night.* London: Allen and Unwin, 1954.

Rolston III, Holmes. *Philosophy Gone Wild.* Buffalo: Prometheus Books, 1989.

Rorty, Amelie, ed. *The Identities of Persons.* Berkeley: University of California Press, 1976.

Roskolenko, H., ed. *Solo.* Chicago: Playboy Press, 1973.

Rousseau, Jean Jacques. *The Reveries of the Solitary Walker.* Trans. Charles Butterworth. Indianapolis: Hackett, 1992.

Rowell, E. "A Man and His Solitariness." *The Hibbert Journal* 42 (1944).

Rubinstein, Robert. *Singular Paths: Old Men Living Alone.* New York: Columbia University Press, 1986.

Ruland, Richard, ed. *Twentieth Century Interpretations of Walden.* Englewood Cliffs: Prentice-Hall, 1968.

Sarton, May. *Journal of a Solitude.* New York: Norton & Co., 1973.

Sartre, Jean-Paul. *Being and Nothingness.* Trans. Hazel Barnes. New York: Philosophical Library, 1961.

Sayre, Robert. *Solitude in Society.* Cambridge: Harvard University Press, 1978.

Scary, Elaine. *The Body in Pain.* Oxford: Oxford University Press, 1985.

Schacht, Richard. *Alienation.* Garden City: Anchor Books, 1971.

Scheler, Max. *The Nature of Sympathy.* Trans. P. Heath. New Haven: Yale University Press, 1954.

Schutte, Ofelia. "The Solitude of Nietzsche's Zarathustra." *Review of Existential Psychology and Psychiatry* 17 (1980–81).

Schutz, Alfred, and Luckerman, Thomas. *The Structures of the Life-World.* Trans. R. Zaner and H. T. Engelhardt, Jr. Evanston: Northwestern University Press, 1973.

Scott, Melissa. *Silence in Solitude.* New York: Baen Books (Simon & Schuster), 1986.

Shanley, J. Lyndon. *The Making of Walden.* Chicago: University of Chicago Press, 1957.

Shelley, Percy Bysshe. "Alastor; Or, The Spirit of Solitude." In *Shelley. Poetical Works,* edited by Thomas Hutchinson. London: Oxford University Press, 1967.

Shephard, Odell. *The Heart of Thoreau's Journals.* New York: Dover Publications, 1961.

Sherover, Charles. *The Human Experience of Time.* New York: New York University Press, 1975.

Sherrard, Philip. *Athos, The Mountain of Silence.* Trans. Titus Burckhardt. London: Oxford University Press, 1960.

Sickels, Eleanor. *The Gloomy Egoist.* New York: Octagon Books, 1969.

Siegel, Jerrold. "Ideals of Eloquence and Silence in Petrarch." *Journal of the History of Ideas* 26 (1965).

Sitter, John. *Literary Loneliness in Mid-Eighteenth-Century England.* Ithaca: Cornell University Press, 1982.

Sitwell, Edith. *English Eccentrics.* New York: Vanguard Press, 1957.

Snowden, Frank. *Blacks in Antiquity: Ethiopians in the Greco-Roman Experience.* Cambridge: Harvard University Press, 1970.

Sophocles. *Antigone.* Trans. Robert Whitelaw. In *Fifteen Greek Plays,* edited by Lane Cooper. New York: Oxford University Press, 1943.

Spencer, Hazelton. *British Literature from Beowulf to Sheridan.* Boston: D. C. Heath and Co., 1952.

Spencer, Hazelton, et. al. *British Literature from Blake to the Present Day.* Boston: D. C. Heath and Co., 1952.

Standing Bear, Chief Luther. *Land of the Spotted Eagle.* Boston: Houghton Mifflin Co., 1933.

Statistics Canada. *1991 Census of Canada.* Catalogs 93–310 and 93–312.

Steere, Douglas Van. *Together in Solitude.* New York: Crossroad Publishing Co., 1982.

Stein, Peter, ed. *Single Life: Unmarried Adults in Social Context.* New York: St. Martin's Press, 1981.

Stevens, Anthony. *Archetypes, A Natural History of the Self.* New York: Morrow, 1982.

Stone, Isidore. *The Trial of Socrates.* New York: Doubleday, 1988.

Storr, Anthony. *Solitude.* New York: Free Press, 1988.

Strunk, Orlo. *Privacy: Experience, Understanding, Expression.* Washington: University Press of America, 1982.

Suckiel, Ellen. "Emerson and the Virtues." In *American Philosophy,* edited by Marcus Singer. Cambridge: Cambridge University Press, 1985.

Summers, Rev. Montague, trans. *The Malleus Maleficarum of Heinrich Kramer and James Springer.* New York: Dover Publications, 1971.

Swan, Jim. "Difference and Silence: John Milton and the Question of Gender." In *The (M)other Tongue,* edited by S. Nelson Garner et al. Ithaca: Cornell University Press, 1985.

Szczepanski, Jan. "Loneliness and Solitude." *Dialectics and Humanism* 4, no. 3 (1977).

Tang, Yi. "Taoism as a Living Philosophy." *Journal of Chinese Philosophy* 12 (1985).

Tannahill, Reay. *Sex in History.* New York: Stein and Day, 1982.

Taylor, Ralph, and Ferguson, Glenn. "Solitude and Intimacy: Linking Territoriality and Privacy Experiences." *Journal of Nonverbal Behavior* 4, no. 4 (1980).

Teale, Edwin. *The Wilderness World of John Muir.* Boston: Houghton Mifflin Co., 1976.

Thomas, Lewis. *Late Night Thoughts on Listening to Mahler's Ninth Symphony.* Oxford: Oxford University Press, 1985.

Thoreau, Henry David. *Walden* and *Civil Disobedience,* edited by Sherman Paul. Cambridge: Riverside Press, 1960.

Tillich, Paul. "Loneliness and Solitude." In *The Anatomy of Loneliness,* edited by Joseph Hartog et al. New York: International Universities Press, 1980. [Excerpted from Tillich's *The Eternal Now.* New York: Charles Scribner's Sons, 1957.]

Triumpho, Richard. *No Richer Gift.* Fort Atkinson: Hoard & Sons Co., 1979.

Tu, Wei-Ming. "The Continuity of Being: Chinese Visions of Nature." In *On Nature,* edited by Leroy Rouner. Notre Dame: University of Notre Dame Press, 1984.

Tymieniecka, Anna-Teresa. *Phenomenology of Life in a Dialogue between Chinese and Occidental Philosophy.* Dordrecht: D. Reidel, 1984.

Unamuno, Miguel de. *Soledad.* Buenos Aires: Espasa-Colpe Argentina, 1946.

Unger, Roberto. *Passion: An Essay on Personality.* New York: Free Press, 1984.

Van den Berghe, Pierre. *Man in Society.* New York: Elsevier, 1975.

Vest, Jay. "The Philosophical Significance of Wilderness Solitude." *Environmental Ethics* 9 (1987).

Vickers, Brian. *Public and Private Life in the Seventeenth Century: The Mackenzie-Evelyn Debate.* New York: Delmar, 1986.

Vincus, Martha. *Independent Women: Work and Community for Single Women, 1850–1920.* Chicago: University of Chicago Press, 1985.

Waley, Arthur. *The Way and Its Power.* New York: Grove Press, 1958.

Walker, Susan, ed. *Speaking of Silence: Christians and Buddhists on the contemplative way.* New York: Paulist Press, 1987.

Ward, Sr. Benedicta, trans. *The Sayings of the Desert Fathers.* Kalamazoo: Cistercian Publications, 1975.

Watts, Beulah. *Solitude: Life on a Louisiana Plantation.* Baton Rouge: Claitor's Publishing Division, 1970.

Wear, Delese, ed. *The Center of the Web.* Albany: State University of New York Press, 1993.

Weiss, Robert. *Loneliness.* Cambridge: MIT Press, 1974.

Welch, Holmes. *Taoism.* Boston: Beacon Press, 1957.

Westin, A. F. *Privacy and Freedom.* New York: Atheneum, 1967.

Wittgenstein, Ludwig. *Philosophical Investigations.* London: Blackwell, 1963.

Wolf, William. *Thoreau: Mystic, Prophet, Ecologist.* Philadelphia: United Church Press, 1974.

Wolff, Cynthia. *Emily Dickinson.* New York: Alfred Knopf, 1986.

Woodward, John. *The Solitude of Loneliness.* Lexington: Lexington Books, 1988.

Workman, Herbert. *The Evolution of the Monastic Ideal.* Boston: Beacon Press, 1962.

Young-Eisendrath, Polly, and Hall, James, eds. *The Book of the Self.* New York: New York University Press, 1987.

Zaner, Richard. *The Context of Self.* Athens: Ohio University Press, 1981.

Zimmerman, Johann. *Solitude.* Boston: Joseph Burnstead, 1804.

INDEX